Fritz Kreisler

FRITZ KREISLER

By

LOUIS P. LOCHNER

PAGANINIANA PUBLICATIONS, INC.
211 WEST SYLVANIA AVENUE
NEPTUNE CITY, N.J. 07753

Fritz Kreisler by Louis P. Lochner was originally published in 1950 by The Macmillan Company, New York. This edition is reprinted by arrangement with Macmillan Publishing Co., Inc.

ISBN 0-87666-575X

Manufactured in the United States of America

Published by
PAGANINIANA PUBLICATIONS, INC.
211 West Sylvania Avenue
Neptune City, New Jersey 07753

To my dear wife
HILDE
who shares my esteem for
FRITZ KREISLER
this book is affectionately
dedicated

Paganiniana Publications wishes to thank the following people and organizations for their cooperation in providing illustrative material and resource information for this expanded edition: Frederick Kreisler, Franz Rupp, Brent Williams of "The Bohemians," Christopher Politis, Jens Nygaard, and RCA Victor Records.

ACKNOWLEDGMENTS

In the absence of any appreciable documentation concerning Fritz Kreisler's life, owing chiefly to the vicissitudes of war, I have had to call upon friends and colleagues of the artist to supply many of the facts contained in this book. The response has been most gratifying. Even persons unknown to me eagerly supplied details when they heard that a biography was in the making. Acknowledgments are therefore made, coupled with heartfelt thanks, to the following persons and institutions (I apologize in advance if anyone has been inadvertently omitted):

For assistance in library and newspaper research: in London, Mme. Marie Mecinska; in Paris, Bernard Sinsheimer, now of Hollywood, California; in Berlin, Fräulein Ruth Bertram; in Leipzig, Dr. Julius Goetz; in Vienna, Dr. Leopold Nowak; in Rio de Janeiro, Miss Franziska Goldmann; in Washington, Harold Spivacke and Edward N. Waters.

For tributes concerning their colleague: Harold Bauer, Adolf Busch, Pablo Casals, Mischa Elman, Georges Enesco, Geraldine Farrar, Zino Francescatti, Jascha Heifetz, Josef Hofmann, Yehudi Menuhin, Nathan Milstein, Albert Spalding, Joseph Szigeti, Jacques Thibaud, Bruno Walter, and Efrem Zimbalist.

For revealing how the accompanist sees the soloist: Ernö Balogh, Hubert Giesen, George Harris, Carl Lamson, Michael Raucheisen, Franz Rupp, and Arpad Sandor.

For editorial aid and helpful criticism in the preparation of this book: Charles E. Cuningham, Warren Potter, William J. Sailer, and Edward N. Waters.

For supplying authenticated episodes, facts, historical analogies, etc.: Clyde Burrows, Grace Hazard Conkling, Beman Gates Dawes, General Charles G. Dawes, Henry Draper, Dr. and Mrs. Zdenko Dworzak, Clarence A. Dykstra, Dr. Peter Eckertz, Oscar Eiler, Charles Foley, Margarete (Mrs. Felix) Frank, Arthur Gereke, Alexander Greiner, Howard Heck, Max Ittenbach, Maxson F. Judell, Dr. Erich Kessler, Edward Kilenyi, Sr., Roman Klier, Dr. Kurt Kreisler, Ernst C. Krohn, Mrs. Henrik Laerum, Marks Levine, Fred Lewis, Louis Ferdinand, Prince of Prussia; Edith Lorand, Daniel I. McNamara, Frank E. Mason, Mrs. Lola Clay Naff, Edward Naumburg, Jr., Mrs. Dorothy Oechsner, Walter Pelz, Louis Persinger, Frau Friederike Henriette Pistor, Ernest R. Pope, Professor Paul R. Pope, Willy Posselt, John Rosenfield, Basanta Koomar Roy, Betty (Mrs. William J.) Sailer, Mrs. Ernest Schelling, Rudolf Semler, Edoardo Senatra, Major General Ralph C. Smith, William R. Steinway, Dr. Wilhelm Strecker, Arthur Swann, Gershon Swet, Dr. Georg Tyrolf, Sylvia Voorhees, Mrs. Channing Ward (Helen La Motte), Bruno Walter, Lee and Rembert Wurlitzer.

For calling attention to valuable sources and archive material: The chiefs of the Music Divisions and their staffs in the Congressional Library at Washington, the Newberry Library of Chicago, and the city libraries of New York, Chicago, Milwaukee, St. Louis, Nashville, Dallas, Richmond, Va., Peoria, Ill., and Des Moines, Ia.

For assistance in photographic reproduction: Mme. Nellys, Gerhard Heese, the Ernest Schelling Collection, and the National Concert and Artists' Corporation.

For meticulous secretarial assistance: Ilse Abraham.

For compiling the Discography: Miss Elsie M. Garrison, Record Department, RCA Victor Division, Radio Corporation of America.

For supplying an ideal mountain retreat in Pennsylvania for writing: Professor and Mrs. Hilbert V. Lochner (Hilbert being my nephew).

For encouraging barks and understanding wagging of tails when words at times would not come readily: Monika the Scotty and Butch the cocker spaniel.

Louis P. Lochner

Fritz Kreisler, 1875-1962

Kreisler and some of his published music

New York City

My dear Louis:

I have read with genuine pleasure the memoirs of my life, which you have so painstakingly written. Thanks to your meticulous research, in the course of which you have unearthed a surprising number of documents, statements, articles you used as a source of factual quotations, and thanks to your conscientious interviewing of fellow artists, friends and others in a position to know, you have recalled many incidents in my life that I had completely forgotten.

On the other hand Harriet and I are glad to have been able to contribute our modest share to your effort, by delving into the treasure-house of our memories and imparting these recollections to you in the course of the many chats we have had together, while your book was in preparation.

Factually it is an accurate account. Naturally the interpretation of the facts is yours. If you and others have been too lavish in your praise of the subject, it is your own doing. But as the work of an old and devoted friend, your book has my blessing, for its honesty has touched me deeply.

Affectionately yours,

P.S. I cannot dispatch this letter without confiding to you that, owing to Harriet's constant endeavor to eliminate or diminish the references to herself, you have been prevented (*to my deep regret*) from properly illuminating the great influence her unfailing love, friendship, wisdom, criticism, vigilance has had in the shaping of my life.

Fritz Kreisler in 1912

CONTENTS

AN APPRECIATION

Perhaps the two persons in the world who are most surprised at the appearance of this biography are Fritz Kreisler and I.

In all the years that we had been friends, the suggestion of a connected story of Fritz's life had never come up, not even by indirection. Fritz knew in a general way of my intense love for music. The questions I asked him during several interviews must have communicated that fact to him. But he was neither aware that, during our Berlin days I was writing under an assumed name for a large American musical weekly, nor that I had wavered, upon graduation from the Wisconsin Conservatory of Music in Milwaukee, between going to our State University to equip myself for a journalistic career, and venturing overseas to become a professional musician, preferably an orchestra conductor. Like Fritz's father, I, too, was in a sense a "frustrated musician." His father's escape from his profession was playing in an amateur string quartet, mine in conducting church choirs and glee clubs and in accompanying amateur musicians.

Our friendship began during the days of the struggling Weimar Republic of Germany, when the ugly backwash of the Great War of 1914-1918 was still but too patently visible. It intensified during that anxious interim period between two gigantic holocausts, when ambitious dictators sought to make themselves masters of the world. It was a time of stock-market panics, ideological strife within nations, nervous efforts of incompetent diplomats to establish international stability after the chaos of war, and headlong rivalry in competitive armaments which were bound sooner or later to be put to appalling use.

During such an exciting period of world history, an active mind like that of my friend Kreisler could not confine itself to discussion of the chosen profession of music. Whenever we met, international affairs seemed the logical topic for our conversation. Besides, Fritz has shied away from having music forever on his mind. He wanted to come fresh to his concert work, and therefore sought to occupy himself with other subjects when off the platform.

Then how did the present volume come to be written? The answer is very simple: I had an entirely unscheduled, unaccountable "brain wave" on January 29, 1948. On that day I learned that the *Goebbels' Diaries*, which I had translated and edited, with interpretive commentary, had been chosen by the Book-of-the-Month Club as its May selection.

Naturally, I felt elated. Although I had had no intention of becoming the author of any more books, I was now spurred on to new effort. But what was I to write about? I had retired from active journalism and could therefore no longer draw upon personal experience to discourse on international affairs.

That night I lay awake, wondering what to do next. Suddenly it came to me: nobody had ever written a book-length biography of Fritz Kreisler! To make sure I was right in my assumption, I went to the New York Public Library the next morning to consult the card indexes. Some seventy magazine articles dealing in some way or other with Kreisler were catalogued, but there was no reference to any book on him.

Two days later we lunched together. "Fritz," I said, "why is it that there is no autobiography or biography of you in existence?" Fritz had no real answer, except that he could not see why anybody should care to read the story of his life.

I shall not weary the reader with the details of how the task of obtaining his consent was finally accomplished. Suffice it to state that it required six full weeks of persuasion to overcome his inhibitions. One of these inhibitions was his fear that the task might involve too much work on my part. For, as he pointed out, the curtain of Allied fire laid over Berlin in 1943 had also burned to the ground the exquisite Kreisler home, and with it all documentary material, correspondence, and photographs in his possession that might have lightened my task.

My researches have, to my happy surprise, nevertheless yielded an amazing amount not only of biographical data but, what is infinitely more important, of statements by Kreisler which reflect his opinions and moods at every stage of his life. These have been supplemented by innumerable personal conversations which I have had with him. He has thus virtually told his own story in this book.

There entered the further problem of the evaluation of Kreisler's place in the era in which he was the unchallenged leader in his profession. Had I contented myself with expressing my own enthusiasm for my friend Fritz, my superlatives might well have sounded like the adolescent adulation of a bobby-soxer. Fortunately, great musicians and expert musicologists, as well as choice spirits like Rabindranath Tagore and Eugène Ysaÿe, have expressed themselves more extravagantly than a biographer dares to do.

But even without such support it is not difficult to show that the story of Fritz Kreisler's life is one of the most fantastic in the history of music.

An infant prodigy who at the age of three could read music and at four fiddled his national anthem correctly;

a boy wonder who when only twelve snatched the coveted *Premier Prix* from Paris Conservatoire aspirants twice his age and then successfully toured the United States as a professional violinist;

an adolescent who finished high school in two years, learned half a dozen foreign languages with playful ease, tried himself at medicine, and qualified as professional soldier, only to return in his late teens to his first love, music, and to a group of Viennese immortals headed by Johannes Brahms, Hugo Wolf, Arthur Schnitzler, and Hugo von Hofmannsthal;

a mnemonic wizard who, without ever taking a piano lesson, learned brilliantly to play all accompaniments to the standard literature of the violin by heart;

a gay young blade who when only nineteen wrote one of the best cadenzas to Beethoven's classic violin concerto and at the same time helped out fellow musicians with sprightly military marches, ingratiating Viennese waltzes, and charming lyrics for light musical comedies;

a Bohemian of the concert platform who picked a life's mate with beauty and intelligence added to an uncanny faculty for activating the best qualities of genius inherent within her husband;

a world-famed artist who was booed off the platform as an enemy during the hysteria of the First World War when, in fact, he was saving scores of his enemies from starvation;

an outcast living in musical exile who, once the war was over, by sheer character, personality, and will power staged a sensational comeback in the United States, Great Britain, France, and other former enemy countries;

a genius of the bow whose annual schedule of concerts in Europe and North America, more crowded than that of any artist in history, hardly permitted him to take time out successively to tour the Orient, Australia, and South America, in each of which he garnered honors seldom accorded any human being;

a man of the world who conversed with presidents, emperors, kings, and statesmen in their respective tongues with the same ease with which he discussed the Greek and Latin classics, incunabula, and philosophical problems with the erudite;

a musician who commanded higher fees than any violinist ever did, yet who considered his huge earnings merely as a trust fund from the Almighty for the relief of human suffering;

a passionate believer in the untrammeled freedom of art who declined, at considerable sacrifice to himself, to bow to ideological interference by Russian Communism and Teuton Nazism;

a master interpreter who even in the seventy-sixth year of his life and his sixty-second year of professional platform appearance still has a message for an audience that rises in reverent tribute to the white-haired composer-violinist who has never ceased to hold the affection of his listeners—

such, in one sentence, is Fritz Kreisler.

Many artists of the bow have been able to hypnotize their audiences temporarily by the wizardry of their mechanical execution, but after this enthusiasm has evanesced, left the hearts of their hearers cold and untouched. Others, with a beautiful and appealing tone, have made their audiences wince at times because of faulty technical execution, so that a feeling of pity for the executant mingled with, and detracted from, the admiration for his noble interpretation. Kreisler, more than any violinist of our time, has combined an amazing technique with a depth of feeling and emotion and a beauty of tone that gripped the heartstrings of every listener.

Many musicians who appeared on the concert platform regularly were able to bask in the applause which, generated by personal admiration for the performer, was accorded their ephemeral compositions that lived and died with the artist's stage career. Fritz Kreisler has enriched the literature of the violin permanently with works of inimitable charm and beauty that are part and parcel of every violinist's repertoire. One need but to turn on the radio for a consistent period to learn how frequently the announcer ends with the words, "Music by Fritz Kreisler." Whether it be a cadenza to a Mozart or Beethoven or Brahms concerto, or one of the so-called "classical transcriptions" like the "Vivaldi" Concerto or the "Pugnani" Praeludium and Allegro, or graceful short pieces like the "Caprice viennois," "Liebesleid" and "Liebesfreud," and "Schön Rosmarin" the name of Fritz Kreisler is being publicized so much that it has become a household word. For an athlete to be complimented for handling his ball as gracefully as Kreisler handles his fiddle seems quite natural. Even the unmusical understands the analogy.

Many a genius is great in his chosen work and eloquent in its exposition, but utterly dull, not to say ignorant, in matters outside his professional sphere. Many a musician can enthrall his listeners with his music and talk about it with captivating enthusiasm. But start a discussion on politics, science, religion, or human relations, and he acts like a fish out of water. With Kreisler the opposite is true: he shies away from musical discussion, fearsome lest it turn into banal compliments on his own art, and seeks to turn conversation into channels far removed from music. It is then that one becomes aware of the profound erudition which he has attained. One then realizes that this outstanding collector of rare books has not acquired a library merely for purposes of window dressing, but has carefully read and absorbed what he has assembled through the decades in the way of books with exquisite taste and rare discretion. When he turns to other subjects, it is not because he desires to display his wide range of knowledge. Quite the contrary: he is always modest, forever eager to learn from others.

Nor is he a high-brow. His vocabulary is simple, straightforward, and easily understandable. He is a grateful listener to both the humble and the exalted. He is a charming storyteller, with a folksy manner of spinning his yarns.

But when, on rare occasions, he sits down to commit his thoughts to paper for publication, there is something about his style and manner of presentation for which many a professional writer might well envy him.

Many great musicians have been blessed for what they gave the world by those who did not know them personally, but have been cursed for their egotism, capricious eccentricity, and lack of personal loyalty by those who came in close contact with them. Fritz Kreisler is selflessness and kindness personified. He is one of the most universally beloved and lovable characters in musical history—the sort of man who induced a Hindu friend to confess that he, a non-Christian, for the first time understood what we mean by a "Christlike spirit" when he saw with what meekness and fortitude and in what spirit of forgiveness Kreisler bore the humiliations of World War I.

Behind all that my friend Fritz says and does, there is a great, warm, humble, human, God-fearing personality. That, indeed, is the "secret" of his unexampled success, of the affection in which he is universally held, and of the unparalleled longevity of his career as a professional violinist.

Fritz Kreisler at seventy-five is still a great voice, a sage elder statesman of music, a wonderful and inspiring personality. Above all, he is a choice spirit.

Were I an Indian, I would call him Mahatma—Great Soul.

Louis P. Lochner

Kreisler with a violin, about 1955

CHAPTER ONE

A WUNDERKIND IS BORN

[1875]

"I WAS born with music in my system. I knew musical scores instinctively before I knew my A B C. It was a gift of Providence. I did not acquire it."

Fritz Kreisler, asked to define more clearly what he meant by this statement, which has been quoted and requoted hundreds of times in music lexicons, biographical articles, special news stories, and even psychological works dealing with the subject of "innate ideas," readily responded:

"One day, when I was three and a half years old, I was standing next to my father as he played a Mozart string quartet * with his friends. It started out with the notes D, B, G.

" 'How do you know you must play these three notes?' I asked him. Patiently he took a sheet of paper, drew the five lines of a musical staff, and explained what each note meant when written between or on given lines. He also showed how a note was raised or lowered by a half-tone by the use of the 'sharp' and 'flat' signs, and how fractional notes are indicated.

"I understood at once what he was trying to teach me. And so it came about that I literally could read music before I learned my A B C."

Fritz heard music virtually from the moment of his birth in Vienna on February 2, 1875. "Father really was a frustrated musician," he said. "He had begged his father, an architect, to let him choose music as his life's work, but in those days that of a musician was not consid-

* Quartet in G Major, K.V. 156, composed toward the end of 1772.

ered a 'gentlemanly' profession nor a 'bread and butter' career. So my father turned to medicine.

"He had no sooner established himself as a general practitioner, however, than he formed a string quartet with a few kindred souls. Every Saturday afternoon these men—full-bearded like my father, as was the custom of the time—would come to our home. At one time the quartet consisted, besides my father, of the local chief of police, a druggist, and the head of the fire department; at another time of a notary public, a produce merchant, and a police commissioner.

"These men would play with great abandon, hour after hour, and give a worthy, if not altogether brilliant, interpretation of the great classics of chamber music. My father and his friends were amateurs in the real sense of the word—lovers of music who expected no material reward for their work. They strove to understand music, and I believe they enjoyed it more than anyone possibly can who has not taken such pains."

Chuckling reminiscently, Fritz continued: "When the quartet produced sour notes, I would flee with a shudder and lock myself up in an adjacent room. Soon I made myself a would-be violin out of a cigar box over which I stretched shoestrings; and I'd pretend I was playing right, thus correcting what damage the quartet performers had done to my sensitive ears.

"These Saturday séances concluded invariably with a rendition of our national air, followed by the clinking of glasses as my mother served the well earned refreshments in the dining room."

His father, Dr. Samuel Severin Kreisler, he said, "was not a man of any unusual aptitude for music, but his courage and persistency were truly admirable. His enthusiasm was boundless.

"Among the early recollections of my childhood is the picture of my father with his violin. Hour after hour he would bend over his instrument with a happy, beaming countenance, playing the same passages over and over again with infinite patience. That I became a professional musician may be due to the fact that he projected, perhaps unconsciously, his own unfulfilled wish onto me."

Dr. Kreisler was gentleness personified. "I don't remember ever having been punished by him," his son maintains. "All he could bring himself to do was to reproach one verbally."

Brown-eyed, dark-haired Fritz, the second of five children, was by no means born into a life of plenty. Dr. Kreisler was a poor-people's family physician of the old school, rich in experience, poor in worldly goods, but imbued with a true love for suffering mankind, and possessed of an artist's soul that craved neither wealth nor glory, provided only his profession left him time to pursue his hobby, music. His income was meager. When he was called to the home of an impecunious family, it happened frequently that he would not only treat the patient free of charge but even quietly leave a gulden on the table for medicine. That the amateur quartet "clinked glasses" during refreshments did not mean that Vienna's famed *Heurigen*, the local young wine found automatically on the tables of all better-to-do burghers, was served in the Kreisler household.

"Our daily meals were pretty scant," Fritz recalls. "In the afternoon we had only tea, into which the grown-ups would put a spot of rum. There was no other alcohol except light beer in our flat."

The house in which Fritz Kreisler's cradle stood was a lowly apartment building in the south-side section of Wieden, a rather drab *Bezirk*, or borough. It had six rooms, with one set aside as medical consultation office, or *Ordinationszimmer*. The parlor, or *gute Stube*, had the equipment typical of that period: a plush sofa and chairs, an elegant cabinet (*Vertiko*) with the inevitable loud-ticking clock, photographs of the grandparents in gilded frames, and little knickknacks displayed here and there.

The *gute Stube* had also to serve as dining room. For "Med. univers. Dr. Kreisler" (as his professional signboard read) needed three bedrooms for his five children (two girls and three boys), his wife, and himself.

Small though the space was that remained after medical and dormitory needs had been taken care of, accommodations were somehow made available for another hobby of Dr. Kreisler's: he was a fancier and breeder of exotic animals, especially of parrots, rare fish, and crocodiles. These pets from tropic and subtropic climes demanded a warm, even temperature and tepid sand. When Fritz thinks of his earliest childhood, there is associated with it the smell of burning oil used for heating the sand.

The Kreisler apartment was located on an unpretentious side street of the Wiedener Hauptstrasse, or Main Street. It lacked warm-water facilities and had no bath. For the weekly bath, as was the custom in Austria, Germany, and France in those days, a firm specializing in this facility would bring a tub with hot water into the house. At times, too, Dr. Kreisler would go to the *Annabad*, a public natatorium.

Anna Kreisler, Fritz's mother, was "completely unmusical." She had a sympathetic understanding, however, for her husband's passionate devotion to his quartet. Although it took careful budgeting, she furnished a tasty, albeit simple, Vienna repast every Saturday to the four hungry amateur musicians.

Also, once little Fritz's evident predestination for a musical career became evident, she sacrificed comfort and health by accompanying him to Paris and later to America, although she was suffering from myelitis. Constant pain seems to have made her rather quick-tempered. Besides, she believed in the adage, "Spare the rod and spoil the child."

Anna Kreisler died in 1909; her husband survived her by twelve years.

Of his older sister, who passed on early, Fritz has only a vague recollection. After him came Ludwig, "a wonderful boy, much more talented than I, but unfortunately killed in an accident when quite young." Finally, ten years after Fritz, came the twins Ella and Hugo.

Ella remained unmarried and died in 1939 in this country. She lies buried in St. Joseph's Cemetery, Hackensack, New Jersey.

Hugo, the other twin, took to the cello and became a highly respected master of his instrument. While studying at Leipzig, his money ran out. Without a moment's hesitation his brother gave him six of his short compositions, with authority to sell them for what they would bring. The money thus realized, about $150, was quite a sum in those days and sufficed to let Hugo finish his studies.

After sitting at the first cello desk of the Vienna Philharmonic

Orchestra for a number of years, Hugo Kreisler was lured to America, where he joined the Baltimore Symphony. He never felt at home in this country, however. A characteristic utterance of his was, "How can one live in a country in which they serve grape juice instead of *Gipferl* for breakfast!" A *Gipferl* is a Viennese species of bun or roll. Soon he returned to Vienna to become professor of cello and cello soloist, and died in 1929 at Baden near Vienna, survived by his widow and an only son, Kurt.

When little Fritz was old enough to venture into the neighborhood by himself, there was little to inspire him even when he reached the Wiedener Hauptstrasse. The traveler of today who goes into the *IV. Bezirk* of Vienna must remember that in those days it lacked the later redeeming attractions of the Grand Duke Rainer Fountain, the Johann Strauss Theater, and the Mozart Fountain with its alluring *Magic Flute* figures of Tamino and Pamina. Nor had the little square or *Platz* near the Theresia Academy as yet been named after one of the greatest influences in the youthful Kreisler's life—Johannes Brahms.

Fritz's early years were spent like those of any other young, healthy lad—playing robbers, vowing he would become a street-car conductor, and the like. When Saturday came, however, nothing could keep him away from his father's quartet. There he stood, his dark brown eyes riveted upon the players, his abundant black hair often unruly from the emotional excitement stirred by the music.

Finally, one day when the tot was four years old, one of the players insisted that Fritz was truly musical, and that he ought to have a real violin instead of the cigar box. So he presented the beaming boy with a miniature fiddle.

"It was a toy violin," Fritz recalls, "but not so much of a toy that it could not produce sounds which I recognized when pulling the bow across the strings. From that time on, the quartet was increased by another musician, for I insisted upon taking my place with the others and playing my tiny instrument. One evening, as we were playing the national anthem, the others stopped quite suddenly, but I, engrossed in my performance, never noticed it and continued in perfect tune and time, I am told, to the end.

"It was decided then and there that I was a musical 'marvel,' and the next day I had a genuine little violin, purchased by my admiring father, who forthwith began to give me lessons."

Among Dr. Kreisler's friends was Jacques Auber, concertmaster at the Ring Theater. He agreed to teach the little boy. Fritz made astoundingly rapid progress. In a burst of youthful frankness, which in anyone less talented would have been regarded as overweening conceit, he soon told his father that he was playing a certain passage incorrectly.

"Listen to me, Father, and I will show you," Fritz concluded—rather patronizingly. It was then that his father gave a lesson in humility which may have been decisive in the boy's life. Dr. Kreisler patted the lad on his head, put his violin in the case, and said: "Now that my son knows more than his father, it is time that I retire. I shall play the violin no more."

The very next day, "Father began to practice the cello, going over passages with the same enthusiasm, the same infinite patience. He was in truth an extraordinary man, for when some years later Hugo, to whom he had in turn taught the cello, remarked with youthful vanity, 'Now, father, I can play better than you,' the cello, too, was locked up in its case and father began the study of the viola, which he continued to play—with one exception—until the end. There were no more sons!"

A fine sense of humor, which his son Fritz inherited to a delightful degree, helped Dr. Kreisler to accept this double "defeat" by his opinionated youngsters without bitterness, even with pride in his sons' accomplishments.

Only once, years later, was the paternal fiddle taken from its case. Harriet Kreisler told the story: *

"He kept to his viola throughout the years, until, one night in the early 1900's, Fritz scored his first great triumph in Vienna with the

* Reprinted from *He Plays on the World's Heartstrings* by Beverly Smith, in the February, 1931 issue of the *American Magazine*, by permission of Beverly Smith and the Crowell-Collier Publishing Company, copyright, 1931, by *American Magazine*.

Viotti Concerto No. 22. Papa never claimed any credit for teaching his sons; but that night, after he returned home, he took down his long-neglected violin. The old man tuned it and drew the bow across the strings. 'That tone,' he whispered, with tears in his eyes, 'that beautiful tone—maybe I taught him that.' "

CHAPTER TWO

THE YOUNGEST PUPIL OF THE VIENNA CONSERVATORY

[1882-1885]

An unheard-of occurrence enlivened Vienna Conservatory life in 1882: Fritz was admitted to its hallowed halls at the tender age of seven. Hitherto nobody under ten had been accepted.

"Mother was grand on that occasion," Kreisler remembered. "When she was asked, 'How old is the child?' she merely mumbled evasively, 'Oh, the usual age for entering the conservatory.' Mind you, mother was so unmusical that she could not distinguish between the violin and the cello. The neighborhood youngsters would come to ask for one of us. Supposing they wanted me to come out and join them in some game, and if Hugo happened to be playing the cello, in all sincerity she would tell the boys that Fritz was busy practicing!

"Also, she was sick much of the time and was partly paralyzed. Yet she gave herself wholeheartedly to the task of getting me into the conservatory, and she succeeded."

According to the Austrian critic Leopold Weninger:

> Admission to the Vienna Conservatory at that time depended upon an examination that was pretty stiff . . . Prospective students were adjudged very critically; only the very best were accepted. The curriculum then comprised six years: three preparatory and three undergraduate classes. The fact that Kreisler was immediately accepted into the undergraduate department indicates that he must have been pretty far advanced in his studies.

One person who recognized that little Fritz was indeed "pretty far advanced in his studies" was Carlotta Patti, sister of the world-famous prima donna Adelina Patti. Adelina, it appears, had agreed to sing a benefit performance in Carlsbad, the celebrated Czech spa, but had to cancel the engagement because of illness. Her less known sister Carlotta—who in the opinion of many contemporaries sang even better, though lacking Adelina's stage presence—agreed to substitute, but felt she could not hold an audience for an entire program of singing only. She asked the small Kreisler boy to play a few solos as supporting artist.

The audience raved. But Fritz was probably even happier than his listeners, for his "fee" consisted of a box of candy, a rare delicacy for a lad brought up in modest circumstances.

"I even remember the box," Fritz said, "because it made such an impression on me. Native Carlsbad pebbles were glued to its top and sides in more or less artistic patterns."

Admission to the Vienna Conservatory brought a radical change in the boy's daily routine of life. It was not that he became a cloistered prodigy; he could still play and romp with the other children. But, as he put it: "I could not engage in sports like tennis, nor soccer, nor even bicycling. I was not to endanger my fingers. Besides, my younger brother Ludwig died of an abdominal injury caused by a playmate during a game. That tragedy naturally made my parents doubly careful about me."

Fritz Kreisler throughout his life has had a penchant for beautiful instruments. Upon entry into the conservatory, for the first time an instrument of high quality became his possession. He wrote for the *Musical Courier* in April, 1908:

> On this occasion our friends presented me with a half-size violin, sweet and mellow—a Thir *—a very old and famous make. I was not altogether pleased with it, for I thought that . . . being a pupil of the Conservatory I should at least have had a three-quarter. This little Thir . . . represents that period of life which I passed at the Vienna Conservatory. Upon it I received my

* This instrument is now in the possession of Kurt Kreisler.

initiation into musical routine. With this little instrument held close to my beating heart I learned that within it was encompassed my fate—my future career.

The teacher to whom young Fritz was assigned with his diminutive fiddle was Joseph Hellmesberger, Jr. (1855–1907), known among his friends and pupils as "Peppi." He was then assistant conductor and concertmaster of the court orchestra of which his father, Joseph Hellmesberger, Sr. (1828–1893), was chief conductor. He also played in his father's string quartet.

"He was a fine young fellow," Kreisler recalled, "but very gay, with a weakness for ballet dancers. He was an excellent teacher. I was so fond of him that, when I was eight years old, I presented him with my first effort at composition—a string quartet. I don't know what happened to it; I haven't even a copy of it.

"Hellmesberger was a composer of parts. Thus he wrote a quartet for four violins with piano accompaniment which four of his pupils performed publicly from time to time. The late Felix Winternitz was one of them; Emil Baré, later second concertmaster of the Chicago Symphony Orchestra, another; I, a third; the fourth died young and I have forgotten his name.

"Occasionally we'd earn a ducat [about $2.25] for playing at some palace of an Austrian nobleman. If in addition we were served chocolate and a piece of *torte*, we'd feel more than rewarded for our efforts." *

Hand in hand with young Fritz's study of the violin there went a course in harmony and theory of music, given by that great master of the symphonic form, Anton Bruckner. This strange, out-of-this-world character with the heavy jowls and the patriarchal face made an indelible impression on young Fritz.

* The early association with Winternitz was one of the few friendships that Fritz was able to carry over into manhood. It started at the conservatory, continued through young manhood, when the two would play violin and piano sonatas, alternating at the instruments, and was transplanted to America, where Winternitz became a concert violinist and teacher of violin. He died in 1948 at the age of 76.

When at the zenith of his career, Fritz Kreisler sometimes played one of Winternitz's compositions, including "Dream of Youth," "Forsaken," and "The Blue Lagoon." He also dedicated his much-played "Old Refrain" to his friend of boyhood days, and arranged Winternitz's "Troika Capriccio" for violin and piano.

Anton Bruckner,
1824-1896

The Hellmesberger
String Quartet

Anton Bruckner in pose showing profile

"Anton Bruckner was a combination of genius and simpleton," Fritz recalled. "He had two coordinates—music and religion. Beyond that he knew almost nothing. I doubt whether he could multiply or subtract correctly.

"Religion was very real with him. If the near-by bells tolled, he would either fall on his knees in the midst of a class lesson and pray or, more often, would leave us and rush over to the church for his devotions.

"He was a man without guile and of a childlike naïveté. We youngsters, I must confess, took advantage of these traits of his. I recall two instances. One day some sort of official imperial commission, headed, if my memory serves me right, by Professor Hermann von Helmholtz, dropped in on our class to see how Bruckner's pupils were doing. I may say parenthetically that Bruckner was not a good teacher, though he was a magnificent, exemplary human being.

"To my amazement the revered *Meister* asked me, as the youngest one in the class, to go to the blackboard and write something in fugue style. 'Fritz,' he said, 'compose a fugue quickly.' I was then only eight years old. I was flabbergasted. My mind was a blank. No theme would occur to me on the spur of the moment. But our teacher had given us a little textbook with about ninety themes for fugues composed by himself. I knew them by heart. I boldly wrote one of them out on the blackboard. Bruckner, completely forgetting that he had composed and given them to us, looked at my product approvingly and observed, 'Not bad at all.'

"My bluff had worked with Bruckner. Not, however, with my classmates, the youngest of whom were three years older than I. When class was dismissed, the boys waited for me outside and gave me a sound thrashing. They were so comradely, however, as not to give me away to the *Meister*."

During this period, a bitter fight was on between the followers of Richard Wagner and Johannes Brahms. The "Wagnerites" of Vienna included, among others, Anton Bruckner.

"Bruckner had a chubby, fat pug dog named Mops," Kreisler recalled. "He would leave us with Mops munching our sandwiches while he himself hastened off to luncheon. We decided we'd play a joke on our teacher which would flatter him. So while the *Meister* was away, we'd play a motif by Wagner, and as we did so, would slap Mops and chase him. Next we'd start Bruckner's *Te Deum*, and while this music was in progress, would give Mops something to eat. He soon showed a convincing preference for the *Te Deum!* When we thought we had trained him sufficiently so that he would automatically run away when Wagner was played and joyfully approach us at the sound of a Bruckner strain, we deemed the moment appropriate for our prank.

" 'Meister Bruckner,' we said one day as he returned from lunch, 'we know that you are devoted to Wagner, but to our way of thinking he cannot compare with you. Why, even a dog would know that you are a greater composer than Wagner.'

"Our guileless teacher blushed. He thought we were serious. He reproved us, paid tribute to Wagner as the unquestionably greatest contemporary, but was nevertheless filled with enough curiosity to ask what we meant by claiming even a dog could tell the difference.

"This was the moment we had waited for. We played a Wagner motif. A howling, scared Mops stole out of the room. We started in on Bruckner's *Te Deum*. A happy canine returned, wagging his tail and pawing expectantly at our sleeves. Bruckner was touched."

At this time of the young conservatory pupil's life there was no piano in the parental home. Not until Fritz's eighteenth year did his father manage to scrape together enough money to afford such a luxury. Absence of this instrument in the home did not, however, keep the young boy from acquiring the art of playing it. He ascertained what the practice-free hours for the students' instruments at the conservatory were, assigned himself to a "free" piano, and, untaught and merely following his own musical genius, acquired a proficiency on the pianoforte which later made Paderewski exclaim to Harriet Kreisler, "Lucky for me that Fritz did not become a professional pianist," and to say to Ambassador Hugh Gibson, "I'd be starving if Kreisler had taken up the piano. How beautifully he plays!"

Pretty soon young Fritz knew, almost effortlessly, the piano accompaniments for all the standard vocal and violin works by heart. When Hellmesberger stumbled upon this fact, he frequently had his

Anton Rubinstein, 1829-1894

Joseph Joachim, 1831-1907

young star pupil play the accompaniments for other students. In this way not only virtually the entire violin literature of the time became indelibly impressed upon Fritz's mind from constant repetition, but he also learned much from the faults as well as the merits of his fellow pupils.

The youngest conservatory student sat more at the piano than he did with his fiddle. Kreisler has all his life been passionately fond of studying scores. Also, from earliest childhood he has had an aversion to practicing on the violin. He always loved to play—but practice? Repeat and repeat and repeat? No! His reasons will be set forth in detail in another chapter.

Kreisler summed up his impressions of his years at the Vienna Conservatory in these words:

"I was much more interested in playing in the park, where my boy friends would be waiting for me, than in taking lessons on the violin. And yet some of the most lasting impressions of my life were gathered there. Not so much as regards study itself, as with respect to the good music I heard. Some very great men played at the conservatory when I was a pupil. There were Joachim, Sarasate at his prime, Hellmesberger, and (Anton) Rubinstein, whom I heard play the first time he came to Vienna. I really believe that hearing Joachim and Rubinstein play was a greater event in my life and did more for me than five years of study."

There were experiences outside his conservatory life which helped to lay the foundation for that broad, universal culture which has astounded followers of Kreisler's career. His father's cronies included, for instance, Dr. Sigmund Freud, who regularly played chess with Dr. Kreisler.

"Freud made a deep impression on me, even though I was unable to grasp fully what he was discussing with my father," Kreisler said. "He was then by no means the famous man he later came to be, but a practicing *magnétiseur*. He tried, in fact, to help my ailing mother by suggesting that she really wasn't crippled at all but would be able to move about after hypnotic treatments. I never saw her walk, however!

"During these evenings with Freud, my father, speaking in that deep but soft and even-tempered voice of his, would often discuss psychoanalysis with his guest. Naturally this talk was above my head. My father's interest in Freud's theories was probably heightened by the fact that he had from time to time substituted for the regular physician of the Police Department, and had thus become acquainted with many cases that the science of today considers as mental.

"Another friend of my father's who left a lasting imprint on my memory was Professor Theodor Billroth, Johannes Brahms's intimate friend, who was not only a great physician but a fine connoisseur of music. It was he, in fact, who some ten years later strongly advised that I drop medicine and devote myself to music."

The diminutive conservatory pupil also profited from the musical discussions that ensued after Carl Goldmark, composer of the opera *Queen of Sheba*, finished playing chess with Dr. Kreisler. Later, as a world-famous violinist, Kreisler was able to thank Goldmark effectively by frequently playing his Violin Concerto and his E Major Suite.

And then there was, above all, the great Johannes Brahms, whose imposing figure Kreisler recalls from earliest childhood. As his direct association with him, however, began only in the nineties, discussion of Brahms's influence on Kreisler's life will come later.

Vienna itself, then a mecca of musical culture, could not but help shape the young prodigy's character.

Fritz Kreisler at seventy-five still recalls the emotion with which he stood at the grave of Beethoven, to which his music-loving father took him one day. A simple cross marked the grave, which was then located in another section of Old Vienna. The idea of a cypress-surrounded, yew-hedge-enclosed Honor Section in the Zentralfriedhof, or Central Cemetery, where the bodies of Beethoven, Gluck, Brahms, Johann Strauss, Schubert, Hugo Wolf, Joseph Lanner, and many famous painters, writers, and sculptors now lie buried, was carried out only later.

He could hardly walk anywhere without being reminded of Vienna's musical heritage, for many an old building displayed an inscription that this or that noted musician had at some period of his life lived there. This was true especially of Mozart, whose body in

Theodor Billroth, 1829-1894

Carl Goldmark, 1830-1915

View of Vienna, about 1870, showing St. Stephen's at upper right and opera house at lower left

Pauper's Row of the St. Marx Cemetery could not be found for re-interment in the Zentralfriedhof. It was also true of various houses in which Beethoven and Schubert had lived.

In conservatory circles there were still old-timers who remembered how Paganini had come there in 1828, Chopin in 1829, Jenny Lind in 1846. Their stories fired the imagination of young Fritz. It was here in Vienna, too, that the paths of the two musical giants of their time, Wagner and Brahms, crossed. Wagner had arrived in 1861 to try in vain to have his *Tristan und Isolde* produced; Brahms took up residence in the Austrian capital in 1862. While the two showed cool detachment toward each other, their followers bitterly contended that their favorite was the one and only true successor to the imposing list of Vienna-bred geniuses that preceded him, and denounced the other as a charlatan and upstart. Even during his early conservatory period, but to a much greater degree in the days of his early manhood, Fritz experienced the violent clashes between the "Wagnerites" and the "Brahmsites."

At an impressionable age he learned the sad story of Mozart's impecunious end, and of the low regard in which musicians were held by some members of the upper classes, as was manifested by the fact that Mozart had to sit at the servants' table with the lackeys, cooks, and barber whenever the Archbishop of Salzburg, in whose employ he was, came to Vienna; and that at this table he received his daily orders as to what Austrian nobleman's palace he was "to make music in" on that particular day. This early impression of an artistic genius's humiliation may have been one reason why the otherwise so modest and unassuming Fritz Kreisler, lovingly prodded by his energetic wife, insisted throughout his professional life upon the social equality of the artist even with royalty.

As young Fritz went to and from the conservatory, he could not but become thrilled again and again at the lofty spires of Vienna's most cherished landmark, the *Stephansdom* (St. Stephen's Cathedral), in the center of the city. "The Old Refrain," one of Kreisler's most popular compositions, is an adaptation of an old folk melody, "Der alte Stephansdom," first sung, as Kreisler remembers it, about the time of the first partition of Poland in 1772. "I took the melody, enlarged upon it, harmonized it, and adapted it to the violin," he explained.

Here, in the Stephansdom, as well as in the *Hofkapelle* (Court Chapel) he could hear his teacher of harmony, Anton Bruckner, play the organ. To see Bruckner approach the cathedral must have been a feast for the eyes of anyone who, like little Fritz, had a keen sense of humor. Bruckner wore upper Austrian homespun clothes, consisting of a heavy, wide jacket tailored in country style and of trousers which "fell in countless wrinkles to his small feet," their bagginess giving his legs "an elephantine appearance. His face was that of an old peasant, wrinkled by air, sun and rain, but it was a peasant face with Roman features and the profile of the Roman Emperor Claudius." * He wore a broad-rimmed artist's hat, which he removed with a deferential flourish as he bowed low to people he knew or whose rank seemed to demand such recognition.

Once Bruckner had reached the organ bench, however, pure gold seemed to issue from the stately pipes of the organ as this unprepossessing man with legs almost too short to reach the pedals poured out his musical soul. Young Fritz, as everyone else, was enraptured.

The three years at the Vienna Conservatory passed rapidly. About two years after his admission, Kreisler played for the first time in a public concert sponsored by the conservatory. He did not remember the exact time. But the Library of Congress in Washington has come into possession of a revealing, hand-written *Journal* compiled by one Paul Löwenberg, who gives his title as *Ober Kontrolor d.Nordb.i.P.* (Chief Comptroller of the Northern Railway, on Pension), and who describes himself as "Investigator, Connoisseur, and Collector." This man devoted ten years to research into the music and dance of the Lanner-Strauss era in Vienna. One of the sections of his *Journal* deals with the date when each violinist made his first public appearance in the Danubian metropolis. For young Fritz the entry is:

Kreissler, Friedr. 9-jaeh. 1884. Mus. Conserv. Czt.

It is interesting to note that the family name is spelled with a double

* Reprinted from *Legend of a Musical City* by Max Graf, by permission of The Philosophical Society, copyright, 1945, by Philosophical Library, Inc.

Fritz Kreisler at the Vienna Conservatory

Fritz Kreisler, about 1917

s.* Also, the more formal "Friedrich" is used instead of the familiar "Fritz." That he was "9-jaehrig," or nine-years old, at the time of this appearance checks with the year, 1884. "Mus." stands for Music Hall, and "Conserv. Czt." for Conservatory Concert.

The fact that young Fritz was soloist in a conservatory recital at the age of nine was nothing completely novel for Vienna. Löwenberg's *Journal* enumerates twelve other youngsters between seven and thirteen years who fiddled there in public concerts during the years of 1805 to 1884, including the thirteen-year-old Henri Vieuxtemps, who played there in 1833.

What was truly sensational, however, was an unprecedented award a year later: Fritz won the first prize for violinists, the gold medal of the Vienna Conservatory, at the age of ten. Most young violinists of his age were at best ready to leave the preparatory classes and start in on their three years of undergraduate work. Fritz, however, had finished his undergraduate work and come out on top of his class!

Not that he was particularly impressed. It so happened that on that very day his playmates had elected him chief of their robber gang. That meant more to him than the gold medal. His parents and the friends of the family were proud and pleased, however. "Fritz must go to Paris for his further musical education," the friends kept insisting to Dr. Kreisler. Also, they united in presenting the young first-laurels winner with a new violin.

Kreisler has described the gift and his reactions to it for the *Musical Courier* as follows:

"As is the custom in my country, a number of artists made a purse, and to commemorate the event presented me, at a charming reception, a three-quarter Amati, an instrument of value and of lovely and penetrating tone. I did not even vouchsafe to bestow a smile upon my generous friends; they thought—and I have never undeceived them—that I was overcome with emotion. I was, in fact, a most ungrateful and sulky boy. At ten years of age, I considered myself a man—I was angry with my father, who would not permit me to wear long trousers

* This spelling occurs also in A. Ehrlich's *Berühmte Geiger der Vergangenheit und Gegenwart* (Famous Violinists, Past and Present), published 1902. Still another spelling, "Kreissle," was used by one of the critics who reported the violinist's first public appearance in Berlin in 1899.

at the reception. I was in a very bad temper that my friends should offer me any but a full-sized violin.

"I—and poor little Amati, whose value I learned to appreciate as I grew older and wiser in my art—now made a trip to Paris with my father."

CHAPTER THREE

PARIS: PUPIL OF MASSART AND DELIBES

[1885-1887]

To send Fritz to Paris was no easy matter for one in Dr. Kreisler's modest financial position. It involved the expense, for himself and his son, of traveling there for the preliminary examinations. True, his boy qualified for a scholarship and thus was educated at the expense of the French government. But there was the further sacrifice of making it possible for his ailing wife to take up residence in Paris in an inexpensive *pension* with her son for over two years.

Had Dr. Kreisler been a better businessman, a physician of his reputation and clientele should by this time have been beyond monetary worries. But business was a book with seven seals to him. The following occurrence, some years after Fritz's marriage, illustrates the point (I use Kreisler's own words):

"One day Harriet and I came to Father's home near Christmas time. He was rather worried about his financial status.

" 'But Papa,' Harriet said, 'you are not badly off. I see by your books that you have a large number of patients.' 'Yes,' admitted my father, 'but they haven't paid.' 'But don't you send out bills?' Harriet pressed. Touchingly naïve, Father remonstrated, 'Aber ich kann doch nicht Rechnungen an Freunde schicken!' (But, after all, I can't send bills to friends!)

"Many of the patients at that time could well afford to pay. There were bankers and successful businessmen among them. So Harriet took matters into hand and sent out bills. Most patients paid promptly; Father was rid of his worries."

In France a new world unfolded for the alert, open minded, inquisitive young Fritz. He was fascinated by the melodious language of the country and soon became as versatile in French as he was in his native Austrian. Paris completely captivated him. He loved the symmetry and beauty of its stately structures, its expansive boulevards, its incomparable Bois de Boulogne.

Throughout his life Fritz Kreisler has been extremely sensitive to beauty and symmetry, and allergic to ugliness, unharmoniousness, and dissymmetry. Here, then, was a city after his own heart, more grandiose and congruous even than his beloved Vienna.

Paris became his spiritual home. Despite his affection for Austria, the land of his birth, and his genuine loyalty to America, the land of his final adoption, Paris has remained the city at the mention of which his eyes sparkle especially brightly and his reminiscent smile becomes especially ingratiating.

Jacques Thibaud, Kreisler's greatest French contemporary violinist colleague, recently remarked: "Fritz's love for France has always been great. How often, when we met again, he would ask me anxiously, 'What can I do for the French musicians?' Paris was the first great city that really recognized his worth. He has never forgotten that."

Many things have been unusual in Kreisler's life. Who, for instance, could have foreseen that a septuagenarian Belgian would become the postgraduate tutor, in Paris, of a ten-year-old lad from Vienna? Yet this is exactly what happened: Fritz became the pupil of seventy-four-year-old Joseph Lambert Massart, himself a student of Beethoven's friend Rudolph Kreutzer, immortalized by the dedication of the "Kreutzer" Sonata.

Massart in his fifty years of teaching at the Paris Conservatoire had had such distinguished pupils as Henri Wieniawski, Franz Ries, and Franz Ondřiček. Fritz Kreisler was to be the last. Dr. Kreisler was immensely pleased when, several years later, he received a letter from Massart informing him, "I have been the teacher of Wieniawski and many others; but little Fritz will be the greatest of them all."

Rudolph Kreutzer, 1766-1831

Joseph Lambert Massart, 1811-1892

Henri Wieniawski, 1835-1880

Henri Vieuxtemps, 1820-1881

In the opinion of Leopold Weninger, "It may be assumed that Kreisler owes the elegance of his bowing and the crystal clearness of his intonation (*Tongebung*) to this teacher."

Kreisler's own version of his Paris tutor is:

"Massart was wonderful. Born in Liège, he had certain charming Belgian characteristics. He was clean shaven and always wore a high cravat. He was passionately devoted to the violin—so much so, in fact, that he apparently was not even curious about what Beethoven may have told Kreutzer, or what the two must have experienced together.

"Massart laid stress on emotion, on feeling, and not on technique. Sevčic, the teacher of Jan Kubelik, was interested chiefly in technique.

"I believe Massart liked me because I played in the style of Wieniawski. You will recall that Wieniawski intensified the vibrato and brought it to heights never before achieved, so that it became known as the 'French vibrato.' * Vieuxtemps also took it up, and after him Eugène Ysaÿe, who became its greatest exponent, and I. Joseph Joachim, for instance, disdained it."

Hand in hand with Kreisler's violinistic training under Massart went lessons in musical composition under Leo Delibes, whose light operas were then very popular in Paris.

"Delibes was a gay blade," Fritz said. "He was rather flighty and irresponsible. Often when we were in the midst of a composition lesson some pretty young damsel would come along and suggest it was time to *déjeuner* or go for a stroll. 'Allons danser!' (Let's go dancing!) was another favorite challenge of his girl friends. Delibes could never resist such a call. He would hand me the beginnings of some composition on which he happened to be at work, suggest that I try to catch the spirit of it, and then charge me with going on from there.

"Even today the 'Coppélia' waltz, taken from his ballet *Coppélia*, is often played. Well, I can truthfully claim that the motif is mine. Delibes, returning from one of his adventures with the fair sex, liked

* *Webster's Dictionary* defines vibrato as "a slightly tremulous or pulsating effect (but not a tremolo) for adding warmth and beauty to the tone or for expressing changes in emotional intensity." The vibrato can be traced back prior to 1636.

it so well that he took it into his ballet unchanged and developed and embellished it."

Within the two years under the tutelage of Massart and Delibes fell, rather by accident, Kreisler's only attempt at conducting. It happened thus:

"To earn a few francs, I would occasionally play at the first violin desk of the Pasdeloup Orchestra in the Cirque d'hiver. One day a Czech violinist came for a rehearsal. The orchestra parts were there, but the conductor's score was missing. I had previously boasted that I knew this score—meaning, of course, the piano version—by heart.

" 'Eh bien, garçon arrogant' (very well, insolent fellow), the conductor, Jules Étienne Pasdeloup, said, turning to me, 'you claim to know the music by heart. You now show us by taking over.' I hadn't the faintest notion as to which instrument was to play what, but I did know all the motifs and every note of the piano score. Somehow I went through my only performance as conductor to the satisfaction of the orchestra and soloist."

While playing in the Pasdeloup ensemble, Fritz for the first and only time met César Franck, whose violin sonata became one of his favorites. Franck, during a pause in the rehearsal of his symphonic poem, *Le Chasseur maudit*, for chorus and orchestra, came up to Fritz, sitting at the first violin desk, to say how he wanted a certain section played. The conductor turned rather abruptly to the unannounced visitor and said, "How dare you tell my musicians how they are to play?" Franck replied, calmly and with dignity, "I happen to be the composer."

Came the day in 1887 when advanced violin students of the conservatory, most of them at least a decade older than Fritz, competed for the coveted Premier Prix of the institution.

The forty-two aspirants faced an extremely exacting jury of professors of the conservatory. Many a young man or woman faltered during the ordeal. Although Kreisler has been shy throughout his life in other matters, stage fright has never bothered him. Once he has his violin in his hand, he feels himself master of the situation. Some people have wrongly attributed a slight twitch of his face muscles in

Cesar Franck, 1822-1890

Kreisler as winner of the Premier Premier Prix with the other first prize winners

later years to stage fright. Anybody who knows him well can testify that this is not so. Audiences never scare him.

During this Paris competition his *sang-froid* and imperturbable musical self-assurance once again stood him in good stead. As the contest continued, it became quite clear that he was likely to emerge as the Premier Grand Prix winner. This was very unusual but not unprecedented. There had been talented under-age students of the conservatory in the tryouts of earlier years to whom this distinction had been awarded.

A far greater sensation, however, was in store for the participants: the jury ranked a mere child, twelve-year-old Fritz, ahead of all other Premier Prix winners. That was unprecedented. The Conservatoire's *Distribution des prix pour le cours d'études de l'année 1887* announced that five violinists that year (the number varied from year to year) won the *premiers prix* for their instrument. The names were given in the following order:

M. Friedrich-Max Kreisler, born in Vienna, Feb. 2, 1875.
Mlle. Berthe-Euphémie-Marie Gauthier, born in Paris, Dec. 7, 1869.
M. Charles-Henry Wondra, born in Constantinople, Aug. 29, 1866.
M. Léon-Darius Herbeuval Pellenc, born in Toulon, Nov. 23, 1866.
M. Charles-Louis Rinuccini, born in Cluny, Sept. 15, 1873.

Kreisler was therefore proclaimed the Premier Premier Prix (First First Prize) winner among five violinists who had made the top grade. A photograph taken on graduation day shows young Fritz as the central figure among seven first prize winners—four men and three women. "The other two ladies," Fritz explained, "were pianists."

The competitions took place on Thursday, July 28, 1887; graduation exercises were held Thursday, August 4, presided over by M. Spuller, French Minister of Education, Religion and Fine Arts.

This authentic version of what took place, taken from the official records of the Conservatoire, explodes the myth that young Fritz won the Grand Prix de Rome. This prize was awarded by the Académie des Beaux-Arts of the Institut de France and not the Conservatoire, and in 1887 went to Gustave Charpentier. It was exclusively for composers. "Obviously at twelve I was not a composer,"

Kreisler commented. Yet one German musicologist represented Kreisler as having attended the University of Bologna during his Grand Prix de Rome incumbency, and various other writers had him studying both music and painting in the Eternal City. Fact is that Kreisler went from Paris back to his native Vienna, and from there on his first concert tour of America.

Winning the Premier Prix of the Conservatoire meant getting rid of the three-quarter violin. It will be recalled how chagrined young Fritz was when the parting gift of his Vienna well-wishers was not a full-fledged fiddle but only a three-quarter Amati. Kreisler said about his Paris experience: *

"Even during the two years of this most interesting and profitable period, my Amati did not altogether succeed in winning forgiveness. It continually reminded me that I was not a man (and that I still wore knee breeches), and this in spite of the fact that it had been my faithful ally in winning the gold medal and the Premier Premier Prix.

"Ungrateful little wretch that I was, I was the happiest boy in the world when I finally held in my arms a full-sized violin.

"It was a Gand-Bernadel and was the usual gift † of the conservatory to a Grand Prix winner. I thought more of that brilliant red instrument, with its gilded inscription announcing the fact that I was the honor pupil, than I did of the gold medal or the even more valuable Premier Grand Prix de Rome.

"Its tone was none too beautiful and it was not long before its loud and strident voice jarred upon my musical nerves, and I would gladly have returned to the discarded Amati, but, as a matter of fact, my big arms and fingers had altogether outgrown it. Fate punished me for my ingratitude. I was forced to play upon that ugly red instrument, which became more and more of an offense to me."

His last lesson with Massart was the last formal instruction he received.

"Since I was twelve I have never had any regular tuition," Kreisler

* Reprinted from *The Story of My Violins*, by Fritz Kreisler, in the April 8, 1908 issue of the *Musical Courier*, by permission of the *Musical Courier*.

† Charles François Gand inaugurated the custom as *luthier du Conservatoire* (instrument-maker for the conservatory).

explained. "But I had an unerring sense of what was right and realized that every great artist was my teacher. So I gathered good impressions wherever I could, and in due time became a pupil of not only every great performer, but of the great minds in literature and art. The Bible, Homer, Goethe, Shakespeare, and Dante were my household treasures of literature."

CHAPTER FOUR

IN KNEE PANTS ON THE AMERICAN CONCERT PLATFORM

[1888-1889]

ONE day in the spring or summer of 1888, Edmund C. Stanton, manager of the New York Metropolitan Opera House, came to Vienna to call on Moriz Rosenthal, whose wizardry on the piano has almost become legendary, though he was only twenty-six years old then. Stanton wanted the celebrated Polish-born Austrian artist to make a concert tour of the United States.

"In those days it was not customary for a pianist to fill an entire evening," Kreisler recalled. "Another soloist was therefore necessary. I had attracted mild attention by winning the Vienna and Paris conservatory prizes. Moriz Rosenthal had heard me.

"The Steinway brothers in New York had suggested that Mr. Stanton go to Vienna personally to see Rosenthal, a pupil of Franz von Liszt.

"Stanton was an impeccable gentleman, immaculately dressed. I remember especially his patent-leather boots. I had never seen such gorgeous boots in my life, and they entranced me. But he was a kindly, considerate gentleman of the old school of American managers, a keen promoter, but a man of integrity in every sense of the word.

"Rosenthal arranged to have me appear with him in fifty concerts, at $50 an appearance. He further agreed that my mother should accompany me.

"A rare treat was in store for me as the parting gift of my father. This dear, good man had economized and saved a sum equal to $1,000, with which he purchased a most beautiful Grancino, an instrument for which he knew I had a huge longing and admiration. This Grancino was the faithful and beloved associate of my musical career for the next eight years. It marked, so to speak, the beginning and subsequent growth of my public life and my reputation as an artist of serious and high ideals. I have naught but affectionate praise to bestow upon this faithful friend, who at the slightest touch of my fingers justified my confidence and responded to my moods.

"We traveled from Vienna to Salzburg, Munich, Frankfurt, and then north to either Hamburg or Bremen. It meant changing cars several times; still, the journey must be considered very commodious for that period, for sleepers had already come into existence.

"Our small, 8,000-ton steamer had but one deck and employed sails in addition to machine propulsion. Our voyage lasted three weeks. I was extremely seasick. In fact, I may interpolate that I continued to have violent attacks of *mal de mer* until about 1906, after which I have never again been seasick.

"Seeing New York was one of the greatest thrills of my life. We stopped at the Hotel Oriental, quite near the old 'Met.' In those days, the Borough of Manhattan didn't go beyond Forty-eighth Street. What lay beyond was suburbs.

"My ailing mother found herself unable to accompany me on my tour through the United States, but Rosenthal took me under his wing and became one of the great influences upon my life. In New York, the Steinways were especially kind to me.

"My two strongest impressions on reaching the United States were: first, the men had their feet on their desks; second, the girls were very beautiful. (Though only thirteen years old then, I had an eye for the ladies!)

"In the concert halls I had this impression: the audience seemed to judge an artist by his looks, whereas I was accustomed in Europe to having music lovers come to listen only."

Young Fritz, fortunately, had both looks and musicianship. The New York *Times* reported that "society flocked to hear him and the name of 'Fritz' was on the lips of all who professed to know music."

But even now his dream of long trousers had not come true. American newspaper accounts of the day reported, "He dresses in a velvet sack and short breeches and wears high, shining boots." Another account added that tassels dangled from the tops of his boots. A third described him as "an awkward youth, and the long Hessian boots which he wore did not add to the grace of his bearing, for they seemed to make him heavy-footed." The photograph taken for publicity purposes indicates, further, that he had very long hair parted in the middle, and that he wore a big, white "butterfly" bow tie.

"Master Fritz Kreisler," as he was billed, made his debut in Boston on Friday, November 9, 1888. The place sticks in Kreisler's memory even today, not so much because it was his first American appearance, but because he there struck up a friendship with Franz Kneisel, concertmaster of the Boston Symphony Orchestra and first violinist of the famous Kneisel Quartet, with whom he had become only cursorily acquainted in Vienna.

"Meeting Kneisel again in Boston was a great experience for me," he remarked.

Two Boston newspapers, the *Daily Globe* and the *Daily Advertiser*, sent their critics, Howard Malcolm Ticknor and Louis C. Elson, respectively, to report in detail on the American debut of Herr Rosenthal and Master Kreisler. Curiously enough, these two musical experts arrived at opposite conclusions about the young violinist. Said Ticknor:

> The lad . . . accomplished his task creditably but gave no evidence of possessing remarkable talent or remarkable training. . . . He plays like a nice, studious boy who has a rather musical nature . . . *but cannot be ranked among prodigies or geniuses.*

Elson wrote:

> *Young Master Kreisler is a genius* who has yet something to learn. . . . *He is, I think, destined to become a very great artist*, if he does not disdain further study.

Master Fritz played the Mendelssohn Concerto for Violin and Orchestra and the "Hungarian Airs" by Ernst at his debut. Walter Damrosch, with whom he was to appear many a time in the future as a world-famous artist, conducted at this performance.

The critic Elson was impressed by something else: He noted that

Franz Kneisel, 1865-1926

'he Kneisel Quartet at Kneisel's summer home at Blue Hill, Maine

Publicity photo of the thirteen-year-old Kreisler

the young artist was plagued twice in the same Mendelssohn concerto by the misfortune common to violinists before the day of steel strings; namely, that of the snapping of the E-string. Young Fritz met the situation in the beautiful andante by continuing on his A-string, and in the rapid finale by seizing the fiddle of the concertmaster.

"That the boy was not made nervous by the accident and played to the end of the andante on the A-string in higher position, proves him already a veteran," Elson observed.

The following night young Kreisler made his first professional bow to New York, in Steinway Hall. He shared honors on this occasion, however, not with Rosenthal, but with Conrad Ansorge from Berlin. The preliminary announcement read:

Anton Seidl's
GRAND ORCHESTRAL CONCERTS
First Subscription Concert
Saturday Evening, Nov. 10, 1888
at 8.15 precisely

Soloists
Mr. Conrad Ansorge, Pianist
Master Fritz Kreisler, Violinist
His first appearance in New York by kind permission of Mr. Edmund C. Stanton, Director Metropolitan Opera Company

The announcement further stated that Seidl would conduct Beethoven's "Pastoral" Symphony, the Entr'acte from Carl Maria von Weber's *The Three Pintos* (first time), Liszt's *Legend: The Bird Sermon of St. Francis of Assisi*, and Edouard Lalo's Rhapsody for Orchestra; Ansorge would render Schubert-Liszt's "Wanderer" Fantasia, and Kreisler the Mendelssohn Concerto.

The critic of the New York *Tribune* had this to say:

> The first impression created by him [Kreisler] was a most favorable one, and throughout the evening admiration was held by the faultless purity of his intonation; unfortunately, however, his tone is exceedingly small. . . . That he has unusual talent is indisputable and we would prefer to postpone judgment until after the appearance at the Rosenthal concert on Tuesday.

Moriz Rosenthal, who was placarded as "Pianist to the Queen of Roumania," naturally had the lion's share of numbers in his debut a few days later with the Metropolitan Opera House Orchestra, Anton Seidl conducting; young Fritz was merely supporting artist with a rendition of Vieuxtemps's "Fantaisie Caprice," which he played with piano accompaniment. That was, however, the moment the critic of the *Tribune* had been waiting for. He burst into this paean of praise:

> Young Master Kreisler, no longer crushed down by the weight of Mr. Seidl's orchestra as on last Saturday evening, made a much more favorable impression. He certainly has a most agile and accurate left hand. If his tone production, i.e., his manipulation of the bow, were as excellent as his tone formation, *he would be a violinist, young as he is, who could measure himself with some of those who stand highest in the world's admiration.*

It was a lucky thing for Master Fritz that he could hold the critic's attention, for on that night many a listener's mind went wandering from time to time. The reason: it was one of the most exciting weeks in the political life of the nation. A fierce presidential election campaign had been fought between the Democratic incumbent, President Grover Cleveland, and the Republican aspirant, General Benjamin Harrison. The ballots had been in for days, but the outcome—Harrison's victory—had been conceded finally by the opposition only that morning. During the intermissions concertgoers talked chiefly about the election.

There was special significance that night in the footnote to programs that was rather standard in the eighties and nineties of the last century:

> The respectful request is made that all attending these concerts will be seated by 8.15, in consideration of the comfort of those desirous of enjoying the first part of the symphony without interruption; also that any one desirous of entering or leaving the concert will kindly do so between the pieces.

As a further side light on the general status of musical culture in America in those days, it may be noted that advertisements of concerts were always run under the heading of "Amusements."

After several additional appearances in New York the Rosenthal party went on tour. The word "party" is used designedly, for there was also the accompanist for young Fritz, Dr. Bernhard Pollak. Among the cities in which Fritz could learn to know the American way of life were Chicago, Cleveland, St. Louis, Kansas City, and New Orleans. A complete list is not extant.

Chicago at that time made a strong bid as musical center. The auditorium was under construction, and plans were already under way for dedication exercises in December, 1889, at which Adelina Patti was to sing "Home, Sweet Home" as the opening number, and Eugen D'Albert, Pablo Sarasate, Lilli Lehmann, and Walter Damrosch were to be among the first artists to be heard in the new temple of music. It was a time when Teresa Carreño, the fiery Venezuelan artist, Hans von Bülow, interpreter of Beethoven and noted conductor, and Chicago's own Fannie Bloomfield-Zeisler vied for pianistic honors in the growing metropolis on Lake Michigan.

Master Fritz's Chicago debut came on March 1, 1889, in the third subscription concert of the Chicago Symphony Society, Hans Balatka conducting. The society numbered among its patrons such familiar Chicagoans as the Marshall Fields, the George M. Pullmans, the Robert T. Lincolns, the Potter Palmers, the Reginald de Kovens, Cyrus H. McCormick, Clarence Eddy, and Victor Lawson. Rosenthal had selected the Chopin Piano Concerto in E Minor for his first piece, and his own arrangement of Liszt's "Rhapsodies Hongroises" for the second; Master Kreisler played Wieniawski's "Fantasia on Themes from Faust."

The Chicago *Times* opined that young Kreisler "plays remarkably well for his years. . . . If his bowing were as good as his left-hand work he would now be one of the most remarkable players of the day."

The Chicago *Tribune*, less favorably impressed, found that "his performance was crude and frequently out of tune." It conceded, however, that "he possesses undeniable talent, but will have to devote himself to severe and continuous study in order to become a really great artist."

As already indicated, the young artist's mother was not well enough to accompany him through America. The lad was not at a loss, however, as to how to spend his time. He did an enormous amount of reading and applied himself assiduously to learning English. Languages have always been a favorite study with Kreisler. Soon he spoke

English with the same ease with which, since his Conservatoire days, he could converse in French.

But what he liked then most to talk about was music—so much so that Rosenthal from time to time chided his young friend: "You are only a fiddler, Fritz. You know nothing but how to play those strings. You can't even talk about anything else." *

With the ending of the 1888–1889 concert season, the Rosenthal-Kreisler American tour came to a close, and Master Fritz started on the homeward journey, with but little money left after expenses had been paid, but enriched by an experience in globe-trotting that could not but have a beneficent effect on as alert and inquisitive and sensitive a soul as his.

* Reproduced by permission of *Etude, The Music Magazine*, from an article by C. D. Isaacson, "Why Great Artists Succeed." Copyright 1930 by Theodore Presser Company.

Fannie Bloomfield-Zeisler, 1863-1927

Kreisler at about 60 years of age

CHAPTER FIVE

THE FIDDLE YIELDS TO THE PEN, SCALPEL, AND SWORD

[1889-1895]

SOME fifteen years ago Kreisler, then almost sixty years old, discussed musical prodigies in an interview for the *Etude* with Carlton A. Scheinert.*

He deplored that people frequently destroy an artist with their "unreasonable adoration" and with too high expectations. Parents, he added, "destroy the incipient artist in a talented child in the same way. Children should grow simply in music and not be forced into it for business reasons. Reaching their early twenties, their physique is gone, their vitality drained." He pointed out that many musical child wonders were being booked merely because one or two of them had proven box-office successes.

Dr. Kreisler had not been moved by mercenary considerations when he let his son go to America with Moriz Rosenthal. He had approved of the tour because of the experience and broadening of mind it would bring, and because he was aware that musical performance was second nature to Fritz, without draining his nervous energies or threatening to retard his growth. No thought was further from his mind than to capitalize in a commercial way on his boy's success in the United States after his return to Europe.

On the contrary, his ailing wife and sturdy son had no sooner arrived in Vienna, than Dr. Kreisler gave his older boy a fatherly talk.

* Reprinted by permission of *Etude, The Music Magazine*, copyright, 1934, by Theodore Presser Company.

"Fritz," he said, "you are now approaching your fifteenth year, and it is high time that you get down to organized study. Besides, in a few years you will have to report for military duty, and if you want to become a *Freiwilliger* (volunteer), you will need your *Abitur*" (the equivalent of qualifying for junior year in college). Young men who had completed their Gymnasium studies and passed their *Abitur* were permitted to volunteer for one year's training as privates, after which they could take a military examination for a reserve lieutenant's commission.

"This meant crowding into two years all the educational training I had missed because of my Vienna and Paris conservatory days," Kreisler explained. "The normal thing would have been to hire a *Pauker* (slang word for tutor). My father was too poor to do this. So he himself taught me Greek, Latin, and physics, sometimes staying up all night to prepare for my lesson. I had to work hard. But through my father's patient teaching I developed a special love for Homer's *Iliad* and Virgil's *Aeneid*."

The high school to which Fritz, who had from childhood been raised in the Roman Catholic faith, was sent was known as the Piaristen Gymnasium. It was conducted by Catholic lay brethren of the Piarist order. One of them took a special fancy to the young artist and taught him to play the organ.

Learning has always come easily to Fritz. Nevertheless he, one of the world's most traveled men, "nearly flunked in geography. As a precondition to entering the army as *Freiwilliger*, we had, as part of our Gymnasium final exams, to demonstrate our ability at drawing maps. Now, all I knew about Italy, for instance, was that in a general way it was shaped like a boot. As to Tyrol, I had the greatest difficulty to draw a map of it. I just managed to squeeze through the geography course with a rating of *schwach* (weak).

"My inability even to draw a map should dispose once and for all of the rumor that I studied painting under Julien of Paris. I have never been able to live that story down. I have not painted a picture in my life.

"It is also not true, as has been claimed, that I studied engineering."

Two years at the Piaristen Gymnasium sufficed to enable Fritz Kreisler to pass his *Abitur*. What next? He was now almost eighteen years old. He had nearly two years to go before enlisting in the army. Considering his environment, it is not surprising that he elected to study medicine.

"I have always been interested in medicine, and am even now," he said. "In fact, when two years later I joined the colors, I was in a quandary as to whether to go into the medical corps or train to become a combat officer.

"In those youthful days I had some very weird thoughts about my future career. I envisaged myself operating on a patient in the morning, playing chess in the afternoon, giving a concert in the evening, and (in anticipation of a glorious military career) winning a battle at midnight."

So he entered the medical school of the university, whose outstanding *Kapazität* (authority) was Professor Theodor Billroth. During this period, he said, "I sat most of the time in a coffee house studying, my only fare being bread, coffee, and cigarettes."

It so chances that a noted physician on the Pacific Coast remembers having been at medical school with Kreisler. This gentleman, Baron Zdenko Dworzak of Santa Monica, California, son of a chief justice of Austria, revealed that nobody in the class, so far as he remembers, spoke of Kreisler as a musician. This is the more surprising when one learns that Dworzak himself was passionately fond of music and was a regular attendant at, and sometimes participant in, the musicales of Billroth. So completely had Kreisler abandoned his instrument, that to his classmates in the dissecting room (in which alone Dworzak and he met) he was just another medical student who, like the others, "had his scalpel in one hand while with the other he held a sandwich and ate." The idea that Kreisler might be an artist with international training and experience was not even thought of, according to Dr. Dworzak. The only unusual thing about him was that "he did not watch his hands at all" while dissecting a corpse.

The explanation for "not watching his hands" is not difficult to discover: Fritz evidently turned his nose as far away as possible. Allergic as he has always been to anything unaesthetic, the odors of a human corpse nauseated him. Billroth one day remarked to Kreisler, Sr., that he did not believe the son would ever become a successful surgeon. "Why," he said, "even the corpse is too smelly for him" (Es stinkt ihm schon der Leichnam).

On one occasion, as young Kreisler was just emerging from the dissecting room, he chanced to encounter Billroth. The noted savant asked him all sorts of searching questions and also requested him to describe what dissecting he had done. "I fear my answers were not satisfactory," the victim of this friendly inquisition recalls.

By coincidence Fritz's father just then was pondering which of three professions his son should make his life's work—should he become an officer, a doctor, or a musician? He confided his problem to his friend Billroth, who remarked tersely: "Als Offizier—na, gut. Als Arzt—bestens mittelmässig. Als Musiker—erstklassig" (As an officer —well, O.K. As a doctor—middling at best. As a musician—first class). He added prophetically, "But his interest in medicine will always remain."

After taking two of the five required years of medical training, Fritz abandoned his formal medical studies. But he never lost his love for the science of medicine. When he became a collector of rare books, ancient medical works figured among those he assiduously acquired. Also, throughout his adult life he has kept a medical dictionary within reach. "I still retain considerable medical knowledge," he asserted. "Whenever I have been ill, the doctors and nurses could not fool me. I could read the medical charts with the fever curves, pulse measurements, and so forth, and knew what the medicines meant."

During his two years of premedical training Kreisler was able to crowd in some courses in philosophy, a branch of learning that has remained a favorite with him until today. When *Human Destiny*, by Pierre Lecomte du Noüy, fell into his hands in May, 1948, he commented, "It is one of the best books I have ever read." As a devout Christian he was cheered at the thought that this eminent scientist chose to "fight paralyzing skepticism and destructive materialism, which are by no means the inevitable consequences of the scientific interpretation of nature, as we have been led to believe. . . . Science was used to sap the base of religion. Science must be used to consolidate it." *

All through Gymnasium and medical school the violinist-prodigy of earlier days never touched his instrument. "I did, however, occasionally go to a concert," Kreisler remembers. Also, as already pointed out, he had a temporary fling at the organ.

Music began to a certain degree to reenter his life when he became a soldier in the Kaiserjäger Regiment of the imperial Austrian army. By a fortunate circumstance the chief of his regiment was Archduke Eugene of Hapsburg, a grand-nephew of Emperor Francis Joseph. The archduke was not only a devoted amateur of music himself, but had chanced to hear little Fritz when he was the youngest pupil of the Vienna Conservatory. Also, he had met him again during his medical school days on an occasion which Fritz recalls with some embarrassment. Hellmesberger had taken him to a reception given by one of the most amusing but also most outspoken personages of the time—the Princess Pauline Metternich.

The princess, an intimate friend of Empress Eugénie of France, was now over seventy, but still a brilliant conversationalist, with a penchant for risqué stories, which she told in beautiful French. During this reception she indulged in her favorite pastime and narrated an anecdote, the ribald point to which came at the very end. Noticing the teen-ager Fritz among the listeners, she turned to him and asked, "Did you understand?"

Of course Fritz did, for he had learned to master French during his Paris Conservatory days. To be polite, however, and to save the princess possible embarrassment, he blushed and stammered, "*Durchlaucht* (Highness), I got most of it, but not the end." Whereupon the uninhibited noblewoman proceeded to explain the point to her naughty story in great detail, leaving out no "fact of life!"

Archduke Eugene remembered that Freiwilliger Kreisler had a reputation as an accompanist. The Hapsburg scion was wont to contribute

* Reprinted from *Human Destiny* by Lecomte du Noüy, by permission of Longmans, Green and Co., Inc., copyright, 1947, by Lecomte du Noüy.

a vocal number to the musical programs given from time to time by members of the regiment to its officers and their ladies. He asked Kreisler to accompany him.

For one such occasion he chose a selection from Halévy's opera *La Juive* (The Jewess). The young accompanist took the piano score to his billet after the concert and forgot all about it.

A few days later there was a knock at his door. The archduke's orderly entered. He handed the young Officer's Candidate a slip of paper on which His Imperial Highness had scribbled, "Schick' mir schnell die Jüdin" (Send me the Jewess quickly). Kreisler complied and thought no more about the incident. Some days later, when he was in Vienna, he received a summons from the archduke's father.

"Come now," said this blueblood sternly, "tell me the name of that Jewess whom my son and you have been keeping between you."

"Respectfully begging your pardon, Highness, I don't understand," was the young man's truthful rejoinder.

"Don't try to stall," the Hapsburg prince continued, icily. "How is it that my son sent you this?" He produced the paper with the ominous words, "Send me the Jewess quickly."

It required unusual muscular control for young Kreisler to prevent his bursting out in laughter, and considerable tact and diplomacy to explain to the irate father that any fears of promiscuous living on the part of his son were unjustified. One must be fair, however, and understand the parental apprehensions, especially when one remembers that the archduke was Grand Master of the Order of Teutonic Knights, a position which enjoined celibacy and continence upon its titleholder. Armies are not aggregations of saints, and Eros was not an outcast to the average Viennese!

Legends to the contrary notwithstanding, Fritz insists that he did take his violin into his hands from time to time while serving his first year of military service, and played for his comrades. "Of course, I did not get much chance to practice," he added.

As to the Archduke Eugene, Kreisler remembers him as an exceedingly democratic, simple fellow: "Far rather than attend court functions, he'd come in mufti to the *Schwemme* ('pub') of the Imperial

Hotel to sit with musicians. Often he'd load all of them into his fiacre and drive out to Grinzing * with them."

"In those days," Kreisler reminisced, "an artist's life was very simple indeed, and those who really cared about music and art shared this simple life with him. That was exactly what Archduke Eugene did. He never 'pulled rank,' though he was the colonel of our regiment."

Whatever else the army may have done to Fritz Kreisler, it certainly conditioned him for the strenuous life of an itinerant artist that lay ahead, and enabled him to embark upon travel schedules that would have floored any less robust and healthy nature. Fritz Kreisler enjoyed his service with the colors thoroughly. He was fond of the outdoor life, of athletics and sports, and of the conviviality of the *Regimentsabende* (regiment evenings). Austrian army life, after all, in the days before World War I was rather *gemütlich*!

His reserve lieutenant's commission was issued in the name of Friedrich Kreisler and was dated December 24, 1900, effective January 1, 1901. His active service in the army as rookie had comprised the years 1895–1896.

* Grinzing is the charming and delightful suburb to the north of Vienna which abounds in *Heurigenschänken*, i.e., wine restaurants dispensing a special young wine, the *Heurigen*, served both indoors and on tables placed throughout the parklike outside. String and dance bands add to the general gaiety, and the folk song and folk dance are at home there.

CHAPTER SIX

BACK IN HIS ELEMENT, MUSIC

[1896-1898]

MORE than six years had passed since the *Wunderkind* had returned from his first American concert tour. These formative years were spent to lasting advantage. Gymnasium attendance further deepened the fathomless fund of knowledge and culture that astounds everyone who comes into closer contact with Fritz Kreisler. Association with the humane and selfless profession of medicine opened the floodgates of compassion in Kreisler for the downtrodden, the unfortunate, the hungry, and the sick. Living the open-air life of the army strengthened his physical stamina and acquainted him with a phase of life that usually lies outside the experience of the artist.

It was inevitable, nevertheless, that a young man so exceptionally gifted with musical talent and so lavishly endowed with an uncanny ability for playing different instruments and for composing, should return to his first love and make the violin the chosen instrument for expressing what his soul felt and strove and yearned for.

His choice to take up music as a life's career met with the wholehearted approval of his father, whose last qualms of conscience had been removed by Professor Billroth's terse judgment. Once the momentous decision had been made, father and son devoted themselves single-mindedly to fulfilling the promise that Fritz's performance as child prodigy had given. In Kreisler's words:

"My father arranged with a *Gastwirt* (tavern owner) on the outskirts of Vienna whose predecessor, as was indicated by a memorial tablet, had similarly offered Franz Schubert refuge, for me to have a

Kreisler in the 1890's

Arnold Schönberg, 1874-1951

Kreisler and Schönberg in the Tyrolese band

room and board in exchange for my fiddling occasionally in the *Schankstube* (saloon). I spent eight weeks there in seclusion and solitude, getting back into my stride and recovering my manual dexterity. I even made one of my arrangements of a Paganini composition."

Thus conditioned, the young man started on a period of about five years of struggle for world recognition—years of pleasant reminiscences but also of sad disappointments. After that, however, his rise was meteoric, especially after Harriet Lies, his future wife, had come into his life.

There was one deed of immortality that stems from this time, incredible though it may seem. At the age of only nineteen, Kreisler composed the two famous cadenzas for the Beethoven Violin Concerto which musicians of greatest rank have pronounced as among the best ever written. The eyes of violinistic contemporaries like Jacques Thibaud, Albert Spalding, Jascha Heifetz, and Nathan Milstein sparkle when mention is made of these cadenzas, especially the monumental one at the close of the first movement.

The late critic Henry T. Finck paid apt tribute to this early Kreisler effort at composition, observing that the cadenzas "sum up the essence of Beethoven's music as a few drops of attar of rose do the fragrance of an acre of flowers."

At the time when the cadenzas were composed, Kreisler revealed: "Arnold Schönberg was by no means the revolutionary of later years. He took the greatest interest in my Beethoven cadenzas, and especially admired my combination, in fuguelike form, of various themes. In those days he was also an enthusiastic Wagnerian." He even played the cello in a jolly Tyrolese band in which Kreisler played the violin.

The same young man who wrote the classic cadenzas also loved to go to the Prater, Vienna's world-famous amusement park along the Danube, to hear a military band in the Third Café—the very café in which Franz Lehár later became band leader.

"A number of us young fellows frequently used to go to the Prater on Sundays," Kreisler said. "We liked to see the elegant equipages go by. We liked to go down to the Danube for a swim. We liked to join in the games that were often played there. And we liked the band music. I even wrote military marches at one time."

When Kreisler felt he was back in perfect violinistic form, he applied for a position at the second desk, next to the first concertmaster, of the Vienna Hofoper (court opera) orchestra.

"My father was in rather straitened financial circumstances about this time, and I considered it my duty to earn money as quickly as possible," Kreisler explained.

The incredible happened: he was denied the position. He, the medal winner of a native and a foreign conservatory; he, the "boy wonder" whom some American critics considered a coming genius; he, the unusual musician who knew not only his violin, but could play dozens of piano scores from memory, was rejected. Why?

Arnold Rosé, founder of the string quartet that bore his name and carried his fame through the concert halls of Europe and America, was then first concertmaster of the court opera orchestra. He auditioned the candidates. His verdict on Fritz was, "Er kann nicht vom Blatt lesen" (He's no good at sight reading).

It is hard to believe that even a jot of validity could have been inherent in this verdict. Young Kreisler was known fairly to devour new and unknown scores. One possible explanation is the jealousy of an older artist who may have sensed the coming man in the young colleague.

Another explanation is that suggested by Dr. Dworzak of California, who moved about in the leading musical circles of Vienna.

"The older generation," Dworzak commented, "the sticklers to the old and accepted tradition, disliked anything that did not conform to their established traditional style and exactness. . . . Individualism was not accepted as such, but was considered rather as a breach of tradition."

This tallies with a remark of Kreisler's: "I have always gone my own individual way. Either people took me to their heart, or they rejected me. To some hide-bound traditionalists I have been anathema."

That experience with Arnold Rosé was but one of a number of indications that Fritz Kreisler was verifying the biblical truth, "A prophet hath no honor in his own country." When one contemplates the love and veneration with which he was treated almost from the beginning of his adult career in France, the British Isles, and the United States, one cannot but notice that his native city of Vienna, which he loved so much, failed for a long time to reciprocate that affection. One critic wrote, after one of his early concerts in Vienna, "He plays very well, but he does much better at tarot than at fiddling."

Fritz commented on this state of affairs to me with a tinge of sadness in his voice: "I fear you are right. I had my enemies and some jealous colleagues in Vienna. I must add in all fairness, however, that official Austria and official Vienna heaped many honors upon me."

Legends have a way of growing. Various biographers have promptly added that Kreisler was not only rejected as applicant to the Hofoper orchestra, but was also refused by Professor Jakob Grün, a noted Viennese violin pedagogue, when he applied to become his pupil.

"That is arrant nonsense," Kreisler stated emphatically. "I never even thought of applying. My formal training ended with my graduation from the Paris Conservatory." *

Failing to qualify for the *Hofoper* orchestra, the young artist henceforth concentrated on solo work. He had a most engaging manner and made friends easily. Men of wealth or in high positions liked to help him. Thus Kreisler remembers with gratitude that an industrialist named Guttmann, who occasionally arranged for a party of friends to go on a tour of the Mediterranean, invited him to go on a cruise.

"Professor Kaspar von Zumbusch, a noted sculptor and painter; Joseph Hellmesberger, my former violin teacher; Eduard Hanslick, the critic, and I were among the participants in one of these Mediterranean cruises. That's how, at an early and impressionable age, I got to know Constantinople, with its unexampled location on the Bosporus; Athens, with its unforgettable Acropolis; and Troy, where Professor Heinrich Schliemann, the famous archaeologist, was then conducting scientific excavations.

"At Constantinople I met Calice, the Austrian ambassador to the Sublime Porte, a native of Trieste. This diplomat somehow 'took a

* The association of Kreisler's name with that of Grün arose from the fact that the critic of the *Neues Wiener Journal*, commenting on Kreisler's first appearance as soloist for the Vienna Philharmonic Orchestra on Jan. 23, 1898, referred to Kreisler as "One of the most talented of the virtuosi graduated from Prof. Grün's school."

shine' to me and suggested that I return to Turkey to play before His Majesty Sultan Abdul-Hamid II. He arranged for my transportation and stay.

"I had to wait until the Turkish ruler was in a mood to hear me. The ambassador at that time had almost daily conferences with the sultan, since a matter seriously affecting both Turkey and Austria was under discussion. Their talks would usually last from 3:00 to 5:00 P.M., after which there was a two-hour pause. Calice hoped to secure an audition for me during such a pause.

"The sultan knew European languages quite well but pretended to be ignorant of them. In this way he could gain time while his interpreter repeated in Turkish what he had already understood when communicated in French or German. Then, when his own words, spoken in Turkish, were translated to the foreign envoy, he could gauge the effect upon the person opposite as the translation went on.

"Weeks passed, and still no command to play. But I didn't mind. I would sit with his courtiers, drinking coffee and smoking cigarettes. We could look into the imperial gardens, where the ladies of the sultan's harem were taking sun and water baths in their birthday suits!

"Then, finally, one day I was commanded to play. There was no time to send for an accompanist. The sultan sat there cross-legged and by a gesture indicated that I should begin. I played a slow movement from one of Bach's unaccompanied suites for the violin.

"After about two minutes of playing, His Majesty clapped his hands. I felt flattered. The ambassador quickly disillusioned me. 'That means you should stop,' he whispered. 'He doesn't like your selection. Play something fast.'

"So I played something quite inane, but with a lot of fireworks. It sounded particularly senseless without piano accompaniment.

"The sultan's eyes danced. He swayed to the rhythm and seemed thoroughly to enjoy the performance. I played several other fast numbers, and then he asked me whether I preferred a decoration or a bag of gold coins—one hundred Turkish pounds! I said I'd gladly take the cash. So one of the sultan's attendants handed me an embroidered bag from which most enticing metallic sounds issued forth.

Abdul-Hamid II, Sultan of Turkey

Kreisler just before the turn of the century

" 'Hold it up!' His Majesty commanded. He felt the contents, nodded in a satisfied manner, and dismissed me.

"The ambassador and I had to leave by boat to row across the Bosporus. The sultan's major-domo, who held the rank of a general, accompanied us to the boat landing. On the way Calice whispered, 'Grab into your bag and fish out a couple of gold coins.'

" 'But he is a general,' I remonstrated.

" 'Here even a general gladly takes a tip,' the ambassador informed me. 'Generals are very badly paid.' He was right. The bemedaled general was only too eager to accept my *douceur*.

"On the way back to the embassy, Calice explained the sultan's action in passing his hand along the coin bag. 'He wanted to make sure his flunkies had actually put the coins in and not filled the bag with worthless rocks. Underpaid people sometimes do things like that.'

"Many years afterward I was told by a Turkish princess whom I met somewhere or other at a social function: 'My mother heard you when you played without accompaniment for the sultan. She was then a favorite of His Majesty's. The ladies of the harem, without your knowing it, had gone up into the gallery of the imperial reception room and there listened to you behind the latticework.'

"When I left Constantinople, I was given a handsome farewell present by a Turkish bey. It consisted of a huge box filled with nougat and with one thousand Turkish cigarettes.

"I displayed this gift proudly when I reached home. The family regarded it with something akin to awe, but father cast a searching glance at me. He examined my eyes, took my pulse, and said gravely: 'Unless you stop smoking immediately, you may soon be dead. There was hashish in all the cigarettes you smoked.'

"That was the signal for me to cease using tobacco. I never smoked again. But to the present day I have a slightly enlarged heart—I had acquired a so-called 'smoker's heart.' "

Eduard Hanslick wrote about the Mediterranean trip in the *Neue Freie Presse* of Vienna on January 25, 1898:

I got to know Kreisler's violin playing on a more modest and less steady platform than that of the *Musikverein* and am happy at the thought of it. It was on the Lloyd-Liner "Argo" which some years ago took both of us, together with a group of friends, from Athens to Constantinople. To be sure, he was not able, like the much-sung-of Arion, to lure the dolphins to the ship (for he played, not on deck, but in a saloon of the ship), but our sailors one after the other sneaked to the door to listen to his beautiful violin tones.

This early period of his adult artist's life, during which he was more or less of a free lance, already made him realize that the literature of the violin was relatively restricted and scarce. Compared with piano literature, it was indeed meager.

So he began composing those incomparable short pieces of his which have filled a gap for violinists the world over. They were at first ascribed by him to composers of the eighteenth and early nineteenth centuries, but in 1935 became revealed as original works of his own under circumstances so dramatic that a separate chapter will be devoted to the "Confession of an Old Hoax."

Kreisler said about these early compositions: "What I composed and arranged was for my own use, reflecting my own musical tastes and preferences. In fact, it was not until years afterward that I even thought of publishing the pieces I had composed and arranged."

His musical tidbits stood him in good stead when an offer came to go on a concert tour through Russia on the basis of obtaining a certain percentage of the box-office receipts.

"I didn't bring home much money," Kreisler remembered. "I was young, liked to drink a good drop, and was happy-go-lucky with money. So the trip wasn't much of a financial success. But I had a glorious time. Though I was a very young man, older people somehow let me converse with them, discuss philosophy, try out various languages. Also, I knew Montaigne by heart and could quote him at will.

"Furthermore, I had some very good introductions. With the aid of letters from Prince Lubomirsky, for instance, I met some influential people. At Cracow the archbishop took a fancy to me. In St. Petersburg (now Leningrad) I met Alexander Glazounoff, César Cui, who was a friend of Tchaikovsky's, and the conductor Ziloty.

"I had given a performance of the Tchaikovsky Violin Concerto, and Cui and I talked it over. Cui was quite excited.

" 'Did you know,' he asked, 'that Tchaikovsky had written quite a different ending to this concerto? It's hard to believe, but the only

Alexander Glazounoff, 1865-1936

Cesar Cui, 1835-1918

reason it isn't used is that some of his friends told him it resembled the finale of another concerto too closely. I know definitely that Tchaikovsky set to work to compose a new ending, but was very dissatisfied with all his efforts. Finally, in despair, he threw up his hands and let the concerto go without an ending.' "

The incident remained in Kreisler's mind, and was perhaps the subconscious reason for his later editing the Tchaikovsky concerto.*

A second trip to Russia resulted in—Kreisler's expulsion! At Warsaw he had become enamored of a luscious Finnish girl, who eloquently persuaded him that all Finland was virtually waiting to hear him and that he would be given a reception at Åbo (now Turku) and Helsingfors (now Helsinki) which would make it more than worth his while to break off his scheduled recitals in czarist Russia.

Violently smitten with this girl, young Kreisler nonchalantly tossed aside a command from the imperial court at St. Petersburg to play before the czar. This honor had come to him through the efforts of Princess Windisch-Graetz. In his infatuation he forgot the implications of a command performance. Unless severe illness prevents, one appears or—

The romantic young violinist had traveled as far as Riga, from where he intended to go by boat to Finland, when there was an energetic knock at his hotel room. The czar's police asked for his passport and blandly informed him that he had outworn his welcome in the Russian Empire by his failure to appear at court; would he please leave the country immediately.

This youthful escapade fortunately had no lasting consequences in so far as his relation with the Russian musical world was concerned. Until the beginning of the First World War, he frequently toured the vast Russian Empire.

At Lódź and Warsaw a man came into his life who several years later made Kreisler's debut in Berlin possible, and in whose hospitable home he became a regular guest even two years before that debut.

* Students of composition who are interested in Kreisler's guiding principles in editing the Tchaikovsky work will find an explanation in the article "With the Artists," by Samuel and Sada Applebaum, in *Violins and Violinists* for Dec., 1947, pp. 367-368.

This benefactor was Ernst Karl Ludwig Posselt, a carpet manufacturer who took pride in helping young artistic talents.

Thus, during the years between 1896 and 1899, the young artist saw many new and strange places, further widened his cultural horizon, revealed his prowess as a composer, and gained considerable routine in platform appearances.

These tours through foreign lands consumed only a part of his time, however. His greatest experience in this period came in Vienna itself, where he was thrown into the company of a galaxy of world-famous musicians and composers, headed by Johannes Brahms, poets, novelists, and biographers. New vistas were there opened up to Kreisler.

Also, he had the supreme satisfaction of appearing with the Vienna Philharmonic Orchestra as its soloist on January 23, 1898. No less a person than the famed Hans Richter conducted. As one critic pointed out, it was Kreisler's first public reappearance in his native city since he had laid aside the fiddle and the bow to finish high school, study medicine, and serve his turn as soldier.

Vienna's leading critic, Eduard Hanslick, wrote in the *Neue Freie Presse* of January 25, 1898:

> Max Bruch's Second Violin Concerto . . . afforded Herr Fritz Kreisler an opportunity to distinguish himself as violin virtuoso. . . . Kreisler has been putting in recent years to perfect himself, so as to enable him now to face the Vienna [concert] public as a finished master. He was recalled a number of times after having played the concerto with brilliant virtuosity. There is no doubt but that this distinction was accorded his playing rather than the Bruch composition.

The critic, A. K., of the *Neues Wiener Journal* wrote a day later:

> Fritz Kreisler, who was the soloist for the occasion, is one of the most talented of the contemporary virtuosi. . . . The sweetness of his tone is excellent for the melodious honey of the first movement. In the recitativo-like middle movement there could be a wider sweep and sharper plasticity. The dashing, effervescing finale found Herr Kreisler easily on top of the technical demands.

Richter provided a fitting frame for his young protégé's debut with orchestra: the orchestral works which preceded the Bruch Concerto were Mendelssohn's Overture *Meeresstille und glückliche Fahrt*, and Beethoven's Sixth Symphony.

Johannes Brahms, 1833-1897

Eduard Hanslick, 1825-1904

CHAPTER SEVEN

CAFÉ "MEGALOMANIA" AND ITS HABITUÉS

[1896-1898]

WHEREVER the German tongue is prevalent, the village tavern, the town *Bierstube*, the Viennese café, and even the elegant metropolitan wine restaurant has its *Stammtisch*. This is a table set aside for a group of people, cronies, who meet regularly, some daily, some weekly or semiweekly, at an agreed hour and continue to sit together, often till closing time.

Vienna's innumerable coffee houses included the Café Grünsteidl, at whose *Stammtisch* an exceptional group of intellectuals foregathered. So positive were the opinions expressed by this unusual aggregation that the coffee house soon was nicknamed *Café Grössenwahn* (Megalomania).

The most distinguished of them all was Johannes Brahms. With him usually sat Max Kalbeck, his Boswell, who for years was at work on a biography of his idol. (His cronies often joked that he was writing Brahms's *Stilleben*, a pun on a famous book on animal life, *Brehms Tierleben*.) Both were frequently joined by "a small man with heavy, bushy eyebrows, white goatee, and hooknose which looked like the beak of an old hawk. This was the famous music critic and Wagner-slayer, Eduard Hanslick." * Musical comedy was represented by Richard Heuberger (1850–1914), whose *Opernball* with its "Midnight Bells," frequently played by Kreisler, is perhaps the best known of his numerous operettas.

* Reprinted from *Legend of a Musical City* by Max Graf, by permission of The Philosophical Society, copyright, 1945, by Philosophical Library, Inc.

Brahms was far too much in demand to be at the Café Grünsteidl regularly. When he did turn up, it was a memorable occasion for the hero-worshiping young violinist Kreisler.

The regulars among the Grünsteidl habitués were to be found more among the writers. There was Hugo von Hofmannsthal, whose name later became prominently linked with that of Richard Strauss as his librettist. Detlev von Liliencron was wont to read his latest poems to his cronies. Arthur Schnitzler, then only about twenty years old, wrote parts of his *Der einsame Weg* (The Lonely Way) at the *Stammtisch* while waiting for the others to turn up. Frank Wedekind and Hermann Bahr belonged to the group, as did Oskar Blumenthal, author of numerous comedies.

Of the younger generation, the most striking personality, in Kreisler's opinion, was Hugo Wolf. Very pale, slender, with restless eyes burning like live coals, this fanatic follower of Wagner and Bruckner would make sure that Brahms was not in attendance before he sat down. Dressed in a brown velvet jacket, with a wide, black artist's tie around his neck, he was often the butt of jokes by his cronies, especially by Schnitzler.

"We did not take Hugo Wolf very seriously," Kreisler recalls. "When he tried to tell us about three songs that he had written, further discussion was cut off by Schnitzler's teasing, "*Ach, ich habe seine dummen Schundlieder gehört*" (Ach, I've heard his foolish trash-songs). Wolf was then writing musical criticisms for some boulevard sheet. He was very censorious of Brahms.

"It was not until about two years before he became obviously insane that we began to appreciate his worth. He came to our *Stammtisch* one day—it must have been in 1897—and claimed he had written songs that were more beautiful even than those of Schubert and Schumann. Our crowd laughed uproariously, until someone challenged him, 'If they are so good, why don't you play them for us?'

"Hugo Wolf sat down at the piano and played. We became simply enthralled and enraptured. Such music! We became suddenly aware that another genius was in our midst.

" 'Why haven't you shown these songs to *Meister* Brahms?' someone asked.

Hugo Wolf, 1860-1903

Engelbert Humperdinck, 1854-1921

" 'I sent him a song of mine five years ago,' was the sad rejoinder, 'and requested him to mark a cross in the score wherever he thought my music was faulty. But Brahms never looked at it. He handed it back to me with the caustic remark, "I don't want to make a cemetery of your composition." '

"Hugo Wolf, alas, was a Wagnerian, and that finished him in Brahms's eyes. Fortunately, he found a patron in Engelbert Humperdinck, composer of *Hänsel und Gretel*, who prevailed upon the great music publishing firm of B. Schott's Söhne, of Mainz, Germany, to publish his songs. By coincidence, Schott later became my publisher also.

"It so chances that I, although fifteen years younger than Hugo Wolf, was close to him when he had his first manifest outbreak of insanity. About a year before he was committed to the same asylum in which Nikolaus Lenau, the poet, spent his last days, Hugo Wolf and I were marching together in the Corpus Christi procession. Suddenly he acted queerly, sang at the top of his voice, and had to be taken into the nearest house until he quieted down. Even then, however, nobody was aware that he was actually crazy. He merely seemed overwrought."

There was a sort of Bohemian camaraderie about the *Stammtisch*, evidenced by the readiness of one crony to help out the other when in need. Kreisler gave the following example:

"One day Heuberger came to us rather excitedly with the score of his *Opernball*. It contains, among other things, a lyric, 'Komm' mit mir ins chambre séparé,' which on that day, however, was still in prose. 'The producer wants me to change the music into a waltz,' Heuberger said. 'But that's impossible. The words aren't in three-quarter time. What would you do, Wolf, if you were in my place?'

" 'The waltz isn't my line,' Wolf replied. 'Here, let Fritz have a look at it. Besides, if it is to be a waltz, the text must be scanned differently. That's something for Hofmannsthal.' And so, while Hofmannsthal was rewriting the text for Heuberger, I quickly composed some bars for the song. 'Not at all bad,' said Heuberger and hurried away.

"Years later the composer sent me back my original manuscript, dashed off on a slip of paper, and thanked me again for having helped him out."

"And the reward?" I asked.

"In those days we didn't think of commercializing our talents," Kreisler answered. "I did suggest, banteringly, that the effort was worth another coffee at Heuberger's expense, but that was about all.

"Nobody then asked the other about royalties and copyrights and profit participation; ours was a real camaraderie. Heuberger belonged to our crowd—so why not do him a favor?"

"Then you are really the composer of the 'Midnight Bells' that you played so often in your concerts?" Kreisler was asked.

"Oh, I wouldn't put it that way," he replied, modestly. "I merely inspired Heuberger by composing the motif, which he then developed. Incidentally, the poor fellow died in want without ever reaping the benefits of his numerous compositions."

In this connection he recalled how another musician, Kapellmeister Komczàk, leader of one of Austria's innumerable military bands, used to come and ask him to write him a march.

"I would dash off something that came to my mind," he narrated, "and was happy if he paid for an extra glass of wine or another *Schale* (cup) of coffee. That's how 'commercial' we were in those days.

"And there was another thing: an artist was not evaluated by the clothes he wore or the apartment he could afford to keep up. He could have frayed trousers and lived in a *Dachkammer* (attic). That didn't matter."

Besides the *Stammtisch* of the Grünsteidl establishment, there was another meeting-place for artists which left indelible impressions on Fritz Kreisler's memory. That was the Tonkünstlerverein (literally Club of Artists of the Tone) of which Johannes Brahms was the revered honorary president. Brahms was naturally showered with compositions sent him for perusal and criticism by contemporary artists. Many a time he would try these out or have them played by fellow musicians in the rooms of the Tonkünstlerverein. On one occasion he also experimented with a revision of a trio of his own—that in B major, if Kreisler's memory serves him right. If the composition happened to be a quartet for strings, or a piano trio, quartet, or quintet,

Joseph Joachim

he Joachim Quartet in the 1890's (Joachim, Hausmann, Wirth, de Ahna)

Albert Spalding, 1888-1953

Spalding in the early 1900's

it frequently happened that Fritz would be one of the artists in attendance who were privileged to play with, and for, Brahms.

Kreisler referred to his days in the Tonkünstlerverein in an interview with Olin Downes which appeared on November 8, 1942 in the New York *Times* under the title, *Talk with Kreisler*:

> "I had the inexpressible good fortune to sit in quartets to whom he [Brahms] more than once brought the manuscript of a new chamber music composition, for us to run through for him. He would stop us, and change a note or two, or discuss the scoring of a passage. To talk to an Olympian like that, actually to be present at the creation of superb music, was priceless—and a lasting possession which does not fade or suffer from comparison made with the perspective of time. We knew then a wine of the spirit. We were preoccupied with beauty. And thank God, the spell did not wear off."

A frequent visitor to the *Verein* was the Nestor of European fiddlers, Brahms's intimate friend Joseph Joachim. Young Kreisler was especially enchanted with his quartet playing. He also respected this distinguished Hungarian, now firmly established in Berlin, for his prowess as a soloist, though he never could agree with him.

"Joachim has been one of the great influences in my life," he said. "He was a queer mixture of generosity and jealousy. He wanted everybody to do exactly as he desired it to be done and was very pedantic about it. But he was a great man.

"He begged me to come to his classes. Maybe he wanted to win me over to his style of playing, which was so different from the French school in which I had been brought up. Even though I never became his pupil, our relations were very cordial, and I never failed, when going to Berlin, to look him up. It was Eugène Ysaÿe, however, and not Joseph Joachim, who was my idol among violinists."

Albert Spalding, when a student of music in Berlin, often heard both Joseph Joachim and his later lifelong friend Fritz Kreisler. He explained interestingly why the two virtuosos did not see eye to eye violinistically.

"Fritz Kreisler," he said, "is as different from Joseph Joachim as the romanticism in architecture of the pre-Renaissance period is different from the Gothic of the thirteenth and fourteenth centuries.

"In a sense Eugène Ysaÿe was the bridge between the two styles of playing.

"Interestingly enough, Joachim's own performance was quite different from what he did pedagogically. He played with a fire which he would never have tolerated in his pupils."

The most memorable event in the Tonkünstlerverein for Kreisler was that day in 1896 when Brahms, Joachim, Hellmesberger, and he happened to be seated at a table, and Brahms and Joachim got into a discussion of Robert Schumann's Fantasie in C Major for Violin and Orchestra, dedicated to, and frequently played by, Joachim.

"The two Olympians were agreed that this work had certain weaknesses due to the advanced state of Schumann's insanity, but that it was also replete with ideas of genius," Kreisler recalled.

"Schumann had composed it in 1853 as his last orchestral work. Joachim now ventured to prophesy, rather sadly, that the composition would be forgotten after his, Joachim's, death. Brahms, on the other hand, argued that the best parts ought to be saved by eliminating meaningless passages and elaborating the middle episode.

"I still remember his exact words. 'Das Werk muss von seinem Gestrüpp befreit werden' (The composition must be stripped of its underbrush), Brahms kept repeating. Then he turned to Joachim and said, 'Joseph, why don't you take that score in hand, trim it up, and put it in condition for others to play after you are gone?'

"Joachim was then well along in years and was rather vague in his promise to do so. Hellmesberger, noticing this, turned to me and said: 'You heard what *Meister* Brahms said. Don't you ever forget it.' "

Fritz Kreisler never forgot. Every time he went to Berlin, he would inquire how Joachim's revision was faring. But he received only elusive answers—answers which, however, led him to believe that Joachim was actually at work on the score. After the great Hungarian's death he pressed the heirs to search for the revision. It then developed that Joachim had not even begun to carry out his vague pledge to Brahms!

"When I learned that Joachim had not attempted a revision," Kreisler continued, "I determined that I would. I approached my task with diffidence, because one does not like to meddle with the work of great artists. But I had to make a choice of meddling or letting the Fantasie die."

He did not take his self-imposed assignment lightly, but regarded it as a sacred trust—the carrying out of an ardent wish by the venerated Brahms. People have often marveled at the speed with which Kreisler has turned out original compositions, transcriptions, and arrangements. In this case he showed anything but speed.

"I had only one thought," he said, "respectfully and scrupulously to clarify the thought of the master, wherever it seemed perfectly evident what was intended by him."

Again and again he took up this labor of love, and not until almost twenty years later, during the concert season of 1915–1916, did he incorporate his revision into his repertoire. The critic of the New York *Times*, who heard it on December 12, 1915, in Carnegie Hall, was enthusiastic:

> Kreisler not only wrought it no injury but has succeeded in accomplishing his purpose. . . . The accompaniment is made more active and given more movement, more significance and more figuration. In the solo part there are numerous improvements in certain of the ornamental passages, which Mr. Kreisler has made more idiomatic for the instrument and hence more effective. . . . The main outlines of the work are practically untouched.

The critic added, however, that Kreisler also rendered a particular service to the Schumann work "by his warmth of interpretation—not all can do that."

Even then Kreisler was not satisfied. Again and again during the ensuing two decades he labored over the Fantasie. Finally, forty years after the Tonkünstlerverein incident, at a recital in Carnegie Hall on October 17, 1936, he produced the revision in the final form in which it is now known.

If that was "meddling," it certainly was scrupulous, reverential, pious meddling. As was inevitable, some musicologists took him to task for it. But Kreisler remained unperturbed, serenely confident that he had acted in the spirit of the unforgettable table discussion in 1896 in the historic rooms of the Vienna Tonkünstlerverein.

CHAPTER EIGHT

ON TO BERLIN—AND FAME
[1899]

KREISLER, as already noted, met Ernst Posselt in Lódź and again in Warsaw during his first tour of the Russian Empire. We hear much these days of chain reaction. The chain reaction resulting from this contact between violinist and industrialist may be epitomized: Kreisler meets Posselt. Posselt invites Kreisler to Berlin. Ysaÿe there hears Kreisler. Kreisler's fame is assured.

Posselt, who had a striking likeness to Joseph Joachim, asked Kreisler one day in Warsaw, "Why don't you play in Berlin?"

"That's more easily said than done," the young artist replied. "It takes money to hire a concert hall, engage an accompanist, and advertise." (He had had to borrow evening dress for his Warsaw concert from a waiter—he had gambled away both his money and his clothes.)

Posselt, whose hobby was that of helping struggling young talents, promised he would see to it that the necessary arrangements were made if and when it seemed propitious for Kreisler to make his Berlin debut.

For the present, he had another proposal: his and his wife's silver wedding was about to be celebrated in style in Heidelberg. The four sons and one daughter, numerous relatives on both sides (Frau Johanna Maria Posselt, nee Peters, came from a distinguished Elberfeld industrial family), and intimate friends were all to come to help inaugurate the second quarter-century of a happy married life. One of the scheduled features was to be one evening of special illumination of the historic Heidelberg Schloss (Castle).

"Why not come with me to Heidelberg before returning to Vienna?" Posselt suggested. "You'll have a good time and you'll make some valuable musical connections." Kreisler needed no coaxing to accept so attractive an invitation.

There were music critics among the guests at Heidelberg. They strengthened the silver bridegroom's belief that Fritz ought to play in Berlin, the mecca of many music lovers who in their enthusiasm called it Spree-Athen (Athens on the Spree River).

Augusta (Mrs. Henrik) Laerum, Posselt's only daughter—"Gustel" or "Gust'chen" to the family—was then a young lass of ten or eleven years. She vividly remembers some of the incidents connected with the Heidelberg and Berlin visits of the attractive but still adolescent young man from Vienna.

"His face was full of pimples," she claims, "so that Mama said to him, 'Fritz, it is impossible for you to appear on the platform that way.' She therefore made him swallow yeast with raspberry juice."

Ernst Posselt arranged for a concert in Heidelberg for his young protégé. According to his oldest son, Willy: "All guests were already assembled in the concert hall, but Kreisler was missing. My brother, Ernst, Jr., was sent to the hotel to fetch him. There he was, calmly resting in bed at 4:00 P.M., and when Ernst reminded him of his engagement, he replied languidly, 'If people really want to hear me, they can wait.' " Though arriving late, he scored a notable success at his Heidelberg recital!

Kreisler's first visit to the Posselts in Berlin occurred in 1897, when the young violinist was twenty-two years old. Frau Laerum recalls that he was then so poorly equipped that her mother, who with loving care and maternal regard always looked faithfully after the struggling artists whom her husband brought from his journeys into the home, "equipped Fritz with shirts, underwear, and handkerchiefs"; also, that she tactfully cured him of his heavy, audible breathing. "Lulu K.," she added, "was at that time also our house guest. Fritz was quite smitten with her."

"Ernst Posselt was fond of buying up discarded violins at never more than $50 apiece in the hope that some day he would find an instrument of real value among them," Kreisler said. "He would ask me to play them. If he liked the tones I drew from them, he tried to impress others with the fact that the instrument was really a valuable one." Posselt also had a genuine Stradivarius, which he placed at Kreisler's disposal for his concerts.

Soon the days when Mama Posselt insisted on his taking yeast to get rid of pimples were gone: Fritz was now a dashing, grown-up young man who sported an ambitious mustache in the style of Emperor William II, with upturned ends. At the suggestion of his benefactor he went to J. C. Schaarwächter, royal court photographer, and posed for a picture which made him look like a wealthy young man about town to whom money was an object of utmost indifference. There is a somewhat mischievous glint in his eyes.

"If I am not mistaken," Willy Posselt wrote, "Kreisler put on the winter paletot of my father's and, to impress people with the fur lining, rolled back one side somewhat."

One of these photos was presented by Kreisler on December 12, 1897, to the then thirteen-year-old "Gust'chen," with the dedication on the reverse side, "Meiner lieben 'quecksilbernen' Freundin Gust'chen als freundliche Erinnerung an Fritz Kreisler" (To my dear "mercurial" friend Gust'chen in friendly reminder of Fritz Kreisler).

Willy Posselt accompanied a photostat of both the photo and its reverse side with the observation that "the dedication seems to me to be of interest in that one can glean from the signature how Kreisler used to draw his bow through completely." On reaching the end of his name, the young artist had drawn a long, slanting line from the final *r* in "Kreisler" gradually downward through the lower part of *z* in "Fritz." He kept up this practice for many years.

Although he played frequently to enthusiastic listeners at the Posselts' private home in the Tiergarten section during this prolonged visit, his professional debut in the German capital did not occur until two years later.

"Posselt kindly offered to the concert agency of Wolff & Sachs to guarantee the sale of 400 to 500 tickets for my first recital," Kreisler said.

Kreisler in Berlin, 1899

Felix Mendelssohn-Bartholdy, 1809-1847

This initial concert in March, 1899, was planned as a sort of visiting card with which the young artist from Vienna was introducing himself, in the hope of qualifying for the engagement that counted most —an appearance with the Berlin Philharmonic Orchestra.

The German musicologist Peter Raabe wrote about Kreisler's Berlin debut in the *Allgemeine Musik-Zeitung*:

> Nothing but most favorable reports have come to me concerning the violinist, Herr Kreissle [*sic*], from Vienna, whose concert I was unfortunately unable to attend. The artist is reported to be an eminent technician and to possess a *verve* such as is common only to outstanding talents. The success was quite remarkable.

Raabe managed to attend a second recital and wrote about it:

> Herr Fritz Kreisler gave evidence of a technical perfection that was simply astounding. He mastered the most unbelievable difficulties with playful ease and with an elegance that was truly fascinating.

Another critic apostrophized him as "Paganini redivivus."

On December 1, 1899, Kreisler finally had the opportunity for which he and his friends were waiting, and which proved a decisive moment in his life: Artur Nikisch presented him as soloist in a concert of the Berlin Philharmonic Society, which had as orchestral numbers the "Faust" Overture by Wagner, the "Pathétique" Symphony by Tchaikovsky, and "Two Pieces" by Alexander Ritter. The young artist from Vienna was invited to play the Mendelssohn Violin Concerto.

A hilarious side light on Kreisler's preparations for this concert is shed by Fritz's "dear 'mercurial' friend Gust'chen," now the still delightfully vivacious and temperamental Frau Laerum, who wrote:

"Fritz was to practice the Mendelssohn Violin Concerto in the guest room next to my home-study room. I still remember every note of that concerto, for I heard him practice for hours at a time.

"Our mother used to say, as we left the table, 'Fritz, now you simply *must* practice.' Hardly had she disappeared, however, when Fritz would say: 'You know, Gusterl, I ought to practice, but I'd like to take a little nap. Before your mother returns, you wake me, and if

I don't wake up, you take water and pour it on me. Don't let me sleep too long.' * Whereupon I, of course, would turn up with a glass of water after fifteen minutes and pour it over him without waiting to see whether he would condescend to awaken without being doused."

When Fritz reached Philharmonic Hall on the night of December 1, he noticed to his happy surprise that Eugène Ysaÿe, who had given a recital the day before, was in attendance. Ysaÿe was then the uncrowned king of violinists.

"When I finished the last cadenza to the Mendelssohn Concerto," Kreisler reports, "Ysaÿe ostentatiously got up and applauded. That generous gesture put me over. I shall never forget it. Some papers then devoted three-quarters of a column to my appearance."

Ysaÿe's gesture was not an empty one. He really meant it. Jacques Thibaud remarked: "I was about eighteen years old when Ysaÿe said to me in Paris: 'There's a young fiddler named Kreisler up in Berlin. You must hear him. He is marvelous. I heard him when I concertized in Berlin!' "

Walter Damrosch quotes Ysaÿe as saying to him in 1891 (although he must have meant 1901):†

> I have arrived at the top and from now on there will be a steady decrease of my prowess. I have lived my life to the full and burned the candle at both ends. For some time I shall make up in sublimity of phrasing and nuance what my technic as violinist can no longer give. *But Kreisler is on the ascendant, and in a short time he will be the greater artist.*

Ysaÿe further indicated his esteem of his younger colleague when he dedicated an unaccompanied Sonata for the Violin to him, which Kreisler played in many concerts.

The admiration of the two artists was mutual and ripened into a lifelong friendship. When on November 1, 1901, scarcely two years

* The words ascribed to Kreisler are in typical Viennese dialect. Readers conversant with this homey idiom will enjoy them: "Weisst, Gustl, ich muss üben, aber ich möcht' a bisserl schlafen. Eh die Mutter kommt, weckst mi auf, und wenn i net wach werd', nimmst a Wasser und schütt'sts mir über. Lass' mi net zu lang schlafen."

† Reprinted from *My Musical Life* by Walter Damrosch, in January and April, 1923 issues of the *Ladies' Home Journal*, by special permission from the *Ladies' Home Journal*, copyright, 1922, 1923, by the Curtis Publishing Company.

Walter Damrosch, 1862-1950

Eugène Ysaÿe, 1858-1931

after they first met, Ysaÿe was indisposed and unable to play the Beethoven Concerto with Nikisch and the Philharmonic in Berlin, Kreisler unhesitatingly jumped into the breach for his colleague. The press acclaimed it a noble, fraternal gesture.

What the critics did not know was that there was much more behind Kreisler's unscheduled appearance than met the eye. Ysaÿe had played on October 31 in what was known as the *Hauptprobe* (dress rehearsal), for which season tickets and individual admissions were sold just as for the main event the following evening. He then fell ill, and Fritz took his place. Not only had he to play without previous rehearsal, but even without previous practice on a borrowed fiddle. The reason was a tragicomedy that had taken place some months previously.

While in Paris in the late spring of 1901, the young violinist had formed an attachment for a certain Parisian damsel named Mimi. So infatuated was he temporarily that he pawned his violin to have enough money to satisfy the rather expensive whims of his lady love. Even this money was exhausted in due time, and Fritz was unable to pay for his room and board. His landlady, used to irresponsible artists, held him virtually a prisoner on the premises. Fritz could neither pay his bills nor buy a railway ticket back to Vienna. An appeal to his father was the only course open.

When Dr. Kreisler came to Paris to get at the root of the trouble, he hardly recognized his truant son, who had acquired a heavy beard during his virtual captivity. The forgiving parent squared his son's obligations and took him back to Vienna. The violin, however, had to remain in pawn for the time being, for the doctor's resources had been drained by the bills accumulated during his son's escapade with Mimi.

From Vienna Fritz went to Berlin in the autumn—sans violin!

But to continue with the Ysaÿe-Kreisler relationship:

Asked for his opinion on his contemporaries, Kreisler on one occasion said: * "Ysaÿe bears a message, a great message, and you must follow closely to receive it. He does not deliver it every time he plays,

* Reprinted from *Little Violin Music of Merit Being Written*, interview with Fritz Kreisler in the December 14, 1912 issue of *Musical America*.

but when he does, it is wonderful! It is only the mediocre artist who plays the same on all occasions, striking a certain level to which he adheres without fluctuation. But the great artists have their moments. They are worth waiting for."

On the humorous side of the Ysaÿe-Kreisler relationship, Fritz's wife recalled the following episode:

"Eugène and his wife Louise had a summer home at Godines on the Meuse River, near Brussels. One day when we happened to be in Belgium, we decided to look the Ysaÿes up and sent them a telegram, telling them when we'd arrive.

"There was nobody to meet us at the little station; our telegram had somehow gone astray. So we trudged along the dusty road with our little overnight bags. At the Ysaÿe home we learned that Eugène had gone fishing; we were told where we would be likely to find him.

"Sure enough, there he sat in the broiling sun, with a large sombrero on his head, seemingly half asleep. We watched him for quite a while. He did not catch a single fish during that time. Now and then, nevertheless, he pulled in one of his lines. It wasn't a fish that he was hauling in—he had fastened beer bottles to this line which he kept on the bottom of the river for cooling purposes."

When complete tragedy overtook Ysaÿe—one leg had to be amputated, and diabetes proved incurable—it was Kreisler who played in one of the last benefit performances for his friend, rendering the Beethoven Violin Concerto and Ernest Chausson's *Poème*, which the composer had dedicated to the Belgian master.* That was on January 27, 1931. Six days later the slowly dying master—he lingered on until May 12, 1931—wrote this beautiful letter to his Austrian colleague:

Brussels, February 2, 1931

My very dear friend:

I have the feeling that I haven't thanked you sufficiently for the cooperation you have so graciously and fraternally given me. To be sure, I haven't

* For a fuller story of the Chausson *Poème*, see "The Brahms and Chausson Manuscripts Presented by Kreisler," by Harold Spivacke, Chief, Music Division, in *The Library of Congress Quarterly Journal of Current Acquisitions*, May, 1949, Vol. 6, No. 3. See also *Eugène Ysaÿe, sa vie, son œuvre, son influence, d'après les documents recueillies par son fils*, by Antoine Ysaÿe (Brussels, Editions L'Écran du monde, 1948).

The Ysaÿe summer home at Godines, about 1900

Louise and Eugène Ysaÿe

ever doubted either your affection for me or your magnanimity and your generosity of spirit. But, although there was no need of it, this last proof which you have just given to your unhappy and old colleague who, alas, is now infirm and who hasn't even the satisfaction any longer of playing himself, touches me more deeply than ever.

I should like to leave a remembrance of this concert with you, and after mature deliberation I have decided to bequeath Chausson's hand-written manuscript to you in my will. I do not wish to die without giving myself the pleasure of offering it to you as of today. You will receive it immediately.

I am sure, my dear Fritz, that it will give you greater pleasure than any other object, and I now yield this autograph of a work you love into your hands of a great artist which I grasp in friendship.

This letter ought to have been written in my own hand, but alas, my dear friend, I should have trembled more in writing it than if I had had to hold an E-flat near the [violin] bridge during a long organ point. Pardon me, therefore, and be satisfied with my signature.

I embrace you, with my heart full of affectionate gratitude.

[Signed] *E. Ysaÿe*

As to Ernst Posselt, the benefactor who made the Berlin debut possible and thus, aided by the happy circumstance of Ysaÿe's attendance, opened the gate to world fame, Kreisler remembers him with gratitude, even though, as often happens in life, both later lost contact with each other. The survivors of the family were cordial, however, in sending greetings and assurances of affection to Fritz and Harriet Kreisler recently through Willy Posselt, the now seventy-nine-year-old senior son, and Frau Laerum, the erstwhile "mercurial Gust'chen."

Willy Posselt wrote that Kreisler twice stayed with him in Riga, Latvia, when he gave concerts while en route to St. Petersburg (Leningrad); also, that they met occasionally in various parts of Europe, including the Black Forest, Carlsbad, and Monte Carlo.

Frau Laerum recalled that she was a collector of view postal cards when Fritz went to America in 1900 for his first appearance there as an adult artist. "I received a lot of view cards from the steamer and from New York," she said.

"Fritz and his wife and their two little dogs lived with us for a few days in Riga," she continued. "Both were quite crazy about those dogs.

"After the concert we all dined together in Otto Schwartz's restaurant. Fritz asked my [husband] Henrik whether he, too, had attended the recital. Henrik replied truthfully, 'No, I wasn't there,' whereupon Fritz commented, 'Very sensible, very sensible.' He was always such a natural person."

CHAPTER NINE

A GAY YOUNG BLADE

[1900-1902]

"FROM that Berlin concert on," Kreisler recollects, "the Konzertdirektion Wolff & Sachs was able to book me favorably. I now earned 10,000 to 12,000 marks (about $2,400 to $2,800) per year, which was quite something in those days." The relationship with these enterprising impresarios, headed by the indefatigable Frau Louise Wolff ("Queen Louise" to all who knew her), was to last until the Nazis dissolved the concert agency and made Germany unsafe for Kreisler. Wolff & Sachs arranged for the bookings on the European continent.

During these years 1900, 1901, and 1902, Fritz gave concerts in France, Italy, Germany, Austria, Spain, and the Scandinavian countries, crossed the English Channel to make professional contacts in the British Isles, and established himself firmly in the hearts of American concertgoers.

In Italy he learned to speak the beautiful tongue of that country unusually quickly. Temporary infatuation with a pretty Neapolitan girl may well have accelerated his linguistic proficiency even though he had to learn to his sorrow that she was a faithless creature who divided her love between him, Antonio Scotti, and a third person.

Scotti, later the famous baritone of the Metropolitan Opera in New York, was then a struggling artist in Naples—debonair, good looking, but, like Kreisler, not blessed with worldly goods. "Toni and I both had a crush on the same girl," Fritz admitted. "She was a little salesgirl in a flower store."

It appears that both young musicians were on good terms with a *friseur* who was the proud owner of an opera cape and a shining topper. Each, unaware of the other, borrowed these swank accouterments from the barber every time he took the beauteous Lucia out. As she was careful about the dates she made, neither learned of the other's infatuation for some time.

Even the most calculating of damsels may slip, however. Early one evening Toni and Fritz appeared at the barber's simultaneously, each asking for the cape and *chapeau claque*. Somewhat embarrassed, the hairdresser informed the two artists that he had rented his costume out to a third person. Then, however, he added mischievously that this *signor* had a date with—Lucia! "Just as you gentlemen have it on other nights," he concluded.

For a moment the two young swains glared at each other. Then they laughed uproariously, embraced in true Italian fashion, with a kiss on each cheek, and from there on became fast friends. Faithless, fickle Lucia was easily forgotten.

Proof of Scotti's friendship came sometime later, when Fritz, during a stay in Milan, formed an attachment for a pretty Austrian girl who, however, had previously formed a liaison with a Polish count with a sizable bank account with which to gratify the temperamental young lady's wishes. But the passionate, irresistible young Austrian artist was more to her taste, and she gave him the desired rendezvous without, however, breaking off her profitable ties to the Polish nobleman. She managed somehow to keep each of the two rivals in ignorance of the other's appointments with her.

The inevitable happened: one evening Fritz left the Viennese girl's apartment just as the co-lover entered the premises. The count, who had for some time suspected that there was another man in the case, immediately thereafter shot himself in the apartment of his faithless love. Toni Scotti heard of it, and in greatest haste that same night saw to it that his friend Fritz could leave Milan and Italy. While Fritz was, of course, not legally responsible for the Pole's suicide, the scandal that might have attended his being summoned into court as a witness might well have wrecked his career. Until his death Scotti delighted to tell the story of this escapade.

But Fritz remained equally faithful to his friend Toni. Few people

Antonio Scotti, 1866-1936, as he appeared in Manon

Jacques Thibaud, 1880-1953, and Harold Bauer, 1873-1951

know that Kreisler supported his friend Scotti, who had saved nothing for a rainy day, during the closing years of his life. The two friends and Harriet spent many a beautiful day together at the Villa d'Este, near Rome.

In Paris about this time, Fritz Kreisler struck up friendships with Harold Bauer and Jacques Thibaud. Thibaud recalls:

"We met the first time late in 1899 in Paris. Right away we became like brothers. I immediately loved Fritz personally. We saw eye to eye musically. Ysaÿe and Fritz were my two idols. We have been intimate now for fifty years. There has not been one difference between us. Later our wives, too, clicked beautifully. We four were all very close."

About Harold Bauer, Kreisler said:

"I have the highest regard and affection for Harold. I first met him in Paris when he helped me very unselfishly out of certain financial difficulties. We traveled together a good deal in Europe—first in the Scandinavian countries and other continental lands, later, with Pablo Casals, as a trio ensemble."

A Scandinavian impresario had arranged for Kreisler and Bauer to give a series of solo recitals in Norway, Sweden, and Denmark. If these tours proved successful, it was agreed, the two artists were to go on a "highly remunerative joint tour" the following year.

Bauer describes the solo tour as follows: *

Fritz started first. Following him some weeks later, I went to Christiania, where his tour had begun. The manager told me that the tour had been a grand success and that Fritz had left me a note and a message. The message turned out to be a few small Norwegian coins which represented the net profits of his opening concert. This was "to encourage me!"

However, his concerts had really attracted a great deal of attention and so, subsequently, did mine, and the manager felt sure that a joint tour the following season would prove financially successful.

It was understood that Kreisler and I would provide money for advance publicity and expense. When the time came it appeared that I had a little money, while Fritz had none. It did not matter; I sent along the funds and the tour was announced. One week before the date of the first concert I was aghast to receive a telegram from a friend of Fritz's in Berlin: "Kreisler compelled to leave

* Reprinted from *Harold Bauer: His Book* by Harold Bauer, by permission of W. W. Norton & Company, Inc., copyright, 1948, by W. W. Norton & Company, Inc.

suddenly for America on urgent business. Regrets inability to join you on Scandinavian tour."

The "urgent business," of which I could not conceive the nature, turned out to be his marriage. . . . So I went off (alone), and the public and critics received me quite cordially throughout the tour.

Another delightful episode involving Harold Bauer and Fritz Kreisler occurred during their week in Madrid devoted to playing a series of sonatas for violin and piano. One of their colleagues proudly showed them a suit which looked like new because it had been turned inside out by a Spanish tailor.

Kreisler trustfully delivered his shabby everyday suit and Bauer his equally seedy overcoat to the garment renovator. Two days later the clothes were returned, looking as though they came from Bond Street, London. But, according to Bauer: *

When Fritz put on his suit, he presented an indescribable sort of twisted appearance. It was impossible to say what was wrong, but he simply did not look natural. And then he discovered that he would have to button his vest and coat from right to left instead of the usual way, from left to right. While he was struggling with this problem, I put on the overcoat, and found, to my fury and disgust, that I, too, was expected to button from right to left. The tailor, in reply to our remonstrances, said that nobody minded that kind of change and nobody would notice it. When we referred to our friend's costume which, although turned, continued to be buttoned in the usual manner, he simply shrugged with one word: "Double-breasted." That was the answer, of course. Fritz's suit and my overcoat were both single-breasted, and it had never occurred to us that the buttonholes would be on the wrong side after the clothes were turned. . . .

I don't know how long Fritz wore his funny-looking crooked suit, but I used my overcoat for quite a long time and developed a first-rate left-hand technique for buttoning it.

The visit to Madrid also included a command performance at court. Here the two artists did not have to struggle much with their newly acquired Spanish: Queen Victoria Eugenia, the young wife of King Alfonso, was British born, a member of the House of Battenberg, and naturally was happy to have an opportunity of chatting with London-born Harold Bauer. Queen Mother Maria Christine, on the other

* Reprinted from *Harold Bauer: His Book* by Harold Bauer, by permission of W. W. Norton & Company, Inc., copyright, 1948, by W. W. Norton & Company, Inc.

Harold Bauer in the 1900's

Maud Powell, 1868-1920

Hugo Becker, 1863-1941

hand, who before her marriage was an Austrian princess, addressed Fritz Kreisler in undiluted Viennese.

During these years Kreisler, for occasional recitals both in Germany and England, joined with the Hungarian composer-pianist Ernö Dohnányi and the German pianist Wilhelm Backhaus.

A seventy-seven-year-old German lady recently wrote from Düsseldorf:

> Fritz Kreisler is one of the treasured memories of my youth. He appeared in the Nether-Rhenish Music Festival at Düsseldorf with Ernö Dohnányi. We all took Kreisler to be the Hungarian, whereas Dohnányi, a blond young man, looked German to us. The fact that [after his number] Kreisler, seated in the first row of the *parquet*, quite unabashedly flirted with a young lady, strengthened our belief that he was the south-European.

Fritz showed excellent taste. The young lady with whom he flirted was his young bride, Harriet!

Fritz Kreisler's London debut took place on May 12, 1902. Most biographical sketches assume that this was his first appearance in the British Isles. However, the British critic Robin H. Legge is authority for the assertion that Kreisler had been in London before 1902, but that he was considered too "unknown" to risk "testing" in an important concert. He further revealed in the now defunct *Saturday Review*:

> But the unknown quantity tried his fortune in the provinces. For an engagement at a South Coast Resort an agent tendered him—Fritz Kreisler forsooth! —the eleemosynary fee of five guineas for a recital for which Kreisler must provide his own accompanist. To him came a then equally unknown pianist-accompanist of quite outstanding ability. His name was Hamilton Harty and his fee was six guineas.

Henry Wolfsohn, the New York impresario, booked Fritz for an American concert tour beginning in December, 1900. Kreisler was in good company, for Wolfsohn also managed Ernö Dohnányi, Jean Gérardy, Belgian cellist; Maud Powell, American violinist; Hugo Becker, German cellist, and Lillian Blauvelt, Brooklyn-born soprano.

In the photograph released for promotion purposes, Kreisler is shown to have a tremendous shock of dark hair and to wear a pointed stand-up collar with an enormous black butterfly tie. A contemporary magazine speaks of him as the "deep-chested Austrian," who had "rather wild hair—not very long, but bushy," looked somewhat saucy, and wore a broad four-in-hand tie, as well as a capelike overcoat. The New York *Times* added the further descriptive detail that he had "pointed mustachios and a pair of intense, flashing dark eyes that tell of a world of passion."

Kreisler had left Europe in the company of the same Dr. Bernhard Pollak who had gone to America with him and Moriz Rosenthal in 1888.

"During that previous trip," he explained, "Pollak had fallen madly in love with our concert manager's daughter. Hence, when he heard that I was going across the Atlantic again, he implored me to take him along as his accompanist—at least on paper—so that he might have an excuse for seeing the lady of his dreams again.

"I naturally agreed, and Pollak actually accompanied me during my New York appearances; but when I started on tour, he calmly remained behind to court his girl, while I often had to look for another accompanist."

At Kreisler's initial reappearance in Carnegie Hall, New York, on December 7, 1900, he played with the Philharmonic Society conducted by Emil Paur, offering Tartini's Sonata for Violin, with the breath-taking "Devil's Trill" as orchestrated by the soloist, and Max Bruch's Concerto No. 1. A few days later he appeared with David Mannes under the auspices of the Musical Art Society of New York, Frank Damrosch conducting, in Bach's Concerto for Two Violins. The critics praised him warmly both times.

The 1900–1901 tour took Kreisler, among other cities, to Philadelphia, where he played the Vieuxtemps Concerto No. 2 with the Philadelphia Symphony Orchestra; to Pittsburgh, where the critic of the Pittsburgh *Post* observed, "Twelve years ago Kreisler toured this city as a 'wonder child'; today he reappears as an 'absolute wonder' with astonishing violinistic powers"; and to Chicago, where he appeared in the tenth season of the Chicago Orchestra conducted by Theodore Thomas. The leading six dailies of the metropolis on Lake Michigan were unanimous in their praise.

David Mannes, 1866-1959

Jean Gérardy, 1847-1929

During the 1900–1901 season Kreisler sometimes gave joint concerts with Jean Gérardy as his cellist colleague.

Occasionally Pollak's conscience bothered him and he would join Kreisler and the Belgian artist. Leonard Liebling has written in the *Musical Courier* of January 9, 1909 of an episode in which the musician-medico was the victim of a jolly prank played by his two friends:

> Kreisler and Gérardy traveled together in this country, and gave joint concerts in various places, assisted by their accompanist, Dr. Pollak. The two artists managed to make Pollak's life miserable, both because of their love for practical jokes and by reason of their propensity for appearing in the dressing room at the last possible instant before their presence was actually required on the stage.
>
> On one occasion, in Chicago, the hour for beginning the concert had just struck, when Dr. Pollak discovered that Kreisler and Gérardy were not in the dressing room and had been invisible all afternoon. The hall was connected with the hotel at which the trio lived and Dr. Pollak dashed around to Kreisler's apartment. He burst in without knocking, and there, in the large double bed discovered the violinist and Gérardy, with the covers pulled up to their chins, and snoring a *fortissimo* and most discordant duet.
>
> "Hi, there, you two, are you crazy?" shouted Dr. Pollak. "The audience is assembled, waiting for the concert to begin." Then he shook the sleepers violently.
>
> "*Lass' mich schlafen,*" growled Kreisler in the language of Wagner's dragon. "*Meine Ruh' ist hin,*' quoted Gérardy drowsily. Then both artists turned over and snored more untunefully than ever.
>
> "Get up, get up," implored the anguished doctor; "I beg of you, I entreat, I insist."
>
> "Never," sputtered Kreisler. "Same here," mumbled Gérardy in sleepy defiance.
>
> Dr. Pollak argued and raved and swore, but all to no use. Finally he became desperate and seized the covers. "I'll make you get up," he shouted, and pulled off the bed clothes. What was his amazement to find Kreisler and Gérardy fully dressed in their concert togs and shaking with laughter at the fright they had given him.
>
> Of course, it was the work of only a moment for the young men to jump out of bed, brush their clothes and their hair, and hurry down the hall, where the concert began ten minutes after the advertised time, without the reason therefor being known to any one except those on the stage.

America from now on was destined to become Fritz Kreisler's habitual resort. The people of the United States took him to their heart as few nations did—certainly much more quickly and generously than his native Austria, and not less so than Great Britain and France, in both of which countries he soon became the idol of the concertgoing public. He was reengaged for the 1901–1902 season. He then not only appeared as soloist but also joined a rare combination of talents for purposes of a trio ensemble: Josef Hofmann, pianist, and Jean Gérardy, cellist. It was a happy association. Reminiscing on it, Fritz said to Olin Downes of the New York *Times*:

"I remember my early tour with Hofmann and Gérardy. Good Heavens, we gave concerts sometimes to a handful, and lucky if we made enough to pay the next place. But we played, and I think sometimes, at least, we played gloriously. So we felt, anyhow."

Adella Prentiss Hughes, the Cleveland impresario, said in her autobiography: *

> In Gray's Armory on April 17 (1902) I presented a trio of artists in a concert that literally made the rafters ring; three young men—Josef Hofmann, Jean Gérardy, and Fritz Kreisler. What a night that was! I gave a supper for them afterward at the Colonial Hotel. Josef and Jean were in high spirits. I missed them from the supper room for a few minutes, but they returned smiling mysteriously. Later a bell-boy came in and asked if there was a gentleman present by the name of Kreisler; he had a cable to deliver. It was from China. Kreisler looked self-conscious enough after reading the loving message from a lady, which his colleagues had faked!

Five days previously this "rare combination of stars" had appeared in New York. The three young artists elicited the following praise from the musical expert of the New York *Times*:

> The temptation to exploit individual skill in such a concert is great and it is much to the credit of these three artists that they were ready and willing to risk their individualities in the performance of a trio in real chamber music style.

One of Kreisler's most important solo engagements of the season of 1901–1902 was his appearance in Chicago in January, 1902. With

* Reprinted from *Music Is My Life* by Adella Prentiss Hughes, by permission of The World Publishing Company, Cleveland, Ohio, Publishers, copyright, 1947, by Adella Prentiss Hughes.

Kreisler with Josef Hofmann, 1876-1957

Jan Kubelik, 1880-1940

the famous Theodore Thomas conducting, he played Ludwig Spohr's Violin Concerto No. 8. The reason for the exceptional importance of this appearance lay in the fact that Chicago seemed to have gone crazy over the twenty-one-year-old Bohemian, Jan Kubelik.

Kubelik even managed to draw more money per concert out of Chicago than Ignace Jan Paderewski. Young girls from Chicago's best society fairly besieged him with offers of marriage. When he was taken on a tour of the Chicago stockyards, or shown a museum or art gallery, or dragged to some social function, his appearance caused traffic jams. He was hailed as the "heir of Paganini."

Kreisler was up against stiff competition. But he was not worried. He was well aware that virtuosity until his and Ysaÿe's day had been considered as something that must be accepted by the audience as an end in itself; whoever possessed it in an outstanding manner must not be expected also to bring great depth of feeling into his playing. Kreisler knew he could combine both.

The Chicago critics gave the answer as to whether he succeeded. They were unanimous in their praise. The musical expert for the *Interocean* put their feelings in these words:

> Fritz Kreisler brings to the platform a personality so vigorous as to make the fragile violin in his hand remind one of a quill toothpick in the hands of a Gog or Magog. With all his robustness of exterior and his apparent vast physical strength, Mr. Kreisler handles his bow with delicacy and finesse, and the touch of his muscular fingers on the strings in the pianissimo passages is as light as the caress of a summer breeze upon thistledown that it hesitates to destroy.

There was something else, quite apart from his art, which made Fritz stand out in sharp relief from his colleagues: he never tried to dramatize himself, to make a show of peculiarities and idiosyncrasies to attract attention, to fly into tantrums in order to give evidence of artistic temperament. His simplicity and naturalness have won him millions of hearts.

Even as Kreisler was stopping in Chicago for a recital, a scene ensued in a downtown hotel which cost Kubelik some of the goodwill that he had created by his technical wizardry. Coming down in an elevator one morning, Kubelik noticed that a printed photograph of Paderewski had been placed in the elevator car. In a rage he tore down the placard, exclaiming, "That's what you do for another artist, when I'm the man who made your hotel famous!"

At that time Marcella Sembrich and Fritzi Scheff were appearing in Mozart's *Magic Flute* in Chicago. The impulsive Sembrich ran off the stage in a huff during one performance because Fritzi Scheff was given a tremendous ovation.

No such outburst can be charged to Kreisler. He is one of the most even-tempered artists in musical history.

Virtually every language has a proverb, the English equivalent of which is, "Opposites attract." The very fact that Fritz Kreisler is a man of exceptional composure is perhaps one reason why, during his return voyage to Europe after the 1900–1901 season, he proposed to the temperamental Mrs. Fred Woerz, nee Harriet Lies, with whom he has shared joy and sorrow now for almost fifty years.

CHAPTER TEN

ENTER HARRIET

[1901]

IT happened on his return trip to Europe in May, 1901. The young artist with the sad brown eyes, the bewitching smile, the Old World grace of manner—Fritz Kreisler—fell desperately and irremediably in love: His relation to the fair sex hitherto had been one of "crushes," of infatuations, of flippant flirtations; nothing really serious. This, however, was different.

His first meeting with his future wife has been described by Kreisler in these words: *

"I met her on shipboard. On coming eastward from New York on the old *Prince Bismarck*, . . . I went into the barbershop of the ship where they also sold knickknacks. She was in the shop buying a small hat. She was looking in the mirror, trying something on.

"As I got up from the barber's chair, I saw the reflection of a beautiful red-headed American girl in that mirror. I fell in love with her instantly, for she smiled at me then and there; and I smiled back. That was the beginning and the end for me.

"She is a very remarkable woman with a fine brain and an uncanny intuition. She is a self-sufficient person and, in that respect, has what I lack. I needed her and she has made the way easier for me all these years, for she has looked after me in a natural, everyday way. When I say such things about her she says: 'That's right, Pop!' She calls me 'Pop' or 'Fritzi'—and I like it.

"We became engaged on that voyage and were married a year later

* Reprinted from *The Human Side of Greatness* by William Leroy Stidger, by permission of Harper & Brothers, copyright, 1940, by Harper & Brothers.

in New York City, and afterward again by the Austrian ambassador in London . . . and our double marriage took!"

As Harriet was a divorcée, a Catholic Church wedding was out of the question. But theirs was a love that knew no barriers. They therefore had a civilian marriage performed, both in America in November, 1902, and in London in 1903. A third marriage ceremony occurred as late as March, 1947, when Harriet and Fritz returned to the Roman Catholic Church in which both had been raised, but of which they had not been communicants for years, because in the eyes of the Church they "lived in sin." As a septuagenarian couple, after a two-month period of instruction by their friend Monsignor Fulton J. Sheen, they now received, in the Church of the Blessed Sacrament at New Rochelle, New York, the sanction and blessing of an ordained priest for their marital status.

The "beautiful red-headed girl" whom Kreisler chanced to meet in the unromantic barbershop of an ocean liner was the only daughter and child of George P. Lies, a tobacco merchant of New York, Brooklyn, and Havana, Cuba. She can point with pride to the fact that she was born at Second Avenue and Tenth Street, a then fashionable district—the east end of which was the much-maligned Bowery—opposite historic St. Mark's Church. The Stuyvesant Fishes, the Schieffelins, the Astors, and others of New York's old families were her neighbors. "I come from one of the oldest Catholic families," Harriet will tell you, "and that goes for both my paternal and maternal side."

Her parents at first were none too enthusiastic about the affair. A divorcée (Harriet was Mrs. Fred Woerz when she met Fritz) always set tongues wagging in those days. Also, George P. Lies, like so many representatives of Old New York's upper merchant class, thought an artist's calling lacked stability and "seriousness." On one occasion Fritz, discussing his relations, said: "My father wanted to become a musician, but grandfather thought it wasn't a gentlemanly profession. The same thing was true of Harriet's father, who had a notion I was playing around at street corners fiddling."

This prejudice was overcome, however, and a happy and affectionate relationship with the gifted son-in-law ensued.

After the *Prince Bismarck* had docked in Bremerhaven, the two young people, madly in love with each other, went to Berlin, where Fritz proudly presented his fiancée to his friends and musical connections, especially the Landekers, owners of Philharmonie and Beethoven Halls, and the Wolffs, chief owners of the Konzertdirektion Wolff & Sachs. Edith (Mrs. Otto) Stargardt, a Wolff daughter, recalls with amusement:

> In my mind's eye I still see ourselves all sitting together in the Rankestrasse of Berlin in mother's drawing room with a round table in the center. Harriet in an exuberance of affection plumped herself on the lap of her loving swain. We considered it at the time less shocking than amazing.

To appreciate this anecdote, the reader must try to envisage the customs and proprieties of that period. In conventional German society sitting on a gentleman's lap, even that of the future husband, just wasn't done in the presence of others.

Kreisler indeed had reason to be proud of his bride: the young matron from America was strikingly beautiful. *Musical America* wrote admiringly on November 9, 1907:

> Mrs. Kreisler is tall, . . . of fine proportion and grace, and with a face whose beauty and evidence of depth of forceful and high-aspiring character grows on one as she speaks or listens when her husband talks of their home, of America, of England, of Germany.

A biography of Fritz Kreisler would not be honest if it glossed over the fact that Harriet has been a controversial figure throughout her husband's career. She is fully aware of it and, indeed, takes pride in it. She can be uninhibitedly outspoken, undiplomatically direct, and on occasion uncompromisingly frank.

Anybody who has ever met Harriet Kreisler recognizes at once that here is an outstanding personality—strong-willed, temperamental, efficient, shrewd, alert, witty, clever, and amusing. Anybody who knows her is also aware that she is completely sincere in saying, "I live for nobody but Fritz."

Harriet completely reshaped her husband's life. This was necessary. An easy-going, dreaming musician who has attained the stature of genius needs a buffer between himself and the rough-and-tumble world. Harriet was just that to Fritz.

She led him into a regular life. That, too, was necessary. An artist, to secure a niche in the gallery of immortals, must pay a price for it. Fritz Kreisler's price was a much more regimented, budgeted, organized life than that to which the carefree existence of a Vienna coffee-house habitué and Bohemian of the world's music centers would ever have led.

Those who do not approve of Harriet's "management" (a word her husband likes to use banteringly) claim that she supervises his comings and goings too closely and leaves him too little choice concerning his hobbies, recreations, friendships, and indulgence in those foibles of which an ancient Chinese proverb says: "It is my imperfections that endear me to my friends. It is my virtues that annoy them."

Harriet's critics assert that in her single-minded purpose of helping him to become the great man that he is, she went too far in cutting her husband off from associations which he held dear. They further hold that some friendships of which she approved and which she also cherished were lost because of her uncompromising directness. They contend that, strong personality that she is—a personality that in her own right might have played a leading part in American life—she becomes irked at always being presented merely as "Fritz Kreisler's wife," and that, to compensate for this frustration, she then at times asserts her "management" of her husband in a way that embarrasses those present.

To all such criticisms Harriet answers calmly: "After all, I know Fritz best. I have made him. The entire world acclaims the result. I knew what was good for him. So what?"

A revealing glimpse of her inner self was made in the course of a bantering interview with the New York *Times* in October, 1934. Her husband had just been trying to explain one of his most recent acquisitions for his noted library. It was a book printed in Venice in 1500 in "borderline Latin and Italian," and as he struggled to describe it he finally said it was something like "striving for love in a dream." It was then that Harriet broke in emphatically:

"There you are! Now how will that sound in the papers, Pop? What with the 'striving for love in a dream' and the way girls already make eyes at him!

Listen, boys, he's been coming here too much without me; he's gotten out of hand.

"Don't let him fool you, standing there, amiable like that. Often other women come to me and say sweetly, 'Oh, the dear Mr. Kreisler,' and to myself I think, 'Oh, boy, if you only had to handle him for six months!' . . . But I like him anyhow."

Harriet was absolutely right in her assertion that the "girls already make eyes at him." It was worse than that, as was humorously pointed out by Howard Heck, who for about fifteen years accompanied him as road manager.

"At the hotels Mr. Kreisler was simply hounded," Heck said. "For this reason we often ate in cafeterias, just to get away from these people.

"We could not always escape them, however. Suddenly some dame would appear in the lobby, approach Mr. Kreisler before I could prevent it, and engage him in a conversation. Mr. Kreisler would listen kindly, say a polite word or two, and shake off the interloper as rapidly as possible.

"But then came the aftermath! The same dame would write a letter, indulging in such familiarity as, 'Dear Fritz: When we were together at the Hotel X . . .' All such letters naturally came into the hands of Mrs. Kreisler, as Mr. Kreisler seldom reads his mail and his correspondence is handled by his wife.

"Poor Mr. Kreisler, of course, hadn't the faintest idea who the lady was that wrote him such a gushing letter. But he had to do some tall explaining to his wife! It took our combined assurances that the obvious infatuation was decidedly one-sided, and that the letter writer was merely one of the many pests that bored Mr. Kreisler to death."

As to Fritz, any jealousy as to what he might do on the road was out of place. "His adoration of her has provoked more gosssip than most men's infidelities do," *The New Yorker* observed, referring to Kreisler's devotion to his Harriet, then continued: *

With the eagerness of a young lad in love, he brings up references to "a person who is very close to me, whose opinion is of great importance in my

* Reprinted from Profiles—*A Gentleman from Vienna* by Helena Huntington Smith, in the November 24, 1928 issue of *The New Yorker*, by permission of *The New Yorker*.

eyes . . . no one will know what a blessing she has been to me." She is his closest companion, and she stands between him and the world, an arrangement which satisfies him deeply, but which perplexes and irritates pretty ladies with a taste for lion-hunting.

The evaluation placed upon Harriet Kreisler by various of her husband's accompanists is especially important, as these men got to know the artist and his wife intimately during rehearsals and travels.

Carl Lamson, for nearly forty years Fritz's American accompanist, pointed out that, without herself being an adept at any musical instrument, Harriet Kreisler has had an uncanny feeling for what was good and what was defective, what was appropriate to the occasion and what inopportune, in her husband's playing, composing, and arranging of programs. "Hers is a healthy, good judgment," he observed.

One of his European accompanists complained that the concert tours were sometimes "somewhat tedious and boring, because Mr. Kreisler had taken a vow never to have anything to do with other women—and I like women so much!"

Another European accompanist, the Bavarian Michael Raucheisen, ended a long letter on his experiences with Harriet and Fritz:

> I cannot complete this sketch without also paying a tribute to *Frau* Harriet. Only the initiated are in a position to judge what this woman has done for her husband and thereby for the world. Kreisler's good naturedness and naïveté drove him in his younger years even to the point of pawning his valuable violin and of occasionally exchanging the concert hall for a coffee house when in distress.
>
> *Frau* Harriet just could not see him gradually deteriorate, and within a relatively short time accustomed this too soft-hearted man to an ordered, regular life. For this initiative he will be grateful to her as long as he lives. One thing is certain—without Harriet Kreisler there would be no Fritz Kreisler.
>
> Only seldom was she to be seen in the concert hall. She stuck to the artist's room to be ever near her husband with her solicitude. She looked after me, too, like a mother during our appearances—that we surely wouldn't catch a cold in winter, that we took proper nourishment, that no music scores remained behind, that the public did not become too importunate. All this she attended to in the most self-effacing manner.
>
> How often did she say to us, spontaneously, between numbers, "Children, you really made beautiful music!" With a satisfied smile Kreisler would then lay his violin aside.

What other woman would thus disappear in the "green room" and desist from sharing the garnering of honors bestowed upon her husband—if for no other reason out of vanity?

Sometimes she had to take unpopularity upon herself just so that people would not take too great advantage of her husband. Whoever, like myself, got to know *Frau* Harriet intimately during many, many tours is alone in a position to gauge how decisive the influence of this precious woman has been upon a soft-hearted artist. May God bless this ideal relationship for many more years to come!

Michael Raucheisen—later, by the grace of Adolf Hitler, Professor Raucheisen—accompanied Kreisler on the European continent from 1919 to 1931, traveling through Germany, Switzerland, Denmark, Holland, Belgium, France, Italy, Spain, and Greece with him. He also shared the podium with him on his trip to Japan, China, and Korea, and played for him in Canada.

Among Kreisler's earliest artist friends and associates four brilliant and distinguished musicians, all of them with world fame to look back upon in their old age, spontaneously paid tribute to Harriet during my talks with them. All four of them knew both the pre- and the post-marriage "L'Amico Fritz," as Giacomo Puccini used to call him. This is what they had to say:

Harold Bauer: "There is no doubt but that Harriet saved Fritz. He was going down the hill a bit when she married him."

Josef Hofmann: "Harriet made Fritz Kreisler. You know how easygoing he was. She didn't have much formal musical education, but was very good in her musical reactions.

"Fritz would accept any fee. Now, you know the trade—it gauges a man partly by the fee he commands. 'So-and-so is a $250 artist, So-and-so, $500; So-and-so, $1,000,' and so on. Harriet knew how to keep Fritz at the very top."

Jacques Thibaud: "Fritz and I were two crazy young men. If we later had the great Fritz, we owe it to Harriet. Harriet saved Fritz. He began to practice, to write, to stop playing poker all night. Wherever he was, in Paris, Berlin, London, or elsewhere, she made him practice, made him do his very best. She can be credited with a great percentage of his success.

"In the Kreisler career there were two capitals: the artistic capital, the genius, was supplied by Fritz; the moral and physical capital came from Harriet. Harriet was absolutely necessary to Fritz."

Georges Enesco: "Harriet is a dynamic woman. But she saved Fritz. She would say: 'Fritz, don't drink any more; Fritz, don't eat any more.' In that way she kept him in check."

Fritz has never ceased to sing the praise of his Harriet. First impressions are often strongest. Our friendship—my wife and I had naturally heard him many times before becoming acquainted with Harriet and Fritz—dates from 1924. Among the first things Fritz said when we were far enough along in our friendship to exchange confidences was, "Everything I am as a violinist I owe to Harriet." That phrase, with variations, I have heard in his home, in ours, in those of third parties again and again during the quarter-century that ensued.

Coupled with it was soon another phrase, "But she is right." Lover and collector of beautiful instruments that he is, it was not exactly easy for him to yield to Harriet's suggestion that he could relieve considerable suffering if he were to sell some of them for charity. "But she is right," he said. "Why should I have violins around which I don't need?"

One day in New York, Carl Lamson, Charles Foley (his impresario for almost forty years), and I were lunching with Fritz. He hospitably suggested we moisten our throats as a starter. He himself declined, however, saying Harriet would not want it. "But she is right," he continued. "I ought not to drink. I had no breakfast this morning but went directly to a Turkish bath. One must not pour a drink into an empty stomach."

Explaining his dependence on his "manager," Kreisler once said: *

"I am self-confident when on the platform with the violin, but essentially shy in everyday life. I go last into a subway.

"The everyday things of life baffle me. Every morning, Harriet says, I ask where my socks are. She looks after my baggage, my violins—and me also. I am impractical. I am afraid of people and life as a

* Reprinted from *The Human Side of Greatness* by William Leroy Stidger, by permission of Harper & Brothers, copyright, 1940, by Harper & Brothers.

whole. I am baffled by problems that most people would face fearlessly."

How badly he needed a wife to look after the "baffling everyday things of life" was illustrated by an occurrence in the United States toward the close of his bachelor days. In Fritz's own version: *

"I was dismayed to find one evening, on reaching a hall where I was to play, that the vest of my dress suit had not been packed with my other garments.

"What was I to do? There was obviously no time to secure another vest. At last someone came forward with the suggestion that I put a large silk handkerchief around my waist. The idea was adopted, and a suitable handkerchief being forthcoming, this was folded and pinned around my waist with a safety pin.

"But that pin belied its name. Halfway through the solo I felt that it had become unfastened. I played on but was in terror, for I feared that my every movement would bring the handkerchief about my feet.

"Good fortune, however, allowed me to finish the piece. Then came the applause. I made one or two vain attempts to bow in response to the reception given my playing, but the thought of that handkerchief checked me each time. At last, with a spasmodic nod to the audience, I rushed from the stage, thankful that I had escaped so easily."

No such trouble beset him after his marriage!

In a discussion on prodigies with a *Musical America* reporter Kreisler explained how he escaped the fate of many *Wunderkinder* who were treated by their friends and relatives as other than normal:

"For myself, I have been protected by the broad intelligence of a wonderful wife, with ideals of life and great good sense in treating me as a man, subject to the same laws of health, of right and progress as any other man."

Few families can boast of having kept their hired help as long as Harriet Kreisler kept hers. Twenty-four years and longer for the same servant has been no uncommon experience with her. One chauf-

* Reprinted by permission of *Etude, The Music Magazine*, from an article by Carlton A. Scheinert, "Kreisler and the Prodigy," copyright, 1934, by Theodore Presser Company.

feur was with the Kreisler household from 1922 to 1934, by which time he had saved enough money to buy himself a garage. In Berlin the same caretaker who had already been on the premises for years when, early in August, 1939, the Kreislers left for Austria with a premonition they might never return, is still there at this writing. He faced the curtain of fire that was laid over the fashionable Grunewald section of Berlin repeatedly during American and British saturation raids and got in touch with his master and mistress just as soon as the American occupation forces reached the city in July, 1945. His wife and a maid, who also remained in the battered, burnt-out remnants of what was once one of the most artistic homes in the German capital, spoke glowingly of how splendidly the household had always been run by "Frau Professor." (In Germany wives are addressed by the title of the husband; Fritz was named honorary professor by the University of Vienna.) She was always especially keen, they said, about punctuality; artists should lead as regular lives as other people, she believed.

People who only think of Harriet as forever finding fault with her husband ought to have been present that night early in March, 1949, when the Overseas Press Club honored the retired Secretary of State, General George C. Marshall, with a testimonial dinner in the Waldorf Astoria Hotel, New York. On the dais with General Marshall sat about two dozen exceptional men, among them Secretary of State Dean Acheson, General Albert C. Wedemeyer, Former Under Secretary of State Robert M. Lovett, Elder Statesman Bernard M. Baruch, Economic Cooperation Administrator Paul G. Hoffman, Former Secretary of War Robert P. Patterson, and, as an outstanding representative of the fine arts, Fritz Kreisler.

Harriet, who sat at the table of the Frank E. Masons, directly under the dais, was so placed that she could not immediately see her husband. My wife, who was seated next to her, said: "Harriet was like a young thing who has fallen in love for the first time. She kept saying to me excitedly, 'I don't see my Fritzi. Hilde, do you see him? Where's my Fritzi?' And when she finally espied him, she beamed with joy."

A few weeks later, she learned during a telephone conversation that Nathan Milstein had paid Fritz a beautiful tribute. I read Milstein's words to her. "Oh, you must tell Poppi that next time you come to talk to him," she said, fervently and lovingly; "that will make him happy."

On one occasion one of the most prominent socialites of New York bragged at a reception that her daughter had married a duke or a prince. Harriet Kreisler remarked tersely, "I didn't have to buy a title."

"What do you mean by that remark?" the dowager asked with ill concealed anger.

"I am already a queen," Harriet riposted with a disarming smile. "My husband was born a king in his own right—he is a king of violinists."

Passing from the purely personal to the public service aspects of Harriet Kreisler's life with Fritz, it can be asserted apodictically that the charities which she initiated, organized, superintended, and often personally managed on behalf of her husband exceed those of any artist in history. They constitute an astounding record of love and compassion for the underprivileged, for those in distress and want.

As Edith Wolff-Stargardt expressed it:

> Harriet's great contribution has been her far-flung charities. There are other artists who have earned huge fortunes, but they had neither time nor understanding for suffering fellow humans. Frau Harriet, however, saw to it that the Kreisler charities were really magnanimous and not superficial.

Musicians in general owe Harriet Kreisler deep gratitude for having insisted from the beginning of her marriage upon the social equality of the artists with the élite in every walk of life. An equality which the generation of today takes for granted was by no means a generally accepted one at the turn of the century. In those days it still happened that celebrated artists like Nellie Melba, Yvette Guilbert, and Paderewski had to stand behind a rope until all the titled personages had entered their vehicles, after which the flunky would call out, rather disdainfully, "carriages for the musicianers."

Perhaps her most daring act in that respect was her insistence that her husband decline a royal invitation. It was during the early years of their marriage, when Fritz Kreisler was establishing himself as firmly in the hearts of the British as he already had in the hearts of the Americans. Queen Alexandra, consort of King Edward VII, in ignorance of Harriet's presence in London, addressed an invitation to him alone to have tea with her.

Now, an invitation from Buckingham Palace, like one from the White House in our country, is a "royal command." Nevertheless, Kreisler had the temerity to decline, on the grounds that he already had an engagement with his wife! This note might easily have wrecked his career in England. But Queen Alexandra was an understanding woman. A note from the palace expressed Her Majesty's regret that she had not been aware of the presence in London of Mrs. Kreisler; the invitation was, of course, for both!

A few years after their marriage, Harriet stated her views about the social status of the artist in vigorous terms:

"It was quite the thing to send invitations to a married artist requesting the pleasure of his attendance at a dinner or soirée, quite ignoring the fact that he had a wife. After we were married, when Mr. Kreisler received one of these, he would reply that Mr. and Mrs. Kreisler were engaged for that evening. If they hadn't known he was married before, they knew it then, and if they had known they were plainly told that an artist's wife was no more a personage not to be considered than any other man's.

"Would they think of inviting (Sir Laurence) Alma-Tadema and not his wife, or any other married man? But if they used to assume that the 'long-haired artist' would be glad to come into society and his wife be rejoiced to sit alone at home, waiting for her husband to return to present her with the sop of a relation of the glories of his evening, they are gradually learning their mistake. An artist is no freak to come to amuse them, while any wife he may happen to have is something not to be thought of.

"I wouldn't stand it. Perhaps it was my possession of American independence that made me assert myself, but with Mr. Kreisler I didn't have to make the assertion, for all these were his ideas, too."

Harriet Kreisler was a pioneer in winning a social position second to that of no one both for the artist and for his wife. In establishing this social standing for herself and her husband, she benefited equally her husband's colleagues and their wives.

CHAPTER ELEVEN

A GLUTTON FOR MAKING MUSIC BUT A FOE OF PRACTICING

FRITZ KREISLER, it will be recalled, showed his capacity for severe self-discipline and continuous concentration when, after serving in the Austrian Army, he withdrew to a suburban Viennese hostelry to practice, and at the age of nineteen composed his superb Beethoven cadenzas.

Now, with his young bride prodding him lovingly but firmly whenever the Bohemianism in his nature threatened to get the upper hand, he again worked intensely, both at keeping himself at the height of violinistic mastery and at composing.

Music was the very essence of Kreisler's life, and for the sake of hearing, writing, or arranging music he was prepared to drop everything else. He was deeply in earnest when he told Beverly Smith: * "I would still play the violin . . . even if I were fined and punished for doing it. There were laws in Russia, for a time, to interfere with some forms of art. Under such laws I would become a criminal. Always I will play my violin."

As a concert violinist Kreisler was indefatigable. Josef Hofmann said: "I believe Fritz holds the world's record for artists: 260 concerts in the course of one year. He then played in the United States, Europe, Egypt, and South America. In America alone he once had 120 concerts." Howard Heck remembered that during one season Kreisler played 57 concerts in 72 days!

Sergei Rachmaninoff, who was one of Fritz's most intimate friends,

* Reprinted from *He Plays on the World's Heartstrings* by Beverly Smith, in the February, 1931 issue of the *American Magazine*, by permission of Beverly Smith and The Crowell-Collier Publishing Company, copyright, 1931, by *American Magazine*.

once remarked jestingly, but with a justified undertone of seriousness, "Fritz gives so many concerts that he doesn't need to practice."

To all the Kreisler platform appearances must be added the innumerable repetitions (especially in the infant years of the phonograph) for recordings, the rehearsals with orchestras, and the long hours of playing with kindred souls just for the pleasure of making music.

The following anecdote is illustrative of this devotion to music for music's sake:

At a party at Victor Herbert's home in Pittsburgh, Schubert's string quintet (two cellos) was played at Kreisler's suggestion. Herbert's wife, Therese, rewarded the players with some of her exquisite Viennese cooking, for which she was noted. Kreisler then said, "Oh, let's play it again, it is so beautiful." So the heavenly but long work was played a second time in its entirety. Assorted libations cooled the throats of the ardent instrumentalists, and the famous Therese Herbert cuisine again lived up to expectations. Everybody seemed ready now to call it a day. Not so the man at the first violin desk. "Come on," Kreisler begged, "we may never be together again like this. Let's play it a third time." And played it was.

"It is true that we performed the Schubert quintet three times that night," Fritz admitted to me with a pleased laugh. "It is one of my favorites. That evening Victor Herbert played the first cello part. I have also played the work often with Pablo Casals as first cellist."

Whether on tour or at home, Kreisler seemed always to be occupied with some composition of his own, or with one of the innumerable transcriptions which have enriched violin literature, or with the orchestration of some score, or with the revision and adaptation of a work like the Schumann Fantasie or the Paganini Concert Piece in One Movement which he constructed out of the Italian wizard's Concerto in D-major.

Once a score had caught his imagination, he was willing to sacrifice the night's rest to finish it. The 1908 series of newspaper and magazine clippings of the Robinson Locke *Collection of Dramatic Scrap Books* in the New York Public Library contains the following undated item:

Victor Herbert, 1859-1924

Pablo Casals, 1876-1973

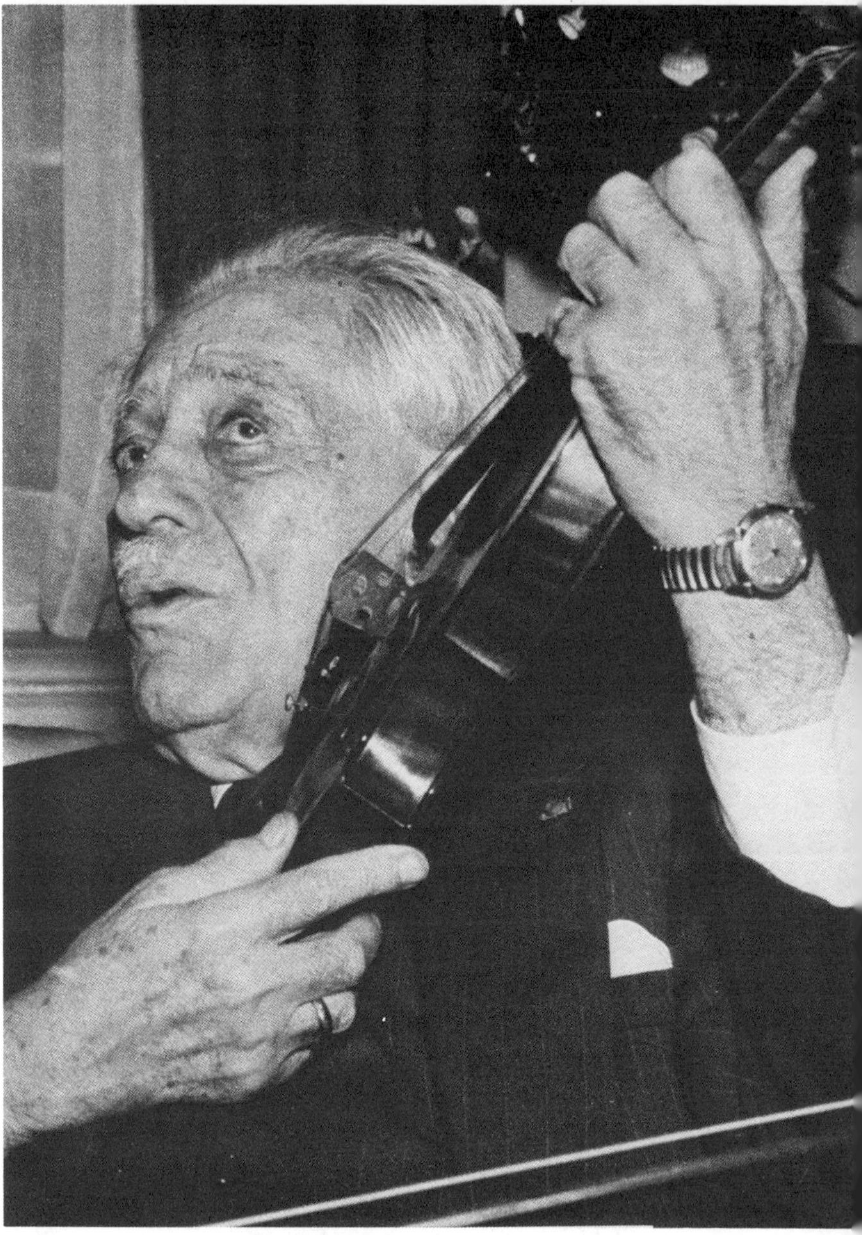

Close-range view of the elder Kreisler's hands

After a most successful concert in Weybridge in the South of England, Mr. Kreisler retired to rest, leaving strict injunctions that he was to be called at an early hour, as he was due to play in another town the next night. On going to arouse him, the hotel porter was astonished to find him busy at work on a score, and it transpired that he had spent the whole night in revising the orchestral accompaniments to Wieniawski's *Airs Russes* for that day's rehearsal, and had, moreover, written a fine accompaniment for the harp.

One of the strangest phenomena about Fritz Kreisler, who was indeed a veritable glutton for making, composing, arranging, transcribing, and orchestrating music, is the fact that he had an aversion to practicing, at least for rehearsing the musical numbers scheduled on the programs immediately ahead. His colleagues have been astounded by it. Critics and fellow violinists agree that Kreisler is unique in his ability to perform without more than token practice. His wife was fond of saying, "Think what a great artist he might be if he had practiced!" She seldom speaks of him as violinist—he is a "fiddler" to her. Kreisler himself is well aware that it is hurtful to cite him as proof that practice is unnecessary. He has always qualified his own position by pointing out that he practiced hard and long in his younger years.

As his aversion to practicing was generally known in musical circles, he was often asked to explain. In the following a series of utterances of his has been combined into a single consecutive statement. Repetition was in that way avoided, but no liberties were taken with Kreisler's words:

"I hesitate to say how little I practice, because young violinists might think they don't need to practice. Yet it is precisely if one practices well in youth that the fingers should retain their suppleness in later years.

"The idea, however, of being *compelled* to practice several hours daily is the result of self-hypnotism, which really does create the necessity. I have, on the contrary, hypnotized myself into the belief that I do not need it, and therefore I do not. I can regain my best form in three hours.

"I believe that everything is in the brain. You think of a passage and you know exactly how you want it. It is like aiming a pistol. You take aim, you cock the pistol, you put your finger on the trigger. A slight pressure of the finger and the shot is fired.

"The same should apply to technique on an instrument. You think before, and not merely as, or after, you fire the note. Your muscle is prepared, the physical conception is perfectly clear in your mind, a slight flash of will power and your effect is achieved.

"But to rely on muscular habit, which so many do in technique, is indeed fatal. A little nervousness, a muscle bewildered and unable to direct itself, and where are you? For technique is truly a matter of the brain.

"How sad it is that in these days the emphasis is on how many hours one practices!

"Long ago I met Kubelik one afternoon. He was worried and excited. He said to me: 'Can't you help me? I have a concert tonight and my fingers are all bleeding. I have practiced twelve hours.' And I asked him, 'But why did you?' When he played that night, it was technically a perfect performance, but yet it was a blank!

"I have not the slightest consciousness of what my fingers are doing when I play. I concentrate on the ideal of the music that I hear in my head, and I try to come as near to that as I can. I don't think of the mechanics at all. A musician who does have to think of the mechanics is not ready for public performance.

"Sometimes I get up from a jolly luncheon party and go to the concert hall cold—cold. Then I awake, and every thought in my brain and every nerve in my body lives—not my life, but the life of the music.

"The secret of my method, if I may say so, consists of my having to concentrate and exert myself, when on the platform, much more than if I had previously practiced the music for many hours. The extra alertness required to master any uncertainties that may exist enables me to play all the better. The fingers are merely the executive organs.

"I never practice before a concert. The reason is that practice benumbs the brain, renders the imagination less acute, and deadens the sense of alertness that every artist must possess.

"I have spent an entire day with Sarasate previous to an evening concert and have seen him go on the stage without having touched the

Jan Kubelik in 1922

Pablo de Sarasate, 1844-1908

violin or even having mentioned the subject of violin playing, and yet his playing was as perfect as if he had devoted the whole day to study.

"The true artistic talent is a gift and not a matter of practice. If the player is an executing artist, the matter of technical acquisition is a matter of early study and, after that, if he has the real violin talent, he does not need to work at the instrument. Paganini is an excellent example of that talent.

"I have never been troubled with stiff fingers. I can get off a train after an all-day ride and go at once to the concert hall and play as well as ever. I merely dip my fingertips in hot water for a few seconds before stepping on the platform. That limbers them up better than if I had spent a couple of hours practicing.

"My greatest need, my greatest anxiety, is to preserve my enthusiasm and to be able to make my playing fresh and buoyant. I never practice compositions I am to play in the near future. I must have them fresh. I must not allow myself to become tired of them. I have to enjoy whatever I play or I can't play it.

"Technical exercises I use very moderately. Too much work along routine channels does not accord with the best development of my art.

"Technique is decidedly not the main essential of the concert violinist's equipment. Sincerity and personality are the first main essentials. I don't believe that any artist is truly a master of his instrument unless his control of it is an integral part of a whole. The music is born—his medium of expression is often a matter of accident.

"To me, music is an entire philosophy of living. What I say in music is that part of my deepest inner being that can never be put in words.

"Words, even with the best of intentions, can be deceptive; a person may misunderstand what you say—a trick of language, an inflection of voice can alter meanings. That is why I sometimes hesitate to put my most cherished thoughts into words! But with music, it is different. Here there is no intervening obstacle of medium. One feels deeply in one's heart and one transfers that meaning into tone.

"When I play, I am completely myself, and I have no fear of being misunderstood. Joy, fear, anger, gladness—all of these can be projected from one human heart directly into another through the medium of music. This is possible, I believe, because music is the most direct and untrammeled exponent of human emotion.

"Approaching music in this way, I believe that it becomes the expression of one's truest self. In this sense, the building of ultimate musicianship involves a great deal more than technical proficiency on an instrument. It involves the qualities that make up self. The things that stir one, the things that anger one, the things that delight one—all these come to light in the music one makes.

"To me, the man who loves justice will 'sound' different from the man who is secretly capable of a mean act; the man who is cruel will 'sound' different from the man who is humane. In neither case is the speed with which he takes his cadenzas too important!

"I never have any trouble memorizing. I know the music so well that I do not even keep the violin parts. In fact, I do not possess any. I study the part from the orchestral or piano score, I get it into my head with its accompaniment. It is all mental. I sometimes play it over on the piano so as to get a general idea of the whole.

"When I memorize, it is as if I engraved the music on a disc in my mind. Once engraved, that disc will reproduce its record for years. Perhaps the record will get a bit dusty or blurred. In that case I take it out and clean it and put it back again to be used when I like.

"I never dreamed that the time would come when I would have to be put to the most severe test of my belief. You know of the accident I had, when I was hit by an automobile and lay unconscious for days.* Even the doctors were uncertain as to what would happen when I regained consciousness, I was so near death.

"Then the day came when I was to play. I took my violin in my hands for the first time. My wife was so worried! I looked at my fingers. They were stiff. They hadn't been used. But my desire was so intense and I told myself: These are my fingers. These are my slaves. I am the general. I order them to play and I will them to action.

"You know—they played."

Examples can be cited of Kreisler's amazing ability to make his fingers obey his will, and of his uncanny musical memory.

Someone writing in the *Musical Observer* in 1912 said that Kreis-

* That was in April, 1941. See Chapter Twenty-Six for details.

ler's playing of a Paganini Caprice was so "easy" that one received the impression that he could play it on his head while bumping down the stairs.

Howard Heck narrated: "Once we got to St. Louis and Mr. Kreisler was to play the Brahms Concerto for the first time in years with the orchestra. He thought he ought to stay in the hotel to go over the work once more while Carl Lamson and I went to the movies. He asked me, however, to report to him before we went.

"When I came to his room to report us out, he said, 'Well, I guess I can practice tonight; I'll go with you to the movies.' The story repeated itself in the evening. Believe it or not, Mr. Kreisler the following day played the concerto without having practiced it again—and he played it divinely."

Michael Raucheisen wrote of an occurrence during Kreisler's only visit to the Orient in 1923:

> When we arrived in Tokio we found the Japanese attached special importance to sonatas. During the eight performances at the Imperial Theater of Tokio, Kreisler was expected to perform virtually the entire existing sonata literature. I still remember as though it had taken place today, how Kreisler had an inquiry addressed to all musical Europeans there, as to whether, perchance, they had any sonatas for violin and piano in their libraries, so that we might fill all eight evenings with them.
>
> Kreisler had, of course, not prepared for such an unusual situation. Imagine, eight different programs! And yet, one—I repeat, one—rehearsal sufficed, and Kreisler played the sonatas which he had not had on his repertoire for many years, by heart, without a single flaw in memory, before this select international public. Usually soloists go on tour with two or three carefully prepared programs for a season. That is nothing unusual. It is absolutely unique and unparalleled, however, to conduct experiments like this extemporaneously.

Carl Lamson says that during their many tours, "Fritz never practiced what was on the program, but something that was scheduled weeks ahead. Often he didn't know what he should play for an encore and would leave it to me to suggest anything, no matter how long ago we had last played it."

At London, this incident took place in 1908 behind the scenes of the hall in which Kreisler was to give a recital:

Just as the concert was about to commence it was discovered that the music of a popular item had not been brought, and there was nothing for the accompanist to play from. It was impossible to procure this anywhere in time, but a way out of the difficulty was soon found by Kreisler. Some music paper was brought to him and he immediately sat down and made a pencil draft of the missing music. The copy was quite sufficient for the accompanist Mr. Haddon Squire to play from.

On another occasion in London during the same year, Kreisler gave evidence of his retentive memory for scores: *

Being engaged to play Mendelssohn's concerto with a well-known amateur orchestra in London, and having traveled all night to be in time for rehearsal, he [Kreisler] arrived, to the dismay of the conductor, minus his fiddle. To the astonishment of all present, he sat down to the piano, and played the entire work from memory, pointing out his wishes so exactly that the evening's performance went without a hitch.

Rembert Wurlitzer, to whose violin shop Fritz always brings his violins for overhauling or repair, recalled an incident which he believes took place in 1937.

"I was traveling westward from Kansas City," he said, "when on passing through one sleeping car I noticed Fritz sitting in his drawing room with an orchestra score in his hands. Fritz explained that this was the first opportunity he had to take a real look at the Sibelius Violin Concerto. Without the slightest show of boasting, he said in a matter-of-fact sort of way that he was sure that by the time he reached his destination at some point out West he would have the whole concerto so completely in his mind that he would be able to play it from memory. Mind you, until then he had not even tried out the violin part!

"Fritz always studied the entire score, so as to master the structure of the composition. If you compared his playing closely with a score, you could notice that here or there he played notes differing from those the composer wrote, but they always fitted in harmonically with the composer's structure."

Even in his high old age Kreisler has retained a manual dexterity

* Reprinted from *Fritz Kreisler* by B. Henderson, in the October, 1908 issue of *The Strad*, by permission of *The Strad*, London.

which astounds his younger colleagues, many of whom are young enough to be his grandsons. Albert Spalding recently spoke of having heard Kreisler in Chicago in November, 1948. "He was still superb," he commented.

Nathan Milstein a few months later said: "There is a natural superiority about Fritz Kreisler which age cannot destroy. Such flaws as there are now stem not from a faulty technique. His technique is still indescribable. They are due solely to the fact that his hearing is slightly impaired."

CHAPTER TWELVE

TWELVE YEARS RICH IN EXPERIENCE

[1902-1914]

When Fritz Kreisler sailed for the United States in the autumn of 1902 to marry his Harriet, he could do so with the unusual satisfaction of having matched his Berlin triumph of 1899 with a similar one in London in May, 1902.

Kreisler will usually mention Hans Richter among his favorite conductors, with Artur Nikisch and Felix Weingartner close seconds. Richter had grown up in Vienna in the same atmosphere as the young violinist. In fact, he had associated with Brahms, Hanslick, Kalbeck, Hellmesberger, and the other older cronies of the Café "Megalomania." When young Fritz returned from his medical studies to his first love, music, Richter on January 23, 1898, had given him his first opportunity to appear as soloist with the Vienna Philharmonic Orchestra. Shortly thereafter the conductor had transferred his musical activities to London, where he inaugurated the famous Richter Concerts. His name remained a legend in Vienna. Broad-shouldered, dignified, strikingly bewhiskered, his was an imposing personality. According to Georges Enesco: "His gestures were sparse—often a mere nod with his beard—yet every player knew he had to do his best."

Richter gave young Kreisler the chance he hoped and prayed for: an engagement as soloist in the first of the season's London Philharmonic Concerts in St. James's Hall on May 12, 1902.

Not that it was a dazzling success, this first appearance in the world's largest city. But that was neither his nor Hans Richter's fault. The English are less mercurial than we Americans and take their time about choosing their favorites. Once they have done so, however, they are more constant than we! Kreisler was a newcomer on the concert platform, and the people of London wanted to be shown, not in one but in a series of performances, what his true measure was.

A part of the London musical press was mildly critical, the greater part, however, flatteringly laudatory. Also, for the first time, the American press correspondents considered the event newsworthy enough to cable an item about Kreisler to America. The critic of the *Musical Standard*, after hearing him with Richter and in a solo recital a few weeks later, named Joachim, Sarasate, Ysaÿe, and Kreisler as "the four artists whose memory violin lovers of the future will cherish. In some ways, perhaps, Kreisler is the most remarkable of the four."

When Fritz returned to England for his December concerts of the season of 1902–1903, he was accompanied by his young bride. She could well be proud of her artist-husband, but also of her share in making him attend strictly to business. For, from that winter season on, Kreisler was the declared favorite of the Londoners. In the musical criticisms of the times, there are numerous references to his "insatiable audiences" which demanded encore after encore of him. He is compared to Robert Browning, the English poet, and Horace, the Latin poet. One reads of "scenes of extraordinary enthusiasm."

During that season Kreisler often appeared in sonata evenings with Ernö Dohnányi, the blond Hungariah composer and pianist.

The twelve years left to humanity to enjoy peace before the first great world war engulfed it were years rich in experience, in triumphs, in friendships, in associations for Harriet and Fritz. Much of their time was spent in England, of which Fritz became so fond that, according to B. Henderson:

> In fact he has been accused of partiality in that respect by some of our cousins across the Channel. Perhaps the robust side of the English character appeals to him, for he is a thorough lover of sport and all manly exercises. . . . He is also a keen motorist and a great lover of country life.

With his stunning young wife at his side as additional inspiration, Kreisler within a few years brought to nineteen the number of enchanting violin solo compositions ascribed to eighteenth and early nineteenth century masters that, as we shall see later, he admitted on his sixtieth birthday to be his own, original works.

Both being persons of vivid imaginations, they invented a version regarding the origin of these pieces that threw musical experts completely off the track. One of the London musicologists even wrote:

I am glad to be able to speak with authority from no less a source than the artist himself, having persuaded him to satisfy my curiosity as to the origin of his works. The violinist discovered a collection of MSS. music in the possession of the monks who inhabit one of the oldest monasteries in Europe, and so anxious was he to have them for his own that he copied one of the pieces on his shirt cuff. To this the monks objected, and eventually Kreisler, after much persuasion, succeeded in purchasing the whole collection for a considerable sum of money. It was a labor of love to arrange the works for the concert room, and having been at so much pains and expense to procure his treasures he naturally considers that, as long as he can play them, they are his sole property. It is only fair, too, to state that others had access to the MSS. but it was left to Kreisler to discover their value and utilize them. "*Palman qui meruit ferat.*" *

As illustrating the point of this argument, the writer of the present article went into a leading publisher's several years ago, after hearing some of these gems, to see if they could be had, and was informed by the gentleman in charge that no fewer than thirty people (many of whom had not waited until the close of the concert) had been in to make the same inquiry, and in the space of an hour the house could have sold a large supply.

In the course of an interview with the New York *Times* on November 9, 1909, Kreisler's fertile mind added a few specific details:

"I discovered the pieces in an old convent in the south of France. I have altogether fifty-three manuscripts of this sort in my possession. Five of them are more or less valueless. Forty-eight of them are gems. . . . In this list are many of the pieces which have attained great popularity—Porpora's Menuet, Couperin's "Chanson Louis XIII" and "Pavane," and Padre Martini's Andantino.

"Naturally, this music was not all written for the violin. I have arranged some of it for my instrument. I have made a few minor changes in the melodies, and I have modernized the accompaniments to some extent, but I have tried to retain the spirit of the original compositions. Nineteen of these forty-

* "Let him who has won it bear the palm!" The motto of Lord Nelson.

eight melodies have found their way to my programs, and they have never been played by anyone else."

In a chat with a representative of the New York *Herald*, Kreisler identified the monastery as located at Avignon, and the price paid the monks for the music scores as "about $8,000 for all they had."

This makes decidedly humorous reading now, in view of his own confession of 1935 and Harriet's statement to me, "That whole yarn about the monastery was pure bunk."

Not all of Kreisler's works of that period sailed under alien flags, however. His most played piece, the "Caprice viennois," as well as his "Liebesfreud" and "Liebesleid," his "Tambourin chinois" and "Schön Rosmarin," were copyrighted as original Kreisler compositions on September 15, 1910.

Describing his method of composing during the early years of married life, Harriet said of her husband: "He never puts them on paper until he has worked them out fully in his head, which is done mostly in the fields when walking. When he is composing he forgets everything else. Often I'd sit for hours playing piquet while he'd write. Fritz sometimes got the names of the old masters to whom he ascribed his works by simply looking in Grove's *Dictionary of Music and Musicians*. Sometimes friends would come and ask, 'What is Fritz doing?' and I'd reply, 'Oh, he's composing Pugnani, or something.' "

Wilhelm Strecker of B. Schott's Söhne, Mainz, his continental publisher, contributed this sidelight on Kreisler's meticulous care in composing:

> Very few people have any conception of the painstaking care and devotion with which he worked up his "small pieces"—how conscientiously and frequently he first practiced them hundreds of times and tried them out on the public before he entrusted them to the printer with the last final touches and nuances and they started on their march through the world in their perfect and authorized formulation.

Fritz's first and subsequent wedding anniversary presents to his wife during the early period of their married life consisted in his learning a violin concerto which he had not played in public before. In due time he thus mastered concertos by Tchaikovsky, Brahms, Mozart,

Erlanger, Elgar, and so forth. Impecunious as he then was, this annual present was as touching as it was inexpensive.

"I kept my watch in my hands, however, while he practiced," Harriet confided to her friend Lee (Mrs. Rembert) Wurlitzer. "I'd make sure he stuck to each passage for four or five minutes, and that he worked on a whole concerto for not less than thirty minutes at a time."

Under the dynamic influence of his wife, Kreisler established a number of precedents in London. It was a hidebound rule, for instance, for artists appearing in an afternoon concert to wear the heavy, cumbersome Prince Albert coat. At Harriet's suggestion and insistence, Fritz appeared in the much more commodious cutaway. As the innovation was accepted without protest, coming as it did from so beloved an artist, other soloists were quick to follow suit. The Prince Albert coat was soon a thing of the past.

Another irksome thing for the artist, especially the violinist, was the high collar, known in Kreisler's native language as *Vatermörder* (father's murderer!). Harriet thought it silly to torture an artist merely because of an established convention. Accordingly, Fritz appeared in Albert Hall wearing a low collar. One more tradition was shattered!

In those early years of the 1900's Kreisler earned only 30 to 40 guineas ($150 to $200) per concert. Then, one day, the manager of Queen's Hall offered him three Sunday concerts at 60 guineas (about $310) per Sunday.

"People all said, 'You can't do that,' " Harriet recalled. "The London correspondent of the *Musical Courier* thought it was dreadful. But Fritz played—chiefly Bach. Soon he was asked to give ten to fifteen concerts. Then Nellie Melba and all the other big artists followed suit. That was the beginning of Sunday afternoon recitals, known as the Boosey-Chappell concerts.

"In Argyll Street there was a huge establishment known as the Palladium. Throughout the week it was the scene of circus performances, but on Sundays the place was closed. So the management came and asked if Fritz would give a Sunday concert there. One hundred guineas (about $520) were offered as a fee.

"Again our friends were scandalized. 'Nobody will come,' they

Kreisler in the early 1900's

Kreisler's signature in 1909

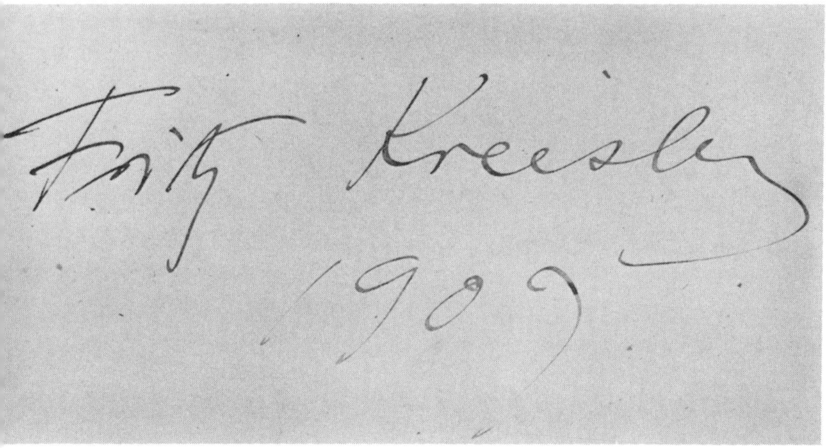

Kreisler with John McCormack, 1884-1945

said. 'Think of the smell from elephants and other animals!' But they came all right. It wasn't long before Sir Thomas Beecham took over the Sunday concerts regularly in this place holding 11,000 people. Later Jascha Heifetz, Yehudi Menuhin, and the rest all performed there.

"One day when Fritz was away on tour I upped his fee for a certain concert from 20 to 60 guineas. When I told him about it on his return, he exclaimed, 'Why, you're crazy; you've ruined me; I'll never be able to get an engagement in that place again.' I waited until he had calmed himself, then held the telegram of the concert management under his nose. It read, 'Accept your terms with pleasure.' "

Harriet Kreisler mentioned the unforgettable Nellie Melba. It was she who replied to someone who asked her about her phrasing, "Hear Kreisler play and you'll know how to phrase in singing."

During those first years in London, when Kreisler was struggling along with small fees, another artist, destined to achieve world fame, was also having a hard time to make both ends meet. He was John McCormack. Baring Brothers of London suggested that Kreisler and McCormack go on a tour of the provinces together, participating in the box-office receipts on a percentage basis. That was the beginning of a long friendship between violinist and tenor, interrupted only by the hysteria of World War I, when Kreisler, because of his Austrian citizenship, was considered a pariah even by some of his best friends.

The two young artists traveled third class. Not so Señor Zulueta, Kreisler's accompanist, who was the proud nephew of a Spanish grandee. Although content to receive £3 (less than $15) per concert, he felt he owed something to his exalted birth and insisted upon traveling first class. He would make the rounds of the swankiest clubs in London and gather up their stationery. On it he would then write his letters.

The tour was not much of a financial success. At first the two artists took in only £10 to £12 together. Their highest "take" was £60. "Why, we could even buy ourselves a bottle of champagne then," Fritz chuckled reminiscently. But Austrian and Irishman had a good time.

Lily McCormack, widow of the great Irish tenor, in the biography of her husband wrote about this association: *

John had what I can only call a loving reverence for Fritz, and among the keenest joys of his musical career was making records with him. They seemed to be perfectly attuned, and when John got a certain sound on a note that pleased him he'd say, "Ah, did you hear that? I got a tone just like Fritz there."

Mrs. McCormack then quotes her husband as writing about his first four weeks' tour with Kreisler in England:

"Financially it was a 'flop,' but in every other way it was of inestimable value to me. The kindly advice and the criticism which I received from Fritz in those few concerts had a greater influence on my work than any other thing before or since. A constructive critic in the true sense, he gave me a piece of advice I've never forgotten. He said, 'John, learn the music as the composer wrote it, be absolutely letter perfect, and then put your own interpretation upon it.' No words of mine can add luster to the name of this great artist. He has always remained my ideal violinist. No one who has not enjoyed his friendship can really estimate the man, as well as the artist. One cannot imagine any field of endeavor in which he could not be a success. He has the natural equipment to fit him for any profession. Add to that his innate refinement, his heart of gold and his musical soul—and you have Fritz Kreisler." *

During his London years Fritz and Harriet frequently saw Pablo Sarasate.

"He was the greatest *grand seigneur* in musical history," Harriet commented. "He looked like a grand duke. He had a mass of gray hair, but his mustache was dyed pitch black. He played with the greatest nonchalance. When he had already placed his violin under his chin and everybody thought he was about to start, he would drop it again, clamp a monocle into his eye and survey his audience. He had a way of seeming to drop his fiddle that would take the audience's breath away. That is, he would let it slide down his slender figure, only to catch it by the scroll of the neck just in time. It was a regular showman's trick of his."

In London as well as on the Continent they also saw much of August Wilhelmj, Richard Wagner's concertmaster for the Bayreuth

* Reprinted from *I Hear You Calling Me* by Lily McCormack, by permission of Jacques Chambrun, Inc., agent for Mrs. McCormack, and The Bruce Publishing Company of Milwaukee, Wis., Publishers, copyright, 1949, by Lily McCormack.

Festival. He was the embodiment of what one commonly associates with the expression "big, blond Teuton." Over six feet tall, his stiff, high collar made him look even taller. His blue eyes completed the picture of a male counterpart to the Rhine Maidens or the Lorelei.

The son of a wine merchant, he found it difficult to wean himself from choice Rhenish vintages when his physicians discovered he was suffering from diabetes. The way in which he would try to deceive himself and his friends often amused Fritz and Harriet.

"One day," they remember, "we came upon him in a London restaurant. Despite doctor's orders, he apparently had already had several bottles of wine—at least there were several empties standing under the table which he thought we hadn't noticed. Fritz ordered coffee. Turning to the waiter, Wilhelmj said, 'You bring what you think is best for me—coffee or a half-bottle of good wine; only, don't ask me any questions.' Naturally the waiter returned with coffee for us and wine for August."

At Wiesbaden during the music festivals the artists used to meet regularly at "Mutter" Engel's Restaurant. Wilhelmj was angry that one critic after his performance had condescendingly written that he now stood so high as to be beside Joachim.

"As luck would have it," the Kreislers recall, "this critic that very day came to Mother Engel's, singled out Wilhelmj, told him he was temporarily broke, and would the artist please lend him twenty marks. With inimitable sarcasm Wilhelmj said: 'Sorry. I'd like to help you out; but I now stand so high beside Joachim that I can't reach down to my pocketbook.' "

What the Café Grünsteidl had been to Fritz in Vienna, Pagani's Restaurant in Great Portland Street (destroyed by air action during World War II) became to Harriet and Fritz in London. As in Vienna, a galaxy of artists and intellectuals assembled in this eating house, which was quite close to Queen's Hall.

There was, for instance, George Bernard Shaw, with his sharp wit and his penetrating mind. "Unfortunately, I never kept a diary, so I don't remember the many witticisms of G. B. S.," Kreisler said. "But did I ever tell you about the wisecrack concerning me? No? Well, when somebody in our jolly group read out a statement from one of the papers or magazines to the effect that the Muses had placed a violin in my arm at my birth, Shaw added dryly, 'And a bow in your leg.' When I looked surprised, he said, 'You're an Austrian cavalry officer, aren't you?" *

Then there was that phenomenon, the Italian tenor Enrico Caruso, who insisted on his open wine and spaghetti and forever kept his cronies in good humor by his expressive cartoons, which he often drew on the cotton napkins if no paper happened to be available. Harriet had assembled a considerable collection of these cartoons, but they, like so many other irreplaceable souvenirs in the Berlin Kreisler home, were destroyed by air action in World War II.

"Enrico Caruso was a grand fellow to have in any group," Harriet said to me. "He was a very simple but truly great gentleman. For five years hardly a day passed, from the end of May until the London 'season' was over, that Caruso, Scotti, and we did not meet at Pagani's."

At a somewhat later date—about 1910—the Spanish cellist Pablo Casals began to join them. To the present day he has not forgotten the help given him upon his advent in America, when Kreisler told the American press, pointing to his Spanish fellow artist, "The King of the Bow has arrived." Lillian Littlehales, Casals's pupil, wrote: † "This spontaneous and stirring tribute was like a trumpet call, a noble and generous flourish announcing the entry of a valued confrère."

Eugène Ysaÿe and Jacques Thibaud never failed to turn up when in town. With Ysaÿe there was usually the stately, black- and full-bearded French pianist Raoul Pugno, whose rendition with Ysaÿe of Beethoven's "Kreutzer" Sonata is still remembered by many American concertgoers. Harold Bauer, with his faculty for mimicry, was often the life of the party.

To this illustrious group further belonged Willem Mengelberg, whose service to culture in developing the Amsterdam Concertgebouw Orchestra into a first-class ensemble will always be recorded in musi-

* In England the idea was widespread that Kreisler was a cavalry officer. Cf. p. 140. As a matter of fact, he belonged to the Austrian infantry reserve.

† Reprinted from *Pablo Casals* by Lillian Littlehales, by permission of W. W. Norton & Company, Inc., copyright, 1929, revised and enlarged edition, copyright, 1948, by W. W. Norton & Company, Inc.

ketch of himself
y Enrico Caruso, 1873-1921

Caruso's caricature of Antonio Scotti

Wassili Safonoff, 1852-1918

cal history, despite his later aberration in collaborating with Hitler and the Nazis.

Another conductor frequenting Pagani's, who also came to America as honored guest, was the Russian Wassili Safonoff, of whom both Fritz and Harriet Kreisler were very fond, and under whose conducting Fritz in 1908 played the "Vivaldi" (in reality the Kreisler) Concerto in C Major and the Mozart Concerto in D Major with the Philharmonic Orchestra of New York at Carnegie Hall. (Safonoff, incidentally, created somewhat of a stir by conducting without a baton.)

Once, during the twelve years under discussion, Safonoff and the Kreislers crossed the ocean together. It was so stormy that the deck chairs had to be fastened with ropes to the railings. Harriet, chipper as ever and unaffected by the heavy sea, kept walking around the deck and, as she was particularly fond of the tune of the imperial Russian anthem, *Bozhe tsaria chrani*, she whistled this song as she strode along. So deep in thought was she and so unconscious was her whistling that she did not notice at first how Safonoff laboriously rose from his deck chair every time she passed him. Finally, at the third turn, Safonoff plaintively interrupted her with: "Oh, please don't whistle our national anthem. I have to get up each time and remain standing until you have finished it—and I am so miserably seasick!"

Safonoff was so patriotic that he always wore a colorful triptych on his breast to show his nationalistic feelings.

Indeed an interesting group—these Pagani gourmets! If it was a simple matter of tea or coffee, and not a solid meal, most of these artists went to the Café Royal. In the evening, especially after symphony concerts, Harriet and Fritz would often go to the beer restaurant Gambrinus, where they would meet celebrities like Hans Richter, Vladimir de Pachmann, Leopold Godowsky, and members of the orchestra.

Hans Richter always spoke English with a Viennese accent and often got his languages mixed. Thus Harriet Kreisler remembered how, during one rough Channel crossing, the great conductor called out: "Steward! Steward! Quick! Get my wife a chair; when she doesn't lie she *schwindels*" (gets dizzy). But the word also means to tell fibs! On another occasion he wanted a round-trip ticket for himself but only a one-way ticket for his wife. He put it thus: "Two tickets, please—for me to London to come back; for my wife but not to come back." The effect of which, Harriet remembered, was that some persons thought the Richters were estranged and would soon get a divorce!

But the best is the story of Hans Richter's turning to his first violins during an orchestra rehearsal and admonishing them: "Will you please play that like a *tausend* Kreislers—not so much *mit* the k-nuckles (pronouncing the *k*); more *mit* the meats" (meaning the fleshy parts of their fingers).

Harriet one day asked Richter why he always declined to go to America. "Are you afraid of getting seasick?" she teased him. "Maybe we can build a bridge over the Atlantic for you."

"No, it isn't that," the conductor replied. "I'll tell you the reason: You are a heathen country. You committed a great sacrilege by taking *Parsifal* out of the hills and mountains and Bayreuth and producing it in the Metropolitan Opera. It should be performed in Bayreuth only.

"You're the only American I like."

Harriet resumed: "Hans Richter and I were indeed great friends, but he was anything but extravagant with his money. And so, when one evening at the Gambrinus he invited me to share a bottle of Rhine wine with him, I think some of the orchestra members nearly fainted."

"Yes, and he would not let me have even a sip of it," Fritz interposed with mock jealousy.

The Kreislers made friends with many members of the London Philharmonic Orchestra at the Gambrinus; among them Gómez, a clarinetist, and Pedro Morales and Achille Rivard, violinists.

"Fritz had his Austrian way of being affable to everybody," Harriet reminisced, "and of forever shaking hands with his friends and acquaintances, although I often told him, 'Stop pumphandling—it isn't done in England; don't forever be affable.' He'd reply, 'But that's the way we always do in Austria.'

"So one day Rivard, Gómez, Morales, and I 'ganged up' against Fritz and decided to watch him on the sidelines, as it were, in the 'green room' of St. James's Hall after one of his concerts. Of course

Hans Richter, 1843-1916

Feruccio Busoni, 1866-1924

Busoni in a less formal pose

the usual scene ensued: simpering ladies approached Fritz with questions like, 'What were you thinking of when you played that divine Andantino?' or 'What was that delicious second encore?'

"It was not long before a gushing dowager swept into the room. Shaking hands with Fritz effusively, she cooed, 'I don't think you remember me.' Fritz, affable as usual, said, 'Of course I do, very distinctly.' Said the dame, 'Oh, really? The time we met in Berlin?' 'Yes, indeed,' Fritz smiled back, 'I remember it as though it happened yesterday.' 'And our mutual friends?' the lady persisted. 'Oh, they're quite all right,' Fritz assured her.

" 'Well,' said the hero-worshiping socialite, 'I must hurry along now. Goodbye, Mr. Busoni.'

"Fritz never heard the end of that. Our friends would tease him on every occasion. As a matter of fact Busoni that same afternoon played at Queen's Hall. It was quite obvious that the gushing lady had never before seen either Busoni or Fritz and merely pretended to know Busoni."

The out-of-town artists in those days for the most part stopped at the same French hotel, the Ronveau, according to Harold Bauer.

Another member of the Bauer family who played an important part in the life of the Kreisler couple during some of the years in London under discussion was Ella Bauer, sister of Harold, who rented them rooms for some time and thus got to know them rather intimately. Now a dainty but chipper, worthy, and white-haired lady of eighty, she loves to tell about the way Harriet supervised Fritz. She recalls:

This energetic guardian angel of her famous husband often had to fight veritable skirmishes with autograph hunters. The crowds which besieged the artist's room after a concert were enough to smother him. He would soften and begin to sign his name, but she would soon put a stop to that.

On one occasion Harriet was quite agitated when, on coming to dinner unexpectedly late, she noted that her "disobedient" husband had begun to eat a "forbidden" pea soup with great relish. "Aber, Fritzi, um Gotteswillen, Du darfst es nicht" [But Fritzi, for God's sake, you mustn't], she exclaimed, and already the plate was snatched from him as from a naughty child. With sad eyes the disciplined husband followed the disappearing soup he loved so much.

People ask whether Fritz practiced much in my home. Why, there wasn't much of an opportunity for that, unless he did it very early in the morning.

The minute the sounds of a violin were heard issuing forth from No. 166, Adelaide Road, people knew: Kreisler is back in London. A few minutes later the street was jammed with listeners who remained as long as he played. Not only the street: one could see admirers oozing from every window of the near-by villas. Those who were standing in the street cared not about the weather. To hear Kreisler "at home" it was worth their while to stand in pouring rain for an hour. This seems hard to believe when one considers how unemotional the English usually are. But what was there that the sorcerer Kreisler could not do! He transformed human character.

I wonder whether Fritz will remember one little happening which comes to my mind as I write. Fritz was to play at an evening concert outside of London and had taken his violin that afternoon to Hill's for some adjustments. He returned in a taxi with Harriet and while he paid the fare she came into the house and the taxi drove away. No sooner were they both indoors when both of them exclaimed, "Where is the fiddle?"

It had been left in the cab! Fritz thought Harriet had it, and she thought he had it. There was, of course, wild consternation, but nothing could be done about it at the moment, and Fritz had to depart for his concert with a different violin.

After about two hours, a time of great anxiety to us all who remained behind, the taxi man brought back the violin, having just discovered it in his car. He "thought the gentleman might be wanting it."

My colleague Marie Mecinska of London, who was kind enough to visit Miss Bauer, wrote that the genteel old lady described Kreisler as the most lovable and charming person thinkable—an artist who was never impressed with his own importance but always insisted (and honestly so) that there were much greater and better artists than himself; and that he was always most generous, especially to children. Mme. Mecinska wrote:

The home in which Miss Bauer received me is still the same in which Kreisler lived with his wife: the same piano and furniture in the parlor and dining room; the same *fauteuils* on which he used to sit; the same table at which he was wont to eat; the same garden with the self-same bench on which he always took his breakfast in favorable weather; the same rose bower that he loved so much. The bench, which one can see from the dining room at the further end of the garden, is regarded as a sort of sanctuary by Miss Bauer, who speaks of Kreisler with reverence and claims that, were he to come to London today, he would be received with the same enthusiasm as of yore.

Only two years after his debut with Hans Richter, Kreisler was awarded the Beethoven gold medal by the London Philharmonic Society, whose recipients, according to *The Strad*, are "a small but distinguished body." During ninety years this medal has been conferred on only five violinists.

A year previously, in 1903, he made one struggling naturalized British musician of French ancestry happy, with a première of his Violin Concerto—Baron Frédéric d'Erlanger, composer of the ballet *Hundred Kisses*; just as, six years later, he gave another Englishman, York Bowen, a lift, by playing the latter's Suite in D Minor for Violin and Piano.

Concerning D'Erlanger, Georges Enesco recalls: "I first met Fritz in 1903 at London, where I heard him play at Queen's Hall. He chose to bring out a Concerto in F-Sharp Minor by Baron d'Erlanger. That rather rehabilitated the baron. I was enchanted."

Kreisler also, in 1904, gave the weight of his authority to a Concerto in E Minor by Jules Conus, a Russian composer then new to British audiences. In 1907 he offered a further novelty to the Londoners, a *Rapsodie Piémontese* by Leone Sinigaglia of the Milan Conservatory.

Above all, Kreisler during this period "made" Sir Edward Elgar's Concerto in B Minor for Violin and Orchestra, which was dedicated to him by the English master.

Elgar promised as early as 1906 that he would compose a violin concerto, for on November 6, 1909, Fritz told a *Musical America* reporter:

> "Like every concert violinist, I should like to get some new concertos. But where are they? Sir Edward Elgar promised me a concerto three years ago. When he writes one it will be a labor of love rather than profit. But I can't get the first note out of him."

On November 10, 1910, the world première of this concerto took place in Queen's Hall during the opening concert of the ninety-ninth season of the London Philharmonic Society. Elgar himself conducted.

Fourteen years later, writing for *Vanity Fair*, Kreisler described his feelings before the première:

> I recall the rapture which I felt, before the concert, when I first played the last movement of the great concerto. I was in the composer's study at the time.

Scattered around on the floor were the sheets of his manuscript where he had dropped them to dry just as they came from his pen. We gathered them together and numbered them hurriedly. I set them, still barely dry, upon the music stand, picked up my violin, and played.

As I played, I knew that Elgar had given the world a work that was full of great music and of inspired passages. When I had finished that last movement, I turned to him and, gripping his hands, thanked him for permitting me to introduce his concerto to the world.*

The *Musical Observer* commented on the first public performance:

> The composer was determined that no ordinary violinist should attempt this work, for the solo part is of great difficulty. . . . There was a memorable scene at the close. Time after time Sir Elgar and Herr Kreisler were recalled amid the greatest enthusiasm from the orchestra and the large audience, which included the principals of our musical institutions, many famous composers and other celebrities in the world of art and letters.

Other reviews were in a similar vein. Again and again, during the ensuing months and years, Kreisler was engaged to play the Elgar work, both in London and in the provinces. Elgar often conducted personally. Kreisler also acquainted audiences in St. Petersburg, Moscow, Vienna, Berlin, Dresden, Munich, Amsterdam, Chicago, and other cities with this work of England's prime composer of the period.

"It is not true that I gave the idea of a violin concerto to Elgar," Kreisler insists, "nor that I initiated some of the motifs or wrote the cadenza. Sir Edward was, in fact, rather proud of having invented a new kind of cadenza, in which the orchestra does a sort of accompaniment.†

"I made occasional suggestions about fingering, and that's all. I suppose I did popularize the concerto by playing it so frequently. Elgar had a way, when discussing the concerto with me, of showing me a page at a time and then scattering the pages all over the place.

* Reprinted from "Stray Thoughts on Modern Music" by Fritz Kreisler, from an article in the August, 1924, issue of *Vanity Fair*, by permission of The Condé Nast Publications, Inc.

† The *Sunday Times* of London wrote concerning the Elgar cadenza that "it is one of the two or three wonders of the music of the last thirty years; there is something Greek, something of Elysium in this return of all the themes of the work, but now ghostly spiritualized and moving about in a larger and purer air, with Aeolian harps wafting faint harmonies upon them from, as it were, the very ends of the earth."

Sir Edward Elgar, 1857-1934, in Order of Merit regalia

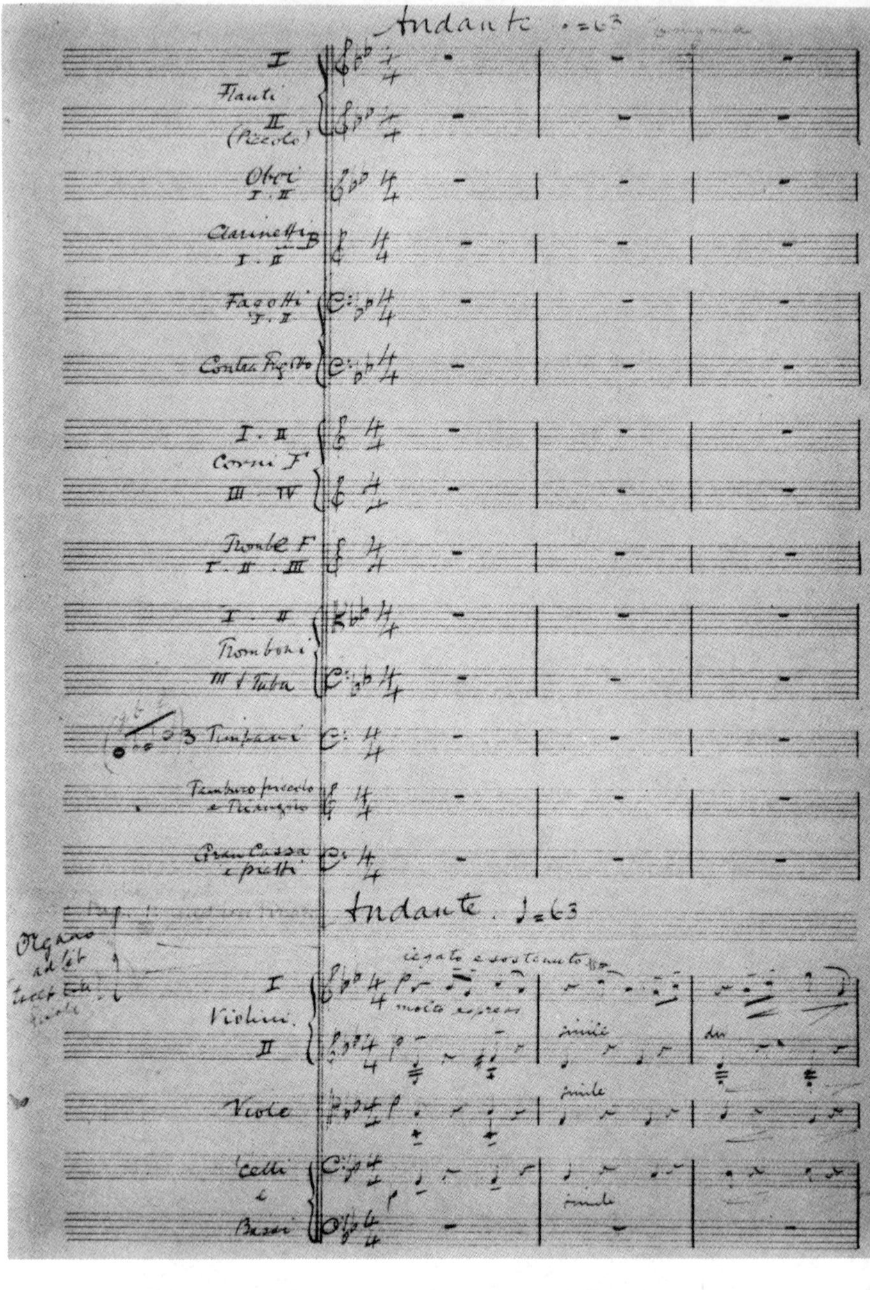

Elgar's Nimrod, Variation IX, of The Enigma Variations

"Elgar often told me that his *Enigma Variations* for orchestra were inspired by his hearing some of my transcriptions."

Joseph Szigeti, who attended the première of the Elgar concerto, wrote: *

> During the stir created by Kreisler's first performance of Elgar's Violin Concerto in London (a furore comparable to a Shostakovich première in our days, though minus plane-transported microfilm and five-figure broadcast fees!) . . . I was impressed chiefly by the fact that it was a *Viennese* who transmitted the Englishness of Elgar to England and the rest of the world; this angle seemed to me to enhance the achievement.

Kreisler always modestly maintained that his friend Eugène Ysaÿe had on one occasion been the best interpreter of the Elgar concerto. He was wont to say: "No one has yet heard the Elgar concerto to ultimate advantage who was not present when Ysaÿe introduced it in Berlin. It was one of the noblest specimens of violin playing in recent years."

As an aside Fritz mentioned in the course of our discussing the Elgar concerto that Sir Charles Villiers Stanford, Irish headmaster; Felix Weingartner, Austrian conductor; Alexander Glazounoff, Russian composer, and Ernest Schelling, New York composer-pianist, also dedicated violin concertos to him, but that Jean Sibelius did not, although some German musicologists have so claimed. Max von Schillings, composer of the opera *Mona Lisa* and intendant of the Staatsoper in Berlin, he said, "wanted to write a violin concerto for me but died before he got around to it." Victor Herbert dedicated "Two Pieces for Violin" (with Piano Accompaniment), "Mirage" and "A la Valse," to his Austrian colleague with the inscription "To my Friend Fritz Kreisler (as a small token of great admiration)."

A year after the Elgar première in 1911, Kreisler for the first time joined in ensemble work with Pablo Casals, the piano partner being their mutual friend Harold Bauer. As with Bauer, so also with Casals a lifelong friendship grew up. The occasion for the debut of the trio

* Reprinted from *With Strings Attached*, by Joseph Szigeti, by permission of Alfred A. Knopf, Incorporated, copyright, 1947, by Alfred A. Knopf, Incorporated.

was a special series of recitals known as the "London Concert Festival."

The Kreisler-Casals-Bauer combination was well received. The *Musical Times* called their playing "a most attractive blend of delicacy and vitality." So excellent, in fact, was the impression created that a tour of the principal cities of the British Isles was arranged.

"Each of us had originally been expected by our impresario, Wirth, to play a group of solos each, in addition to our ensemble numbers," Harold Bauer recalled. "But we were obdurate. Such a program would have lasted entirely too long. So it was finally agreed that we play trios only. We were never advertised as a trio, however. Merely our individual names were given, without mention of the instrument each played or of the numbers to be rendered. The impresario feared the public would not attend 'mere' chamber music concerts.

"The audiences were quite surprised when they found us playing together, but took it in good spirit and applauded generously. On one occasion the hall was so crowded that the seats on the platform almost touched the piano. After the last piece, Mendelssohn's Trio in D Minor, a man who had sat impassive and puzzled all evening, said to his neighbor, 'I suppose that man with the large fiddle would be Casals?' "

Another musician of first rank with whom Kreisler appeared during this period was Ferruccio Busoni, with whom he played sonatas for violin and piano. In November, 1912, the *Musical Observer* wrote:

> The association in chamber concerts of Messrs. Ferruccio Busoni and Fritz Kreisler ought for the sake of the higher interests of art long remain undissolved. . . . They afforded delight as pure and unalloyed as can be recalled. . . . The marriage of the violinist's fiery fervency with that commanding "fundamental brainwork" which puts Mr. Busoni in a place apart from all other pianists produced a performance the noble, masculine intellectuality of which must for weeks leave the listener impatient of that mere toying with great music which passes for interpretation in the usual concert-giving round.

British royalty fell no less under the spell of Fritz Kreisler's personality and music than did the less high-born. Harriet's and Fritz's recollection of the tea at Queen Alexandra's, to which reference has already been made, is:

"The invitation had been arranged by a mutual friend whose husband was a minister to a European country. When we got to the palace, we were instructed to speak in a low voice, because Her Majesty, being hard of hearing, was sensitive about her infirmity. Our obedience to instructions led to many a misunderstanding, in that the queen frequently replied in a manner indicating that she had understood us completely wrongly.

"After a while King Edward VII turned up in plus-fours. He did the very opposite from what we had been told to do: he shouted at the top of his voice. But the most striking thing was the fact that he spoke English with a heavy, broad German accent. After a while he left us and reappeared in a sack suit. He called out to his royal spouse, 'I'm not going to be here for dinner; so don't expect me.' " This was rather shocking to Fritz as he had been raised in the atmosphere of the Austrian court, where breaches of etiquette never occurred.

On more than one occasion Kreisler played at a command performance in Ascot, as for instance during a visit of English-born Queen Maud, wife of King Haakon VII of Norway.

In 1904, Princess Alice of Albany, granddaughter of Queen Victoria and niece of King Edward VII, married Prince Alexander of Teck. Kreisler was honored with a request to play at a court concert given in honor of the wedding guests, mostly royalty, at Windsor Castle on February 9. He received a written appreciation and link cuff buttons with a large diamond "E" and a ruby "R" (Edward Rex) on each button.

A week previously King Edward and the Prince of Wales—the later George V—had "lent their presence," as the language of the court had it, to a concert of the Royal Amateur Orchestral Society at which Kreisler was the soloist. The king presented him with the Gold Brown Badge of the society, thereby making him an honorary member.

In the spring of 1904 the Kreislers were asked to Frogmore, to play for the Prince and Princess of Wales.

Socially, too, the Kreislers had certainly arrived in London!

It may not be amiss to remind the reader that violinists had not always enjoyed such a favored position in England. An ordinance promulgated in 1658 read:

> And be it enacted that if any person or persons, commonly called fiddlers, or minstrels, shall at any time after the said first of July be taken playing, fiddling, or making music in any wine, alehouse or tavern, or shall be proffering themselves, or desiring, or entreating any person or persons to hear them play . . . they shall be adjudged rogues, vagabonds, and sturdy beggars.

While it is true that this ordinance stems from the year of Oliver Cromwell's death, and that the Commonwealth of England which Cromwell founded gave way to the Restoration soon thereafter, yet the prejudice against artists persisted, in a degree, to Kreisler's time, as Harriet Kreisler eloquently pointed out in Chapter Ten.

CHAPTER THIRTEEN

AMERICA AND CONTINENTAL EUROPE

[1902-1914]

Although during these twelve years London was the center toward which he and his wife gravitated, Fritz Kreisler by no means neglected America. Tours to the other side of the Atlantic became an almost annual affair.

Two striking figures are indicative of Fritz Kreisler's popularity in our country: thirty-two concerts in thirty-one days during the month of October, 1912, and seven appearances in New York alone in 1913! Cordelia Camp commented on the crowded Kreisler schedules in the *Musical Observer*:

> The most trying railway jumps have no terror for him. A combination of automobile, steam boat and railway to make a certain date affects him as the trumpet sounding at the post affects a race horse, but let him have three or four days idle and he begins to mope.

Only a man with a very robust constitution and excellent nerves could stand such a pace. Kreisler gave an interesting exhibition of both in 1908. The press reported:

> At the concert [with the Pittsburgh Orchestra in Buffalo] Kreisler's playing made such a hit . . . that they stormed him for an encore. Kreisler was due to leave on a train for the East immediately following his number on the program but . . . he decided to play an encore. When he had done this there remained but ten minutes to get . . . to the station, a distance of about ten blocks.
>
> Louis W. Gay, manager of the orchestra in Buffalo, had a cab waiting. He and Mr. Kreisler drove at break-neck speed . . . and passed through the

gates just as the heavy vestibuled train was starting up. Without a moment's hesitation and to the amazement of Gay and the station employees, Kreisler leaped on a platform of a vestibuled car and clung to the handles with one hand while he pounded on the closed door with his fist. One of the station guards rushed up to the moving train and by main force pulled the artist off the steps.

Nothing daunted, Kreisler waited until the rear car passed and seeing that the doors were open leaped again for the platform and scrambled on. Gay tried to restrain him but failed, and seeing that the violinist was determined to have his way, the orchestra manager and one of the porters seized his handbag and violin case and, running after the now rapidly moving train, threw them on the rear platform, giving the priceless violin a violent jar.

Kreisler stood on the platform and waved a smiling farewell to Mr. Gay and the furious guard who had pulled him from the train.

On one occasion during this period his recklessness cost Kreisler his driver's license. Not that he ran afoul of official regulations! It was his loving wife who decided the end of his motoring days had come.

There is a published photograph in existence which shows the Kreisler couple and Josef Hofmann sitting in one of the early models of open passenger car—the kind on which the steering wheel was still on the right and the brakes and gearshift levers on the outside, to the right of the driver. All three are wearing dusters and goggles. Fritz is at the wheel. The caption reads, "Kreisler handles the steering wheel of his car with as much courage and skill as he does his bow, and he admits laughingly that some of the *tempi* he has taken in his car are faster than any of those he ever attempted on the violin."

Kreisler had forgotten the picture, but when reminded of it, recalled the end of his days as gentleman chauffeur:

"I used to be an enthusiastic motorist," he said. "One day, however, about 1908, we were driving from the Yosemite Valley upward to one of the gorgeous summits in the Sierras. By this time we no longer had the old type of car like that shown in our photo with Hofmann, but a much more modern Willys-Overland. As we climbed higher and higher, the scenery became grander and more overwhelming all the time. We turned a certain corner, and a scene of indescribable beauty unfolded before our eyes. In my enthusiasm I took both hands off the wheel and with a sweeping gesture said, 'Oh, Harriet, isn't that wonderful?'

"You know the roads up the California mountains. Deep chasms often yawn directly under you. One false move at the wheel and disaster may be there. We were now at an altitude of 12,000 feet. One tire of our car was already hanging suspended over the abyss, and I brought the car back on the road not a second too soon.

" 'That'll be the end of your driving,' was Harriet's brief but expressive comment. She was right, of course. I have never driven since."

Harriet added this detail: "When Fritz made that sweeping gesture, I got out of the car then and there and said, 'And if there were a diamond necklace ahead, that wouldn't tempt me.' I got into another car and let Fritz drive alone the rest of the way. I knew that if he hadn't anybody to talk to, he'd keep his hands on the wheel. Somehow he got back in safety. But that ended his career as gentleman driver."

Josef Hofmann, who remembered the occasion, quipped dryly, "Oh, Fritz was a very good driver in his day, but it is always wise to keep one's hand on the wheel, especially in the mountains."

During a tour of the Pacific Coast a year later an incident occurred that soon made the rounds in musical circles both in America and Europe. Fritz Kreisler had played the beautiful "Kreutzer" Sonata by Beethoven with Harold Bauer in Portland, Oregon. A large reception was given in their honor afterward. As the gayety of the evening wore on, the Portland hosts kept entreating their distinguished guests to "make a little music." The obliging duo did—but not in the way everybody expected. In a spirit of high glee Harold seized Fritz's fiddle, Fritz sat down at the piano, and the "Kreutzer" was repeated, but with the artists in changed roles! It created a furor. Bauer wrote: *

> Nobody ever knew how it happened that the report of this impromptu performance was circulated all over the country. Even in Europe, years later, I was asked to tell about the concert I gave in America wherein Kreisler had played the piano, and I the violin.

From Portland the two traveled to Seattle for another joint appearance. They reached this thriving Northwest metropolis when it was

* Reprinted from *Harold Bauer: His Book* by Harold Bauer, by permission of W. W. Norton & Company, Inc., copyright, 1948, by W. W. Norton & Company, Inc.

in the midst of a tremendous real-estate boom. Agents swarmed about them, trying to sell them land at fancy prices with the assurance that Seattle was on its rapid way to becoming the world's greatest seaport. In their mad competition these promoters fortunately so effectively destroyed each other's claims that the two artists kept their hands securely on their purse strings.

Not that Fritz Kreisler minded a little speculation! Money at last was coming rather easily—the newspapers of this period speak of his grossing $1,000 per night—and he began to play the stock market. A rumor that he risked $80,000 in a speculation and came out minus $18,000 led the New York *Evening Sun* to warn him "not to indulge in Wall Street caprices but to adhere to the Vienna variety."

Musical America commented on February 4, 1914, on the *Sun's* admonition:

> That is not bad advice. However, it is doubtful whether it will be heeded either by the Vienna violinist or other artists. Many of them love to woo the dangerous goddess of chance. . . . Here's to Kreisler! Let him continue for many years to make money by playing his violin and not lose it by playing the ticker.

These were prophetic words, both as to their going unheeded and as to Kreisler's losing disastrously during the great stock market panic in 1929 when well meaning Wall Street friends successfully urged him to buy heavily on margin after the first big crash.

Reckless though he proved about his own investments, ironically enough he warned a fellow artist earnestly against stock gambling. Gregor Gaitz-Hocky, a Russian violinist, complained to the police of being fleeced of $50,000 with bogus stock. He added he wished he had taken the advice of his friend Fritz Kreisler, whom he met on the day he took his last dollar from the bank in order to purchase a piece of a Colorado gold mine.

"Fritz Kreisler shook his head sadly," the Russian artist was quoted by the press as commenting, "and said: 'Stick to your fiddle, Gregor. Take my advice, Stick to your fiddle.' "

Fritz is not averse to good cooking. In fact, his wife was in constant fear that a Falstaff instead of a Kreisler might walk onto the platform some day. He would not have been human had he not departed occasionally from the austerity prescribed by his "manager." A tempting opportunity for evading slim rations seemed to present itself when, in February, 1910, his concert tour brought him to Montreal, Canada. A news item from there informs us:

> Fritz Kreisler was perhaps the most disappointed man in Canada on Friday last when he started out in search of some real French cooking in what he considered a French city.
>
> "For goodness sake," he said to his local manager, Mr. Veitch, "take me somewhere I can get a French dish with some decent seasoning in it. Wherever I go in America it is always 'roast beef' or 'broiled steak,' and an eternal bottle of tomato ketchup the first thing on the table; I am tired of tomato ketchup and raw cow. I want something cooked, something artistic—something Parisian."
>
> So Mr. Kreisler and Mr. Veitch and a select party of friends started out to do up Montreal for a French cook. Four-fifths of the population of Montreal talks French all day and every day, but it does not cook *à la Parisienne*. French-Canadian cookery is the product of Breton and Norman ancestry modified by generations of life in an intensely cold climate far away from the refinements of high civilization. It is pleasant when you get used to it, but very greasy. All the best French-Canadian restaurants are run in the American style. Everyone of them had a ketchup bottle as its most conspicuous adornment.

At the end of a tour of eight highly recommended places Kreisler gave it up in disgust. "Let us go back to beer and pretzels," he said, and they did.

During his appearance in America in these twelve years, Fritz Kreisler's programs were thickly studded with those exquisite short pieces which he ascribed to old masters, but which he later confessed to be his own. In America, too, nobody suspected their origin. In fact, the critic of the New York *Post*, for instance, on January 4, 1908, wrote about the so-called "Vivaldi" Concerto:

> Kreisler offered . . . an admirable Concerto in C Major by an eighteenth century composer named Antonio Vivaldi, a real jewel. During the intermission several persons in the back of the hall were heard humming the melodies!

Two days later the New York *Sun* complimented him:

> Mr. Kreisler as a student of history has never exhibited higher scholarship and intuitive grace than in his own writing out of the accompaniments, which the ancients merely sketched in continuo.

The imagination can play funny tricks. The critic of the Boston *Transcript*, on October 23, 1909, discerned that "the singular Kreisler" was so wrapped up in these seventeenth and eighteenth century masters that he had even "acquired their look." He continued:

> Consciously or unconsciously, Mr. Kreisler . . . caught something of the manner of these *virtuosi* whose music he so cherishes, meditates, and practices. He, too, is of grave and "elegant" aspect when he plays. He bears himself with quiet dignity and his manner in all things suggests the qualities that the eighteenth century liked to call "taste."

How the artist thus apostrophized must have chuckled when he read it! But he kept the secret of these compositions to himself for another quarter-century.

He did not even rise to the bait which the *Musical Courier* cast to him in November, 1913. This was apparently the only periodical during that period which suspected there was something not genuine about Kreisler's story concerning the origin of his musical tidbits. It still accepted them, however, as having originated with seventeenth and eighteenth century classical masters. The *Musical Courier* commented:

> Whether or not Kreisler unearthed the pieces in a Benedictine monastery, as has been claimed, matters very little. The *Musical Courier* never has believed the story, particularly as some of the staff of this paper are acquainted at first hand with Kreisler's propensity for perpetrating harmless hoaxes, musical and otherwise. All the Kreisler arrangements of the old numbers are provided with modern harmony in the solo setting and the accompaniment, and as the original music does not seem to be easily available, it is difficult to say how much of the versions played by Kreisler belongs to the composers and with what share the clever adapter should be credited.

Kreisler remained silent!

An illness which befell the otherwise so unusually healthy artist caused him to publish some of these "monastery" pieces much sooner than he or anybody else had anticipated.

Music lovers learned through *Musical America* on May 2, 1908:

> It is not generally known that Fritz Kreisler has been suffering for many weeks with what his physicians call "walking typhoid," with a temperature at 100. As he would not allow it to interfere with his concert engagements, how-

ever, it was not until his temperature rose to 104 in Chicago a short time ago and he was forced to cancel some of his engagements that the public became aware of his illness. It was against the urgent advice of his physicians that he appeared at the first of the two recitals he has given in New York with Josef Hofmann during the past fortnight.

"I had been engaged for a tour with Hofmann," Kreisler recalled, "but had to drop many of these engagements. In New York I literally had to get out of bed and take a shot of strychnine to play. Hofmann had naturally fallen sole heir to the evenings of six or seven weeks during which I could not appear with him.

"The doctor ordered me to go to Mexico to recuperate. While there I met young Wilhelm Strecker, son of the Councilor of State Strecker, the right-hand man of B. Schott's Söhne, music publishers in Mainz, Germany. Strecker, Jr., suggested that his firm would be interested in bringing out, say, twenty of my short pieces and 'arrangements,' and offered $50 per item. Twenty items meant $1,000, which was an awful lot of money just then, what with our living without an income in a strange land. We accepted. Later Charles Foley, my American manager, regulated the matter of the copyrights with great skill and there was a reevaluation and relegalization."

Within six months of their first appearance in 1910, seventy thousand copies of the Schott edition of these items were sold.

Kreisler, as already pointed out, received $1,000 per concert as an average fee toward the end of this period. Not always, however—nor did he care. Mrs. Lola Clay Naff, for many years manager of concerts in Nashville, Tennessee, recalls that early in 1914 Charles Foley came to her to offer Geraldine Farrar, Ernestine Schumann-Heink, and Fritz Kreisler for the Ryman Auditorium concert series for the 1914–1915 season.

"Miss Farrar and Mr. Kreisler always seemed to bring bad weather for their Nashville appearances," Mrs. Naff recalls. "There was a terrible blizzard the night of the Kreisler recital, and I tried in vain to get the contract cancelled. It was too late, and the concert took place nevertheless. The box office 'take' was only $1,000 for the big auditorium.

"I stood with Kreisler in the ticket booth after the concert, where he was to get his percentage of the receipts. I felt embarrassed at its meagerness. But it didn't feaze the artist one bit. He seemed totally indifferent to the money. On the contrary, with a gracious flourish he insisted that I take the large bouquet of yellow chrysanthemums which someone had sent him backstage."

Blushing prettily, the white-haired but still extremely energetic "M's Lola," as everybody down south calls her, added, "He was a very handsome young man then."

One thing which impressed music critics again and again during these twelve years was Kreisler's adherence to high musical standards in his programs. *Harper's Bazaar* for January, 1910, put it thus:

> A deserved tribute should be offered to the courage which makes Mr. Kreisler ignore an appeal to "popular" taste in the preparation of his rare and exquisite programs, and leads him to hold firmly those high musical ideals for which he is noted on both sides of the ocean.

Kreisler can further claim for himself that he "sold" the Brahms Violin Concerto to the American concertgoing public. As every violinist knows, it is so difficult that it has often been apostrophized as having been written "not for but against the violin." Kreisler, who at various times in interviews has placed the Brahms concerto ahead of all others written for the violin, set out to prove what a great work it is, and also wrote another of his matchless cadenzas for it. "It is not a concerto 'against the violin,' " he said on one occasion, "it merely calls for a new kind of technique."

It did not take him long to prove his point in America. As early as March, 1910, the *Musical Courier* observed:

> Kreisler has become the supreme exponent of the Brahms concerto and has succeeded in making the work peculiarly his own as a concert asset. No one else plays it with Kreisler's breadth, insight, or technical finish.

If during this period Kreisler appeared in the same recital with other artists, it was always with celebrities like Johanna Gadski, Lina Cavalieri, Enrico Caruso, Geraldine Farrar, Josef Hofmann, Harold Bauer, Jean Gérardy—to mention but a few. The Vanderbilts, the Mackays, the Payne Whitneys, the Robert Colliers, and other socialites vied in arranging for private musicales with him as their star.

The children, too, of whom Kreisler has always been touchingly fond, took to him with ebullient enthusiasm.

Lucy and Richard Stebbins wrote about this period: *

> It was his [Damrosch's] practice at each children's concert to present a soloist whose performance would familiarize listeners with the character of his instrument. Many a child, fascinated by its tone and shape, conceived the bold idea of playing it himself.
>
> Kreisler played to the children at a gala Christmas concert where the pretty programs were garlanded with delicately tinted holly and the Musical Art Society came to sing carols. But it was the violinist who enchanted the youngsters. They called him back again and again and noisily begged for encores.

A further testimonial of his popularity with the rank and file of average citizens came to Kreisler during a trip to Los Angeles in 1908. As he told it:

"The most spontaneous tribute I ever received was from a band of American cowboys when I was on my way to play in Los Angeles. They came on board the train at a wayside station, whooping and firing off their revolvers, and were kind enough to inform me that they 'were riding 180 miles on the kyars to hear you scrape the fiddle.' "

The more often Kreisler came to America, the more he was impressed with its musical development. In December, 1912, he said:

"There are tremendous possibilities here musically, and I recognize the growth since my last tour. Everywhere I find a keener interest displayed in serious musical art and also an advance in the maintaining of orchestras, operas, and so forth, in the several cities."

That this was not mere flattery is attested by the fact that, on arriving in London sometime later, he warmly praised American orchestras as "superb" and lauded American audiences as "highly critical; they are spoiled because they hear all the world's best. If they do not like your work any longer they frankly tell you so."

Toward the close of the period under discussion, late in 1912, Kreisler found himself in the unusual role of converting a cub reporter into a music critic.

* Reprinted from *Frank Damrosch: Let the People Sing* by Lucy and Richard Stebbins, by permission of Duke University Press, copyright, 1945, by Duke University Press.

No less a person than Fulton Oursler vouches for the following occurrence:

Oursler was passionately fond of music and, by way of self-education, had read up on classical and romantic composers, on operas and musical comedies, on oratorios and string quartets, on sonatas and symphonies. He had never in his life, however, been to a professional concert, and the only opera selections he had ever heard were delivered to his ear by a hurdy-gurdy man.

Then, in 1912, the city editor of the *Baltimore American* called the young cub reporter into his sanctum. "Can you play the piano? No? Can you sing? No? Fiddle? No?" thus his questions ran in double quick succession. He concluded:

"You're just my man. Our music critic is ill and I want to see what you can do with a concert at the Lyric. Fritz Kreisler is to give a violin recital."

"This was the chance I had been hoping for and craving for years," Oursler confided to me. "I don't mind telling you that I went out on the fire escape and prayed, for I badly wanted that job. And how diffident I was! I knew that my opposite number on our competitor, the *Baltimore Sun*, was a very able critic whose style was fluid and whose technical vocabulary was such that he could master any musical situation. I could just see him writing a masterpiece."

When the concert—a charity affair—was over, Oursler, who had listened to a program of composers he had never heard of, knocked at Kreisler's door.

"I found him rather exhausted, for as always he had given himself completely," Oursler narrated, "and told him of my predicament."

" 'And what can I do for you?' he said with a kindly smile when I had finished.

" 'Help me write my review,' I pleaded.

"Anybody else would have thrown me out and would have complained that a paper of our standing dared send an ignoramus to act as critic. Not so Fritz Kreisler—and that shows you what a big man he is. He not only virtually dictated my story to me, but showed me what mistakes he had made. 'Take the piece, *The Lagoon*,' he said. 'I slipped up in it.'

"The next day my criticism appeared, pointing out that Kreisler had not had his best day, as was evident from the fact that in *The Lagoon* certain passages were somewhat faulty.

"My editor liked the piece so well that he actually made me music critic—all because Kreisler had so generously shown me how to write a music review. My older colleague, who had been ill the day I took over, generously gave me books to read, showed me how a piece of music is constructed, and in other ways helped me. Well, it wasn't so very long before I found myself as editor of *Music Trades* and *Musical America*.

"But that is not the end of the story. Later I became editor of *Liberty Magazine*. When I went east again after resigning from this position, a lady reporter from a prominent weekly magazine came to interview me. I told her various things and finally gave her the story of how Kreisler had helped me to become a music critic. Strangely enough, the young lady never published that part of my chat with her.

"Rather disgusted, for I thought it was a fine story, I then sat down and wrote the episode out for *Reader's Digest*. The editor-publisher liked it so much that—well, now I am one of the Senior Editors of *Reader's Digest*! I am told it was the story about Fritz Kreisler which attracted attention to me.

"So for the second time I am indebted to him for a turning point in my career."

People have often wondered why, neither during these years nor later, Kreisler never had promising violin students as pupils. There are four principal reasons why he refrained from teaching: First, he knows that his case of needing no practice in the ordinary, formal sense is unique and not generally applicable, yet what would be more natural for a pupil than to challenge him with, "Why practice? You don't do it yourself!" Second, he is aware that his fingering is unorthodox and might confuse an advanced student brought up under regular conservatory training. Third, he is so kindhearted a person that he shrinks from hurting the feelings of anyone, even a sour-note-playing pupil. For this reason, too, he consistently shies away from giving auditions to allegedly talented violin students. He just cannot bring himself to say bluntly to a nontalent, "You'd make a better mail carrier or bricklayer or butcher than an artist." At the same time he knows that the kind and approving word which he is likely to speak out of pure compassion may be taken as a nod to continue on a career that is bound to end in disappointment. Fourth, he believes real talent should go on its own individual way after the technique of playing has been mastered. It is better, he holds, for an artist to be not quite so good and perfect, but to retain his own personality, than it is for him to be an excellent imitator of his teacher.

Although he never had formal pupils, Fritz has always been generous in showing the "tricks of his trade" to aspiring colleagues. The most informal lessons he ever gave probably took place in the Auditorium Hotel of Chicago. The amusing episode is told by Henry Draper, first violinist of the WSM radio station at Nashville, Tenn.

Draper in his adolescent years was a bellboy at the Auditorium Hotel. As a future violinist, he was naturally more than curious about everything that pertained to the famous Fritz Kreisler when he was a guest there. Also, he understood what was going on in one corner of the hotel lobby. There Jacques Gordon, who idolized his older colleague, would sit and have Kreisler show him how he fingered this or that passage. No instruments were used; the two would hum the tune under discussion, hold their left hands out as if they were fingering a violin keyboard, and with their right hands make the long and sweeping movements that fiddlers make when their bows move across the four strings.

To young Draper this was extremely interesting and quite understandable, and he watched the two with rapt attention. Not so, however, some of the hotel guests who knew little about music and less about fiddling. Seeing two grown-up men going through weird motions and singing complicated tunes to boot, can one wonder that they asked the bellhop: "Say, who are those two goofy guys over there in the corner? Hadn't the manager better call a doctor?"

Before taking the reader to the European continent to highlight the events in Kreisler's life there during the years of 1902–1914, one unusual American tribute should be recorded, at least in part. Writing in the Chicago *Tribune* for January 9, 1908, the music critic W. L. Hubbard said:

A master gave a recital last evening in Music Hall. The voice is one of the loveliest to be heard in the world today. In range it is virtually limitless, its depth being of wondrous warmth and richness, its middle portion brilliant and vibrant, yet filled with a sympathy and nobility that charm, and its upper tone being of a clarity, a sweetness and an exquisite fineness that ravish the sense. In volume it is full and strong, capable of voicing of the most intense emotion and dramatic feeling when these are demanded, and yet when the master owner wishes it, sinks down to the softest possible *pianissimo,* and while remaining unfailingly audible sings but the slightest breath of a tone. . . . It is a voice without a superior in the world today, and its equals are found only among those chosen few which mankind has recognized as supreme, and therefore designated as "great."

And back of this voice is an artist and a personality. A fine, big, virile nature, strong with all the strength of a true man, yet tender, poetic, and sane in sentiment as a true man also may be. There is in the mere presence of the artist the subtle that compels attention, commands respect, and wins liking, and coupled with this personality are the temperament of a large nature and the sound intelligence of a splendid mind. . . .

Who was the singer?

Fritz Kreisler.

It is true that it was the voice of his violin that sang, but that fact makes him none the less a Master Singer (*Meistersänger*).*

The two principal cities of continental Europe with which Kreisler became especially identified during these twelve years before the First World War were, quite naturally, Berlin and Paris. Two of America's most popular violinists remember Berlin as their first contact point with Kreisler: Joseph Szigeti and Jascha Heifetz.

Szigeti wrote: †

When I came to Berlin in 1905 . . . I heard for the first time . . . also Kreisler and Ysaÿe. To make clear the impact of their playing on me—a playing of a fire, an elegance, a rhythmic incisiveness which I had never imagined—I should have to be able to convey the style of playing of the only virtuosos I had heard during my conservatory days: Burmester, Kubelik, Marteau, Hugo Heermann. It is obviously impossible to do this. These first impressions were

* Kreisler is here represented as a singer. Conversely, his friend John McCormack was twice complimented as a fiddler. Karl Muck once said to McCormack, "You sing exactly as Fritz Kreisler plays." And Jan Kubelik remarked after hearing him in Prague, "His voice comes nearer to the violin than any I have ever heard." See also page 401.

† Reprinted from *With Strings Attached* by Joseph Szigeti, by permission of Alfred A. Knopf, Incorporated, copyright, 1947, by Alfred A. Knopf, Incorporated.

too amorphous, too lacking in critical perception, too biased by schoolroom prejudices. In Berlin I was on my own, and I was bowled over by Ysaÿe, Kreisler, and Elman.*

Heifetz said: "I met Kreisler for the first time in 1912 in Berlin. There was a gathering of critics and musicians at the home of a man named Abell. I simply worshiped Kreisler, and when, somewhat later, I gave a recital in Bechstein Hall, Berlin, I tried to imitate my idol.

"During the gathering at the Abell home someone suggested that 'the young man from Russia play a number or two.' I was willing enough, but what about an accompanist? What about the piano score? Fritz Kreisler kindly jumped into the breach and played my accompaniments from memory. I chose the Mendelssohn Concerto and Kreisler's own 'Schön Rosmarin' for that informal but portentous introduction to the musical world of Berlin." †

A year after his marriage, Fritz Kreisler made his first phonograph recordings in Berlin. He has thus virtually grown up with the industry. "In those days the cylindrical disc was still used, and the trumpetlike horn for the reproduction," Kreisler recalls. "Often we would have to try a piece over and over again before a relatively good master record was obtained."

Some youngster who chances to read this biography may have an opportunity in the year 2007 to hear what recordings of this period were like. Harriet Kreisler remembered that somewhere about this time a number of artists, including Caruso, Kubelik, Geraldine Farrar, and her Fritz had been asked to make recordings for deposit in the vaults of the Paris Opéra. They were to be preserved for posterity. She suggested writing to Paris for confirmation. The following reply

* When Szigeti came to America in 1925 for the first time, he was happily surprised at the sympathetic reception he was given from the very beginning. Many other artists from Europe had to come up the hard way with the critics. Only later he learned that Kreisler, on arriving from Europe somewhat earlier, had done him a tremendous turn by heralding him to the press as "the best young violinist abroad." Szigeti gratefully acknowledged this lift in his autobiography as an act of "characteristic generosity."

† Heifetz as late as the spring of 1949 played Fritz Kreisler's Recitativo and Scherzo Caprice for unaccompanied violin in Paris, certainly an indication of his continuing esteem for his older colleague.

Joseph Szigeti,
1892-1973

Jascha Heifetz,
1901-

Scene of Berlin in early 1900's

came from the secretary of the Réunion des Théatres Lyriques Nationaux, with offices in the Théatre de l'Opéra:

> It is true that the discs of great artists were registered with the Opéra in 1907. They were locked up and, in accordance with the wishes of the donor, M. Clark, manager of French Gramophone Company, the urns in which they were enclosed may not be opened until one hundred years after the signature of the agreement, that is to say, not before December 14, 2007. There is only one single recording by Kreisler among the discs: No. 07959, *Allegretto* by Boccherini. It is contained in the fourth urn.

Fritz quipped, when he heard Harriet telling about this unusual collection, "The Unknown Soldiers of the Phonograph."

In 1910 the Gramophone Company of London (Victor) announced that Kreisler had signed an exclusive contract for recordings. He has remained with Victor ever since.

The concertgoing public of Berlin is quite as sophisticated as that of New York. Critics are not wont to wax lyrical over an artist. Yet Otto Lessmann, editor in chief of the *Allgemeine Musikzeitung*, on November 25, 1904, used this unusual language in describing Kreisler's recital in the Beethoven Saal:

> The public was quite beside itself and not only demanded encores during the concert but also succeeded in extracting a whole series of them at the close. Herr Kreisler played . . . as a final number the "Devil's Trill" Sonata by Tartini, for the last movement of which he had composed a cadenza for himself which probably constitutes the *non plus ultra* of this specific technique of trills. The artist rendered the works that I was able to hear with a captivating *bravour* and an amazingly temperamental greatness and majesty of expression.

In Europe as in America his programs contained many of the "rococo" pieces ascribed to Corelli, Francœur, Couperin, Pugnani, and others. In Europe as in America no critic questioned their authorship.

In Germany, Kreisler's concert itinerary regularly included, besides Berlin, such music centers as Frankfurt, Dresden, Stuttgart, Mainz, Leipzig, Hamburg, Wiesbaden, Hanover, Königsberg, Magdeburg, Munich, Nuremberg, Mannheim, Düsseldorf, Bremen, and

Cologne. In Switzerland, Zurich, Berne, Basel, and Geneva were visited regularly.

Frequently recurring numbers on his programs at this time were the two violin concertos by Max Bruch. But, although Kreisler was in Berlin often, it was not until one day in May, 1912, that composer and master interpreter met in the home of the same Mr. and Mrs. Arthur Abell where Heifetz had first become acquainted with his Austrian colleague. The Norwegian composer Christian Sinding and his wife, as well as American Ambassador John G. Leishman, attended the soirée.

Max Bruch, then an old man, sat at the piano to play his "Scottish" Fantaisie with Kreisler. According to one of the guests present: "At seventy-four Bruch was still a magnificent pianist. His fire and vigor inspired Kreisler."

On one occasion, Fritz played in a charity concert under imperial auspices in the Charlottenburger Schloss, or Castle, of Berlin.

This castle, badly damaged by air action during World War II, had a famous Golden Gallery, a beautiful rectangular hall with imposing rococo decorations, and with Venetian crystal candelabra that still held candles instead of electric light bulbs. Musical events in the *Goldene Galerie* always had a flavor all their own, not only because the soft, subdued candlelight seemed particularly conducive to musical receptivity, but also because the performers were often clad in the colorful gala costumes of the eighteenth century. Most of the audience tried to dress as nearly like those of 150 years ago as possible. Further charm was lent to occasions of this nature by the fact that even the approaches to the castle were lighted by candles.

In the year 1905 a Russian musician who had married the daughter of a wealthy industrialist of Imperial Russia took up residence in Berlin: Serge Koussevitzky! The young musician and his bride rented an apartment in the Tiergarten section, on one of the most aristocratic streets in Berlin, entertained lavishly and frequently, and soon were on terms of friendship with everybody of importance in the musical world of the German capital. Fedor Chaliapin, Leopold Godowsky, Ferruccio Busoni, and of course Harriet and Fritz Kreisler were among those frequently seen in the Koussevitzky home.

Max Bruch, 1838-1920

Serge Koussevitzky, 1874-1951

It is said that when Koussevitzky's father-in-law asked the young couple for suggestions about a wedding present, the young lovers requested "an orchestra for Serge." So an orchestra they got, and their Berlin residence was partly devoted to making the right contacts with soloists. On October 31, 1909, Fritz Kreisler was able to announce:

> I have just closed a contract for the most marvelous tour I have yet undertaken. This will be a trip next year down the Volga in Russia for about 1,600 miles. Mr. Serge Koussevitzky, a remarkable contrabass player and conductor, of Moscow, has chartered a steamer that will take an orchestra. We shall stop at twenty large towns and see the interior of Russia from the north to the Caspian.

Although the Volga trip did not materialize, Koussevitzky arranged for his friend Fritz to appear in eight concerts in St. Petersburg and Moscow in 1910. Violin recitals were also given in a number of other Russian cities. Harriet accompanied her husband. The two stopped en route with the Posselts at Riga.

In the course of the ensuing years, and until the outbreak of the First World War, Harriet and Fritz got to know more of Russia than most tourists and even inquiring Western writers did.

"Every year during this period we stopped in the Koussevitzky home in Moscow," Harriet said. "Natasha, Serge's wife, was a perfect hostess, a woman of great charm, and of concealed but very pronounced intelligence. We led a most interesting life at the Koussevitzkys'—a typically Russian life. The finest composers and musicians came to this artistic home, as did great painters and writers."

In the course of one of the tours of Russia, a grand duke requested Fritz Kreisler to give a private recital. Kreisler accepted on the one condition that it be made possible for him to catch the express train for Paris, which regularly left the nearest Russian station at 10:00 P.M. His Imperial Highness assured him there would be no difficulty about that.

The concert, however, did not get under way until nine o'clock, and Kreisler became worried and made serious representations about the imperative necessity of boarding the train. Thereupon he was shown an official document of the Russian railway administration, certifying that the express had orders to wait until he had finished his program!

The train actually waited and Kreisler could keep his Paris engagement.

During a concert tour of Holland in 1908, Fritz Kreisler became better acquainted with Gustav Mahler, with whom he had already crossed the ocean a few months previously. Always eager to broaden his musical culture, he attended as many Mahler rehearsals as possible, so that the composer of the *Lied von der Erde* wrote to his wife: *

Dearest Amscherl:

. . . The orchestra is magnificent—balm after the experience in New York. Kreisler is giving concerts here at the moment and haunts my rehearsals. I like him extremely both as a man and an artist.

The Mengelbergs are as warm-hearted as ever. . . .

Concerning his ocean voyage with Mahler, Kreisler told the *Musical Courier* on November 9, 1909:

"I crossed the ocean with Mahler and had occasion to spend hours and hours with him, going over his remarkable scores and hearing them explained by the composer. I can truthfully say that in certain effects of orchestration Mahler has no superior, nor does any writer of music exist who outdoes him in sincerity and in the desire to express only what is in him without the slightest conscious use of sensational or extraneous means.

"The whole world is bound to give him unreserved and enthusiastic recognition before long, and the signs of this attitude already are becoming visible in many cultured centers."

With Kreisler's tours to Holland were usually combined concerts in Belgium. Many a friendly visit to the Ysaÿe home then ensued. At Brussels, a series of recitals was known as the "Ysaÿe concerts," and Kreisler appeared in that series under the conducting of Frank van der Stucken in 1909. He also played at a command performance of Prince Philip, Count of Flanders, a brother of King Leopold II.

Tours through the Scandinavian countries during this period meant, for instance, that in Oslo—then Christiania—"Kreisler's audience last night was so completely carried away that they had actually had

* Reprinted from *Gustav Mahler: Memories and Letters* by Alma Mahler, by permission of John Murray, London, and The Viking Press, Inc., New York, copyright, 1946, by John Murray and The Viking Press, Inc.

Gustav Mahler, 1860-1911

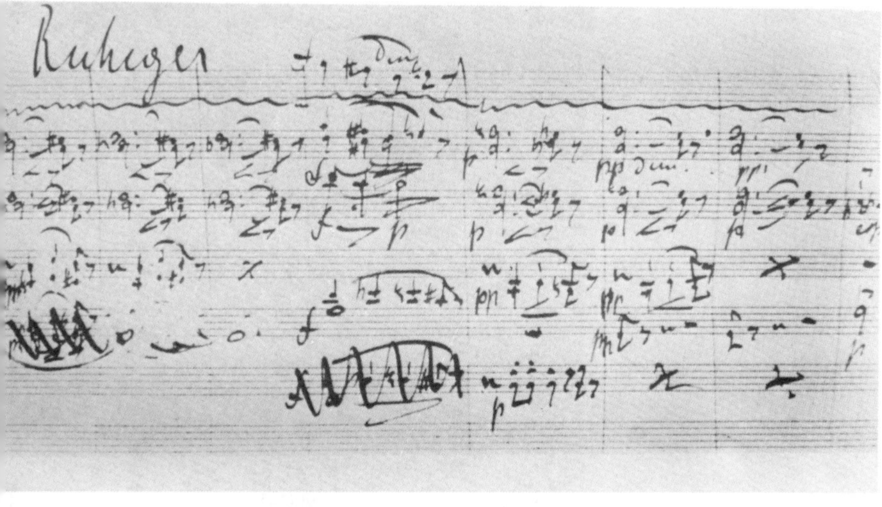

Sketch for a portion of the Lied von der Erde

Sergei Rachmaninoff, 1873-1943

Antonin Dvořák, 1841-1904

to be put out of the hall by force; hardly ever had the old concert hall been the scene of such enthusiastic admiration."

"A greater violinist is not in existence today," opined the Danish *Nationaltidende* of Copenhagen in 1908.

An experience in Scandinavia convinced Kreisler beyond peradventure of doubt of the much-heralded honesty of the successors to the Vikings. It was reported in these words by *Musical America*:

> On arriving at Copenhagen Kreisler opened his trunks at the custom house and later in the day discovered that his keys were lost. After a long search he finally found them sticking in the trunk lock, which in the meantime had been handled by different carriers and baggage porters. To the key ring was chained a gold *casette* containing ten English sovereigns, but none of these had been touched in transit.

Upon one of his reappearances in his native Vienna, Kreisler learned that a long, lank, serious-looking composer-conductor from Russia who was being mentioned in the same breath with Tchaikovsky was to play his Second Piano Concerto with the Vienna Philharmonic Orchestra. He was Sergei Rachmaninoff. One of the closest friendships of Kreisler's life was formed with the somber, meticulous Slav, who in many respects was the very antithesis of the happy-go-lucky Austrian.

Another important meeting between two musical geniuses in the first years of this century was Fritz Kreisler's call on Antonin Dvořák in 1903 in his impoverished home in Prague.

"It was like a scene from *La Bohème*," Kreisler remembers. "Dvořák was lying in bed, sick and in visibly bad shape. He had sold all his compositions for a mere pittance and now had nothing to live on. Even the emoluments for his brilliant American tour had for some reason or other been used up.

"I had been playing some of Dvořák's 'Slavonic Dances' and visited the old man to pay him my respects. I asked him whether he had nothing further for me to play. 'Look through that pile,' the sick composer said, pointing to a mass of unorganized papers. 'Maybe you can find something.' I did. It was the 'Humoresque.' "

What happened to the "Humoresque" after Kreisler took hold of it, arranged it for the violin, and played it countless times is a matter of history. It became world famous. The "Humoresque" was to young violinists in the early 1900's what Paderewski's Menuet was to the aspiring teen-age piano student.

According to Carl Lamson: "Fritz Kreisler wanted the Dvořák family to have all the royalties accruing from his arrangement, but some lawsuit was started over it." Whatever may have been the outcome of the legal squabble, Dvořák's widow was provided for from funds which were at least alleged to have been royalties due.

During his tours in Italy, as occasionally elsewhere in Europe, Kreisler met the Italian composer Giacomo Puccini. The two struck up a friendly acquaintanceship, epitomized by Puccini's always calling the violinist "L'Amico Fritz," with a side glance at Mascagni's opera by the same name. Although Puccini was sixteen years older than his Austrian fellow musician, there was in those years a striking resemblance between the two. This led to all sorts of complications, especially with autograph hunters.

"In Budapest, for instance," Kreisler recalls, "a group of celebrity hunters swarmed into my hotel and would not believe that I was not Puccini. They wanted a Puccini and not a Kreisler autograph. On another occasion a man came into the artists' room after my recital and addressed me as 'Maestro Puccini.' The worst experience was in Italy, where naturally Puccini was a demigod. I'd sit down in a café and suddenly a bevy of girls would come up and kiss me. At first I couldn't figure it out, until it dawned on me that these *baisers* were intended for the great Italian."

The death of Puccini in 1924 put an end to this case of mistaken identities, of which there have been many in Kreisler's life.

Paris, as already pointed out, is the European continental city Fritz has loved most. There was a particular reason why it should be especially dear to him during the twelve years before the great European conflict of 1914–1918:

Early every summer, beginning in 1910, a galaxy of musical stars, the like of which was not to be found anywhere else, foregathered in Paris. They got together, not to entertain a cheering public or to garner box-office receipts, but simply and purely to play their instruments for the joy of interpreting the great masters of chamber music.

Giacomo Puccini, 1858-1924

Kreisler with Eugène Ysaÿe (sitting) and Mathieu Crickboon

Alfred Cortot, 1877-1962

They were Eugène Ysaÿe, Jacques Thibaud, and Fritz Kreisler, violinists; Pablo Casals, cellist; Raoul Pugno, pianist; and somewhat later, Georges Enesco, primarily violinist and composer, but, like Kreisler, so excellent at the piano that he assumed the piano part in the last period of these musical meetings when Raoul Pugno, who died in 1914, was no longer available.

Kreisler said in January, 1910 to the *Musical Courier:*

> "Ensemble playing is a luxury for which I now have very little time. And so I look forward to every summer, when Ysaÿe, Thibaud, Casals the cellist, Pugno, and I meet in Paris. Ysaÿe and I alternate in playing viola, but the queer thing about it is that we all want to play second violin."

Thibaud added to our knowledge of this rare combination.

"Every day we'd lunch and dine together," he said. "We played all the quartets, changing round, now playing first or second violin or viola. We'd play till three or four o'clock in the morning. It was heavenly. We needed no rehearsals. We understood each other perfectly. Our music could have been recorded right then and there for release to gramophone fanciers."

"The unforgettable chamber music sessions were held in a little parlor in Jacques Thibaud's house," Harriet Kreisler recalls. "How informal these parties were you may gather from the fact I sometimes, in fun, tied little blue ribbons into Eugène Ysaÿe's hair. Thibaud's wife was a charming hostess and deserves great credit for these get-togethers."

Enesco contributed further interesting details covering the later period when he participated:

"There was a collector of instruments named Reifenberg who lived in Paris and at whose home many musicians met. That's where we sometimes played. When it came to piano quintets I played the piano part—for instance, in the Brahms quintet.

"Fritz was particularly happy because he rather missed chamber music playing. Ysaÿe had his organization, Thibaud had a trio with Alfred Cortot and Casals, and I had plenty of opportunity for chamber music work. But Fritz not, and that's why he was so particularly happy. Even then one of his favorites was the Schubert quintet for two celli.

"Of course we fiddlers changed around, and there was always a particular struggle to play the second violin. One can 'duck under' so nicely and hear the whole ensemble. As first violinist you must set the pace and watch yourself; at the second violin desk you can just relax, only to play with greater intensity when a passage comes in which you carry the tune."

One impresario who attended some of these informal chamber music evenings waxed so enthusiastic as to suggest that the unusual ensemble go on tour. He soon found, however, that the costs would be prohibitive, considering the fee each artist was wont to command for his concert appearances.

As to Kreisler's standing in France as an artist, Enesco asserted: "He was tremendously popular. On one occasion I heard him give a joint concert with Alfred Reisenauer in the Salle des Agriculteurs in Paris in which, despite Reisenauer's superb playing, Kreisler was distinctly the hero of the occasion."

The very fact that he soon gave all his concerts in the imposing Paris Opéra was an acknowledgment of this stature. For only the greatest artists were given the opportunity to give concerts of their own there.

Suffice it to say that Paul de Stoecklin wrote in *Le Courrier musical* for December 1, 1911:

> M. Fritz Kreisler is incontestably the most perfect king of the violin, the most accomplished virtuoso of our day. We know it. But he succeeded in reaffirming it with an incomparably inspiring authority.

Stoecklin was commenting on a concert with the Société Philharmonique.

During the twelve-year period on the European continent, there was only one occasion when Fritz Kreisler was made really nervous on the stage.

"I am very allergic to unrhythmic movements," he said. "Playing in Berlin one day under the conducting of Artur Nikisch, I was almost ready to give up because in the first row there sat a lady with a big

eorges Enesco, 1881-1955

rtur Nikisch, 1855-1922

Kreisler in 1914,
by English artist Edmond Kapp

The opera house in Paris

fan which she manipulated quite out of rhythm with our music. It nearly drove me crazy. Nikisch whispered, 'Just don't notice her.' But that was more easily said than done. Even when I tried to look beyond her, that fan stuck out like a sore thumb and made me nervous."

Surveying the twelve years of 1902–1914, Harriet Kreisler said: "It was a great era. Those were remarkable days of music in England, with their London 'season' and the music festivals in Leeds, Norfolk, Norwich, Birmingham, Bournemouth, and the rest. In Germany, too, the music festivals in Bonn, Jena, Wiesbaden, Cologne, and other cities were unforgettable experiences.

"Equally outstanding were the French music festivals in Lyons and Marseilles, and the wonderful concerts at Cannes and Monte Carlo which gave the lie to the general impression that these Riviera resorts are merely towns for pleasure-loving 'sports.' Nor can we forget the music festivals in Florence, Italy, and the incomparable concerts in the St. Cecilia Academy in Rome. There was a dignity about the musical performances of that period which today is lacking."

These were also unheard-of years of triumph for her "Fritzi." But, though they carried him to dizziest heights, they also entailed great sacrifices. Less than a year before this period ended, Kreisler revealed his craving for real home life. This is how he put it to a New York *Sun* reporter on October 28, 1913:

"You know my home is now in Berlin, because of its geographical situation. I have my apartment there and that is where my official home is supposed to be. And do you know where I have spent my Christmas during the past seven years?

"Last year I spent it in the middle of the ocean, crossing on a steamer. And what a Christmas! I should call it a continuous earthquake rather than a Christmas. The year before that it was at St. Moritz in Switzerland. That was pretty nearly a real Christmas. I was on a three weeks' holiday. . . .

"The others during the last few years have been involuntary exile. One was in Finland, another in Madrid. Then there was one in London and another in Pasadena, California. The present, as you see, is in New York, and it appears now from my bookings that next year's will be somewhere in Russia. So that in the last seven years I have not been able to have one Christmas in my own home.

"My home has to be anywhere I happen to find myself, whether it is a train, a hotel, a taxicab, or a concert hall. For long stretches of time such places as these are the only home I have; and generally I sleep badly.

"Out of last year I spent a total of about three weeks, adding up the days as they came, in my home in Berlin. There were over two hundred concerts and they took me to Russia, France, Germany, Holland, Belgium, Italy, England, Rumania, Austria, and America.

"That is a pretty wearying schedule. I find my refreshment of strength comes from playing. That is at the same time my business and my recreation.

"The greatest streak of luck in the whole thing is my wife. She is a New York girl, you know. My wife is a very integral part of my career, and she is responsible for at least 50 per cent of all that I do. . . . She has traveled with me during these seven Christmas seasons. That is why Christmas away from home loses some of its terrors."

At various earlier stages of Fritz Kreisler's life, it was possible to communicate to the reader a picture of him as he looked to an observant contemporary. How did he appeal to Europeans shortly before World War I?

A graphic description is supplied by E. Honold, a musicologist of Düsseldorf, who wrote in part:

His figure is middle-large and powerful. There is something soldierly about his bearing. His face is sharp-cut and forceful, contrasting markedly with his black eye-brows and a short-cropped moustache. His eyes are brown and warm, with an open expression, over which there is occasionally something like a veil.

His hair is somewhat wavy. His neck is strong, as is the jaw, which holds the violin as if in a vise. The ear has a big opening for the sound—decidedly a musician's ear.

He is a complete personality. He is a musician first, even ahead of being a fiddler. He is one of the greatest violinists the world has produced—unassuming, great and without blemish. No other artist gets so much out of a piece of music. His is the ardent fervor of a high-priest. He has the inspired ability to give structure and form to music—from the high-striving Gothic (as in Beethoven) to the elegance and *esprit* of the French school. He is truly universal.

It will be noted that Honold refers to Kreisler's "soldierly" bearing. During all these years he regularly went through his military exercises as an Austrian reserve officer, often at considerable sacrifice.

In 1912, his American tour was even interrupted because of trouble

Kreisler at age 37 in 1912

Fritz with Harriet in 1914

brewing in the Balkans between Austria and Serbia, when he was ordered to join the troops of his native land mobilized along the frontier. He was released in time only to fulfill his many European engagements. Returning to New York the following autumn, he said:

> "The mobilization of nearly 500,000 men and the maintenance of this stupendous army on a war footing for about six months has left Austria in a deplorable condition. The financial drain and the partial paralysis of her industries by the retention of most of her available men on the Serbian frontier have been keenly felt in the Empire. Added to this, there is a considerable popular dissatisfaction with the outcome of the maneuvers—a general feeling that it was all for nothing. The people do not look back with any gratification on the cabinet chess game of Europe that called for a mimicry of war involving all the hardships of the real article and bringing no results."

On one of the maneuvers directly following the Russo-Japanese War, Kreisler was permitted to take his wife along as the only woman tolerated. A photograph released in August, 1908, for publication shows her standing beside her husband and surrounded by officers of lower and higher grades, with her "Fritzi" garbed in a lieutenant's uniform. All wear the smart but decidedly uncomfortable parade dress of the period, with high choke collars and much gold braid. Commenting on this episode, Fritz continued:

"When the success of night maneuvers had been demonstrated in the Russian-Japanese War, the Austrian Government decided to adopt these tactics and we were accordingly sent to the northern part of the Empire to rehearse them. Mrs. Kreisler, being somewhat timid about remaining alone, asked that she be allowed to accompany me. I gained the necessary permission and Mrs. Kreisler took to the field with us—the only woman in the army! She marched with us, twenty or thirty miles a day, and even shared the terrors of a military mess. In a word, she became a full-fledged soldier.

"One night, in the absence of my superior officer, I was ordered to take the regiment back to a certain village. Arrived there I asked the sentinel whether anyone had come in. 'Yes,' he answered. 'The archduke, the general, and the beautiful American lady.' He did not know that the 'beautiful American lady' was my wife.

"One night she was quartered in a lonely old mill. The watchful guards, pacing their quiet rounds underneath the stars, were suddenly aroused by a terrified screaming within.

"As I was located not far away, I heard in the still night air the insistent thumping of musket butts on the ground. I rushed to the scene. 'What's the matter?' I inquired anxiously.

" 'The lady inside,' replied the guard, 'has been awakened by mice and she has ordered us to pound the ground with our muskets to scare them away until she has had time to dress and come out.' "

That Kreisler was doing his military duty year after year was, of course, a matter of public knowledge, and inspired a British critic in Brighton to write a piece for *Musical America* entitled "The Military Violinist," which was published on November 19, 1910. It read in part:

> When he [Kreisler] strode on to the Dome platform you at once saw a man who was like no other musician you had known. Six feet high and brawny to boot, with military erectness, with something of military imperiousness in the quick-flashing glance of his eyes, he crossed the platform, filled with members of the Municipal Orchestra, and he did so with the mien of the captain who is about to lead his men to battle.
>
> He led his cavalry charge when he came to the finale of Max Bruch's Concerto. With a mighty downstroke of his bow that was like the first slash of his sword as it sprang from his sheath, the violinist was in the saddle of a charging gallop, and behind thundered the orchestra in emulation.*

There was an Austrian Cassandra who did not take Kreisler's military service, nor indeed the general European preparations for war, lightly. She was the Baroness Bertha von Suttner, who with her epochal novel *Die Waffen nieder!* (Down Arms) had so profoundly stirred the lovers of peace everywhere that in 1905 she was awarded the Nobel Peace Prize by a committee appointed by the Norwegian Storting, or Parliament.†

Speaking in the Berkeley Lyceum, California, on December 2, 1912, she used Kreisler as an example of how horrible it would be if men were compelled to substitute the sword for instruments of peace in

* Cf. p. 104.

† The Peace Prize was the only one of five annual Nobel prizes awarded by a Norwegian committee. Those for chemistry, physics, medicine, and literature were awarded by Swedish learned bodies.

the event of war. Kreisler, she announced, had only a few days previously received an official notification from the Austrian Government to be in readiness to respond to a call to arms.

The baroness continued: "Among the terrible effects of the present Balkan War is this, that all the forces, all the faculties of a great genius may be sacrificed to this modern madness of universal slaughter."

The baroness's fears proved justified: Fritz Kreisler was mobilized for World War I.

CHAPTER FOURTEEN

LIEUTENANT KREISLER

[1914]

FRITZ and Harriet Kreisler had been vacationing in Ragaz, Switzerland, to benefit by the medicinal waters there, when the summons to the colors came on July 31, 1914. They hurried back to Vienna, rapidly canceled all concert engagements, including another tour of Russia with Koussevitzky, and bade goodbye to Dr. Kreisler. By about August 10, Fritz, now a simple army lieutenant, was on his way to Leoben to join the Fourth Battalion, Company 16 of the Third Army Corps, Imperial and Royal Austro-Hungarian Army. Harriet went with him as far as Leoben.

The news that the great violinist was sent into the combat zone evoked different emotions. In Vienna, according to Dr. Dworzak, who lived in the Austrian capital at the time, "there was quite a sentiment against sending Kreisler into the actual fighting zone to the trenches. Yet there was an idea prevalent that it had to be." Expressions of regret were then invariably followed by that typical Austrian outlet for all unpleasantness—a shrug of the shoulder and the exclamation, in Viennese dialect, "Da kann man halt nix machen" (There's nothing one can do about it).

The *Outlook* of New York commented that it was "exasperating to find that, for the sake of having one more officer at the front, Aus-

Harriet and Fritz before his departure

Officers and their wives in Leoben before departure

Kreisler's battalion taking the oath at Leoben

Concert at Leoben before departure for the front

tria was willing to throw away, if need be, the life of a man who had already won for her more than she could gain by any feats of arms."

Kreisler himself took the call to military service calmly and in his stride. He said later:

> It was just the cold-blooded call of the army routine delivered to me through my father, who still lived in Vienna. Mine was one name on a long roster. No one cared who was sent out. . . . I was but a cog in a great wheel—an atom in that big mass.
>
> Sometimes I am asked why the Austrian Government called me, an artist musician, to duty in the trenches. Why, the Austrian Government never moved a hair's breadth to concern itself with me! I was called in by the commanding officer of the regiment I had belonged to in a provincial town. I was a reserve officer by law. My name was on the rolls, that was all. . . . Every one is cannon fodder there, you know. There are no national idols in the ranks of the Austrian Army.

Once more before he faced the grim realities of front-line fighting, Kreisler took his violin into his hands. That was at Leoben, near Graz, of which he wrote:

> In Leoben my wife and I remained a week, which was spent in organizing, equipping, requisitioning, recruiting, and preliminary drilling. . . . Many of the officers had brought their wives and soon delightful intercourse, utterly free from formality, developed, without any regard or reference to rank, wealth, or station in private life.

On the night before his regiment left for Galicia to face the Russians, he gave a concert in aid of the Red Cross. A photograph taken of the event shows him, with hair cropped shorter than usual, in officer's uniform, whereas his accompanist wears civilian evening clothes. The men in the auditorium are chiefly in uniform, with their shining swords at their sides, their military hats on their laps.

The troops the next morning, August 19, entrained at nearby Graz, traveled by way of Budapest to Galicia, and left the train at Strij, an important railroad center in the Carpathians, south of Lvov (Lemberg).

The war had hardly got under way when, on September 7, 1914, a brief cable dispatch stated that Fritz Kreisler had been killed in action. Details were lacking. For weeks nothing further was heard. The

Musical Courier, scooping newspapers and news associations, was the first to tell the world that Kreisler was still alive.

Under the date of September 13, 1914, Harriet had written a letter to New York, addressed to "My Dearest Papa and Mama," which reached her parents after the usual wartime censorship delays. They offered it to the *Musical Courier* for publication. After a first paragraph with some purely personal remarks it stated:

And now about Fritz. I went through fearful times about him. As I wrote you, he left for the front on the 19th by way of Graz-Buda Pesth to a little place in Galicia. There they were supposed to remain two weeks, but upon their arrival found that the battle of Lemberg had begun, and thereafter the horrors proceeded. Up to the 23rd I received daily field postcards from him, but from then until midnight of September 9 not a sign of life, and none to be had anywhere. I didn't know what to do; the only thing that sustained me was constant work, so that when midnight came each day I couldn't stand on my feet. The sounds through the night also were fearful, the constant clanging of ambulances bringing in the thousands of wounded from the different stations to the hundreds of hospitals.

Finally, at midnight of the 9th, I received a telegram from Fritz saying he expected to be home the next afternoon in a hospital train. Of course, between joy and anxiety, we none of us could sleep. The next day at noon he arrived. When I finally saw him limp off the train, my knees went from under me from shock. He had a three weeks' growth of beard, which was more gray than black, and was hollow-eyed and cheeked. He had lost about twenty pounds in weight, and limped from a bruised nerve center in his leg. Well, I was so glad to see him alive that I soon recovered my courage, for he was my first thought. Thank God, it is nothing serious; it is really more soul and nerve shock than anything else. Such dirt you can't conceive of. It seems he didn't get out of his clothes for over eighteen days, and in all that time slept under the heavens, in the damp and marsh. On the 23rd of August through a night alarm all the officers' trunks were lost and have not up to date been found, so that they had for the twenty-one days only what they carried on their backs and in the knapsacks. Some times it was two or three days before they had anything to eat.

The accident to Fritz was the following: One night when the regiment was in trenches, in horrible dirt and mud, there was a sudden alarm and they were suddenly attacked by Cossacks. Fritz's only recollection is that of being suddenly overridden and of shooting the second horseman, when he lost consciousness from pain. It seems that he was missed by his military orderly, and finally was found and carried to safety, although his orderly was shot in the

Kreisler shortly after arriving at the front

Members of Kreisler's company

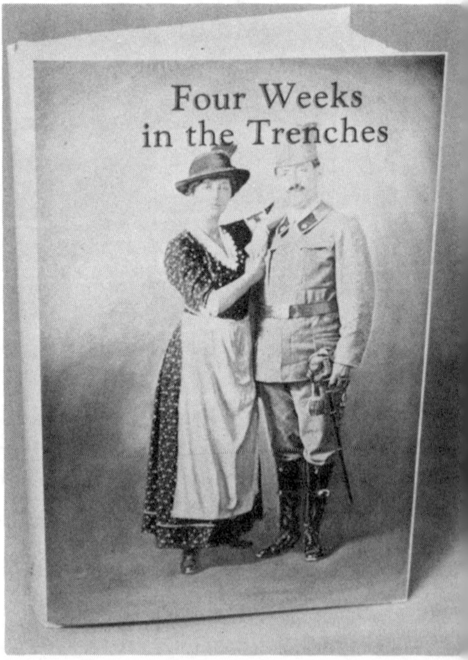

Reissue of Four Weeks in the Trenches *by Paganiniana Publications*

back, but was saved by his knapsack. Fritz continued with his company two more days, but the pain in his leg was so bad that he was sent back. He was sent from field hospital to field hospital until finally, after a four days' journey, he arrived here. Now, thank God, he is getting along nicely. The leg bothers a lot, but we will go tomorrow for three weeks to some hot sulphur baths (Baden, near Vienna), where I hope he soon will recover.

The day after Fritz was sent away another terrific battle took place, and every single officer was wounded; many died and Fritz's own particular company was almost depleted. They were simply mowed down by the Russian artillery. No one has an idea of the horrors of such war. But most extraordinary, the officers are all anxious to get back again. . . .

If you get an opportunity, read my letter to newspaper people, and all influential persons, and beg them to help stop this European war.

I hope, dear folks, that you are both safe and well. Kindly give our best love to all near and dear, also to all friends, and you, dear Papa and Mama, accept much love and kisses from Fritz and your very loving daughter,

Hattie

One detail which Harriet omitted in her letter, obviously in order not to alarm her parents unduly, was the fact that the telegram from her wounded husband, dated September 9, was preceded by two other messages which might have driven to distraction anybody less robust in mind and body than she proved to be. The first was the news dispatch asserting that Lieutenant Kreisler had been killed in action. She simply would not believe it—and her faith proved justified. The second, from the chief surgeon of Fritz Kreisler's regiment, was cryptic and exasperating: "We are sending Fritz to you." What could it mean? Harriet steeled herself for the worst interpretation. The chief surgeon—so she reasoned—was a friend. He had seen to it that her Fritz was not cast into a mass grave after the battle, but had rescued the remains and was now shipping them to her. Forty-eight hours after the unfortunate first news dispatch she finally knew that her mate was still alive. But there was nothing in the message to indicate how seriously he was wounded.

The full story of what happened to the musician-soldier has been charmingly told in Fritz Kreisler's only book, *Four Weeks in the Trenches*, with the subtitle "The War Story of a Violinist." Unfortunately, it has long been out of print. It is dedicated as follows:

TO MY DEAR WIFE
HARRIET
the best friend
and staunchest comrade in all
circumstances of life
I dedicate this little book
in humble token
of everlasting gratitude
and devotion.

The book contains descriptions of poetic beauty, and Kreisler's deep humanitarianism is once again revealed. His fighting is shown to have been without a trace of hatred. He evinces a remarkable command of both medical and military terms.

One naturally asks: Could a sensitive artist who is living in the world of sounds and not swords be worth anything in a fighting army? The answer in Fritz Kreisler's case is a decided Yes! And it was his ear attuned to sounds which enabled him to make a positive contribution to his regiment. He later explained: "I found that I could, with a trained musical ear, mark the spot where shells reached their acme, and so could give the almost exact range of the guns." *

While *Four Weeks in the Trenches* is Kreisler's personally written story of his military experience, an abridged version, based on various interviews in different newspapers and periodicals, was skillfully put together by the New York *Times*. In presenting this summary on November 29, 1914, the *Times* observed:

It should be borne in mind that Mr. Kreisler is recognized as a keen observer and a close reasoner, and that the impressions of such a man, pointed as they are by the vision and imagination of a highly sensitive artist, should afford some interesting first-hand evidence on the psychology of the battlefield.

Here is Kreisler's abridged story as it appeared in the *Times*:

"We got to the fighting line about Aug. 16. Our orders here were to hold our positions at any cost—and you know what that means. We were two army corps to seven of the Russians, and our task was to hold them back until our reinforcements came up. That meant fighting day and night without rest.

"It is all a vague, blurred impression in my mind. I cannot call it even a nightmare, for it lacks the definite impression that a nightmare sometimes cre-

* For details, see Chapter Eighteen, p. 204.

ates. You will see what I mean shortly. For instance, when you hear the first shell burst. It is a terrible thing; the whining in the air, the deafening crash, and the death it spreads around it. That is what you think of your first shell. But you think less of the second and third, and after that they pass out of your mind.

"The first man you see die affects you terribly. I shall not forget mine. He sat in a trench and suddenly he began to cough—two or three times—like an old man. A little blood showed at his mouth and then he toppled over and lay quiet. That was all.

"Very shortly none of these things affect you. It has made me mournful when I have thought how quickly we all threw over everything the centuries have taught us. One day we were all ordinary civilized men. Two or three days later our 'culture' had dropped aside like a cloak and we were brutal and primeval.

"I was in the trenches three weeks, for instance, without a single change of clothes of any kind. But I never thought of it. For all of us the things that were considered necessities in civilization simply dropped out of existence. A toothbrush was not imaginable. We ate instinctively, when we had food, with our hands. If we had stopped to think of it at all, it would have seemed ludicrous to bother using a knife and fork.

"A certain fierceness arises in you, an absolute indifference to anything the world holds except your job of fighting. You are eating a crust of bread and a man is shot dead in the trench next to you. You look at him calmly for a moment and then go on eating your bread. Why not? There is nothing to do. In the end you get to talking of your own death in the trench with as much excitement as you could get up over a luncheon engagement.

"Why? Because there is nothing else left in your mind but the fact that hordes of men you belong with are fighting with other hordes and your side must win. That is your complete psychosis. It is only some tremendous force like this warfare that can so destroy the individual's conception of himself while he still lives.

"It becomes terribly dreary waiting in the trenches, with no incident but the occasional wounding or killing of a man near enough to see. Actual fighting is, under these conditions, welcomed by the soldiers as a great relief.

"For the officers there is perhaps a little more variety, since they must keep thinking about and safeguarding their responsibility. It began to get very hard for us to hold back our men, for instance. We had been in a trench in a swamp for three days. The water gradually drained in and finally reached our knees. We resorted to bailing with our hats, but that did not help much. Under these circumstances it became difficult to convince our men that it was wise to stay intrenched, rather than try a charge.

"On the modern field of battle the soldier of infantry is a small unit. We could look out and see the clouds of smoke and hear the thunder of the guns, but there was little else except now and then the sight of an aeroplane. You could hear the whirr of the motor, but they generally flew so high we dared not fire at them for fear that the hail of bullets would fall back among our own men.

"Amid this absence of all signs of life it was hard to convince our boys that their time had not yet come.

"In the trenches we were generally without food, several times for three days at a stretch. I have more than once licked the dew from the grass to moisten my throat because I could get nothing to drink. The roads were impassable and the supply trains moved only with great difficulty at the outset of the war. Now and then a cow would be found, shot, butchered on the spot, and then we could roast portions in the trenches and eat where we were. In the night time they would bring the field kitchens up, when they were available, and then we would have soup.

"Somehow the physical discomfort—that is a tame word to apply—does you no harm. Indeed you feel better physically. I am of a nervous temperament. I would never have given myself credit beforehand for being able to get through what I went through. But when I was in it, I found it did me no harm. On the contrary it improved me in some ways. For instance, my eyesight was far better on the battlefield than it ever was before. I could see like a hawk, for long distances; better than I can now. My nerves disappeared. The horrible, shocking sights that were seen hourly did not affect me as much as some letter I get now from a friend or well-wisher expressing sympathy.

"Coming back to comfort and safety has been more of a shock to the nervous system than I suffered while I was fighting. And I dread my first concert appearance here, where I have friends, more than I did the shells of the enemy. I think you can understand what I mean on the mental side.

"On the physical side does it mean that we moderns under civilization do not live rightly? Do we eat too much, do we get too much sleep, do we fail of proper exercise? For my experience has shown me that the soldier on the battlefield, suffering crippling physical discomfort and mental shock that must almost have a pathological effect, is really a healthier man than even the one who uses civilization's best hygienic experience under the most favorable conditions.

"That is part of what goes with the primeval condition that war reduces us to, I suppose. I have learned my lesson in the trenches. When we have war, the centuries roll away and we are back at beginnings at a bound.

"But there is another side to the picture. War may bring unspeakable horrors, but it does not fail to unfold the finest flowerings of humanity.

"From the moment war was declared all ranks disappeared in my country. No one knew who the other was. He was satisfied that they were brothers in their devotion to their country. That is why it has made me angry sometimes when people have said, 'How could they take an artist and let him fight?' They should rather not think it worthy of any comment. I am an Austrian. As soon as war began the last thing I thought of was a violin or that I had ever played one.

"Next to me in the trenches were a Prince, a sculptor, a mathematician, and a professor, and nobody asked them who they were, or cared. We forgot everything except the work we had to do. Why should I claim immunity as an artist?

"I have seen people whose houses stood in the way of our artillery fire and therefore had to be razed, put the torch to the houses cheerfully themselves. I, too, lost everything I had invested in the regions touched by the fighting.

"Before the war we thought the human race had deteriorated. We often said so. We thought it had gone tango mad and destroyed itself in frivolities. But the war proved among all the nations engaged that the race is just as sturdy as it ever was. There is that side to it.

"I have seen acts of the most tender sympathy and kindness, and real heroism, with my own eyes, go hand-in-hand with grim, stalking war.

"For instance, it was good to see that the hatred of one foe for another was only an impersonal thing. In the mass we hated our enemy, but as soon as we were confronted with him in person, all was kindness to the individual. I have seen emaciated Austrian soldiers—and I well knew how long it had been since they had had enough to eat—hand a crust of bread to a Russian prisoner.

"And we know from Austrians who were taken prisoner that the Russians had exactly the same feelings. Often our wounded would be captured and removed to a Russian field hospital. Then a sudden temporary change in the battle line-up would force the Russians to abandon these prisoners and they would come back to our hands. So we well knew how the Russians acted and felt toward us.

"Then there were innumerable little incidents of the honoring of bravery in a foe. We took one trench, for instance, after the enemy had put up a gallant fight. The first act was a salute to the foe in acknowledgment of his bravery. And there were the little things like returning the arms of an officer who had fought well but been forced to surrender by the fortunes of war.

"There were all those fine flowers of courtesy to show that, perhaps, after all, it was not utterly brutal and primeval, but that finer feelings had survived and been cultivated.

"I remember once that a Russian officer tottered out of one of their trenches waving a rag on the end of his sword. The firing ceased. He came to our lines. Under his arm was a bottle of wine. He said he had had nothing to eat for five days and could stand it no longer, and proposed that we exchange some bread for his wine. We scraped together some mildewed pieces of bread and gave them to him. He stumbled back to his lines. He had spoken to us and we to him, and I remember we gave him a handful of cigarettes for his comrades. When he got back to his trenches the firing was resumed, but there had been an unofficial truce for twenty minutes.

"The next morning, I am sorry to say, I stumbled across his dead body.

"Another incident of pure human kindness being brought out on the battlefield concerned a soldier who was in charge of one of the horses that carried our ammunition. The soldier had become deeply attached to the animal he was in charge of. One day a fragment of a shell hit the horse and made a deep gash along its side. The man also was wounded.

"He stopped a civilian surgeon and asked him to bandage the horse's wounds. The surgeon gasped in amazement at being asked such a thing when there were so many wounded men, and refused. Thereupon the soldier drew his bayonet and forced the surgeon to bandage the animal. They were in a hellish fire all the time and the man was wounded, but he asked no attention for himself.

"The acts of heroism were innumerable, of course. I remember a case where three soldiers were sent with a very important message to the division commander, in the hope that one of them would get through. They had to cross an open space where they were exposed to a heavy fire, and progress was impeded by barbed-wire entanglements charged with electricity. They had to cut their way through this with insulated wire cutters. Two of them were shot dead. The third found himself nearly through when his arm, which had been shot badly, caught in the entanglement and he could not get it out. Thereupon the soldier drew his bayonet and finished the work the enemy's fire had begun, amputating his arm himself. He got clear and delivered his message.

"I have seen artillery caught in an exposed place and the horses killed. The men who tried to work the guns were shot down; then the non-commissioned officers went, and, finally, there were none left but the officers to fire the guns. But they kept at it. The instances of devotion of soldiers to officers under fire were numerous.

"Without doubt, I owe my life to my orderly. The trenches my regiment was holding were rushed by the Cossacks on the night of Sept. 6. The cavalry only dares attack intrenched infantry at night, when they have some protection from rifle fire. It was about 11:30 when they attacked us.

"I can remember being hit by one horse and knocked down. While I lay I saw a second Cossack reach down to finish me. He got me in the hip, but as he struck me I fired my revolver. I remember seeing him fall and the riderless horse gallop on. Then I became unconscious.

"My orderly retired with the rest of the company. After the fighting had moved on he came back and started to look for me, using a pocket flash lamp to examine the faces of the dead and wounded. He says that several times he was nearly caught by Cossack patrols, but escaped by dropping to the ground, where he was taken for wounded or dead. He found me about 3 A.M., so I must have been lying there about four hours.

"He says I was lying on the dead Cossack who had wounded me, and that I must have grappled with him and then used him for a pillow. He gave me some brandy and revived me and then assisted me back to our lines and to a field hospital. I was wounded near Komarano, a village a little way to the southwest of Lemberg. After being in the field hospital I was taken to Vienna.

"During the three and a half weeks my wife, who had been acting as a Red Cross nurse, had not heard a word from me. The first word she had was that I was dead. That was probably the same report which reached this country. She says that when she heard I was dead, she received that as good news, for at least she had found me.

"The report of my death originated through a mistake of the surgeon. Next to me in the hospital was lying a man who was dying. After the surgeon had looked at him an officer in the hospital said, 'Did you know that was Kreisler, the violinist?' The surgeon thought he referred to my neighbor, and when he unfortunately died, reported my death.

"I was in the hospital three weeks after reaching Vienna. Then I took the cure at the sulphur springs near Carlsbad. After this a commission of surgeons examined me and pronounced me unfit for further military duty. My trampled right shoulder has healed and does not bother me much now. I suppose I will always retain at least a stiffness in my leg, however.

"I shall always remember my days in Vienna after I was invalided. I think it was impossible to have lived in Vienna in war time without loving it. There was an air of seriousness, of solemnity, of dignity, and yet thorough resolution that was striking. Perhaps, after all, if war can bring about that feeling of unity that was so apparent through all the classes of Vienna, it may have a great value as a purifier of the dross of human sentiment.

"It is my fond hope that after the war has ended we artists will be in a position to carry first the message of peace through all the countries. Surely art and religion will be the first forces that will set about the great reconstruction of world sympathy.

"If, for instance, the dignified figure of Ysaÿe were seen on the concert stage of any country which had been hostile to his in the war, would there be any one equal to expressing animosity? I don't know what I myself will be able to do, because I have fought, and they may not be able to forgive me at first. Can we tear down the great walls of hatred that have been erected between the nations? It will be a gigantic task.

"I fear art will suffer. When peace comes, although art will try to speak its message, will not all the energies of the nations be devoted to reestablishing the material things that are of first urgence? I fear all other things will have to wait for these. Then there are so many artists who have fallen. They may not be world-famous, but, after all, the art of a country is the sum of what all the artists are, and the individual does not loom large."

Kreisler did not state in his various interviews that, just before being discharged because of permanent disability, he was promoted one grade and left the army as a captain.

Interest in Kreisler's fate was so keen that the Boston *Herald* wrote, somewhat plaintively:

> The bulletins concerning Mr. Kreisler's military achievements and misfortunes have been more frequent and more circumstantial than reports about Gen. Joffre, Gen. French or any commanding officer in the German, Austrian or Russian army.

It was not America alone that was concerned about Kreisler. The Berlin correspondent for the *Musical Courier* cabled his editors:

> While Kreisler and I were walking down the Friedrichstrasse . . . we met a great number of German officers and soldiers. They one and all saluted their Austrian comrade with great respect and reverence. In going about town Kreisler in his Austrian uniform attracted a great deal of attraction.
>
> The great violinist now walks with a pronounced limp. Marching or even standing for a long time is now quite out of the question with him, so he has been compelled to renounce all further military aspirations. This is news that the musical world will hail with joy; there are thousands of lieutenants, but there is only one Kreisler. . . . The musical world cannot afford to lose a Kreisler.

Just as soon as Kreisler could move, he and his wife started for the United States. As Fritz put it:

"My wife being an American and having a mother who was then alive in this country, we came back here immediately. I had absolutely no trouble getting a passport. I had received an honorable discharge as a complete invalid unfit for any further service.

"We went to Holland. There we boarded a Dutch steamer for America, the same boat on which came Dr. Henry van Dyke, American minister to Holland. On the way we were stopped by a British cruiser. The British officers were very cordial, courteous, and charming to me. They sent a wireless to London and the Admiralty allowed me to proceed. The naval officers showed absolutely no ill feeling, though they knew I had fought in the Austrian Army—and that was only two weeks after I had been discharged."

Fritz and Harriet Kreisler arrived in New York on the *Rotterdam* on November 24, 1914. Fritz walked down the gangplank with the aid of a cane.

Although declared permanently unfit for military service, this sensitive musician, who once described himself as an ardent pacifist, has always retained an astonishing interest in military affairs.

An incident on March 15, 1949, indicates that at the age of almost seventy-five Fritz Kreisler still liked to think in military terms. He had been kind enough to invite me to go with him to a luncheon of the Dutch Treat Club of New York, where we happened to be seated at the same table with Major General Ralph C. Smith, United States Army.

Smith then told of his first meeting with Kreisler some months before, in the cocktail room of the Waldorf-Astoria Hotel. To his amazement, the famous violinist discussed artillery technicalities with an understanding and insight so great that he, Smith, turned to his friend Frank E. Mason saying, "Kreisler may be a great artist; he certainly is an artillery expert." He concluded his recital of the episode with the words: "One realizes very soon whether another fellow has the 'feel' for military things. Fritz Kreisler has it."

The Waldorf-Astoria chat, incidentally, came to an end rather abruptly, and to the regret of all participants, when Kreisler was motioned to imperiously by a rotund figure of a man who was seated at another table.

"I'm afraid I must leave you," Kreisler told his group with a chuckle. "My boss is calling." It was James Petrillo, the aggressive president of the Musician's Union, who had made him an honorary member of Local No. 10, Chicago, on February 27, 1941, introducing him with the words, "That's my boy."

CHAPTER FIFTEEN

BOUQUETS, BOOS, AND WAR HYSTERIA
[1914-1917]

FRITZ KREISLER's first reappearance as artist after his army service—his concert in Carnegie Hall, New York, on December 12, 1914—caused considerable advance speculation. Although America was still technically neutral, the sympathies of the American Government and people were decidedly hostile to Germany and her ally Austria-Hungary. How would music lovers regard a man who had fought on the Teutonic side?

Dr. Algernon St. John-Brenton wrote in the New York *Telegraph*:

> Many of his [Kreisler's] good friends were under the impression that this advent on the concert platform would be the signal for an impassioned demonstration semi-political in nature, and therefore of rousing and provocative proportions. To the honor of New York be it said that hitherto all attempts to poison music and the fine arts with the gall of the present quarrels and discontents have proved failures, in whatever sense they originated.

On the same day on which Kreisler filled Carnegie Hall, another famous artist enraptured a huge throng at the Metropolitan Opera House with her unique interpretation of Puccini's *Madam Butterfly*: Geraldine Farrar. She, too, had been identified with both the German and the Austrian courts during her meteoric career as prima donna of the Berlin Staatsoper. She was American-born, however, so that she was spared some of the humiliations later heaped upon her co-artist Fritz. She stuck loyally to her Austrian friend and his American wife when, some two years later, the Kreislers were shunned by many of their friends of better days.

Geraldine Farrar, 1882-1967

Farrar and Kreisler Give the Beautiful "Mignon" Air

Geraldine Farrar, Soprano—Fritz Kreisler, Violinist

Twelve-inch—$3.00. *In French*

88538 Mignon—*Connais-tu le pays?* (*Knowest Thou the Land*) *Act I*

Ambroise Thomas

Kreisler

Mignon, *opéra comique* in three acts, subject from Goethe's Wilhelm Meister, was first produced at the Opéra Comique, Paris, November 17, 1866. The opera has always been a success, and will doubtless always keep its place on the stage by virtue of its picturesque story, as well as by the beauty and freshness of its melodies.

Farrar

The *Connais-tu le pays*, sung by *Mignon* in Act I, is full of tender beauty and rare expression. The opening passage—

gives us an idea of the melody, one of the most beautiful in the entire range of opera. *Mignon's* passionate longing for her childhood home is expressed in a superb climax—

in which she seems to pour forth her whole heart in a flood of emotion.

Knowest Thou the Land

MIGNON: Knowest thou yonder land where the orange grows?
Where the fruit is of gold, and so fair the rose?
Where the breeze gently wafts the songs of the birds?
Where the season round is mild as lover's words?
Where so calm and so soft, like Heaven's blessing true,
Spring eternally reigns, with the skies ever blue?
Alas, why afar am I straying, why ever linger here?
'Tis with thee I would fly!
'Tis there! 'Tis there! my heart's love obeying,
'Twere bliss to live and die!
'Tis there my heart's love obeying,
I'd live, I would die!

Miss Farrar renders this longing cry of the sad and unselfishly loving *Mignon* most beautifully, singing it with tenderness and simplicity, while a highly effective obbligato is furnished by Mr. Kreisler.

12

Promotion piece for a Kreisler-Farrar recording in 1915

Kreisler's reappearance in New York provoked much discussion. The New York *Evening Post* for December 14, 1914, even devoted an editorial, "Fritz Kreisler Very Much Alive," to the Carnegie Hall concert. It read in part:

> How unreasonable these apprehensions [of hostile demonstrations] were he [Kreisler] learned in the most agreeable and impressive manner in Carnegie Hall on Saturday afternoon. Since that hall was opened in 1892 it has held many crowded and enthusiastic audiences, but none more so than that which greeted him when he played his violin in public for the first time since last July. To be sure, New York is more or less American and neutral; but in that audience there were more women and men who were descended from the British, French, and Russians than from Germans and Austrians; yet all united in bestowing on him plaudits that rose in crescendos like storm-winds, both when he first appeared and after each of his numbers. . . . There were as many men at Saturday's recital as there are usually at Paderewski's.
>
> It is to be hoped he will not overdo—but he needs the money, not only to cover his own losses *but to support the forty-three orphans he has adopted*—the children of comrades who fell at Lemberg (Lvov). The big heart which prompted him to assume this burden shows in this playing—that, after all, is the secret of his success.

The editorial is slightly incorrect in one detail: it was not only children of comrades who fell at Lemberg whom Kreisler adopted, but rather the children of the soldiers who died in the field hospital where Harriet Kreisler was serving while her husband was fighting. Harriet had eased the death of each of them with the promise that she would care for their children. These included Russian and Serbian children in addition to Austrian. The New York *Times* later revealed: "As for Kreisler himself, there are at least 1,500 men and women, artists and would-be artists, in the war-stricken capitals of Europe for whose support he has made himself responsible."

Two days after the Carnegie Hall concert, Kreisler offered to aid the Penny School Lunch Fund for New York's underprivileged school children. He even agreed to address a gathering of youngsters to tell them about the war children of Europe. Shy as he is about public speaking, this was more than a gesture; it was a sacrifice.

Nor did he forget his fellow artists amid the personal triumphs he was achieving. He wrote out in longhand a statement for *Musical*

America which this magazine reproduced in facsimile in its edition for January, 1915:

> The strained artistic conditions in the old countries may force a great many musicians from over there to seek a new field in America. I feel sure that the country's splendid hospitality and immense receptive capacity will amply take care of them, and the ultimate result should be a strong expansion of America's artistic resources.

It was inevitable that a sensitive soul like Kreisler's should be deeply affected by the experience of war, and that a change should come over his playing as a result of it. The music critic of the Boston *Transcript* sensed it after hearing him in December, 1914, and in January, 1915. Writing on "The Changing Kreisler," he said in part:

> The fine-spun beauty of his tone has warmed and deepened. The old suavity and smoothness have become a graver richness. The pile of the tone, so to say, has thickened. Its warmth is less bright, but soberly glowing. It is still the voice of instrumental song; but of song . . . that is the voice of human longing. . . .
>
> And this tone is the fruit of a technique that in itself has changed and ripened. It is as variously resourceful as it ever was and the end of its resources is the end of the resources of the violin. . . . But now intc it has come a new mood of rhapsodic impulse, of creative fire. Under it the music undergoes a new birth.

During the years 1915 and 1916 the American papers were filled with photographs of Kreisler showing him in military uniform and his wife in the garb of a Red Cross nurse. The public, far from taking offense at this time at his having served in the Austrian Army, seemed to enjoy these pictures. The demand for him was greater than ever. As Henry T. Finck pointed out in *The Nation* for March 18, 1915: "Kreisler has already played fifteen times in Greater New York to overflowing houses. He could continue if other cities were not clamoring for this."

In St. Louis, "the women shrieked and the men stamped" after Kreisler played. In Richmond, Virginia, where he appeared with John Powell, the pianist (himself a native of Richmond), and with Elizabeth van Endert of the Berlin and Dresden operas, the critic of the Richmond *Times-Dispatch* decided that, "Until last night, Ysaÿe

Popular photograph of Harriet and Fritz Kreisler

Efrem Zimbalist, 1889-

Enrique Granados, 1867-1916

stood alone and exalted in our appreciation; now Kreisler stands with him, or he with Kreisler; in either case they stand together." His appearance in Milwaukee with Efrem Zimbalist to play the Bach Concerto in D Minor for Two Violins was most enthusiastically greeted, as was his appearance in Boston with Josef Hofmann in a program of sonatas for violin and piano.

Adella Prentiss Hughes wrote about Kreisler's concert in Cleveland early in 1915:*

> February 15 was a red letter day because of the return of Fritz Kreisler. . . . Gray's Armory was filled almost to suffocation. . . . When the great artist came out, limping with slow, dragging steps, the applause was hysterical. Wilson G. Smith painted this picture:
>
> "Kreisler is no longer the debonair man of the erstwhile. His pale, firmset face and air of repression gave evidence of the fact that he has stood in the shadow of a great tragedy whose memory has left a lasting imprint on his life, and as the limpid tones issued like jewels from his instrument, sparkling and iridescent with the fire of genius, they seemed laden with a sadness that converted them into tears falling upon the graves of the martyred thousands."

The musical circles of New York were especially thrilled when, in March, 1916, an unusual trio combination made its appearance: Kreisler, Casals, and Paderewski. Lillian Littlehales wrote: †

> Much affected by the tragic death of his friend Enrique Granados in the torpedoing of a Channel steamer the *Sussex*, in March, 1916, Casals helped to arrange a concert for the benefit of this victim of the "humanitarian" methods of modern warfare, and a New York audience had the unique experience of hearing Ignace Paderewski, Fritz Kreisler, and Pablo Casals in trio—the great *B-flat* of Beethoven. All the musical world and more crowded into the Metropolitan Opera House that night, while many others tried in vain for entrance.

During that same March of 1916 Kreisler gave a recital for the benefit of St. Mary's Free Hospital for Children at the New York

* Reprinted from *Music is My Life* by Adella Prentiss Hughes, by permission of The World Publishing Company, Cleveland, Ohio, Publishers, copyright, 1947, by Adella Prentiss Hughes.

† Reprinted from *Pablo Casals* by Lillian Littlehales, by permission of W. W. Norton & Company, Inc., copyright, 1929, revised and enlarged edition, copyright, 1948, by W. W. Norton & Company, Inc.

home of Mrs. James Speyer. The effort netted a handsome sum for the institution and a laurel wreath for Fritz with the dedication, "From the Grateful Little Children of St. Mary's Hospital."

A month later he filled Carnegie Hall to capacity in a benefit concert for the relief of destitute musicians, music teachers, and music students of all nationalities then stranded in Vienna.

A rather novel item of news reached the public on August 27, 1916. The press then reported that "Fritz Kreisler . . . is at work on the score of an operetta." Later it became known that he had signed an agreement with Charles B. Dillingham for its production. War hysteria, however, compelled him in 1918 to ask for a release from the contract.

One of Kreisler's most lovable traits is his unflinching loyalty to friends, to beliefs he holds, to convictions he cherishes, to causes he espouses. This loyalty was put to an unusual test when the aged Emperor Francis Joseph I of Austria died on November 21, 1916, at the age of eighty-six after a reign of sixty-eight years.

America, to be sure, was not yet in the war. But her sympathies were decidedly anti-German, and the press did its best to put the deceased emperor down as an ogre. Was Kreisler to alienate sympathies by speaking up for the man under whose banner he had served? Might that not wreck his career in America for good?

Kreisler knew but one thought: I must defend my emperor. He threw caution to the winds and committed himself in an interview with the New York *Times*, the salient passages of which follow:

"I knew the Emperor. . . . I have played for him. And always, after the hifalutin music, which his masters of ceremony thought they must have on the court concert program, he would come to me as simply as any child and in a half apologetic whisper, as if he were afraid of those same masters of ceremony, ask me to play simple little tunes that he knew and understood. . . .

"The Emperor had the same qualities that make children love the right sort of a grandfather, only he was that sort of a grandfather to all his people. The farmers knew that as well as anybody else, and the demands which they and others made on his generosity were the despair of his treasurers, for he insisted on knowing, personally, about all appeals to him, and he never denied a request for assistance.

"He never carried money, but gave to each petitioner his personal IOU, and all sorts of queer odds and ends of paper bags, and what not, with the Emperor's initials, would be presented after a hunting trip for payment.

"He was a hard worker and no lover of luxury. All his life he slept on a camp cot, and in the same bare apartment was his working table, where he spent the greater part of his time.

"One of the things in his own room was a small cabinet containing the first pair of shoes worn by each of his children and many other little family mementos, including—the most prized treasure of all—a poem written to her father by the Archduchess Gisela one Christmas, many years ago, when she was still a little girl.

"The birthdays of all his relatives and friends were marked a year ahead on his calendar and to each of them, as the day came round, he always wrote a personal letter.

"Another annual custom of the Emperor was to give an uncut, unset diamond to every woman, young or old, in the Hapsburg family on Christmas.

"He was a great newspaper reader and his habit was to put aside all the clippings that his secretary cut out for him each day and then go through the papers for himself over his breakfast of tea, toast, and cold roast beef, invariably followed by a cigar, called the Virginia, which cost him about a cent and a half apiece. . . .

"In spite of all the arguments to the contrary recently adduced, the fact remains that all people living within the boundaries of the Austro-Hungarian monarchy have received, and have been safeguarded by all means known to modern culture, their nationalistic political representation as well as all moral and nationalistic possibilities of development. This is true of all these people, whether they are Poles, Ruthenians, Czechs, Croats, Slovenes, Rumanians, or Italians. The first five of these owe their political existence, and future especially, to the policy of free national development adopted by Kaiser Francis Joseph."

Kreisler could not know at this time that thirty-three years later none other than Winston Churchill would castigate the dismemberment of the Austro-Hungarian monarchy as a grave historical mistake!

It is a rare tribute to the general esteem in which Kreisler was held that his unconditional praise of his emperor was not held against him. Even when war hysteria a year later forced him off the stage, his apology for the aged ruler to whom he had sworn allegiance did not figure among the "crimes" laid at his feet.

As late as January 17, 1917—only three months before America's entry into World War I—Kreisler participated with Paderewski in a gala concert for the benefit of the Vacation Association given by the

Boston Symphony Orchestra under the conduction of Dr. Karl Muck. Kreisler played the Mendelssohn Violin Concerto, Paderewski the Schumann Piano Concerto—both works by German composers! The receipts totaled $25,000.

A week previously he had made his friend, the pianist-composer Ernest Schelling, very happy by playing this artist's Concerto for Violin and Orchestra at a performance of the Philadelphia Symphony Orchestra at Carnegie Hall, New York, under the auspices of the Friends of Music. (Josef Hofmann had been the other soloist.) It was thus given what amounted to a world première, for an earlier rendition, on October 17, 1916, at Providence, Rhode Island, with the Boston Symphony Orchestra, had gone by rather unnoticed.

Lawrence Gilman said of this concerto in a program of the Philadelphia ensemble: "Mr. Schelling wrote this work for Fritz Kreisler at Bar Harbor, Maine, in the summer of 1916. . . . The concerto is in one movement, which might, however, be divided into two sections." Kreisler, to whom the work was dedicated, in a letter to Schelling dated from Carlsbad, July 27, 1923, authorized the notation on the published edition, "Violin part phrased and fingered by Fritz Kreisler."

Early in 1917 he, Harold Bauer, and Pablo Casals were heard together in the Triple Concerto by Beethoven with the New York Symphony Orchestra, Walter Damrosch conducting.

Meanwhile World War I did not produce the result desired by Henry Ford, "Out of the Trenches by Christmas." As it progressed, nationalism in each country became more pronounced. Even the arts did not escape the recrudescence of chauvinism. Ernest Ansermet was quoted by the New York *Times* of January 7, 1916, as saying that Richard Wagner and Richard Strauss had caused the war by their music and predicting that international music would disappear after the war!

Dispatches from Paris on February 4, 1916, indicated that the question had been put to various prominent Frenchmen as to whether Wagner should be produced. Auguste Rodin, the sculptor, replied: "Beethoven, yes. But Wagner is too near our time." Camille Saint-Saëns answered from his organ bench in the Madeleine, Paris: "No,

Jose Iturbi, Walter Damrosch, Willem Mengelberg, Fritz Kreisler, and Ernest Schelling (host)

Camille Saint-Saëns, 1835-1921

because Wagner will symbolize Germany in the eyes of the French people and besides his beauties are a pretext for getting his inferior work accepted."

For anyone who knew the American temperament it was obvious that even as respected and beloved an artist as Kreisler was apt to encounter trouble once the United States had entered the war.

However he himself may have felt, he gave no outward indication that he foresaw an early end to his American platform appearances. He continued his tour across the American continent after Woodrow Wilson had elicited a declaration of war on Germany from the Congress on April 6. In a letter to Ernest Schelling from San Francisco he made no mention of any plans to cancel his concerts for the season of 1917-1918. His worry then was his wife's health and the state of mind of the Schellings. The letter is reproduced in full from the Ernest Schelling Collection because Kreisler wrote so seldom that but very few communications from him are available.

San Francisco, Cal., May 9, 1917

My dear Ernest:

Please forgive my answering you by a typewritten letter, but I am just at the present time being almost overwhelmed with work of all kind, and I do not like you to wait for an answer any longer.

I was awfully glad to hear from you, and both Harriet and I are very sorry that you feel so down and out, and that Lucie is feeling badly again. We always were of the opinion that Lucie did not sufficiently take care of herself, and that her numerous activities were bound to have a bad effect on her health and her nervous system. We both feel, however, now that she is in the hands of Dr. Cast, that everything will be done in the right way for her. We only hope that Dr. Cast's instructions will be minutely and closely obeyed.

As for us, there is nothing particularly good to report. Harriet has been almost continually ill since her arrival on the Pacific coast, and after a series of minor ailments she finally succumbed to a very serious recurrence of her former kidney trouble, which necessitated her immediate removal to a hospital, hereby undergoing an atrociously painful and severe local treatment. She is getting slowly better now and if it were not for her renewed worry about her Mother's health, who contracted pneumonia three weeks ago and almost died, she might now be on a secure road to recovery. As it is, the Doctor now has hopes that Harriet will be alright in about three weeks; but then her nervous system will be so worn down by the painful treatment that she will have to be very careful in restoring her health completely over the summer.

I have been living with her for the last two weeks at the hospital, occasionally taking a night trip in order to give a concert on the Coast.

Next Thursday is my last recital in San Francisco, and then I am at least free of artistic worries for the time being.

We have retained the little house in Seal Harbor and shall, in all probability, be there by the end of June. We are looking forward to seeing you both and spend a quiet and as uneventful a summer as possible.

I am very much interested to hear that you made a new Coda to the Concerto, but with all respect to your genius, I hardly believe you can improve on the last one which in my mind is as fine as possibly can be.

Please let us hear from you again as soon as possible.

With lots of love from Harriet and myself, as always,

Cordially yours,

(Signed) *Fritz*

Mr. Ernest Schelling
New York.

To Kreisler, citizen of the world that he was, it was incomprehensible that anyone should object to his continuing his even way of giving concerts, chiefly for charity.

"Why hate any people because of disagreement and disapproval of the political government of that people?" he asked in an aside during his Kaiser Francis Joseph interview, then continued:

> "I am not only an Austrian but, more than that, I am a human being and have no right to hate anybody, because we are all brothers and should be able to think of individual men as such, no matter what we may be doing to each other as members of political groups. I have not cut off a single friendship because of the war and I have friends who are of every belligerent country."

Undisturbed, he started out on the 1917–1918 concert season even earlier than customary. On August 19 he appeared in Ocean Grove, New Jersey, in a joint concert with his old friend John McCormack, to which ten thousand music lovers flocked while another three thousand had to be turned away. His first Carnegie Hall recital of the season in New York on October 29 was again "a sell-out, platform seats included."

After that, however, trouble began. Led by a leader in the Dolly Madison Chapter, Daughters of 1812, and by the president of the Pittsburgh chapter of the Daughters of the American Revolution, a movement was started to protest against Kreisler's appearance at

Carnegie Hall, Pittsburgh, on November 8. An appeal was made to the director of public safety who refused the usual license to the concert management on the grounds that Kreisler's appearance would constitute a disturbance of the peace. The Woman's Club of Sewickly, a suburb of Pittsburgh, canceled its Kreisler concert even before the director of public safety had taken a stand.

The first that Harriet Kreisler, who had remained behind in New York, heard of the trouble in Pittsburgh and Sewickly was an item in the newspapers to the effect that her husband had been attacked in an alley while taking a stroll. She took a train immediately for Pittsburgh to be near him.

"He was completely calm," Harriet recalls, "and was drafting his celebrated letter, released some days later in New York, in which he replied to various charges made against him. The situation was so tense that at 7:00 P.M. that night—November 7—the police visited us and escorted us through a rear entrance of the railway station to our train for New York.

"Fritz took the upper berth of the sleeping car while I had the lower. Suddenly I heard him laugh uproariously. Well, that's it, I thought. The excitement, after all, has gone to his head. He is out of his mind. I called to him: 'Fritz, are you all right? Are you sick?' Quite surprised, Fritz called down from his berth: 'What's the matter? What makes you think so?'

" 'You are laughing like a madman,' I replied. 'Oh, that,' he said. 'I've just been reading one of the funniest books I ever laid my hands on. It's by Alexander Moszkowski, and full of excellent jokes.'

"And then this husband of mine, who only a few hours previously had been in real personal danger, proceeded to read some of the jokes to me just as if nothing whatever had happened."

Other cities followed the lead of Pittsburgh. Youngstown, Ohio, barred Kreisler from his scheduled joint recital with Frieda Hempel on November 10. Williamsport, Pennsylvania; Buffalo, New York; Morgantown, West Virginia, followed suit. New York and Brooklyn, however, refused to succumb to the general hysteria, as did Baltimore, Maryland; Washington, D. C.; Hartford, Connecticut; Fall River, Massachusetts and Cleveland, Ohio.

"Kreisler Wildly Cheered—Sailors and Soldiers at Violinist's Second Recital Here" the New York *Times* reported on November 25. The soldiers and sailors, according to this account, filled the huge hall "with a tumult of roaring acclamation rarely heard in a concert hall."

Several music critics noticed something else: the loudest cheerleader of them all was a Frenchman—Jacques Thibaud, technically an enemy of the soloist.

Thibaud had come to America for the concert season of 1917–1918, after his property in France had been blown to atoms by shellfire and he himself had fared rather badly as a mere private condemned to driving military trucks through fire and over shell holes. At his first recital he had been so overcome by emotion when he attempted to play the celebrated *Poème* by Chausson that the critic Konrad Bercovici had to take him to his lodgings—the same Wellington Hotel in which Fritz and Bauer were also living. Kreisler had attended his French friend's concert but, to avoid any possible embarrassment, had taken the elevator up to his rooms just as Thibaud entered the hotel.

A few days later, the two happened to meet on the street, both limping. They merely saluted each other. During his friend Fritz's concert, however, Thibaud finally threw conventions to the wind. After Kreisler's tenth bow, when the others had already stopped, Thibaud still stood there clapping his hands and crying, "Bravo! Bravo!"

As Bercovici described the scene,* Thibaud turned to him and exclaimed: "I have never heard such playing in my life. Fritz is wonderful! Magnificent! Superb! He has never played like this before." Bercovici continued:

> We met Kreisler in the lobby of the hotel as we came in. The two men hesitated for a moment, then rushed at each other with outstretched hands. The war was ended as far as they were concerned.

On the day of his great Carnegie Hall triumph, Kreisler released the statement drafted in Pittsburgh on November 7, in which he stated

* Reprinted from *Little Stories of Big Men* by K. Bercovici, in the January, 1934 issue of *Good Housekeeping*, by permission of *Good Housekeeping*, copyright, 1934, by *Good Housekeeping*.

his position concerning the criticisms directed against him. It is an unusual pronouncement and was characterized by the New York *Times* as a " 'White Paper' of an Artist's Life in America in War-Time." The complete text follows:

There have been continuous statements in Pittsburgh papers designed to prejudice and arouse public opinion against me. It has been said that I am an Austrian officer on furlough and that my funds were sent abroad to give comfort to enemy arms. In this morning's papers these statements are intensified by positive and violent accusations to that effect.

These statements are utterly baseless and untrue.

I am not on furlough here. At the outbreak of the war in July, 1914, I served for six weeks as a reserve officer of the Austrian Army on the Russian front and after receiving a wound was pronounced an invalid and honorably discharged from any further service. There has been no attempt whatever by my Government to recall me into service.

It is true that I sent money to Austria.

I have sent a small monthly allowance to my father, a medical doctor, who has been prevented by a subsequent paralytic stroke from exercising his profession. He is 74 years old.

I have sent monthly allowances to the orphan children of some artists, personal friends of mine who fell in the war.

In fulfillment of a pledge undertaken by my wife, at the deathbed of some Russian and Serbian wounded prisoners whom she nursed during my stay at the front, I have sent eleven individual monthly allowances to their destitute orphans in Russia and Serbia through the medium of the Red Cross in Berne, Switzerland.

The bulk of my earnings, however, has gone to the Brotherhood of Artists, founded by me for the purpose of extending help to stranded artists and their dependents regardless of their nationality. For fully three years my contributions were the sole and unique support of seventeen British, Russian, French and Italian artists and their entire families who found themselves stranded and utterly destitute in Austria at the outbreak of the war.

I have been bitterly and violently attacked by chauvinists in Vienna for diverting my earnings to that channel. On the other hand, I am in honor bound to state that I have never been rebuked for my actions by any official of my Government.

I have not sent a penny to Austria since the entrance of the United States in the war, and I have not had a word from abroad for fully eight months.

The ironical aspect of the situation is that some threescore of British, French, Russian, and Italian children may now be actually dying of want because I, technically their enemy, am prevented by the laws of this country, their friend and ally, from saving them.

During every minute of my three years' stay in this country I have been conscious of my duty to it in return for the hospitality. I have obeyed its laws in letter and spirit and I have not done anything that might be construed in the least as being detrimental to it. Not a penny of my earnings has ever nor will it ever, contribute to the purchase of rifles and ammunition, no matter where and in whatsoever cause. The violent political issues over the world have not for an instant beclouded my fervent belief in true art as the dead center of all passion and strife, as the sublime God-inspired leveler of things, as the ultimate repacifier, rehumanizer and rebuilder of destroyed bridges of understanding between nations.

It is to the cause of crystalizing and purifying this true vocation of art and to the preservation and marshalling of its forces, the priesthood of artists all over the world against the coming day of their mission, that every penny of my earnings has been and shall be devoted as long as I shall be permitted to exercise my profession. No sordid consideration of my material welfare enters for a moment into my mind. After four years' successful tour of this country I have less money to my name than many a prosperous bank clerk. I have no personal interests at stake. I shall serve the cause I am devoted to undismayed by personal attacks as long as I shall be permitted to and so long as the deep sentiment and feeling I bear this country will not be thrown into conflict with the fundamental and unalterable principles of my honor as a man and artist. I make no appeal for sympathy, but for justice and respect.

But come what may, my deep gratitude for past kindness, hospitality and love shown me by the American public will be forever engraved in my heart.

November 7, 1917. (Signed) *Fritz Kreisler*.

Elaborating later on his refusal to contribute to the purchase of rifles and ammunition, Fritz said: "I was criticized at the time for not buying Liberty Bonds. True, I bought none. But neither did I subscribe to Austrian war loans, because, as an artist, I considered war unjustifiable, and held that not a cent of my money must go to its support."

Kreisler's lofty statement may well have provided the spark for the demonstrations of affection given him during the few additional engagements which he was able to fulfill. It had the opposite effect, however, on the Reverend Dr. Newell Dwight Hillis of the Plymouth Church of Brooklyn, a man of narrow nationalistic views who had succeeded such broad-minded liberals as Henry Ward Beecher and

Dr. Lyman Abbott in the time-honored Brooklyn pulpit. Dr. Hillis delivered a sermon on November 26 in which, according to the New York *Times*, he said in part:

"Our Government forbids trade with states at war with us. Would a merchant enter into contract to buy goods from a German he would straightway be arrested; but what shall we say about men who enter into business contracts with Muck and Kreisler? It is well known that Kreisler is an Austrian captain; that to obtain his release from the army he entered into an agreement to send back to the home government a large percentage of his income. An Austrian gun costs approximately $20. Every night that Kreisler is paid $1,000 Austria can buy fifty rifles with which Germans can kill American boys.

"Young Albert Spalding obeyed the call of his country and is serving in France for $30 a month. To do this he cancelled contracts for $45,000 for his winter's work. Last night over in New York men and women who claim to be patriots bought for an enemy state some thousand dollars' worth of pleasure and with the receipt Kreisler can send enough money to buy fifty rifles with which to kill Albert Spalding."

This was too much for even the soft-spoken, peace-loving Fritz. His dander was up. He issued this statement:

In his cowardly, irresponsible and unethical attack upon me, Dr. Hillis said, "It is well known that Kreisler is an Austrian captain and to obtain his release from the army he promised to send a large percentage of his income back to the home government." This is a baseless and malicious lie. Knowing Dr. Hillis to be a minister of the Gospel I refuse to believe that he uttered this lie in full cognizance of its falsity and import. I expect him to retract his misstatement publicly and without delay.

Hillis was nowhere to be found for comment. He was "somewhere in New Jersey," his office said. Nor did he emerge when Kreisler demanded that he be given an opportunity to "meet him man to man."

Utterances like Dr. Hillis's did not fail to arouse chauvinistic passions still more. Carl Lamson told me: "Vile stories were circulated about Fritz. One man testified he had seen Kreisler shooting at him. Another wrote that Fritz Kreisler refused to play on one occasion because there was an American flag on the rostrum. I personally traced this man and asked him for his evidence. 'Someone told it to me somewhere in a hotel lobby,' was the evasive reply. 'Is that the way you play with men's reputations?' I challenged the man. He had no answer."

To the honor of Yale University it must be recorded that even after chauvinism had begun to ride high, it refused to cancel the Kreisler concert scheduled for December 12.

The chief of police of New Haven, Connecticut, wrote to the treasurer of Yale:

I am in receipt of protests against the appearance of Fritz Kreisler, Austrian violinist. Under the law governing licenses of concerts etc. I cannot refuse a license for this concert, but I believe the stand taken in this protest is a perfectly good one.

The treasurer replied:

The contract was made long before the United States and Germany broke off diplomatic relations. It would not be good propaganda to reneg on contracts when we tell Germany she failed to live up to agreements. In effect this would mean to declare war on art. . . . For any educational institution to encourage a community in such action would be for it to prove unfaithful to the ideals of its founders.

From England an English officer wrote to the New York *Times* to the effect that it was indeed true that Kreisler had given aid and comfort to the enemy—but in reverse, and not in the way the Reverend Dwight Hillis had envisaged it. "Our British soldiers," the officer observed, "go to battle with Fritz Kreisler's tunes."

Despite such courageous support, Kreisler decided that, no matter what he might do or how he might explain his actions, he would be misunderstood if he continued to appear in public. He therefore drew the logical consequence of withdrawing from the concert stage. On November 26 the press announced: "Kreisler Quits Concert Tour—Violinist Finds That He Cannot with Self-Respect Accept America's Money—Loses $85,000 Contracts." The news story contained a formal statement by Kreisler:

Bitter attacks have been made upon me as an Austrian and because at the outbreak of the war I did my duty as an officer in the Austrian army at the Russian front. I have also been criticized for fulfilling engagements under contracts made long ago. I therefore am asking all concerned to release me from my obligations under existing contracts. My promise will be kept to play, without compensation, for those charities to which I have already pledged my support. I shall always remain deeply sensible of my debt of gratitude to this country for past kindnesses and appreciation of my art.

To the reporters he added: "I propose to live quietly and devote myself to composing some serious works I have long had in mind."

His manager, C. A. Ellis of Boston, was quoted as "frankly telling friends that an artist belonging to a nation allied with this country's enemy in the war could not fairly and with self-respect continue to accept America's money."

In a special editorial the New York *Times* the following day lauded Kreisler's decision in these words:

In taking the action he has, Mr. Kreisler has acted wisely. His retirement is a recognition of facts and conditions as they are. . . . Mr. Kreisler can withdraw temporarily from view and he will take with him an amount of approval as a good musician who was a good soldier and who has a sense of propriety and expediency that not all artists possess. This appreciation will be of value to him and to his country when come the better days for which we are all hoping.

CHAPTER SIXTEEN

MARKING TIME

[1918-1919]

THE generous interpretation placed upon Kreisler's attitude and acts by the New York *Times* was unfortunately not shared by a number of men and women whom Fritz had considered his friends. Helen L. Kaufmann and Eva vb. Hansl in their book *Artists in Music Today* summed up Kreisler's fate during the ensuing anxious years in these words: *

> And now this lovable artist, who knew no hate, who invited the hungry enemy into his own dugout to share cigarettes and sausages between battles, and suffered as only the sensitive can at the horror he was compelled to witness, found himself reviled by former friends as a *Boche*.

"Fritz remained serene about everything except when friends turned on him," Carl Lamson commented. "That always really got him down."

During the winter of 1917–1918 the Kreisler couple continued to live at the Wellington Hotel. "British and French officers did not hesitate to come to my suite there," Fritz recalled, "whereas some of my American friends were afraid even to greet me."

"During our retirement," Harriet remembered, "and until the war was over, many of our friends suddenly got shortsighted; or they would dodge around corners so as not to have to recognize us. They weren't all Americans, either! Some were mighty eager later, when the

* Reprinted from *Artists in Music Today* by Helen L. Kaufmann and Eva vb. Hansl, by permission of Grosset & Dunlap, Inc., New York, copyright, 1933, Grosset & Dunlap, Inc.

conflict had ended, to have Fritz do favors for them, which he with his forgiving spirit then did."

A top British diplomat felt so outraged at the treatment accorded Kreisler even by alleged friends that he extended a formal invitation to Harriet and Fritz to take up residence in England, where, he promised, they could live unmolested and, in fact, highly respected.

Harriet recapitulated a scene at Carnegie Hall which has been deeply engraven upon her memory.

"It was the afternoon of the Armistice," she recalled. "We had been invited to share the box of friends. In a box opposite us sat a famous tenor, who pretended not to notice us. Elsewhere sat others, some composers, some pianists, who developed sudden myopia. The center box, however, was filled with highest Allied officers in full regalia.

"During the intermission the door to our box was suddenly opened, and in came four Allied officers. Such a scene of hugging and handshaking and mutual demonstrations of affection—the whole house watched breathlessly, and you could have heard a pin drop. 'Thank God, Kreisler, the war is over,' an English general exclaimed. 'Elgar and Nellie Melba and scores of other friends all send you greetings. And don't you think we stopped playing your music during the war!' I was so deeply stirred I could not utter a word.

"Then came the irony of it: after the officers had left our box, the persons who only a short while previously had been bothered with bad eyes suddenly regained their eyesight and tried to greet Fritz. By that time, however, we had temporarily lost our eyesight and for some time had difficulty regaining it.

"I thought the performance of these people disgusting. If they had sent us word at the time of Fritz's retirement to the effect, 'We're unfortunately now enemies technically, and perhaps we ought for the present not to see much of each other,' he would naturally have understood and thought nothing further about it. But for them first to pretend not to see us and then to come forward, when they thought it was respectable to do so, without a word of apology or explanation—that I consider contemptible."

It goes without saying that the Kreislers also retained many of their friends who courageously stood by them. One such loyal friend was Geraldine Farrar. In her autobiography she commented: *

> One man who had enjoyed long and well deserved popularity, both as artist and lovable personality, was Fritz Kreisler; but he, too, came under the ban. Friends turned aside when he passed on the street; and because he and his wife were honored guests at a Christmas party in my home, their presence brought me a sheaf of scurrilous—and of course anonymous—letters about the occasion. I was taken to task as well by a recently naturalized citizen, for my loyalty to old friends. I pointed out that this country was not, at the moment, at war with any other. I had too many forbears listed in the accounts of our various wars to preserve this democracy to warrant self-invited criticism offered in the first blush of recently acquired patriotism. And my birthplace, almost at the foot of Bunker Hill, should sufficiently guarantee my own integrity—as well as my sense of fair play.

On another occasion during the period when Kreisler was out of circulation, Miss Farrar gave a jolly party to which she invited the Kreislers, but at the same time cautioned them that this or that superpatriot might inadvertently have been included in the list of those invited. But she laughingly said: "Fritz saved the situation beautifully. When he saw that I had engaged a band for dancing, he joined it and had a good time fiddling dance music. In that way he did not have to be presented, hence risked no rebuffs."

Another loyal friend was the Hindu journalist and essayist Basanta Koomar Roy. "I was intensely fond of Kreisler's art," he told me shortly before his death. "Often while he was playing I would try to put into verse what he was saying in tones.

"On one occasion Kreisler did me the honor of saying to Artur Bodanzky, who was lunching with our group, that I was an intuitive critic. 'Roy doesn't know anything about the technique of Western music,' he said, 'yet he arrives intuitively at the same conclusions as we do.'

"One day in 1916 I saw Rabindranath Tagore to my surprise sitting in a box at a Kreisler concert. I did not even know he had come to America again. I asked him what he thought of Kreisler and his music. 'Wonderful,' he replied, 'he is a spirit.' I asked whether he'd

* Reprinted from *Autobiography: Such Sweet Compulsion* by Geraldine Farrar, by permission of The Greystone Press, copyright, 1938, by Geraldine Farrar.

like to meet the artist. 'By all means,' he replied. After a pause he added, however: 'But of what nationality is he? This is war-time, you know.' 'He is an Austrian,' I answered. 'Well,' said Tagore, 'it doesn't matter to what nation he belongs; I want to see him anyway.'

"Kreisler was equally enthusiastic about the prospect and said he had read many of Tagore's works. Unfortunately both men had so many engagements outside New York then that the meeting did not come off until much later. When these two great minds finally met in the artists' room after a Kreisler concert, their greeting was most affectionate. Each hailed the other as a great spirit."

The Hindu poet's obvious fondness for Kreisler and his art inspired Basanta Koomar Roy to publish an interview with Rabindranath Tagore on "The Music and Personality of Fritz Kreisler." It more than deserves rescue from oblivion. Its most important passages follow:

Eventually we began talking about eastern and western music. During the course of this conversation I asked him: "What do you think of Kreisler's music? You have heard him twice."

"I like Kreisler's music very much," said Tagore, as his magnetic eyes were electrified, and his face was lit up with a reverent smile. "I like it more than words can tell," continued the poet. "I shall never forget his music. It has moved me deeply. It has shaken me profoundly. It so simply carries us to the very beginning of things. I have heard many musicians, but no music has moved me so fundamentally as Kreisler's playing on the *behala* (violin). It is something more than marvellous execution, it is, in fact, a cosmic cry of the soul from the realm of the eternal. I do not know how to express it adequately in ordinary words. Psychic language is necessary to express such feelings. How soulfully he plays! He most mercilessly lances one right through the heart with the inexplicable somethingness of his music. It is simply superb.

"Kreisler ought to come to India and study our music and then give it to the world. A man with his brain, training and feeling would grasp the spirit and technique of our music in no time. And what a contribution it would be to the art and science of music! No such attempt has yet been made. A few western novices have tampered with our music with disastrous results, but no artist has yet given it a careful study, not even a serious thought. Our music has something to give to the world. From the union of the music of the east and the west a new form of music may be developed, perhaps much richer than any now in existence."

And again, on the eve of his departure for Europe, while discussing the saintly personality of Mahatma (Great Soul) Gandhi of India, Tagore said to me: "I have known him for a long while, and the longer I know him, the better I like him. . . . Gandhi has what is known as a Christ spirit," . . . and he looked at me inquisitively as if to see how I would take the remark.

"I have not yet met Mahatma Gandhi," said I, "and I have only read of Christ and his idealism; but I have . . . heard the voice of God most eloquently in Kreisler's music. The longer I know him, the better I like him. During the wartime I saw him bear his cross like a Christ."

"Yes, I understand," said Tagore pensively, as he shook his unique head and opened wide his wonderful eyes, as if to seek a glimpse of something that eyes cannot see. "Yes, from the quality and message of Kreisler's music I can readily understand what you mean. . . . Kreisler plays a cosmic music. His music is a positive spiritual affirmation. He must think in terms of the infinite. He ponders over the varied expression of the universal in sound and color. He is enveloped in his heavenly music; so nothing can affect him. . . . Kreisler rests on the lap of the eternal, and this makes him invincible."

True to his pledge, Kreisler continued to fulfill charity engagements to which he was committed. He went to Boston in December, 1917, to play with the Symphony Orchestra at a benefit for the Halifax victims. When his friend Franz Kneisel was unable, because of ill health, to continue his quartet, he joined the other members, Hans Letz, second violin, Louis Svecenski, viola, and Willem Willeke, cello, for a series of three benefit performances on behalf of the Needy Musician's Fund of the Bohemian Club of New York. The first of these concerts, on December 21, 1917, in Aeolian Hall, New York, drew the following comment from the music critic of the New York *Times*:

Mr. Kreisler has spent his life hitherto in solo performance. Ensemble playing necessarily means for such an artist a great change of ideal and method. There was nothing in his doings last night to suggest the great artist slighting the task or the great artist condescending to it. He is, indeed, a great enough artist to realize that what he was doing was in some ways greater and in some ways more difficult than he was accustomed to.

The critic of the New York *Herald* wrote:

Mr. Kreisler by no means "plays solo" in the new combination. Yet by his extraordinary beauty of tone he seems sometimes unduly to dominate the ensemble. . . . On the whole the tonal eloquence and the interpretive vigor were so distinguished that these minor faults are hardly to be remembered. Mr.

Kneisel String Quartet in 1915

Fritz Kreisler, about 1917

Kreisler will serve as a salutary pacemaker in those respects in which the Kneisel ensemble has sometimes fallen short in the past.

The second concert also took place as arranged, but the third had to be called off because meanwhile even Kreisler's charity engagements were being interfered with. He then decided to remain off the platform altogether for the duration of the war. He even canceled an engagement to accompany Reinhold von Warlich, baritone, on the piano at a concert of the Passaic Philharmonic Society of New Jersey. He also asked Charles B. Dillingham, the theatrical producer, to release him from the contract to write a comic opera. He wrote to Dillingham:

> Since the day on which you did me the honor to enter into an agreement with me, great changes have taken place. In due regard to the ethics and propriety of the situation created by these changes and in order to avoid any possible embarrassment to my friends, I have at the beginning of this season cancelled all my public appearances and engagements. My request to you is but the final step toward the realization of my sincere desire to refrain from any public activity whatever in this country in which I am a guest.

The withdrawal of Fritz Kreisler was now complete. He and Harriet went to Seal Harbor, Maine, to spend the summer of 1918.

At Seal Harbor they found kindred spirits and the freedom from anxiety and persecution that they had craved for so long. Before describing the Seal Harbor sojourn, however, it should be mentioned that Fritz Kreisler in this time of misunderstandings and hateful aspersions also had some pleasant surprises. Among other incidents, persons completely unknown to him were moved to write verse on hearing him during World War I.

There was, for example, Nathaniel Ferguson, a successful businessman in Reading, Pennsylvania, who wrote a poem of twelve stanzas which *The Musician* for March, 1917 thought worthy of printing in its columns. It was entitled, "When Kreisler Played," and began as follows:

> I heard Fritz Kreisler play tonight—
> His music made me mute,
> An orchestra in but one bow;
> With harp, oboe, and flute.

He touched the changing shores of sound
  Where sands of time are heaped;
And struck the waves of harmony
  Where shades of tone are steeped.

Another poem, "Fritz Kreisler Plays," by Grace Hazard Conkling, was published in *The Touchstone* in November, 1917. The following four lines are a fair sample:

Since music is your spirit's own,
Since you are overlord of tone,
Oh tell us, Master, you who know,
What secret way does music go?

A unique group of musical stars vacationed at Seal Harbor during the summer of 1917. Josef Hofmann, Carl Friedberg, Ossip Gabrilówitsch, Leopold Godowsky, Walter and Frank Damrosch, Leopold Stokowski and his wife, Olga Samaroff, Harold Bauer, Ernest Schelling, Carlos Salzédo, Fannie Bloomfield-Zeisler—these were some of the colleagues with whom Kreisler could associate there. Fritz and Harriet had, as a matter of fact, also spent the summers of 1915 and 1916 in this New England summer resort.

One might have expected that the air at Seal Harbor would be ringing with ensemble music—a repetition of the Paris experience of Ysaÿe, Kreisler, Thibaud, Casals, Enesco, and Pugno. Such, however, was not the case. Everybody was there for complete relaxation.

To Fritz and Harriet, Seal Harbor was especially dear because it reminded them of the scenery of Germany and Austria. Fond as they were of walking, this was a hiker's paradise. Even the colored signs on the trees which guided them in their wanderings reminded them of Switzerland and Central Europe.

Clara Clemens, only daughter of Mark Twain, has provided a vivid narrative of some of the exploits, in which Kreisler also figured, of this rare aggregation of musicians. In her *My Husband—Gabrilówitsch* she wrote in part: *

A remarkable assembly they formed, and were exceptionally vivacious in

* Reprinted from *My Husband—Gabrilówitsch* by Clara Clemens, by permission of Harper & Brothers, copyright, 1938, by Clara Clemens Gabrilówitsch.

Ossip Gabrilówitsch, 1878-1936

Leopold Stokowski, 1882-1977

the hospitable home of Walter and Margaret Damrosch, where everyone ignored general customs and initiated new ones. . . . Harold Bauer, for instance, though intellectually superior, could make faces that defied all competition. One dreamed—or rather nightmared—about them in sleep. . . . When the Schellings and Walter Damrosch added their bubbling mentalities to histrionic exhibitions, it was hard to say who was funniest.

Ossip . . . entered the house with not a hair left on his head. Shaved smooth. Gone—each lovely lock! Why had he done it? When would it grow? Did he mean to play in concerts looking like that? My consternation delighted Ossip and he proceeded to shatter the peace in other families where long-haired musicians lived.

The first to follow suit was Stokowski; then came Bauer; others also joined the cult and finally the colony was known as the convict camp. Someone was inspired to dramatize this hair-shedding plague and the scene was performed on a yachting party to the hilarious enjoyment of the audience:

Gabrilówitsch was discovered reveling in the comfort of his shorn locks and admiring the new shape of his head. Stokowski entered and noticing his confrère's transformation, tossed his hat into the air and triumphantly displayed his own glistening dome. They embraced in rapture when Bauer appeared with a haughty stride. Seeing his companions' ecstasy he flung his hat overboard and joined the others in a wild dance of exultation. Who then should appear but the heavy-maned Carl Friedberg, with a self-confident, self-preening mane that aroused the brute in the three bald gentlemen and with one leap they pounced on the newcomer, determined to operate at once.

But Friedberg was equal to the emergency. With a graceful flourish he thrust a contract into their hands that disclosed a concert engagement he had to play during the summer. Naturally without his hair he would have no success, and so his enemies retreated, just as Josef Hofmann stepped onto the stage courageously exhibiting a complete head of hair. This was scandalous indeed! No soft treatment here! Off with the scalp! Throw him into the sea! A noisy attack and then—lo and behold, Hofmann became eloquent. He implored them to remember his poor health, his children, and above all the millions of circulars that had been printed and paid for representing him as he normally looked. Or did the convicts—perhaps—intend to pay for a *new* circular?

Before they could recover from this shock, a bold creature with forests of hair on his head, stalked in as though he were the chief of anarchists. Fritz Kreisler it was, and no mistake. Like infuriated beasts the trio fell upon him, but he was a match for them. Like Hofmann, Kreisler used the overwhelming weapon of pathos. With tears in his eyes and trembling hands, he pointed to his World-War wounds and routed the savages in this capillary slaughter.

The strictly chronological sequence of events will now be interrupted to recall another hilarious party, twenty-three years later, at which Albert Spalding and Jascha Heifetz were the comedians and Fritz Kreisler the butt of their joke.

The Bohemians, New York musicians' club, is wont to honor outstanding musicians from time to time with receptions and dinner parties, in the course of which excellent music is produced and some speeches, usually of a humorous nature, are delivered. Among the many musicians of distinction whom the Bohemians have singled out in the course of years are Gustav Mahler, Engelbert Humperdinck, Arturo Toscanini, Victor Herbert, Ignace Paderewski, Artur Nikisch, Karl Muck, Serge Prokofieff, Eugène Ysaÿe, Sergei Rachmaninoff, Ferruccio Busoni, Marcella Sembrich, Josef Hofmann, Carl Flesch, Leopold Auer, Pablo Casals, and Mischa Elman. The list could be extended indefinitely.

Kreisler had been honored by the Bohemians with a "Reception and Supper, Ladies' Evening," as far back as December 6, 1913, at which music was rendered by the University Mixed Quartet, Carlos Salzédo, Michael von Zador, and the Longy New York Modern Chamber Music Ensemble. Also, his string quartet, composed early in 1919, had been played for the first time in America by the Letz Quartet after a dinner by the Bohemians in honor of Alma Gluck-Zimbalist and Efrem Zimbalist on April 26, 1919.

The dinner in honor of Fritz Kreisler, during which Heifetz and Spalding played their joke, took place on December 22, 1940, at the Waldorf-Astoria Hotel. Ernest Hutcheson, president of the Bohemians, and Albert Spalding were the speakers, and Gregor Piatigorsky and Lotte Lehmann, the soloists. At the large guest table with Fritz and Harriet, besides the speakers and soloists—to mention only a few—were the Adolf Busches, the Walter Damrosches, the Mischa Elmans, the Emanuel Feuermanns, the Carl Friedbergs, the Jascha Heifetzes, the Alexander Kipnises, the Josef Lhevinnes, the Emanuel Lists, the Yehudi Menuhins, the Sergei Rachmaninoffs, the Theodore E. Steinways, the Joseph Szigetis, Raya Garbousova, and Fabien Sevitzky. Charles Foley was also at their table.

Hans Letz, 1887-1969

The Letz Quartet

Gregor Piatigorsky, 1903-1976

"THE BOHEMIANS"

(NEW YORK MUSICIANS CLUB)

•

DINNER IN HONOR OF

FRITZ KREISLER

•

SUNDAY, DECEMBER TWENTY-SECOND
Nineteen Hundred and Forty
WALDORF-ASTORIA

Program for the Bohemians dinner in honor of Fritz Kreisler

"THE BOHEMIANS"

(NEW YORK MUSICIANS CLUB)

Administration 1940 - 1941

34th Season

OFFICERS

Ernest Hutcheson..........President
Willem Willeke..........Vice-President
Francis Rogers..........Vice-President
Georges Barrère..........Vice-President
Walter L. Bogert..........Secretary
Carl Deis..........Treasurer

BOARD OF GOVERNORS

Adolfo Betti
Clyde Burrows
Gaston M. Dethier
James Friskin
Paolo Gallico
Hugo Grunwald
Edwin Hughes
Marshall Kernochan

•

THE MUSICIANS FOUNDATION, INC.

Willem Willeke..........President
Walter W. Naumburg..........Vice-President
Emil Goldmark..........Recording Secretary
Carl Deis..........Secretary-Treasurer

BOARD OF DIRECTORS

Harold Bauer
Hugo Grunwald
Lewis M. Isaacs
Marshall Kernochan

SPEAKERS

ERNEST HUTCHESON

ALBERT SPALDING

●

onatina .... Mozart

Andanto Minuetto Rondo

ntroduction et Polonaise Brillante .... Chopin

GREGOR PIATIGORSKY, Violoncello

VALENTIN PAVLOVSKY, at the Piano

●

n die Musik .... Schubert

ie Post .... Schubert

er Nussbaum .... Schumann

) liebliche Wangen .... Brahms

he Shepherd's Madrigal .... Kreisler

he Whole World Knows .... Kreisler

MME. LOTTE LEHMANN, Soprano

PAUL ULANOWSKY, at the Piano

●

... AN EXTRAVAGANZA ...

Dedicated to a Great Master
by two of his admiring
and affectionate colleagues

(All characters herein represented are purely imaginary
and have no reference whatsoever to actual people)

●

Dancing in East Foyer

Entertainment Committee

CARL DEIS, Chairman
JAMES FRISKIN
CLYDE BURROWS

Kreisler (center) with George Barrère (left) and Ernest Hutcheson at the dinn

Kreisler (center) with Albert Spalding (left) and Jascha Heifetz after the prog

After announcing the menu and the musical numbers, the program continued:

. . . AN EXTRAVAGANZA . . .
Dedicated to a Great Master
by two of his admiring
and affectionate colleagues
(All characters herein represented are purely
imaginary and have no reference whatsoever
to actual people)

The curtain went up. The diners could not believe their eyes: Were they seeing double, or what? At the head table they saw Fritz Kreisler; on the stage was another Fritz Kreisler, with the movements and mannerisms that every concertgoer who has heard him knows.

The soloist on the stage worked hard, but not a tone issued from his instrument. And yet the diners heard a typical Kreisler performance, note for note, of a Chopin Mazurka as arranged by the guest of honor.

As if by accident, the curtain was suddenly drawn back further than it should have been. The audience saw a man in shirt sleeves and suspenders, with his back to the audience and facing a music stand, who was playing the Chopin-Kreisler Mazurka as nearly like the phonograph recording which Kreisler himself had made as it was humanly possible for one artist to imitate or copy another.

Again as if by accident, the shirt-sleeved fiddler, whose motions matched those of the "Kreisler" in the center of the stage and the Kreisler at the guest table, turned about to see whence the hilarity that visibly irritated him was coming. When he noticed the distinguished audience, he fled like a scared rabbit, the mute Fritz Kreisler II disappearing with him.

"Spalding had been made up exactly like Fritz by the *friseur* of the Metropolitan Opera," Jascha Heifetz explained. "He had soaped his bow so that not a single tone came from his fiddle. I, however, stood slightly offstage, with my back to the audience, and imitated Kreisler's own recording of his arrangement of the Chopin composition. Fritz nearly laughed his head off."

Following this bit of buffoonery, the two artists became serious and offered the audience distinctive performances. "Spalding and I,"

Heifetz said, "made a number of arrangements, among them Kreisler's 'Liebesfreud' and 'Liebesleid,' for two violins. Also, Albert transcribed the Tartini-Kreisler Variations for us to play as a violin duo, and I arranged the slow movement of Kreisler's Quartet in A Minor for two violins. Fritz seemed so pleased that he said afterward it sounded as though a quartet had played."

Two other amusing incidents of a distinguished artist "ribbing" Kreisler were told by Carl Lamson. Everybody knows that Fritz was about as tired of having to respond to the demand for his "Caprice viennois" as Paderewski was of his Menuet and Rachmaninoff of his Prelude. One day in Boston, Kreisler had finished his regular program and the mad clamor for encores set in. High above all other voices rose what seemed to be a teen-age boy's strident falsetto: " 'Caprice viennois,' 'Caprice viennois.' " It was so insistent and it so effectively started others in a demand for this most often played "Kreisleriana" that the composer-violinist, with a weary smile in the direction of Lamson, returned to the platform to play it for the nth time.

Lamson learned soon enough who owned the improvised falsetto: it was Jacques Thibaud, who "knew his old friend's dislike for old chestnuts" and had played a practical joke!

On another occasion Kreisler felt for his mute in his vest pocket. As he pulled it out, a dime dropped to the floor. Quipped the irrepressible Thibaud, who was sitting in the front row: "Look out, Fritz, you're losing your fee."

After this digression, let us go back to Seal Harbor and the summer of 1917.

It was by no means all play at Seal Harbor. The European war was ever uppermost in Fritz Kreisler's mind. He devoured every news dispatch from Europe avidly. His sensitive soul suffered with the suffering millions in that war-torn Continent.

Instead of composing heavy, serious music, as he thought he would when he went into musical exile, he found relief in the lighter muse. He began work on his operetta *Apple Blossoms*. It is one of two comic operas he has composed, the other being *Sissy*, written in 1932.

The genesis of *Apple Blossoms* is interesting. Harriet and Fritz

Jacques Thibaud in the early 1900's

Jascha Heifetz, Efrem Zimbalist, Alma Gluck, and Kreisler at Fishers Island in 1919

were the house guests of Efrem Zimbalist and his wife Alma Gluck, at Fishers Island off the coast of Connecticut. Zimbalist and Kreisler, according to the former, agreed to try their hands at a comic opera. The result was Kreisler's *Apple Blossoms*, which was produced first and ran for over a year on Broadway, and Zimbalist's *Honeydew*, which also had a very fine run.

Though *Apple Blossoms* was started during Fritz's involuntary exile, it was, for obvious reasons, not produced until almost a year after the Armistice of November 11, 1918.

The music is not entirely Kreisler's. Assisting him was Victor Jacobi, a writer of light comic opera, who contributed eight of the nineteen musical numbers while two are ascribed to the two co-writers jointly. The book and lyrics were by William Le Baron. It is an operetta in three acts. The cast consists of these parts:

Polly Stewart	Annabelle Mason	Harvey
Julie	Molly	Philip Campbell
Nancy Dodge	Johnny	Mrs. Anne Merton
Dickie Stewart	Chauffeur	Premier Danseur
Lucy Fielding	Uncle George	Première Danseuse

Schoolgirls, Bridesmaids, Ushers, and so forth.

Act I takes place in the garden of Castle Hall School, Clifton-on-Hudson; Act II at Philip Campbell's house near Fifth Avenue, New York; Act III in the ballroom. The time is the present. In Act III Kreisler's "Tambourin chinois" is introduced as an additional number.

The story was summed up for theatergoers:

In a garden at a fashionable girls' school, Castle Hall, Dickie Stewart ostensibly calls on his sister, Polly. Actually he visits the school to see Nancy Dodge, Polly's best friend. In the midst of Dickie's proposal to Nancy, her uncle appears and carries her off to marry Philip Campbell. Nancy hasn't seen Philip since her childhood.

On their wedding day, neither Nancy nor Philip take the event seriously. The bride receives a letter from Dickie in which he vows he will overlook her marriage and continue to love her. The bridegroom receives an equally endearing message from a young widow.

After the ceremony, Nancy tells her husband about Dickie and Philip tells her about the young widow. They hardly finish their stories before Dickie arrives, followed shortly by the young widow. The honeymoon becomes a

convention. Nancy's uncle, seeing that his ideas about marriage are too old-fashioned, revises them during an effort to keep Philip and Nancy together. He now does his best to bring about a divorce, but the bride and groom find married life more pleasant than they had expected. They stay married, much to the uncle's happiness.

The story was to Kreisler's liking not only because it gave him a chance to extend himself in beautiful valse tunes but also because he likes the theater as a form of amusement and not as a means of solving problems or raising pertinent questions. Also, this master of classic interpretation believes in the comic opera per se. He does not turn up his nose at it, but regards it as a true form of art.

"An operetta is a homogeneous work in which everything is based on a central idea," he said. "No work of art can be without that. There should be dramatic impulse, good scenic effects, and a romantic touch. It should be a combination of musical charm and dramatic idea. Art is not great because it is austere, and you cannot measure it by its seriousness. A good operetta deserves its place in art. Art in itself is in a large part accidental. At least it is involuntary."

Referring specifically to *Apple Blossoms*, Kreisler revealed to the New York *Times* on October 12, 1919:

"I'm very fond of light music. I adore waltzes and have always wanted to write them. Into an operetta one can put all the fire and verve, all the charm and color, which have made this form of entertainment so popular abroad. We are not pioneers. Gilbert and Sullivan, Victor Herbert, Reginald De Koven showed what can be done. And the public greeted them with delight. In the meantime, too often musical comedy has been so vulgarized that many have lost sight of its artistic possibilities.

"I admit that I wrote my part of *Apple Blossoms* quite as much for my own sake as for the public. Torn and weary with the sorrow of war, I fought my own depression in the work of composition. It was the only thing which saved me. In seeking to write songs which should amuse people and make them happy, if only for a moment, I found I could forget myself.

"You must not speak of 'the Kreisler work,' however. Mr. Jacobi must have at least what you call in this country 'fifty-fifty.' His love duet in the second act is entrancing. I should be proud to say that I had written it."

Although Kreisler had been compelled by the prevailing war hysteria to request Charles Dillingham to let him out of his contract, it was Dillingham, nevertheless, who acted as producer when *Apple Blossoms* went on the boards of the Globe Theater, New York, beginning on October 7, 1919.

Kreisler took a most active interest in the preparations for the production. Victor Jacobi gave a graphic description to the New York *Times*:

"It was no uncommon sight to see the famous violinist with a dozen of the beauties of the chorus clustered around him as he hummed a bit of refrain, marking time with the nervous right hand which has thrilled thousands as it wields a violin bow. Or, again, to see him sweep aside the man on the piano stool with an impatient gesture and seat himself, to swing into a dashing accompaniment for a pair of little dancers who remained quite unmoved at the extraordinary spectacle of a world genius willingly accepting suggestions as to tempo, while they went through their steps without a quiver.

"At these rehearsals Kreisler would play not only the score itself, but snatches of music ranging from a Beethoven concerto to the latest popular syncopation."

Came the night of the première, October 7, 1919. Heywood Broun, writing for the New York *Tribune* the morning after, commented:

It is good music, pleasant to hear, melodious and interpretive of the lyrics. Some of it is exciting . . . all in all, the new operetta is pleasant, high class entertainment. . . .

Kreisler was tumultuously applauded. That seemed to us the most gratifying event of the evening. We were glad to observe that the war on violinists has ended.

The critic for the New York *Times* added that Wilda Bennett as Nancy nearly fainted backstage at the thought that Kreisler himself was present at the opening night!

Three now well known artists found it decidedly to their advantage to have appeared in the original cast of *Apple Blossoms*: Adele and Fred Astaire, as Molly and Johnny, literally danced into fame to the tunes of Kreisler waltzes, and John Charles Thomas became established as a singer of note through the fact that he was chosen to sing the role of Philip.

The *Times* society reporter gave this interesting information concerning the "Who's Who" of notables in attendance at the première:

> The name of Kreisler attracted . . . such an audience of musicians as rarely is seen in a theater. There were orchestra conductors Josef Stransky, Walter Damrosch, Edgar Varese, Theodore Spiering, and singers, such as John McCormack, Sophie Braslau, Andrea de Segurola, Paul Reimers, Herbert Witherspoon. Pianists present were Sergei Rachmaninoff, Ossip Gabrilówitsch, Alexander Lambert. Violinists were less observed, but there were those who discovered Franz Kneisel, Ysaÿe, Elman, Jascha Heifetz.
>
> Kreisler himself, in a dark corner furthest from the stage, had to be called out and finally dragged out to answer a curtain call with John Charles Thomas, Wilda Bennett, and Jacobi.

The operetta was produced in scores of American cities.

CHAPTER SEVENTEEN

THE COMEBACK

[1919-1924]

WORLD WAR I ended with the armistice ceremony in the forest of Compiègne, France, on November 11, 1918. But peace with Germany did not come until June 28, 1919, when the Treaty of Versailles was signed in the Hall of Mirrors in Versailles, and peace with Austria was concluded at Saint-Germain even later, on September 10, 1919.

Kreisler made no effort to reappear in public during the interim between the Armistice at Compiègne and the signing of the peace treaties. But he saw no reason for not resuming his concert work during the season of 1919–1920. The Austro-Hungarian monarchy was now a thing of the past.

His first reappearance on the American concert platform occurred at Carnegie Hall, New York, on October 27, 1919. It was a benefit for the Vienna Children's Milk Relief, for which all the outstanding artists in New York and many of the city's socialites had bought boxes at $100 each. An overwhelming ovation was given him. For five minutes the audience stood, cheered, and applauded before he could begin, and the conclusion of every number was the signal for new and increasingly enthusiastic demonstrations. As the individual voices surged up to the podium, on which I chanced to sit, from the electrified crowd below, French, Italian, Spanish, Russian expressions were heard just as frequently and exultingly as were words in English or German. Wreaths were deposited on the platform in profusion. Encore after encore was demanded, until the management saw no other recourse save that of turning out the lights. It was, indeed, a rare triumph for a man whom war hysteria had forced off the stage, and an unforgettable scene for all of us who were privileged to attend.

Thus it seemed that Kreisler's comeback was an assured fact. It remained for a new, militant organization, born of the World War, to rob the distinguished Austrian of this illusion: the American Legion started a campaign to keep Kreisler off the American concert platform.

In Ithaca, New York, the legionnaires announced that if Cornell University persisted in having Kreisler play on December 9, they would storm the auditorium. The electric-light cable was cut while he was in the middle of a number; he calmly continued playing in total darkness.

The late Professor Paul R. Pope, who was at that time chairman of the music committee at Cornell, wrote me about the incident:

> I spoke to Kreisler during the intermission of the concert after the lights had been cut off and Kreisler had played his cadenza without a sign of nervousness until the usher came on the stage with a flashlight to light up the accompanist's music. Later I sat next to him at the Ithaca Hotel dinner, where we discussed incunabula and other rare books.
>
> The newspaper reports had got the affair twisted. They said that the Cornell students had staged a protest against Kreisler's playing in a university hall. On the contrary, the concert was sold out and the student athletes had been strategically distributed in and around the building to prevent any action on the part of any rowdies who might try to prevent the concert. The student stalwarts easily disposed of the rowdies, but someone was able to cut off the electricity temporarily. Kreisler was magnificent and completely calm when I spoke to him in the intermission.*

The New York branch of the Legion, thinking the Cornell episode un-American, invited Kreisler to participate in a benefit of theirs in the Hippodrome on December 28. Kreisler graciously accepted. But the Legion's national office ruled adversely, even though a general, Robert Alexander, had personally asked the Austrian ex-lieutenant to play!

In Lawrence, Massachusetts, the local American Legion Post an-

* The American Legionnaires of Ithaca made handsome amends to Kreisler fourteen years later, when they entertained him at their post and accorded him a rising tribute as he entered the concert hall in 1933.

nounced it would not interfere with the concert scheduled for the following day (November 23, 1919), but asked Kreisler not to play any German music!

The mayor of Lynn, Massachusetts, bowed to the American Legion and canceled the license for a Kreisler concert. Thereupon those in charge of arrangements obtained a state permit for a "sacred concert." The mayor next announced that he would have a jury of twelve musicians present at the concert to determine whether the visiting artist played anything but sacred music, and that he would have the police present to arrest him in case a worldly note crept into his performance! Kreisler would not make a fool of himself by bowing to such a regulation, and the concert at Lynn, like so many others, was canceled.

A celebrated case of Legion interference was that of Louisville, Kentucky, which the Louisville *Courier-Journal* characterized as "a test of the Americanism of everybody. One was either for the Legion and what it represents, or for an Austrian on tour." Louisville's response in preventing the concert, it thought, was "good for its soul."

Mrs. Lola Clay Naff of Nashville, Tennessee, was glad to pick up the available Louisville date, and her Kreisler concert in the Ryman Auditorium came off successfully.

The *Outlook* on December 24, 1919 entered the lists on behalf of Fritz Kreisler. It observed, concerning the attitude of the American Legion:

> Action of the enthusiasts . . . is not representative of a general sentiment, particularly among the men who actually went overseas and fought. True, he was an officer. But honorable. He fought because he owed allegiance to his country. He fought not as a Hun but as a man and gentleman. Now that his country is not only defeated but rendered powerless, Mr. Kreisler, like every other Austrian, ought to be considered on his record and merits as an individual. . . . Mr. Kreisler is primarily an artist. Those who do not wish to attend his concerts need not do so; but there is no public service to be rendered in preventing his appearance.

In Philadelphia two society women spearheaded a movement for a "silent protest" against Kreisler's appearance with the Philadelphia

Symphony Orchestra on January 9 and 10, 1920. But the Philadelphia concerts passed off without disturbance.

In Battle Creek, Michigan, the Ministerial Association launched so effective a protest that the Kreisler concert had to be canceled. Whether the pastors sought divine guidance before deciding upon their protest was not revealed.

At Pittsburgh, where the trouble had started in 1917 which ultimately led to Kreisler's banishment from the platform for the duration of the war, the first postwar concert was not even advertised for fear of hostile demonstrations. Yet the audience filled every seat in Carnegie Hall. Twenty patrolmen in plain clothes were scattered through the building. Nothing adverse happened. Appropriately enough, one of Kreisler's numbers that evening was C. C. White's arrangement of the negro spiritual "Nobody Knows the Trouble I See."

The music critic George Seibel, who was present, recalled, under the pseudonym of the "Quiet Observer" (Q. O.): *

Kreisler's admirers presented him with a laurel wreath the size of a wagon wheel, with a poetic tribute not up to the level of his concert. It was in "Austrian" *à la* Schiller, with an English translation by the Q. O.:

"To Fritz Kreisler:
"Ulysses' bow no other hand could conquer,
Nor Kreisler's bow another hand can wield:
So, when the Master fell in bloody battle,
Apollo raised o'er him his mighty shield.

"The lord of music, who with magic touches
Awakes the soul to rapture, sad or gay;
The patriot, who heard the trump of duty,
Him shall this wreath of laurel crown today."

But it was still deemed inadvisable to let him venture into the streets. Those were the days when the "*Caprice Viennois*" and *Wiener Schnitzel* were both dangerous to democracy; *Sauerkraut* became "Liberty Cabbage" and *Koenigsberger Klops* turned into "Kingsbury Clubs." Dachshunds were stoned in the street, and S. Monguio, a piano teacher of Spanish blood, was warned by the "Gestapo" not to eat *Sauerbraten* or teach pupils Schubert and Schumann. . . .

* Reprinted from *Kreisleriana* by George Seibel, in the December, 1946 issue of *Musical Forecast* of Pittsburgh, by permission of George Seibel and *Musical Forecast*.

After that mad tarantelle of war came that complication of remorse, repentance and headache known professionally as *Katzenjammer.*

Out in Duluth, Minnesota, where some "hyper-Americans" were likewise trying to stir up trouble, their efforts were squelched by an editorial in the Duluth *Tribune,* which reviewed Kreisler's services for marooned Allied musicians when America was neutral, then continued:

After war came to the United States, as well as before, he contributed to the Red Cross, in which his wife was a worker. He also . . . gave concerts in our cantonments to our soldiers, and that without charge.

Does it not impress all true Americans that a man whose music was American enough for our boys in khaki in the camps . . . is good enough and his violin American enough for all the rest of us?

Thus the battle of words raged to and fro concerning Fritz Kreisler. He himself retained that enviable imperturbability that is an integral part of his nature. "Little pinpricks" he called the attacks against him. The trouble he had been having was only to be expected, he said, as the "convulsive after effects" of World War I.

"In every case where I have been able to meet those who have objected to my being permitted to play, their opposition has passed immediately," he added. It was in the nature of news, he pointed out, for the public to read about the places where attacks were made on him, but not about the thirty or forty cities in which he was cordially received. "People have the idea that I am a hunted man. I'm not. They do not hear of the many times I'm welcomed."

Attacks or no attacks, Kreisler continued to play for charity in addition to making a livelihood. He participated, for instance, in a benefit concert for the Catholic Big Brothers at the Hippodrome, New York, given jointly with Frances Alda, the Metropolitan Opera star, and Mischa Levitzki, the pianist; also in a benefit for the Babies' Dairies Association at the Waldorf-Astoria Hotel, with himself as the soloist. In June, 1920, Fritz and Harriet sailed for Europe to aid in the distribution of food and clothing donated in America for relief in Austria. Naturally, he also wanted to see his aged father, now an invalid.

Before he left, however, he was called upon by a committee of

American citizens to define his attitude toward the United States and also to consider the possibility of becoming an American citizen. His reply, revealing the man Kreisler and what he stands for, answered specific questions:

The principles of true democracy are the basis of my political faith. I held these views and expressed them openly abroad at a time when their confession required a great deal more courage and self-abnegation than it does now. My feelings toward the United States of America are expressed in complete and whole-hearted endorsement of its political institutions; deep admiration for its generous and unselfish international policy; everlasting personal gratitude for individual and collective marks of hospitality, kindness, and friendship toward me.

There are two potent reasons why I have not reaffirmed this my sentimental allegiance to this country by a more significant and political allegiance, and I leave it to the fair judgment of your committee to pass upon their honorability.

In the first place, the country to which I belong has passed out of existence, with the exception of a small remnant which constitutes the Republic of Austria. As a native of Vienna I have automatically become a citizen of this small democracy, which just now is in the throes of abject misery and starvation. To sever under existing conditions my allegiance to that country would be an act of poor sportsmanship that no true American could possibly endorse.

In the second place, the personal advantages I would derive by becoming an American citizen are so obviously patent that it is repellent to me and incompatible with my true and deep respect for this country to brave the suspicion that I might be one of those who put their personal welfare above all else and thereby prejudice an act which, in my estimation, must be the outcome of a clear, deep conviction and chemically free from any other consideration.

I confess that in my actions I have been guided by the desire to appear in this country in the same light as every true American would like one of his countrymen to appear in my country were he placed in a similar position to mine. I can only repeat that as an artist I consider myself purely a messenger of a sublime principle expressed in the international language of music, and that I shall try honestly to fill this my vocation as long as my honor as a man and my ideal as an artist are untouched.

Kreisler's loyalty to his fatherland in the time of its greatest anguish led to a movement by some friends to suggest to the new republican Austrian government that he be made Austrian minister to America. Nothing was further from his thought than to enter upon a diplomatic

Kreisler, about 1920

ACADEMY OF MUSIC . . PHILADELPHIA

Saturday Afternoon, October 23, 1920, at 2.30

KREISLER

(Direction C. J. FOLEY)

PROGRAMME

I. Fantasy (for violin and piano) C-major (Op. 159) Fr. Schubert
(Andante molto—Allegretto—Theme and Variations
Tempo 1—Allegro vivace)

II. Concerto No. 4, D-minor (Op. 31) . . H. Vieuxtemps
Andante—Adagio religioso
Scherzo—Finale marziale

III. (a) Introduction and Scherzo-Caprice (for violin alone) . . . . Kreisler
(b) Siegfried Paraphrase . . . Wagner-Wilhelmj
(c) Valse Caprice . . . . . . Chabrier-Loeffler
(d) Hindoo Chant (from "Sadko") . Rimsky-Korsakoff
(e) Wienerisch . . . . Godowsky
(f) Two Caprices . . . . . . Paganini-Kreisler
1 B-minor
2 A-minor

CARL LAMSON, Accompanist

Tickets, $2.50, $2.00, $1.50, $1.00, 75 cents. Box seats. $2.50, on sale now. Mail orders to Geo. T. Haly, care of Heppe's, 1119 Chestnut Street, promptly filled.

STEINWAY PIANO USED

Program for a Kreisler concert in 1920

career, even though his friend Paderewski had become Polish premier and was in the very thick of politics and diplomacy.

"My friends," he laughingly recalled, "knew that Karl Renner, the chancellor, and Vienna's burgomaster, Karl Seitz, were old acquaintances of mine who would undoubtedly have supported the move. I was told that with my beautiful wife I would go places as a diplomat. I told them that Harriet was so straightforward that she would never do for the double talk of diplomacy. Then my friends tried to tempt me with the advantage of having a diplomatic passport. I retorted, 'You forget that Apollo signed my passport.' "

When Kreisler returned for the concert season of 1920–1921 sold-out houses and enthusiastically cheering crowds were again the order of the day for him.

More than that, early in 1921 he received a tempting offer: the St. Louis Symphony Orchestra asked him to become its conductor. Many virtuosos, if offered the opportunity, accept such a call eagerly as a chance to show the musical world how they believe the great works for orchestra should be interpreted.

Kreisler never had the ambition to exchange the violin for the baton. "You must have the 'it' to be a successful orchestra conductor," he said, "and I never felt I was predestined for such a career." He wrote George D. Markham, chairman of the board, from Chicago on March 17, 1921, declining on the grounds that "I have contracted for appearances as a violinist for almost two years ahead, which engagements will, of course, have to be faithfully carried out. This disposes of any possibility of accepting a permanent engagement for the present."

A second country that had a great claim on Kreisler's affection was England. It was natural that he should yearn for the day when he could measure the postwar temper of the British people toward himself and his art.

An almost unbelievable and certainly unparalleled reception was given Kreisler when he appeared on the podium of Queen's Hall on May 4, 1921, to resume his solo performance.

The *Daily Express* reported:

Kreisler came, he played and he conquered. He received the reward of Caesars. At the close of the Vivaldi and Viotti concertos Dame Nellie Melba and Mr. Albert Sammons—England's leading violinist—presented him with laurel wreaths.

The final *dénouément* was simply hero worship. Men and women waved hats and handkerchiefs. At length, after a demonstration lasting a quarter of an hour during which few left the hall, Kreisler stepped to the front with a single red rose in his hand and in a low voice said: "I thank you very much. I am too overcome to say more. Thank you."

The *Sunday Times* musicologist added this touch:

He gave us such violin playing as we have not heard for years. . . . The audience's reception of him was something to restore much of the idealism and the belief in human nature that we have lost during the last few years.

The *Daily Graphic* went more into the political aspects of Kreisler's comeback:

Kreisler, the great Austrian violinist, wafted us up to the heavens yesterday on the wings of the magic of his music. . . . Those people who think there should be forever a wave of unspoken hatred between enemy people and ourselves may take a lesson from yesterday's wonderful reception, of which Fritz Kreisler was the hero.

But what of the meticulous, austere critic Ernest Newman? Here are his words:

The scene in Queen's Hall was the most extraordinary I have ever witnessed. . . . In the whole of my concert going career I can recall no such welcome to any artist. . . . Kreisler comported himself through it all with the simple dignity one might have expected of him. . . . Kreisler is greater than ever. There is not a violinist in the world who can approach him.

In no human community, however, are all people of like mind. There were writers in London, albeit very few, who were critical, not of the artist as artist, but of the welcome extended to an Austrian. As an example, the critic of the *Musical Standard* wrote:

I consider it [the hero worship] a veritable disgrace to the hall in which it took place, to the public taking part in it, and to our general musical sensibilities. For there can be no doubt that, had the soloist been of our own blood, and the audience uninfluenced by totally extraneous considerations to the music, such a scene would not have been witnessed. . . . The fact is, certain of our petty cult-followers and would-be intelligentsia do not realize that this sort of thing is only an inverted jingoism, and equally vulgar and repulsive.

Ardent zeal for Fritz Kreisler, far from having spent itself at that first reappearance in Queen's Hall, continued throughout his four recitals that marked his stay in London.

In retrospect Kreisler's London triumph seems quite natural and easy. One must not forget, however, that events might well have turned out differently. Kreisler himself confessed that his walk onto the platform of Queen's Hall was "the tensest moment of his career," and that he had visions of eggs being thrown at him. His wife recalled that certain London papers so pointedly used nothing but photographs of her husband in Austrian officer's uniform in the advance publicity that the conductor of the evening was hesitant about stepping onto the podium because he had received intimations that a hand grenade might be thrown.

Archer Wallace thought he had discovered the secret to Kreisler's unexampled London comeback: *

He [Kreisler] once said, "No man can accomplish great things unless he has a heart full of love"; and so that is why, when the World War ended, the people of London gave Fritz Kreisler one of the greatest receptions ever accorded a visiting musician. They know that the finest thing about this man is his strong and tender love for all humanity.

Kreisler's "strong and tender love for all humanity" manifested itself positively during the memorable London days of 1921. A writer in the *Daily Telegraph* stated that he was eager to obtain Kreisler's opinion on the violins made by ex-service men at the Polytechnic Institute in Islington. "It is hardly necessary to point out that Kreisler, the greatest violinist of our time, had had very exceptional opportunities of knowing the worth and quality of all the best violins made today," the writer observed. "With characteristic courtesy Mr. Kreisler acceded at once to my request."

Kreisler's reply read:

The violin you sent me and which I understand was made by disabled

* Reprinted from *Hands Around the World* by Archer Wallace, by permission of Harper & Brothers, Publishers, copyright, 1930, by Richard R. Smith, Inc.

soldiers at the "Music Training Center" has an excellent tone quality and the workmanship is surprisingly good considering the short training the men have received. It is to be hoped that the public will generously support this commendable effort.

Effective use was made of this endorsement in admonishing the public to buy these British fiddles.

When Kreisler started for the British Isles from New York in April, 1921, he had carried in his baggage the String Quartet in A Minor which had been privately performed in April, 1919, at the Bohemian Club dinner in honor of Alma Gluck and Efrem Zimbalist.

The London Symphony Quartet was glad to offer this composition to the Londoners in a recital on May 9, 1921. Among the musical celebrities who, according to the press, attended the première were Sir Edward Elgar, Sir Henry Wood, Frederic Lamond, Albert Sammons, and Benno Moiseiwitsch. Each movement was loudly applauded, and at the close the composer was recalled many times.*

The critic of the *Daily Telegraph* came closest to understanding what the composer meant to convey in the quartet. He wrote in part:

There are four orthodox movements. Of these the first is a curious, tragic fantasia, in which the cello seems to be asking some profound question that the remaining strings answer with a pathetic but at times a joyous humor. Then there is a burst of purest happiness in the fascinating scherzo, the lightheartedness of which is most attractive. On this again there follows a piquant romance, and on this an amazing dance of pure Viennese color which, however, is interrupted by the cello's questionings once more, and the pathetic reply of the other strings. The final note is that of tragedy and pathos intermingled with the outbursts of frivolity and fun.

Is there perhaps a story attached to the quartet? Is it Vienna—Vienna in the lively, lovely days and in all its tragedy, or is it the Viennese, then and now? Is it personal to the composer?

It is all three: it is Vienna and the Viennese, then and now; it is most decidedly personal to Fritz Kreisler. "Es ist mein Bekenntnis zu

* Discussing the quartet forty years after its first performance, Kreisler said: "It is played a great deal in South America but, strangely enough, not in the United States. It is also often to be found on chamber music programs in Australia. I made a recording of it with William Primrose, violist; Laurie Kennedy, cellist, and Thomas Petrie (who has died meanwhile), second violinist."

Wien" (It is my avowal of Vienna), he said to me, using his native German rather than the language of our country, as he wanted me to know precisely what the quartet stands for. And indeed, no English translation can quite convey the thought.

The unique position Kreisler now held in England was epitomized by an appeal which the learned musicologist Percy A. Scholes addressed to Kreisler in the *Observer* for May 12, 1921, in the course of which he apostrophized the returned Austrian as a man who wields the power of life and death in the musical world. It is an unusually interesting document, entitled, "Kreisleriana," and merits partial quotation:

> In London music Kreisler is the hero of the moment.
>
> If in what follows I seem to make still further demands on this great player I must not be understood as depreciating the value of what he has already done for us.
>
> The first question I have to ask is this: Cannot Kreisler do something to help us to widen the violinist repertoire? . . . Our public performers seem to me to narrow down unnecessarily the circle from which they choose pieces they play to us. To take a few examples, why always the *Chaconne?* . . . What of the modern classics? And what of the younger composers who are trying to get a footing? Are any of these worthy of Kreisler's help?
>
> There is another matter in which Kreisler might help us greatly: the matter of applause. We have a bad habit in this country which Kreisler can help us to kill, that of clapping in the wrong place. . . . Last week we forced Kreisler to break . . . the performance of the Franck *Sonata.* But should he allow himself to be thus forced?

Quite an unusual occurrence: the national of one country asks the national of another—and that, too, very recently an "enemy" country—to help cure the defects of his people!

Of the many social engagements in Kreisler's crowded London calendar of May, 1921, there is one event that looms especially large in his wife's mind.

David Lloyd George, who was very musical, gave a party for the Welsh Singers, and invited the Kreislers, too, to this event, which happened to fall on the day on which he and the Irish leader Eamon de Valera had finally agreed on a treaty for the establishment of an Irish Free State.

Lloyd George had always regretted that his duties had prevented him from attending a Kreisler concert. Harriet therefore thought it a gracious idea to have Fritz bring his violin to the party and to have his accompanist, Haddon Squire, also in readiness. After the Welsh Singers had performed, she told the British prime minister that her husband had a surprise in store for him: he would play.

"Lloyd George was delighted," Harriet remembered. "After Fritz had rendered three or four numbers, I said to him, 'Why not play the "Londonderry Air"?' Fritz had heard a street fiddler play it in Dublin and had hastily scratched down the tune on a piece of paper. To it he had that very day added a sketchy accompaniment on the same slip of paper.

"Somehow Haddon Squire was able to figure out the accompaniment and the 'Air' was played.

"Lloyd George then asked for attention, and said to those present: 'I realize that you must be awfully tired having me deliver speeches. But I'm going to make one more. All I want to say is that if this air had been played six months earlier by Kreisler, the treaty with Ireland could have been concluded six months earlier.' "

After his great comeback in the British Isles, Kreisler went to the Continent in the summer of 1921, chiefly to Germany. His String Quartet was performed in Berlin by Professor Karl Klingler's ensemble in December of that year. Kreisler also arranged for a number of personal appearances in Berlin, for none of which did he take a fee, for all were devoted to charitable purposes. When he played with Berlin's famous Philharmonic Orchestra, the proceeds went to that struggling organization. When he played his own recital, the beneficiary usually was the Mutterhilfe (Mother's Aid), sponsored by Harriet. This organization also profited by many concerts he gave in the German provinces. In the midst of the suffering and privation of a beaten country, the Mutterhilfe established soup kitchens in various sections of Berlin and other population centers. Whenever he was in Berlin, Fritz would visit these kitchens, talking to the impoverished, underfed children and distributing chocolate to them.

In October, 1921, there was a terrible mine explosion at Oppau, in Upper Silesia. No sooner had the Kreislers read of it, than Harriet telephoned the *Berliner Tageblatt* that her husband would play a benefit concert for the Oppau victims. Would the noted liberal daily appeal to the population to contribute money, clothing, bedding, linens, and other necessities for the relief of distress in Oppau? The newspaper gladly cooperated, and not only was the benefit concert a sellout, but bundles upon bundles of things similar to those which the stricken families had lost were delivered to the *Tageblatt* offices.

That concert took place on October 28, 1921. Two weeks previously Kreisler had been in Vienna, where the Lord Mayor of his native city conferred the title of professor upon him, saying, "for you have long been known to us Viennese as an excellent *professor caritatis et humanitatis*."

On November 25 Kreisler played again in Berlin for charity, this time for the children of Upper Silesia. The concert was again a sellout. A few months later he contributed the proceeds of a concert to enable especially gifted students of the Hochschule für Musik in Berlin to continue their studies. The critic Heinz Pringsheim wrote:

> I suppose the people are still applauding. At any rate it looked, after I left the Philharmonie after the nth encore, as though the thick walls of an enthusiastic public would never give in.

Harriet and Fritz returned to America on January 18, 1922, for a four-months round of concerts. The artist's appearances were by no means limited to big cities. Kreisler has always been meticulous about giving smaller communities an opportunity to hear his message. Thus Peoria, Illinois, and Richmond, Virginia, were included in his itinerary. One of the numbers then appearing on his program was a "Melodie" by General Charles G. Dawes, who became Vice President of the United states in 1925. Later Fritz told the story of how he came to play it: *

> Ten years ago I was looking through a great bundle of music sent for my consideration by a Chicago publisher. I came across a little piece that immediately took my fancy because of its tunefulness and its strong musical value. I called my wife and played it for her. She liked it, too. I accepted it for my

* Reprinted from *He Plays on the World's Heartstrings* by Beverly Smith in the February, 1931 issue of the *American Magazine*, by permission of Beverly Smith and the Crowell-Collier Publishing Company, copyright, 1931, by *American Magazine*.

program the next year. The piece was simply marked "Dawes." I never associated the name with that of the general.

The next year, when I met General Dawes, he informed me that I was making him famous. I was astonished and pleased. It was an especial pleasure for me to play the Ambassador's piece in London last spring.*

It goes without saying that there were no more anti-Kreisler demonstrations. When the Kreisler couple sailed for Hamburg on May 3, 1922, to take the cures in Carlsbad, rest in the Engadine, and tour Venice and points on the Dalmatian coast, they could depart with the comforting feeling that Fritz's dramatic comeback, in America as well as in Europe, was complete, except for Paris and France.

The reconquest of Fritz's "spiritual home" was not attempted until the autumn of 1924. Why so late? Fritz Kreisler had a good reason:

"I can remember a concert that I attended in Paris, in 1887, when I was a boy. It was learned by the audience that one of the musicians, who had been announced as a Bohemian, was really a German, and he was booed from the stage. That was seventeen years after the war of 1870 between Germany and France. The bitterness of those years was nothing, I am afraid, compared to now."

He therefore bided his time and let five years elapse after the signing of the peace treaty, before attempting to concertize again in Paris.

Even in 1924 not all Parisians were ready to forgive and forget that the Austrian violinist had fought on the opposite side. Perhaps the date selected for the first recital was unfortunate: Armistice Day, November 11. Kreisler had meant his initial performance as a gesture of reconciliation, but this gesture was as little appreciated as was the sculptor Émil Derré's marble group "Reconciliation," to the showing of which in the annual 1924 art exhibition chauvinistic French super-

* Mr. Dawes had become Ambassador to the Court of St. James in 1929; Kreisler played the "Melodie" in London in 1930, precisely as written by Dawes, without alteration or adaptation. The New York *Times* reported on May 21, 1930:

"Charles G. Dawes, the diplomat, was introduced to London tonight in the unfamiliar role of music composer. Prime Minister MacDonald was present for the debut in London music of the ambassador. 'Melodie' was one of the chief attractions of Fritz Kreisler's first London concert. He played it for the first time tonight abroad. He even played it twice.

"Ambassador Dawes sat in the audience looking immensely pleased with the performance. He looked a little self-conscious when people sitting near by recognized him."

patriots objected, so that it had to be moved to an inconspicuous place.

Kreisler's concert, too, was shifted to a less conspicuous date, November 9.

The first reappearance after an absence of ten years was an undeniable success of the first order. A great crowd at the Opéra "cheered him for hours," the press reported. The expected nationalistic disturbances did not occur. *Le Courrier musical et théatral* of Paris devoted the cover of its issue of November 15 to a photograph of Fritz, and one of its editors, Raymond Balliman, wrote:

> M. Kreisler . . . has returned even greater—though this might seem impossible—than he was.
>
> The vast auditorium of the Opéra was *comble* [chock-full]. The success of Mr. Kreisler was triumphal during that remarkable evening when we were in the presence of a master who left most of his confrères, even the most celebrated, far behind him.

A second concert at the Grand Opéra followed. A noted French violinist, Yvonne Astruc, reported for the *Courrier*. She wrote in part:

> I went to the Opéra not without emotion. Twelve years had elapsed since I last attended a Kreisler concert. It was an unforgettable *soirée*, which brought us a joy the impression of which will long remain with us as a fruitful precept [*enseignement fécond*] not only for violinists but for all who are devoted to their art.

More than ever, she continued, the recital of November 15 made her realize what the personality of an *artiste de génie* can do to an entire hall of listeners. She had wondered, she said, whether Kreisler had changed, whether her own attitude had changed, whether the same things that used to charm her would now still charm her. But she was not disappointed.

> The auditorium of the Opéra, absolutely jammed, bore testimony to the ardor and zeal of a public predominantly cosmopolitan. On the platform which, in accordance with a delicate thought of M. Kreisler, was reserved for his old comrades of the Paris Conservatoire and for those who lost their eyesight in the war, there was a spirit of fraternity aflame with enthusiasm. . . . He himself seemed to be seized by intense emotion, and the wonderful expression of kindness that illuminated his features made a striking contrast with his imposing stature.

Truly, the last objective of his comeback had been attained. In Paris, too, Kreisler had triumphed. Less than two years later he was made an officer of the French Legion of Honor.

In the French-speaking section of Switzerland, in Geneva, the impresario who had engaged Kreisler became frightened at the initial protests of the French metropolitan press and canceled the concert. Thereupon an enterprising promoter in the little resort town of Vevey, at the other end of Lake Leman, snapped up the date, hired the largest hall available, and advertised the concert throughout the resort region —at Montreux, Territet, Villeneuve, Glion, Caud, Clarens, Lausanne, and of course also Geneva. The result was a sellout. Michael Rauch-eisen wrote me: "All Geneva seemed to be on its way to Vevey. In all my life I have not seen a cavalcade of automobiles like that on the Geneva-Vevey highway."

Busy and nerve-racking though the struggle for a comeback had been, Kreisler nevertheless took out time for one of the few major literary efforts of his career. He wrote "Music and Life" for *The Mentor* late in 1921. It is an article so full of lofty ideas and keen observations that it will follow directly as a separate chapter.

CHAPTER EIGHTEEN

MUSIC AND LIFE

By Fritz Kreisler

[1921]

"*All one's life is music, if one touches the notes rightly and in time.*"—Ruskin.

LIFE begins and ends with music. It envelops and permeates the world we live in. Land, water, and sky are full of elemental music of many kinds and degrees of intensity. The wind sings through the responsive leaves, and plays on the harp-strings of the waving reeds by the rivers; birds pour forth their lyric tunes to charm the waking morn; and the ocean waves swell in rhythmic chorus as if at the command of a master conductor.

The potency of music has been acknowledged in all ages and by all races. And it was so from the beginning of time. It is said that long, long ago Orpheus charmed all things animate and inanimate with the strains of his lyre. He even went down to Pluto's domain, Hades, and coaxed back the soul of his dead and lost love Eurydice with his music. And everyone knows of the Sirens who bewitched sailors with their songs in the Grecian Isles, and the Lorelei maiden on the rock above the Rhine.

This suggests the thought, often stated, that good music ennobles and bad music degrades. It seems clear to me, however, that there is only one kind of music, and that is *good* music. When music can be called bad, it ceases to be music. It simply becomes rhythmic noise.

I do not think that music, in itself, produces good or bad effects, but rather that it enhances and intensifies existing ideas and instincts, good or bad. To a man in love, music may deepen the feeling of romance; a man suffering from melancholia may have his sorrows dyed a shade deeper; a warrior may have a heightened feeling of war fever. In this connection music may be compared to *hasheesh.* That powerful drug produces good or bad dreams in keeping with the mental condition and environment of the drugtaker. In a room furnished in good taste, he dreams of things beautiful, but in ghastly surroundings he dreams frightful dreams. That alluring composition, *Humoresque,* to a religious man may mean devotional ecstasy; to the frivolous, a sensuous dance. I have even been told that some highway robbers once were heard whistling it before they started on a daring escapade.

I do not think that there is such a thing as *absolute* religious or sacred music. What is true of other things in life is true of music. It is relative. What is true in art to-day may be deemed quite untrue by the next generation. Take, for example, the musical consonance and discord once recognized as essential elements in music. Modern composers and musicians do not recognize the old order of things. The Gregorian chant has been associated in Christian nations with religion for hundreds of years, so it invokes within us religious feeling. In a non-Christian land the same chant might rouse martial sentiment, if it had been used there for that purpose *traditionally.* Play the Gregorian chant to an Australian bushman and it may not affect him devotionally at all—but a certain crude melody of his own will; at the same time, his wild music may inspire feelings of a quite different nature in others in a different environment.

The same is true of the music of different musical instruments. The horn has been associated with the chase. When we think of the chase we instinctively think of the horn. The guitar is associated with romance—a gondola under the Rialto in Venice, or a young man under a window in Seville. Nowadays, we associate war with trumpet and drum—the instruments of fire and fury. But in ancient Greece the bards were wont to lash the country into feverish martial activities by singing and playing on the lyre. The Gaelic bards did the same.

Now, the lyre is to us an instrument of tender tones and romantic feeling.

During the exciting days of the French Revolution the singing of the Marseillaise was thought more dangerous by those in power than incendiary speeches or weapons of war. It inspired people to make sacrifices, it roused them to fight and to die fighting. I am certain that, in a country that knows nothing about the French Revolution, or of this great song of France, the Marseillaise could be effectively used for religious revival.

Art, then, is influenced by environment, education, and association of ideas. Art, like love, is a state of mind and heart, and the art of music more so than other arts. The arts of poetry, painting, and sculpture have tangible forms. But music is formless—it is all feeling. For that reason it is the more dynamic, and produces a deeper emotional effect.

A beneficial act, like healing, is quite often accomplished by the art of music. The world is destined to hear more and more of this practical side of music. I shall not be surprised if a book on musical therapeutics, written by a scientist, shall have, before long, a place on the shelves of the medical libraries of the world. In the ancient scriptures of the Hindus, the Christians, the Egyptians, and the Chinese, there are references to the healing power of music. Thus we read in the Bible: "When the evil spirit from God was upon Saul, then David took an harp, and played with his hand. So Saul was refreshed, and was well, and the evil spirit departed from him."

My father was a physician, and I studied medicine for about two years—so I know a little about medical science. I do not think that it is unscientific to say that, in certain instances, music can be effectively used as a healing agency. Scientists have just begun to investigate this matter. Healing is largely a normal adjustment of the maladjusted molecules of the body. Recently a case was brought to my notice. A young lady was sick with high fever in her home on a ranch in one of the western states of the Union. The doctor's home was far away, and he could not be summoned readily. A friend asked the mother to give her daughter a "music cure." A certain record was played on the phonograph a few times. The young lady's temperature came down, and, I am informed, she was soon on her way to recovery. A case has been cited recently of a young woman, suffering from sleeping sickness, who was brought to consciousness and health through the ministration of music. She was a Russian, and when she recovered she declared that what recalled her from her long siege of sleeping was the violin playing Russian melodies.

The effect of music not only upon the ill, but also upon the insane, has been noted and considered by physicians. For my own part, I believe in the soothing, comforting, and healing effect of music. We all know how thought affects the human body. An embarrassing remark causes a rush of blood to a woman's face, and she blushes. If you look at something sour your mouth waters, or if at something tragic, tears rise in your eyes. Think of your absent beloved, and your body and mind ache with the bitter pangs of separation. Happy thoughts make the body buoyant, and melancholy thoughts depress it. If the mind is "low," if the nerves are weak, the power sent to the muscles is diminished. Now every musical note is a living thought current. If electrical waves in air can carry a wireless message over thousands of miles, a musical wave may also find a response in the physical and mental being. The musical waves no doubt act and react on our nervous system. And surely they do adjust or maladjust, disturb or harmonize, the atoms and *ions* of our natures.

I found my musical ear of value in war service. I soon got accustomed to the sound of deadly missiles—in fact, I quickly began to make observations of their peculiarities. My ear, accustomed to differentiate sounds of all kinds, had noted a remarkable discrepancy in the whine produced by different shells as they passed overhead, some sounding shrill, with a rising cadence, and others rather dull, with a falling cadence. Every shell describes in its course a parabolic line, with the first half of the curve ascending, and the second one descending. Apparently, in the first half of its curve, while ascending, the shell produced a dull whine, accompanied by a falling cadence, which changed to a rising shrill as soon as the acme was reached, and the curve turned down. I was told that shells sounded different when going up than when coming down, but that this knowledge was not of value for practical purposes. I found that I could, with a trained musical ear, mark the spot where shells reached their acme, and so could give the almost exact range of guns.

Music affects even the animal world. The flute pleases and thrills the horse. The drum and trumpet awaken the spirit in this noble animal so that he plunges headlong on to the battlefield. The Hindu snake charmer plays on his *poongi* flute, and deadly cobras crawl out and weave their sinuous way toward their seductive charmers. Not long ago a musical experiment was tried out at the New York Zoological Park. The animals were tested on the "jazz music" that so many modern human beings seem to fancy. The animals did not like it. The monkeys, in particular, went wild in anguished revolt.

It is passing strange that some would like to nationalize music. Music belongs to no nation. The spell of music is the same whether it is sung and played in America or England, in France or Italy, in India or China, in Russia or South Africa. Music, like art and literature, is universal; it transcends all national boundaries. Rodin belongs just as much to Russia as to France; Shakespeare just as much to Europe and America as to England; Kalidasa just as much to England as to India; and Brahms just as much to Paris as to Vienna. As from the mountain top the world below is bereft of all national distinctions, so, viewed from the peak of higher understanding, nationality in art disappears.

It is cultural background, intellectual training, specialization, and execution that make the difference in the appreciation of music. If badly played, even Beethoven's symphonies would be a deadly drag. From my earliest days I have been interested in music, and music is my life; and yet, if I do not like the music of a negro in Darkest Africa, that does not make that music less vital, less real to the African. It is my own fault that I do not appreciate such music. The first time I heard Chinese music I did not like it at all. But later on, when I heard a Chinese scholar sing, the deeper and inner message of Chinese music was revealed to me. To understand music of this sort we must study national background and tradition.

In examining the cubist and futurist arts of to-day, one may fail to understand the meaning of lines and surfaces. One may scorn a picture, and call it grotesque, but to the artist it is real. Adherents to the traditional laws of pictorial art scoff at him, but he does not care. He looks at the picture he has produced from the angle of a highly accentuated imagination.

The same is true of music. The last movement of Beethoven's Fifth Symphony, played to an untutored listener, may be no more than a crude march, but to one trained in music it is sublime revelation—as though the soul of a mortal had burst through the shell of egotism to stand face to face with the Infinite. When I hear Beethoven's symphonies, I think I know why he became deaf. It seems to me that he must have been so saturated with exalted music feeling that a little more would have devastated him physically. It seems almost as if he *had to become* deaf, to be shut in, in order to gain an intensified hearing of the musical inspiration within him. No sound from outside could help him any more. The sonatas that he wrote while deaf are the very essence of music.

Here it may be mentioned, by the way, that with the growing complexity of music, really great compositions are growing less in number. Haydn wrote one hundred and fifty symphonies, Mozart over forty, Beethoven nine, Tchaikovsky six, Schumann only four, and Brahms four.

The international animosities of the past few years have retarded the progress of music in the world. But in the task of reconstruction, of the regeneration of the human race, music will play a prominent part. I have, however, somewhat modified my views in this matter. Before the war I was enough of a dreamer to exaggerate the importance of music for the elevation of society. But I know Europe to-day, and I have seen things with my own eyes. Now I hold that when men, women, and children actually die of starvation, or eke out an existence of lingering death, music, even the very best of it, cannot help them! The artist himself cannot sing or play on an empty stomach. Give the hungry musician a slice of bread and a glass of water, if a cup of sugarless coffee is too much to expect—then his spirits will rise and he will produce good music. Give the hungry lover of music a bite of food—then he will enjoy music and smile. Music glorifies life but cannot preserve it. Music is the dome, a very beautiful dome, but not the foundation of the edifice of humanity.

As in music some notes mingle, so in life some vibrations are in accord. The underlying principle of this accord in life may be called love. Music and love are like twin sisters. Like flames of fire they both burn into the very core of our being. Music has often been defined as "the language of emotions," and the profoundest of all emotions is love. The dominant note of most of the beautiful songs is love. Most of the grand operas strive to unfold this glowing principle in life. Love invigorates art. One who cannot love greatly and unselfishly cannot accomplish great things in life. "Music," says von Weber, "is the purest, most ethereal language of passion." "I can grasp the spirit of music," says Wagner, "in no other manner than in love."

Most of the great musicians have been great lovers, for music creates love; it deepens and sanctifies love. Love has been the rudder to guide the ship of their lives.

In spite of all human thoughts and theories, life is still a mystery, love is a mystery, music is a mystery. No one can really define them. It is a supremely happy thing, nevertheless, that we can realize love and music in life. Both music and love blend with life as does color in a rainbow.

CHAPTER NINETEEN

A GLIMPSE OF THE ORIENT

[1923]

Fritz Kreisler was somewhat surprised to learn that the Far East was clamoring for him to make a tour of the principal cities of Japan, China, and Korea. He was well aware of the difference between Occidental and Oriental music, and had grave misgivings as to whether his message on the violin would be understood by peoples used to quarter-tones and sounds that to Western ears seemed weird.

He learned later, and often spoke of it, that the phonograph had performed a tremendous cultural missionary task in the East, in that, among other things, his recordings were known quite as well in Tokyo, Shanghai, and Seoul as they were in Chicago, Munich, and Birmingham.

Fritz and Harriet arrived in New York from Germany on January 13, 1923, and a busy schedule of concerts awaited them in eastern America before they could depart for the West Coast on April 3. Fritz as usual had a crowded house for his Carnegie Hall recital, in the course of which he offered a novelty: C. M. Loeffler's arrangement of Chabrier's Scherzo-Valse. It is well to recall that through the years, Kreisler has brought out at least one new contemporary work each year.

Carl Lamson remembers an incident which shows how Fritz was constantly alert for new things. The two musicians had gone to the movies—it was in the days before sound pictures—when they heard the young organist play something that struck Fritz Kreisler as worth while.

Fritz Kreisler, about 1920

Leopold Godowsky, 1870-1938

"Please go and find out what that is," Kreisler suggested. Lamson went to the console. The organist was Elmer Owens. "It is my own composition," Owens said modestly. Fritz Kreisler then arranged it as a violin solo and played it often.

Newsmen who regularly met Fritz Kreisler at the dock in New York usually reported either that the artist was returning from Europe with a number of new works that he had incorporated in his repertoire for the tour, or that he stated, "Nothing worth while has been composed in Europe for the violin since my last visit there."

Fritz and Harriet with the accompanist Michael Raucheisen arrived in Yokohama on the afternoon of Friday, April 20, 1923—the birthday, incidentally, of a man who was to attract world-wide attention by an ill fated beer cellar *Putsch* in Munich seven months later. His name was Adolf Hitler.

Three launches loaded to the gunwales with reporters and camera men had come out to meet the distinguished artist on the deck of the *President Grant*. Kreisler, who never before had set his foot on Japanese soil, was immediately asked the stock journalistic question, "What are your impressions of Japan?"

He was also asked, among other things, "What do you value your violin at?" To which he replied genially, "I don't place any price on my violin, for I wouldn't sell it; it is a Stradivarius."

To the question, "What kind of music do you think Japanese like best?" he naturally could give no authoritative answer as yet.

When he thought he had complied sufficiently with the proprieties of the occasion, he brought the interview to a close with a polite, "Thank you very much," whereupon there was ceremonious bowing and lifting of hats on the part of the Nipponese newsmen.

The port authorities were no respecters of persons. Noting that the Kreisler party was now getting off merely to travel overland to Nagasaki to catch a boat for Shanghai, the artist had to give assurances that he was not going to China to connive with the Bolshevik agents there, but merely to play the violin! A. Strok, their impresario for the Far East, escorted them to Nagasaki. When they passed through Tokyo, Leopold Godowsky was at the station to greet them.

Before leaving America, Harriet Kreisler had repeatedly said, with the unusual intuition for which she is noted, "Mark my words: we're going to have bandits, a typhoon, and an earthquake." She was to have all three, as we shall soon see.

The first concert took place in Shanghai on April 28. According to the *Celestial Empire*, an English-language newspaper, there was "incessant cheering, clapping, and shouting for further encores. It was a remarkable scene, for Shanghai audiences are not disposed to be demonstrative. Nobody ever received such a wonderful reception as he on Tuesday."

Fritz Kreisler was well pleased with this first taste of Oriental concert-giving. He expressed himself to the Shanghai press in these words: "Shanghai to me has always been a city of golden dreams, of high emprise and great adventure. It has long been my ambition to visit it, since it is one of the greatest cities of the world, and my arrival now is the fulfillment of many years."

One shadow, however, was cast over their stay in Shanghai, thrilling though it had been. "Our sojourn at the hotel was not exactly a pleasure," Raucheisen wrote. "There were rats galore in both the dining room and in our bedrooms. They were a veritable plague. Mrs. Kreisler suffered especially in this situation and implored the manager at least to let her have a cat for her room."

"Yes, that's true," commented Harriet Kreisler. "They did get a cat for me. It was a semiwild animal. In the night I awoke and saw two eyes glaring at me. The cat had taken up quarters on Fritz's chest!"

After two recitals in Shanghai, the Kreisler party had to return to Japan for an extended series of concerts. Their reentry was unique. The Japanese representatives of the Victor Phonograph Company had ordered all their employees out to the dock, where they appeared carrying "transparents" (luminous signs) which they held high in a parade all the way from the dock to the hotel. Representatives of the Japanese and international press were there in full numbers, as were movie and still-camera men.

In Tokyo alone, Kreisler gave eight recitals in the Imperial Theater, which had a capacity of 2,500 to 3,000. Japanese audiences were gourmands for classical sonatas for violin and piano. This meant preparing programs quite different from what Fritz had in mind. Raucheisen has already described how Kreisler's phenomenal memory played an important role in meeting the situation (see page 93).

The first six days of May were taken up with one concert each day at the Imperial Theater. A two-column spread on the first page of the *Japan Advertiser* reported after the first performance: "Japanese enthusiasm never ran higher for music of the West than last night for Fritz Kreisler." After his "Caprice viennois" the "applause was so deafening that he had to repeat it."

During an intermission he was ceremoniously presented with the Gold Medal of the Alliance Musicale du Japon. Kreisler responded to this honor by playing his arrangement of Tartini's "Devil's Trill" Sonata.

A prominent German violinist, Willy Burmester of Hamburg, also on tour in Japan, came to the artist's room after the concert to congratulate his Austrian colleague warmly.

On the second evening Prince Kuni and Prince Chichibu sat in the imperial box. Again there was tumultuous applause, and again a gold medal was presented, this time by the *Jiji Shimpo* (Tokyo daily newspaper), through Kyusaburo Yamamoto, manager of the Imperial Theater. Kreisler thanked him in a brief speech.

The following day Prince Kuni came to the hotel as an emissary of His Majesty the Mikado to bring a present as an expression of the sovereign's appreciation. It was a modest little jewel box containing a tiepin in the form of a small chrysanthemum. There was much scraping and bowing and thanking and assuring of mutual esteem, whereupon the emperor's envoy left.

Harriet with her practical sense calculated: "A mere chrysanthemum? Not very much for my Fritz!" But when they started out that evening, she pinned the piece of jewelry on her husband's tie.

The very first Japanese they encountered took one look at the flower, then bowed ceremoniously three times, and insisted upon escorting the couple to their vehicle. Wherever they appeared that night, the chrysanthemum was the center of attraction. Fritz and Harriet were treated like royalty.

Late that evening they learned at last why the chrysanthemum was such a miracle worker: when Fritz asked for his dinner check, he was told that he was the guest of the Mikado, the proof of which was the chrysanthemum!

Thus it went day after day, until the final concert of this series, on May 6, "eclipsed everything. From the main floor to the roof the house was literally packed." Afterward Marquis and Marquess Yorisada Tokugawa entertained the Kreislers at a dinner graced by the presence, among others, of Prince Kuni-Asaakira. Joseph Hollman, the Dutch cellist, was also invited.

Marquis Tokugawa was one of the last descendants of the Shoguns. He and his wife, besides having inherited an old culture, had also acquired the most graceful forms of European living, spoke French and English exceedingly well, and were of extraordinary intelligence and lovableness. The Marquis had assembled a remarkable library of Western music and musical literature, and had bought many choice rarities in England, especially from the famous Cummings Collection. Catalogs were printed of the marquis' collection.

The Tokyo days were as crowded with social functions as the nights were with concerts. Typical Japanese entertainment was usually provided. Thus two or three geisha girls of highest grade would perform, or some entertainer would arrange flowers artistically in charming designs as the guests watched, or an artist would appear with a box of sand and within a short time conjure up a tiny Japanese garden, with Japanese trees and a little bridge, all made by hand.

At the home of Count Otard the Kreislers viewed the most marvelous collection of Oriental art they had ever seen, a collection for which a prominent New York art collector had unsuccessfully offered upward of $10,000,000. Unfortunately, six months later Nature took from the Japanese count what dollars were unable to accomplish: the priceless collection was destroyed in the earthquake.

At the German Embassy the jovial ambassador, Dr. Wilhelm Solf, was the chief of mission.

"In that connection," Michael Raucheisen wrote, "I should like to mention that I heard Fritz Kreisler play Viennese waltzes on the piano during an evening at the German Embassy. Never before or after have I heard Johann Strauss played so charmingly."

Before starting for Yokohama for a series of concerts, Fritz was the honored guest at a dinner given by Prince Kuni and attended by many members of the diplomatic corps and leading musicians.

It was then that the first of Harriet's three premonitions proved well founded.

"While we were sitting at the Prince Kuni dinner," Fritz reported, "the chandeliers suddenly began to rock. I said laughingly, 'I suppose that's one of your funny earthquakes.' 'That is a very silly remark,' an English diplomat reprimanded me. He was right—my heart began to beat wildly when I realized it was in truth an earthquake."

This was, however, merely a warning tremor compared with the earthquake that took place shortly after.

Harriet had been invited with Ambassador and Mrs. Solf to the residence of the German consul general, Dr. Müller, in the hills outside the capital while Fritz was busy with his crowded schedule of rehearsals and concerts.

"Suddenly the earth swayed," Harriet said. "It is not possible to describe what the rocking of the ground does to your stomach and otherwise. You feel nauseated. You feel as though the end of things had come. The air is as in a conservatory. You feel steaming hot. Then the plaster comes down and scatters all over you. Next, you are knocked over.

"Later we received a remarkable picture. Dr. Müller had stepped out of his house with his kodak to photograph his garden. At that very moment the earthquake came, and the unusual exposure on his film showed a wide chasm in the earth, his home crumbling like a house of cards, and Mount Fujiyama visible in the gap made by the falling roof."

But it was not only the élite of Japanese and European society in the Nipponese capital that hero-worshiped Kreisler. Even jinrikisha men would unwrap phonograph records and ask him to autograph their Kreisler discs.

After the Yokohama engagements there followed concerts, usually two in each city, in Kobe, Osaka, Nagoya, and Kyoto. The Japanese provincial press indulged in superlatives in describing these recitals.

At Kyoto the high priest of Shintoism, Count Kozui Otani, a brother-in-law of the Japanese empress, had come to honor Kreisler by his presence. It was most unusual for this high ecclesiastic dignitary to come to a public function of this sort. He did not mingle with the crowd, but even during a reception which followed remained in a small adjoining room, where he presented the artist with two vases on which he had written two poems of his own. Writing under the name of Kubutze, he was one of the leading poets of his country.

Raucheisen thinks of the Shinto high priest's attendance at the concert with some embarrassment. He wrote:

> During the reception in some enormous hall, I noticed that a Japanese gentleman was standing quite by himself in a salon adjoining. Bavarian boor that I am, I was seized with compassion for the lone figure. I seemed to sense that nobody was looking after him. In my naïveté I decided to keep him company. So I slapped him on the shoulder and said, familiarly and in poor English, "Hello, my dear friend." I was later told very politely what a *faux pas* I had committed: the man was none other than the highest priest of the Shinto religion, whose rank may be compared to that of the Pope in Rome! It was not customary for him to mingle with common mortals, and of course I had no right to address him thus familiarly.

The self-confessed "Bavarian boor" might have added that not even the brothers of the high priest, although they were also Shinto ecclesiastics, were allowed to look him in the face, but had to keep their heads bowed low in his presence.

Count Otani not only attended the concert but invited Kreisler to see the Buddhist temple Nishi-Honganji, and he asked Harriet, at the end of her husband's visit, to come into the Royal Messenger Court. Harriet thus became one of the few women in the world to be entertained by the highest Shinto dignitary. She was even photographed with the count.

"I had remained in our carriage outside the temple compound," Harriet said, "as women are not permitted inside. After a while, however, I was sent for to meet the high priest in the Royal Messenger Court. I had to remove my shoes before entering.

"Count Otani was an impressive person, with a wonderful, spiritual face. He had studied in Europe and spoke German and several other Occidental languages well. He was adorned with jade and amber. At the end of our visit he presented my husband with a scroll on which he had written a poem, based on his hearing Fritz play the Dvořák 'Humoresque.' It was beautifully done in gold cloisonné enamel. To me, too, he gave a present—a little brooch which had hundreds of wraps around it. We were naturally not required to follow the Japanese custom of not looking him in the face, but could converse freely with him.

"If there is anything about present-day Japan I am happy about, it is that the position of women is changing. At the time of our visit Japanese women had to sleep with their heads on wooden blocks because of their coiffures. They were virtually the chattels of the men. In their presence they sat on the floor cross-legged like tailors.

"At the temple compound of Kyoto the buildings are arranged in fives. They cover two city blocks. Twice a year, I learned, there is a gigantic ceremony at the Shinto shrine, up to which huge steps lead. As many as 100,000 people take part. For hours they lie flat on their faces, prostrate on the steps of the temple, and wait for the supreme moment when the temple screens are opened and the high priest appears."

Fritz has described his impressions of his meeting with Count Otani, of his sensations in the temple, and of his experiences generally in Japan in an article, "A Violinist in the Orient," which follows at the conclusion of this chapter.

During their stay in Kyoto, Harriet had become interested in a particularly beautiful kimono at Yamanake's, the leading store. When she tried to purchase it, she was told it could be worn only by royalty and therefore could not be sold to her.

News of the unusual reception of the Kreislers by Count Otani in his private quarters, however, traveled rapidly throughout Kyoto. As Harriet and Fritz were about to depart that evening, a Japanese emissary of Yamanake's in full regalia came to the train to bring her the imperial kimono as a present. When Harriet remonstrated and said she could not accept it unless she were permitted to pay for it, he bowed low and said, "If you do not accept it I shall have to destroy it." That clinched the argument.

During their stay in Kyoto they met many painters to whose studios they were invited. The greatest among them was Seyto. He presented Kreisler with one of his famous works, painted as usual on a scroll. When Fritz and Harriet reached their hotel, the first motif that struck their eyes as they unrolled the gift was a mouse nibbling at cheese. Allergic as Harriet is to rodents, that settled the painting as far as she was concerned, and it was never displayed on the walls of her Berlin home.

Fritz had now been in Japan long enough to be willing to express an opinion to the press on a variety of subjects.

"I love Japanese art, especially Japanese painting," he said. Japanese paper, he claimed, was the best in the world, and he said that he would like to send some to Berlin and Vienna to etchers there. "I greatly admire Japanese music and one of these days I shall want to create a new music of my own by combining the Western with Japanese music," he further stated. He eulogized the ability of Japanese artists in following foreign music. At a concert at the home of Marquis Tokugawa in Tokyo, he pointed out, he had heard a Japanese vocalist who could equal any first-class musician in the West.

He spoke further of the deep impression a *koto-shakuhachi* concert had made on him at the mansion of Viscount Mishima in Tokyo. The Japanese artists were Micho Miyage, who performed on the *koto*, or zither harp of thirteen strings, and Saifu Yoshida, the *shakuhachi*, or bamboo clarinet player. They offered a piece called *Ochiba-no-Odori* which, he said, was modern music with much foreign element, and developed from purely classical Japanese music. He had been so charmed with it that he tried to get a phonograph record of it. He hoped to transcribe it into a new Western-Oriental music.

The Kreisler party returned once more to the Tokyo area for farewell concerts in Yokohama on May 19, and in Tokyo on May 18 and 20. As a parting gift Fritz was presented with beautiful woodcuts by Hokusai and Harunobu. From there he departed for the Japanese coast, engaged passage through the Straits of Korea, and sailed for

Seoul, the capital of Korea, the unhappy land that was absorbed by Japan in 1910 and renamed Chosen—"Land of the Morning Calm." En route, he and his party passed through the various points from which tiger hunts start. From there they traveled by way of Mukden in South Manchuria to Peking (Peiping) and Tientsin.

At Mukden, Harriet's second premonition—about bandits—proved justified. General Chang Tso-lin, who held sway in this region, unceremoniously put the Kreisler party out of its sleeping-car compartments, ejected other passengers with equal dispatch, and commandeered the train for military purposes.

"We didn't know what to do," Harriet Kreisler said. "The Germans resident in Mukden, however, came and helped us. They assured us that this sort of thing happens from time to time and that one must get used to it.

"They also asked, however, whether Fritz would not play for them during our enforced stay that day. So at 3:00 P.M. a concert was hastily improvised at the Deutscher Klub. The whole German colony turned out.

"We were later put in a cattle car, where we stepped on each other's toes, and were allowed to continue to Peking. The police had to guard us with machine guns, as an attack by bandits might come any moment. In a certain sense we profited by the fact that a train recently had been held up and Mrs. John D. Rockefeller, Jr.'s, sister had been taken off and held for ransom. The precautions were now all the greater."

Fritz added philosophically: "Yes, we were made rather uncomfortable on that trip, due to the regulations of Chang Tso-lin. But it was Chang Tso-lin's way of doing things; and as he seemed to be in charge there, his instructions had to be accepted whether we liked it or not."

The unforeseen delay in Mukden meant that the first concert in Tientsin, scheduled for May 25, could not be given. Instead, Kreisler played the next day at 9:15 P.M., the regular hour for performances in the Orient, in near-by Peking. (The advertisements in both Tientsin and Peking newspapers always carried announcements of concerts in both cities, so close are they. They have a common airport.) According to the Peking *Daily News*, the "audience was spellbound and enthusiastic. . . . There was such silence that you could hear the hearts beat, and the charmed life ceased only when Kreisler's bow stopped."

These concerts, it must be remembered, were attended by the Europeans and not the Chinese, and were given in the European compound. The Chinese, out of a feeling of national pride, remained aloof from "European" concerts.

Two days before the Kreisler party left the Peking area, a representative of the Chinese intelligentsia came to the Embassy at which the artist was staying and asked if Kreisler would please give a concert for the Chinese exclusively in the Chinese quarter of the city. Had he any objections?

"But I thought my concerts were for Chinese as well as Europeans; neither my manager nor anybody else has told me that Chinese could not come to the concerts at which I have so far played," Kreisler responded, astonished.

He was then told that no European artist before this had played or sung for the Celestials and that the Chinese did not desire to go to any function that was not their own. "Could you play tomorrow night?" the young Chinese asked.

"But is it possible to arrange for a concert within twenty-four hours?" Kreisler queried, incredulously. "Of course I'd be happy to play, but I am already billed for a recital in the European compound."

"What about tomorrow afternoon?" the young Chinese persisted. Kreisler agreed. "And the fee?" "The same as always." The Chinese was surprised and happy. He had expected that Kreisler would ask a much higher fee for this special occasion.

After the Chinese had left, Harriet asked her husband, "What kind of a program are you going to play?" To which Fritz replied, "The same as I give in Carnegie Hall." It seemed rather daring.

The next morning the wife of the British ambassador called to complain that she had tried in vain to secure a ticket to the concert: the Chinese would not sell one to her. Harriet assured her that even she would not be able to attend except for the fact that she was the artist's wife, and that she had no way of getting her in except to take her

The Temple of Heaven in Peking, China

Sun Yat-sen, founder of the Chinese republic

along into the artist's room where she herself would sit during the concert, and which was no larger than a closet.

"Never in all my life have I seen a stage more beautifully and artistically decorated," Harriet recalls. "It looked like a huge altar. And then the gowns of the ladies! One seemed to look out upon an ocean of silk. There were most gorgeous colorings of the silk costumes, and the ladies' jewels were too lovely for words—not set in elaborate Western style, but simply and thereby most effectively. The stools on which the audience sat were in variegated silks. It was an unforgettable sight."

Before the concert began, a young Chinese lady, a niece of Sun Yat-sen, who had been educated in London, delivered an admonition to the Chinese audience as to how it should conduct itself during a Western musical recital, and how it should show its approval. She illustrated her words by clapping her hands.

Kreisler played an unaccompanied Bach Suite as his opening work. For the first time in his long career the initial selection had to be repeated, so enthusiastic was the response. Bach was followed by a Beethoven sonata; again there was fervent appreciation. Then followed the traditional group of small pieces. Kreisler included Cyril Scott's "Lotus Land" in this group, and Scott's composition must in some curious way have reminded the listeners of their own shepherds with their shawms. Kreisler had to repeat it.

Then something like an act of sleight of hand ensued which the Kreislers are at a loss even today to explain. "How the Chinese did it is a mystery to us," they say. "But although the Embassy was only a short distance away, and although we were taken there in a car, the flowers that had adorned the stage so marvelously had already been transferred to, and artistically arranged at, the Embassy."

The concert was followed the next day by a tea party in the Chinese Chung Yang (Central) park, in the course of which the visiting artist became profoundly impressed with China's intelligentsia.

Raucheisen, who in Kyoto had caused himself and the Kreislers some embarrassment by glad-handing the Shinto high priest Otani too familiarly, in Peking suddenly became lost for a day and gave Fritz some anxious hours before one of his evening concerts. It appears that Michael had started out for a walk along the ancient City Wall, then had lost his way and drifted into a lepers' colony. Quite unconcerned about the danger of contagion, he not only had remained interestedly for a considerable time among the unfortunates but, when he finally found his way back to his European quarters, in his exuberance and happiness tried to throw his arms around Harriet, at the same time telling her with a beaming face about his experiences among the lepers!

Besides Kreisler, another distinguished person was enthusiastically acclaimed at this time in Peking: Jane Addams of Hull House, Chicago, whose devoted efforts on behalf of world peace are a matter of history. Another popular Occidental was Dr. Jacob Gould Schurman, former president of Cornell University, then American minister to China. Kreisler was to see Dr. Schurman frequently some years later in his capacity of United States Ambassador to Germany.

The four public and several private recitals and concerts in Peking and Tientsin proved so overwhelming a success that Fritz Kreisler on the last day of his stay in Peking was asked by the Chinese Government whether he would agree to play in the Gobi Desert in places where no European had ever before been heard. The government offered to place a special train at his disposal, to provide European food to his liking, and to arrange concerts wherever the train happened to be when evening came, producing audiences virtually as a magician produces a rabbit from his hat. Money was no object, the government emphasized. It also promised to furnish military protection against bandits.

Harriet was eager to accept, but Fritz felt he could not let down the music lovers of Shanghai, where he had promised to give two more recitals. "We now both regret we did not accept the offer," Harriet said.

The trip from Peking to Shanghai was described by Raucheisen in these terms:

From Peking we traveled the notorious stretch via Tientsin to Shanghai, on which eight days before that same train had been raided by bandits. On the train and at the various railway stations Chinese soldiers with bayonets drawn were on patrol duty. Next we learned that the bandits were quite near. They were even pointed out to us on the stone heights above us.

When we asked how such bandit armies come into existence we were told that determined generals from time to time go on their own and exercise authority and power.

Shanghai was in a turmoil when the Kreisler party arrived there for the second and final series of concerts on the Asiatic continent. Mass meetings were being held throughout the city, demanding of the government that it put a stop to banditry. There were meetings of the Europeans, of the Americans, of Orientals and Occidentals together. Some twenty thousand Chinese assembled at one of these numerous demonstrations of protest against a weak government.

Nevertheless, the two Shanghai concerts were a tumultuous success, and Kreisler could leave China with the comforting feeling that he had created a lasting impression.

As the Kreisler party left China, the third of Harriet's premonitions came true: the typhoon. As she tells the story:

"Fritz had come to me quite elated a few days previously and said, 'I've got a lovely boat for us to go back to Japan; you'll be quite happy.' I went aboard ahead of him, as he still had his final concert to give. However, it took much longer than he had anticipated, and the captain, unable to wait any longer, started out without him. You can imagine my feelings! But after finishing at about 11:00 P.M., Fritz managed to charter a Chinese bark which caught up with us nearly twenty-four hours later at some little port before we reached the open sea.

"When we got closer to the Japanese side the following day, I said, 'I don't like the looks of the water.' To me it seemed like the quiet before the storm. Though the water was unusually smooth, you could see it vibrating as if shaken by an ominous force. Fritz, however, turned to some other passengers and quipped, 'My wife won't be satisfied until she has her typhoon.'

"And then it came—our ship acted as though it were plowing through lava. At about 2:00 A.M. I awakened Fritz. 'I suppose you've got your typhoon,' he said tauntingly. But when he got up he realized it was indeed a typhoon. For twelve hours we were tossed about and became completely water-soaked. When we reached Nagasaki, that port was badly damaged."

This time the return to Japan was private and, as it were, incognito. The Kreislers tarried only long enough to catch the *Empress of Canada*, which sailed for Vancouver on June 9.

Just before sailing, Fritz Kreisler once more met the Japanese press. "I have had a wonderful trip through the Orient," he said, "and have seen many beautiful places; but the prettiest of them all is the City of Kyoto, with its spirit of old Japan and a quietness which is entrancing to the man who will allow himself to sense the things that have come and gone. That city is the heart of Japan. I am in love with it.

"I think Peking is by far the most fascinating and interesting of the Chinese cities we visited. Korea and Manchuria have an alluring charm, but my trip was so hurried that I did not have the time to see it all.

"I have found things in Japan, Korea, and China different from what I thought they would be, but they have nevertheless been pleasing. . . . As I received such a wonderful reception everywhere I went, I am leaving with none but pleasant memories of my visit here. The ovations I received almost swept me off my feet. The applause during my first few appearances came as a total surprise to me. Later, I became a little accustomed to them, but they continued to be one of the great surprises which I received during my trip through the Orient."

The Orient tour had a painful aftermath: Harriet Kreisler fell ill and had to go to Carlsbad, Czechoslovakia, for a cure. In a letter to his friend Ernest Schelling, dated Carlsbad, July 27, 1923, her husband wrote: "Harriet is not well and I am rather worried about her just now. She had quite a break-down after the return from China and Japan and somehow does not seem to get better."

Later that year in Berlin, Kreisler went more deeply into his impressions in an article for the Berliner *Tageblatt*, an article so full of wisdom and keen analysis that it is here reproduced in full. It is entitled "A Violinist in the Orient":

The echoes of a tour through China and Japan which I undertook some months ago are still ringing in my ears, and before I set out again upon the journey across the Atlantic, after a short time in Germany, I am glad of the opportunity to set down the sum of the impressions that I received in the storied lands of the East.

Not from the standpoint of the investigator of conditions, but rather in an artistic nearness to the men with whom the artist so gladly comes in contact, not with the attitude of a mistrustful adventurer, but rather with a mind open to beauty and in quest of it, did I submit myself to these foreign nationalities and age-old cultures. From this standpoint I do not hesitate to make known my deep admiration for the intellectual life of the Far East.

Even if the keen intelligence of the Japanese and Chinese were not well known, it would nevertheless be instantly apparent to any European artist who comes into spiritual contact with them. A Western European finds an extraordinary charm in what we are likely to regard as a quality of the heart—I mean their fine tact in the common life of men together and the quickness of perception with which they treat one another and their foreign guests.

I hasten to admit that I am personally a great admirer of the refined forms of social life, and of ceremonial that is really sincere; but even crude natures coming from Western Europe to Eastern Asia will feel the charming lightness with which the game of life is played there, thanks to the friendliness and courtesy of the people, partly innate and partly taught. One hears no rudeness, traces no discourtesy, finds no irritation, feels no sense of hostile coolness, and yet one does not seem oppressed by an unnatural degree of politeness. One enjoys the bloom of a social culture that has been shaped and formed for centuries, and one thinks, not without regret, of Western Europe, where, quite the reverse, men so often make life unbearably dull because they have no technique of social existence and have not learned to control their temperaments.

The relation of the Japanese and Chinese to art in general, and to German art in particular, is of special interest. For several years both nations have been devoting themselves with especial enthusiasm to the comprehension of German music, and I may add that a field of action lies open to German art and German artists in the Far East which will in the future bear rich fruit. The manager of the Imperial Theatres in Tokyo, Mr. Yamamoto, is the prime embodiment of the aspirations of the Japanese people, who seek to make Western music their own and have sought to emulate its achievements at a distance. Each year Mr. Yamamoto arranges concert tours of the most important European musicians, and it was at his invitation that, in addition to other engagements, I played each evening for a week in the Imperial Theatre at Tokyo. The house, which seats about twenty-five hundred persons, was sold out at every concert, and in the course of seven I presented all that is best in violin literature—so far as I have mastered it. The effect of my artistic efforts was so clear and of such inner strength as I have seldom experienced.

The music of the Chinese and Japanese is not for a European to discuss.

There is a kind of nasal twang about it, and it lacks all the properties that form the very essence of a European composition—rhythm, harmony, and structure. All the greater are the demands which our European music places on the Oriental's capacity for understanding, and it is scarcely for me to say how broad or how deep a comprehension my Eastern hearers really achieved; but in the thousands of faces that looked up from a sea of white silk garments I saw a tension of the will, an effort to penetrate into a foreign world of tone, and a feeling of reverence for art as such. That the Chinese and Japanese do take pleasure in our music was proved, in my eyes, by the enthusiastic reception which I had at the end of every concert, quite after the European manner, and also by one very special experience.

In Peking I gave my first concert at the Embassy, and the audience which assembled consisted chiefly of the most prominent white residents. One morning a young Chinese appeared at my hotel, speaking excellent English but clearly belonging to the less exalted classes of the people, and said, 'We are informed that you are to play only for the foreigners, but we beg that you will give us also the pleasure of your art.' To such a wish I quite naturally was very glad to accede, and the very next afternoon I played Bach, Beethoven, and Brahms before an exclusively Chinese audience. Seldom have I been in society of such exquisite good manners.

In this and in other experiences I saw and felt that, quite apart from my own individuality, art and the artist were being honored; and I could see clearly that in both of the great States of the Far East art, the artist, and above all the intellectual life, are valued far more highly than in Europe. The writer, the philosopher, is regarded as a leader of the people, who, in Schiller's words, together with the political leader, directs mankind toward the heights. The artist is regarded as a man possessing a kind of mystic power which he has received and which he now gives out in turn. In the East gold is not the measure of all values as it is in Western Europe. One does not there look askance at an artist who has met with no pecuniary success, nor does one mock him as a useless member of human society.

In Kyoto an old man of no great outward distinction came to my first concert, treated with great deference and accompanied by other gentlemen. It was Count Otani, the chief intellectual dignitary of Japan, who is related to the Imperial family. Before the concert began he sought me out and begged permission to present me with two vases bearing poems that he himself had written, inscribed upon them. According to Japanese usage, this was an almost incredibly high honor. After the concert he visited me again, and invited me to visit the great temple. It is impossible to describe the beauty of the altar and the holy shrine, which are usually kept closed and are opened only to the eyes of artists; and equally indescribable is the sweet odor of the incense that was burned—in order to give pleasure to an artist. On my way out of the temple, I was led through an arch that is opened only on the rarest occasions, and was last used on the visit of the Prince of Wales. As Count Otani said good-bye to me he murmured: "We wished to do honor to an artist."

Fritz elaborated upon one point of his visit to the Shinto temple with Count Otani. "Before one reaches the arch through which I was escorted," he said, "I found myself before two big screens with boats embroidered on it. As these opened, I entered a temple courtyard which, I was told, was known as the Royal Messenger Courtyard. The last one to pass through it had been the Prince of Wales. I was told that I was in Japanese eyes a king among artists, and as to them there was no higher king than an artist, I must leave by the Royal Messenger Courtyard and the sacred arch." When Kreisler went to America the next time after the unique experience of his tour of the Orient, he spoke so eloquently of it that John McCormack planned and undertook a similar tour in 1926.

Fritz was touched and pleased when, during the late summer of 1949, he received a letter from Viscount Takatoshi Kyogoku of Tokyo, who assured him that the Japanese people still remembered his 1923 tour of the Orient. The count requested that Kreisler send him news about himself, which he would be pleased to place in Japanese musical organs.

The viscount informed the artist that the Marquis and Marquess Tokugawa were in good health, and that the managing director of the Imperial Theater, Yamamoto, had resigned his position and was enjoying life at seventy.

CHAPTER TWENTY

A PERMANENT HOME AT LAST

[1924]

WHEN Fritz Kreisler returned to his flat on Berlin's busy Kurfürstendamm after his tour of the Orient, German economy was in a state of chaos. The value of the reichsmark was dropping from hour to hour, so that price tags in the afternoon were often more than double those of the morning for the identical articles. By the time inflation had run its mad course in the late autumn of 1923, one could buy 4,200,000,000,000 reichmarks for one American dollar.

The wage earner was in despair. The contents of his pay envelope within a few hours dwindled to a mere pittance as far as purchasing power was concerned. After every payday there was a mad scramble to get to the stores and shops first and to convert the money into *Sachwerte* (things of value).

If ever there was need of aid to the poorer classes, it was now. Accordingly, Harriet and Fritz found themselves almost completely absorbed by their charities and benefit concerts.

Fritz's personal inspection of conditions in the proletarian sections of Berlin happens to have furnished the occasion for my first meeting with him. The press had been invited to the great festival hall of Bötzow's Brewery in southwestern Berlin to report on a Christmas celebration for some six hundred to eight hundred poor children. We did not know until we arrived there that these children were being fed one warm meal day after day at the expense of the Kreisler couple. On this day, of course, the place was replete with Christmas decorations, and the meal was in every respect "Christmassy," with a gift package beside each plate for the emaciated youngsters to take home.

While the newsmen were taking notes for their story, who should turn up but the compassionate benefactors themselves! There they stood, Fritz and Harriet, taking in the scene with deep emotion and then, as the children departed, handing each of them a big bar of chocolate as an extra Christmas greeting.

We chatted together for a while. With a somewhat tired smile Fritz said: "Life was so much simpler when I had nobody to look after but myself and my wife! I think I was never so carefree in my life as when I had to worry about the next month's rent. My whole mind seemed to be concentrated on this one thing, and I worried in a wholesome sort of way until I could come home with a contract in my pocket for a concert that would pay for the rent. What happiness to be able to tell Mrs. Kreisler that our next month's housing problem was settled!

"The less one must worry about material things for oneself, the more do the problems of others encroach upon one. Also, our desires become much more complex as our material wealth increases. There is no longer one single thing filling my mind as did the necessity of providing next month's rent in my younger days.

"Then, too, in proportion as one gets interested in the problems of others, one sees how little, how very little one can do to solve them. You know my wife—how she is constantly looking for some new opportunity to be of service to her fellow men. Both of us become so engrossed in her work that there is often little time to think of anything else. And yet—how little can we do, and how immense are the social problems lying at our very doors!"

A few days later the Kreislers could be seen in action again—this time in their own home; not yet the beautiful residence into which they were soon to move, but a rented flat. Fritz and Harriet had invited some sixty children, the poorest among the poor of the German metropolis, to a Christmas party. Sixty had been invited, but when the Kreislers completed their count, they found that eighty-five had appeared. "My business is going splendidly," Fritz observed with a chuckle. "We certainly can't turn the poor uninvited youngsters away," Harriet declared, good-naturedly.

So they were all asked to stay and gather about the long festive tables arranged for them. There were cripples and emaciated faces and underfed tots, also boys and girls eight, nine, and ten years old who looked like four- or five-year-olds. They were all dressed in their Sunday best, which often meant a patched suit of clothes or a garment borrowed from some neighbor who was a bit better situated.

Presently the candles on the Christmas tree were lighted. At a signal from the hostess the whole crowd joined in singing "O Tannenbaum," which her husband tried to direct. He did not get very far, though, for not only were the lads and lasses quite able to sing by themselves, but he was too deeply moved to proceed. Tears rolled down his expressive face.

When the song had ended, the children were told to lay hands on the toys, most of them musical instruments, lying on the tables. Such a cacophony of whistles, trumpets, mouth organs, and tiny drums ensued that our ears rang for a long time afterward. It was truly "atonal" music, which Kreisler otherwise abhors, but which on that day, judging by his beaming face, must have sounded to him like music of the spheres. Later, by way of further amusing the children, he turned on a large phonograph standing in the parlor, and alternated Christmas carols with jolly marches and bright waltzes.

To one crippled tot Fritz said, "Won't you have another cup of chocolate and some more cake?"

"No, uncle," the urchin replied, "I've already had two helpings."

"But you may have a third," Fritz encouraged him.

"I could get it into my mouth, all right," the youngster explained, "but I couldn't get it down."

At the conclusion of the party, and after the children had had an opportunity to enjoy the cocoa, the Christmas cookies, and the sandwiches to the full, each invited child was sent on his way with a package containing a complete suit of clothes with underwear, shoes, and stockings, as well as nourishing things to eat. The youngsters departed laughing and telling each other about the surprise their fathers and mothers would have when they brought the treasured packages to their dingy homes.

But what about the twenty-five uninvited "extras"? The problem of providing for them was no easy one. Fortunately, a friend of the family, the Lieder singer Julia Culp, had foreseen just such a "catastrophe" and had sent bales of cloth to the Kreisler flat as her contribution to the children's party. And so, while the host measured each youngster, his wife cut the cloth for a suit or dress. Thereafter Fritz disappeared into the pantry and brought out cans and cans of milk and bars of chocolate, and the servants fetched toys and fruits and sweets from God-knows-where. Thus even the uninvited guests went home with the happiest of faces.

"And yet, it is but a drop in the bucket," Fritz Kreisler sighed as the last tots disappeared. "What a civilization that makes conditions like these possible!"

Someone remarked how tired Kreisler had appeared to be at the Christmas party in the Bötzow Brewery Hall. He explained: "You see, I had played the night before at a benefit of the Berlin Press Club, and when I got home, I found so much correspondence accumulated that I decided to work right through the night. So it was not until six o'clock that morning that I lay down for a few hours' sleep."

A series of winter engagements in England and America beginning in January, 1924, made the weary Kreisler couple pick up their baggage and Fritz's fiddle soon after Christmas and go on tour once again. Just before leaving London in January for New York after his unusual successes, Fritz told a reporter of the "extraordinary poverty of Central Europe, particularly of Germany," and especially of the "class which is suffering most—the musicians, the artists, the professors, and the *rentiers* generally. . . . They are absolute beggars."

"One cannot really imagine what it is like," he continued. "Think of it: the man who had, say, a capital of £20,000 before the war, with a comfortable income for life, cannot buy a tram fare. First the *objets d'art* of these people went. Then their furniture. Then their clothes. Then there is nothing. Then they die."

He was somewhat more hopeful about Vienna: "I find Vienna incredibly improved. The Allied credits have largely done that, of course. But not that alone. Self-confidence has been restored—that is the great thing. All that previous orgy of spending was merely because people were afraid that their money of Monday would be worth nothing on Tuesday."

Of his concerts in America two deserve mention: both at Washington, D.C., on February 6, and at Richmond, Virginia, on February 9, Kreisler offered a special tribute to the memory of Woodrow Wilson, who had died on February 3, in the form of his violin arrangement of the Largo movement in Dvořák's "New World" Symphony.

During his stay in America he also granted an interview to Henrietta Malkiel for the April 26, 1924 issue of *Musical America*. Kreisler told her:

"You know, Bruno Walter and I were just talking about the artist's lot. We decided that we should be the happiest of men; not only he and I, but all artists. I think the happiest person in the world is the successful artist and the next happiest the unsuccessful one. He is really almost as happy as his more popular colleague. I'm not talking in paradoxes. I really mean it.

"Imagine the man who wants to be a poet, let us say, who has to earn his living balancing books. He can only write at night and all day he is a bookkeeper. He doesn't know very much about it and he doesn't do it very well. He is an unsuccessful bookkeeper and he wants to be a poet. Shouldn't an artist, even an unsuccessful one, be happy? For at least, as Bernard Shaw says, 'his profession is his hobby!'

"Success isn't all-important. It is fine, of course, to step before an audience. But it is the enjoyment that the artist gets from doing his work well and trying to do it better that really matters. That satisfaction an artist who believes in himself—and every true artist must—gets whether the public appreciates him or not. I was once an unsuccessful artist. I had almost no money and very little appreciation. Nobody wanted to hear me play, but I enjoyed doing it and I felt that I could make people listen to me, so I kept on working until I did."

Kreisler had some fatherly advice to give to young people headed for a career in music. "The younger generation hasn't learned to sacrifice for the sake of art," he claimed. "Their self-confidence, their conceit is appalling. They think the world is theirs. They are all geniuses. They have no humility before art. They worship not art but the material gains of art. They work not to accomplish something but to make others acknowledge that they can."

Since his return from his trip to the Orient, he said, he had looked in vain through a hundred manuscripts for good music. "I have heard a lot of modern noise," he stated, "and very little modern music. . . . In the realm of the violin there has been nothing since the Elgar Concerto. This is a period of interpretation rather than of creation."

On another occasion he said: "These are the times for commercial and scientific advancement. Humanity, I believe, advances on one or two fronts at a time but not on all fronts at once, and today it is simply not the turn of art to go forward."

Fritz and Harriet started back for Europe late in April, but spent only one day on the other side of the Atlantic. Hardly arrived, they received a cable telling of the death of George P. Lies, Harriet's father, in New York, of cancer, which had already taken his wife some time previously. Naturally Harriet, the only child, returned to America immediately with her husband.

The *Berengaria* brought them back to New York on May 10, 1924. It happened that Cardinal Mundelein of Chicago was also a passenger, and the papers reported that he administered spiritual consolation to the mourning daughter.

While the *Berengaria* was on the high seas, it received a distress signal from a small steamer, the *Major Wheeler*, to the effect that the assistant engineer, Albert Anderson, had met with an accident. When the man was transferred to the large ocean liner, Harriet Kreisler immediately took up a collection among the passengers on behalf of the stricken engineer. She was able to turn $1,200 over to him.

Not many months elapsed before a dream of Harriet and Fritz's came true: these two wandering globe trotters, who had for years been compelled to live mostly in hotels and Pullmans, and for brief intervals in a rented flat, at last acquired a property they could call their own: a wooded piece of land of several acres in the quiet, residential Grunewald section of western Berlin had become available, and here they built a residential mansion for themselves, a comfortable house for the caretaker and his wife, a conservatory for hothouse flowers and vegetables, an Italian rose garden which was Harriet's special pride, and a parklike terrace with a lawn slowly undulating away from the veranda of the mansion and ending some hundred yards beyond in a sort of grotto with a large marble bench and several seats in white Italian marble.

For the Italian rose garden Fritz would bring home to his Harriet from his concert tours in Italy, now a hand-wrought cast-iron gate, now a charming piece of statuary, now the artistic superstructure for an Italian well.

It was a joy to be a guest of the Kreislers at lunch or dinner during the summer, when the meals were served on the spacious veranda that ran along the rear side of the house, and from which one could overlook the entire idyllic *buon retiro* of this artistic couple.

The estate was so secluded, lying as it did at the end of the Bismarckallee, which seemed to terminate in an attractive little church directly opposite the Kreisler property, that visitors had difficulty finding it the first time. It thus gave Fritz Kreisler that seclusion which he craved for his leisure hours.

The spacious parlor, or music room, which occupied much of the ground-floor space and overlooked the parklike estate, was a veritable museum. There was part of Fritz's priceless library (the rest was in his study on the floor above); there were *objets d'art* from every corner of the globe; there were enticing oil paintings; there was rare China, beautiful tapestry. On the grand piano stood photographs of crowned heads and presidents, of world-famous artists, poets, and philosophers, all of them personally autographed with dedications most flattering to the recipients.

Next to the parlor was a hall decorated exclusively with Chinese and Japanese prints and silks, and ornamented with beautiful Oriental vases and other artistic treasures. The furniture was French.

The adjoining dining room was so arranged that when Fritz and Harriet Kreisler were alone, or when, as they were fond of doing, they entertained only one or two people, the table was set in inclement or winter weather in the alcove facing the spacious lawn.

"Home at last!" Carl Lamson emphasized how frequently Fritz Kreisler spoke enthusiastically about his new abode. Musical contemporaries who chanced to visit the Kreislers in their Grunewald mansion, too, became enchanted.

Fritz and Harriet hoped and expected that this would be their permanent home to the end of their days. Alas for the vicissitude of human life: when they left Berlin in 1939, it was for good. The curtain of fire which the Allied powers laid over Berlin in 1943 and 1944 was

The Kreisler home in Berlin in 1933

The Kreisler home in Berlin in 1945

no respecter of persons, and one of the appalling sights for the first American occupation troops and for me as war correspondent entering Berlin on July 3, 1945, was the totally bombed-out, burnt-to-the-ground, gutted, and demolished Kreisler home.

Soon after Harriet and Fritz moved into their choice new home I was received for an interview, in the course of which three questions were posed: What has the European upheaval following the Great War done to musical art? What of "atonal" music? With what country does the future of music lie?

As to postwar music in Europe, Kreisler described the difference between audiences before and after the Great War in these terms:

"The same radical change that has taken place in other realms is also to be observed in the case of concert audiences. Certain strata of society have suddenly risen to the top, replacing the former representatives of culture. At first I found these new audiences rather dull and unresponsive. This was true particularly of audiences in Austria, Italy, and Germany—less so of England and America, which countries were less directly affected by the war.

"The people who were cast up, as it were, from the bottom—people who 'took up culture'—were a dead weight at first, and it was difficult to play to them. It is surprising, however, how quickly this changed. After all, even the most uncultured person cannot hear Beethoven or Tartini or César Franck with impunity! The ennobling quality of classical music wrought a quick transformation. The audiences became more and more refined, until today concert-goers are as cultured and appreciative as they were before the war."

The second topic was then much debated in Germany—"atonal" music, or music without any reference to euphony and key, and written, in fact, with an apparent intent to revel in cacophony. Kreisler said:

"The atonalists fly in the face of all that we have accepted as standards and as conceptions of beauty and harmony. Their music has little or no relation to these standards.

"Now, I am the last one to insist that art must forever move in the same grooves. If an artist, a composer, has gone with the rest of us for a certain stretch of the road, and then gradually walks off the beaten path and finds paths of his own, I am quite willing to concede that right to him. Beethoven went with the established standards of his time and then blazed new trails. Likewise Wagner in his time; Brahms ditto; Scriabine, Richard Strauss, Mahler, Debussy, and Ravel in our day. But all these men lived up to certain standards of harmony and beauty even when, out of a creative impulse within them, they branched out beyond the conventional. It is a significant fact, however, that these men always had a devoted following of contemporaneous musicians who could understand and keep up with them. Brahms, for instance, had no less a patron than Schumann.

"But take some of our atonalists. They know little about the classical traditions of music, and think that by just putting down a succession of disharmonious and discordant noises which have no integral relation to each other, they have evolved something new in the realm of music. Some combinations of dissonances do not constitute music, in my opinion. After all, art connotes beauty, assonance, harmonic symmetry, and not cacophony. And the atonalists can hardly expect others to understand them when they do not understand themselves.

"I had an amusing experience not long ago. An atonalist handed me a composition of his for perusal. I said to myself, 'If this man really knows what he is doing, he must have written every bar with a purpose, and he will detect alterations of his score immediately.' I therefore tested him out by changing his composition in a number of places. But what do you suppose? He never even noticed the changes!

"Let me put the atonalist case in another way: supposing I learn to know a man intimately and hear him converse, say, in English, German, French, Italian, and Spanish, and that I find he speaks each of these poorly, though claiming to be a linguist. If suddenly, overnight, that man claims to have written marvelous poetry in, say, some dialect spoken by the tribes of Western Africa which I am in no position to control, I think I have a right to doubt his claims. The fact that his knowledge of the languages I know and which he claims to have mastered, is decidedly faulty gives me a right to doubt whether he is a genius in the language which I don't know." *

With what country does the future of music lie? was the third question.

"America," Fritz replied unhesitatingly. Noticing my look of interrogation, he developed his reasons:

"America is a young country, with untold possibilities still before it. I expect great things from it from an artistic standpoint. The same surplus energy which in the earlier days of the Republic went into the acquisition of money

* Later, after he had learned what Nazism is like, he described atonality pithily as "a pogrom in the arts" in an interview for the *Vossische Zeitung* of Berlin for Jan. 10, 1934. He then added: "What surprises me in all these new efforts to achieve effect is that so many instruments and devices must be used when our greatest composers with simple instruments and the human voice did things that remain beautiful."

and the provision for material things is now finding an outlet in the espousal of art.

"In the pioneer days of America it was but natural that men's minds should be filled with material things—the development of railways, the rearing of buildings for service rather than beauty, the construction of bridges and tunnels, the acquisition of money.

"Now America has the leisure and the culture to foster beauty and artistic design. Look at the Woolworth Building in New York, for instance! It is not only a skyscraper—it is also an expression of architectural art. Look, too, at modern bridges in America—they are built with an eye not only to service but also to beauty.

"The traveler who visits the United States at intervals is also struck by the development which artistic city planning and the building of beautiful homes is making. All these are straws which indicate which way the wind is blowing. America is entering upon an artistic period. In music, too, it wants the best that can be furnished from anywhere in the world. American musical audiences are now of high order."

Edoardo Senatra, now of the Italian news agency ANSA, visited Kreisler at about the same time for an interview for the Italian press. Fritz then was still so completely under the impression of his tour of the Orient that he spoke of nothing but his impressions of Japan and China. "In fact," Senatra wrote, "he even wore a picturesque kimono made of wonderful silk and embroidered most artistically."

The matter of atonality must have been very much on Kreisler's mind in 1924, as his chat with me has already shown. To a representative of *Vanity Fair* he stated in August, 1924: *

We live in a world that is in a state of flux. Everything is changing. These unsettled conditions are nowhere more strongly reflected than in the arts. Poets, painters, playwrights, musicians, are casting aside the artistic dogmas which hitherto governed them, and striving for new ways of expressing themselves. To these men—the leaders of the new movements in art—the old forms seem obsolete, utterly antiquated.

The modernists have something so new to express that they look upon the old technical modes as hopeless to convey to the public the ideas of which their work is the embodiment. The consequence is that we now have—among the painters—the modernists, the cubists, and vorticists, and other offshoots of the new movements, with strange pictures, pictures not of material things

* Reprinted from *Stray Thoughts on Modern Music* by Fritz Kreisler, from an article in the August, 1924 issue of *Vanity Fair*, by permission of The Condé Nast Publications, Inc., copyright, 1924, by *Vanity Fair*.

as they appear to our eyes, but of something all but incommunicable—the sensations and impressions that visible objects have created in the painters themselves. They seem to be striving to paint the very moods of their souls on canvas; but to most of us, lacking the key to their minds, these pictures remain without meaning.

I cannot refrain from thinking that the world would be the poorer by far if Rembrandt had sought to express himself in the manner of the modern painters!

Some poets are as difficult to follow as the painters. The stress and turmoil of the day has reacted upon them and colored their work sharply and vividly, so that they have invented new rhythms to replace the old ones, a new vocabulary and new images. These modernist formulae, for they are that as much as the older ones, are, to most of us, a little distracting and disquieting. Strangely enough, those poets among us who write of the bitterest and cruelist phases of life, are often the greatest idealists. They are so haunted by their instinct for beauty that the misery around them revolts their souls. So they seek to remake the world, "to remould it nearer to the heart's desire," and think that only by shocking people out of their smug complacency, will the misery and ugliness of life be swept away.

As it is with painters and playwrights and poets, so is it with musicians. The ultramodernists seek to express their genius in new and experimental ways. For melody and harmony they have but little use; euphony is regarded as a sign of positive weakness. They are casting classic tradition into the dustbin of the past. Those composers who give us melodious sounds to delight the ear, are regarded as unawakened children chanting the alphabet of music. The forms which to Bach were all-sufficient, to them mean nothing. Their ideas refuse to be imprisoned in the old musical moulds. They are inventing their own scales and calling for new instruments, because the old instruments are unable to produce the series of sounds required. They seek to replace harmony with dissonances. They argue that combinations of sounds hitherto looked upon as ugly, are, when one has become accustomed to them, more beautiful and satisfying to the ear, and much more significant to the imagination, than are the harmonies woven in the music of the past.

I frankly admit that there are some of the modern composers whom I do not understand. They speak a language different from what I have learned. These men are many of them fine musicians—some have true genius—but they seem to me to be leading music into an uncharted wilderness.

To me the leaders of the new movements in music, painting, and poetry may well be symbolized as potters crouching over their wheels with formless lumps of clay before them. The curves and flowing lines of the pots that were made in the past do not satisfy them. They desire to mould their lumps of clay into shapes never seen, never imagined before, that will make the onlooker gasp, or shudder with surprise.

With Keats, I hold that "a thing of beauty is a joy for ever." The fundamentals of beauty are still, I think, form, balance and harmony; and these still satisfy me. Other men, of course, are entitled to think differently. We can only watch their experiments sympathetically and see what comes of them. But it is to be regretted that some men who can make real music are today contenting themselves with making noise. Although the composers on the continent of Europe (a good many of them at least) seem to have gone more or less mad in their effort to break away from musical traditions, the English composers seem to be retaining their sanity in spite of the universal upheaval in the world of art. Conspicuous among these is Sir Edward Elgar, whose idealism shines through his music like sunlight through a cloud. The *Dream of Gerontius* is certainly the work of a genius, and many pages of it are full of sheer inspiration. In *Gerontius* Sir Edward Elgar has written music that we shall love when most of the contemporary music of Europe is forgotten.

Fritz and Harriet were not to enjoy possession of their new and beautiful home for long that first year, for the tour of the Orient, the many charitable undertakings and the excitement of furnishing and moving into a new house had proven too much for even the indomitable Harriet. They had, therefore, to go to Carlsbad, Czechoslovakia, to continue the cure which she had begun the year before after her return from the Orient.

Fritz interrupted his stay there to hurry over to London, "just because I want to, because I love that city and it loves me and I don't want to lose the contact with it," as he said to an interviewer.

On December 17, 1924, Kreisler gave his only concert of the year in his native city of Vienna. The New York *Times* correspondent cabled laconically, "The applause was in Carnegie Hall fashion." Nothing more was needed to tell American music lovers the story.

He now hastened back to Berlin for the first Christmas in the beautiful new home. Frau Friederike Henriette Pistor, who with her husband was one of the most intimate friends of the Kreislers in Berlin, wrote about the annual Yuletide observation in the Kreisler home:

Fritz and Harriet always arranged a Christmas celebration for their help. The two would light the Christmas tree, invite the servants, the chauffeur, and the caretaker and their wives to come into the spacious parlor, and there distribute the gifts. Fritz would personally pour the champagne for them.

After that, year after year, they came over to our house for our Christmas observance. As I have a son, it was self-evident to them that they would come to us, rather than we to them. Fritz would play the Christmas song on our grand piano. Later he would sit down at the spinet and there was something profoundly touching in the expression of his face as he would softly play old sacred music.

Sometimes the Kreislers would come to us on foot, without their car. One day Fritz came that way, wearing his beloved mountaineer's cape [*Lodenmantel*]. My old servant who put away the wraps afterward said, "I suppose the gentleman is a mountain climber." "No," I replied, "he is the famous violin virtuoso Fritz Kreisler." The name registered immediately and she said, "What? Fritz Kreisler? Why, he talks so naturally and simply to us as if he were one of us." She was deeply impressed with his humaneness.

Harriet at one time brought three velvet jackets home from a trip to America, of which Walther Kirchhoff,* my husband and Fritz each received one. They would occasionally appear in them as the Fraternity of Velvet Brothers, the purpose of which was to emphasize their friendship but also, while thus garbed, to give each other an unvarnished piece of their minds. The result was inevitable—it took all the diplomacy of Velvet Brother Fritz to settle a quarrel into which they got!

* A famous German opera tenor.

CHAPTER TWENTY-ONE

A TOUR "DOWN UNDER"

[1925]

RELATIVELY few European and American artists have gone to what, in an adaptation of Churchill's famous war phrase, is the underbelly of the earth—the Australian continent and the two islands of New Zealand. Yet there was a teeming musical life there in the twenties, and teachers of great merit formed the staffs of ambitious conservatories. Percy A. Grainger was not as yet the world figure in 1925 that he became later, but Nellie Melba and Frances Alda had placed Australia securely on the musical map of the world.

Fritz Kreisler was booked for a strenuous tour "down under." Eleven concerts in Sydney, four in Melbourne, three in Auckland, three in Wellington, two in Brisbane, and one each in Adelaide, Christchurch, and Dunedin were crowded into a stay that began May 1 and ended June 29.

Before going to our antipodes, however, Kreisler had his usual busy season in America. He arrived with his wife on January 10, 1925. When asked the stock question as to new compositions that he might have in his suitcase, he replied that "Music in Europe is in a transitory stage and very little is being done."

"What about jazz?" someone asked.

He answered:

"Jazz, too, is transitory. To me it seems that it is a clever caricature. We do not think of pen-and-ink caricatures as art. Jazz has the same relationship to music. The majority of the jazz composers pilfered their themes and motifs from the masters.

"Those jazz writers who steal all the old-time melodies which came from the brains of others and turn them into syncopated time because it means a quick return of money are nothing better than thieves.

"The 'Hindoo Song' in its original version is one of the principal themes in the opera *Sadko* by Rimsky-Korsakoff and ranks as a classic among modern melodies. The jazz merchants, however, laid their unholy hands upon it several years ago and it has since appeared as a fox-trot dished up in various different ways and under various titles.

"I had loved that song and often played it. Somebody turned it into popular jazz dance music. Hundreds know it for the first time in that form. One night I played it during a recital and some of the audience were astounded. 'Why, Kreisler is playing jazz,' was the comment I heard on every side. They thought that lovely thing was the creation of some popular music writer, though to me it was only a very dear old friend who had been shamefully slandered.

"Writers can be protected from plagiarism, but poor old Beethoven, Bach, Tchaikovsky, and Chopin cannot rise up in their graves and flay the thieves who turn their wondrous music into such syncopated paths that the composers themselves do not recognize it."

To digress for a moment: six years later Fritz Kreisler modified his opinion about jazz. He said to Horace Melvin of the Richmond *Times-Dispatch* in November, 1931:

"Jazz is characteristic of the people of America in the mass—it is the expression of their vibrant stimulating spirit, vigorous and direct. Gradually it is being advanced to a very distinctive style of music. The efforts of several American composers in 'popular music'—and 'popular music' is the music of the people—are to be lauded and encouraged. There have been notable contributions from Mr. George Gershwin, Mr. Jerome Kern, and Mr. Irving Berlin, among others, and I am especially impressed with the work of young Mr. Vincent Youmans. These comic opera composers are sincere in their work, and are giving generously to American music, which some day will attain its full stature and will receive the recognition it deserves.

"Even now the prejudice of tradition is being dissipated. Leading musicians and artists, slowly but nevertheless surely, are giving more attention to the possibilities of American music as a school of expression."

Still later, on October 9, 1936, he said to a representative of the New York *Times*:

Percy A. Grainger, 1882-1961

olas Andrejevitch Rimsky-Korsakoff, 1844-1908

Jerome Kern, 1885-1945

George Gershwin, 1898-1937

"Jazz is the expression of primeval instincts. Don't think jazz is bad. There is good and bad music, and do you think all classics are good? Who can tell, a gifted man like Gershwin, had he been born in some other environment, might have written great symphonies, but it happened that his expression was in the field of typical American syncopated music."

When New Yorkers heard Kreisler was leaving for Hawaii and Australia, they decided to turn his final New York recital on February 21, 1925, into a farewell demonstration. The New York *Times* reported:

> In the lobby hung a wreath, inscribed to Kreisler, from the Bohemians. In the hall an audience which exhausted every inch of its capacity, including a crowded stage, listened spell-bound. . . . Kreisler was never a man of one or six composers. He seems to meet all of them with nearly equal felicity and to bring to each work the technic and interpretive manner due to its author and period.

At Honolulu he appeared in three crowded concerts, but also ran into something of a storm—not a physical one, as on the tour of the Orient two years previously, but a musical one. The Chicago *Tribune* reported in a copyrighted dispatch from Honolulu on April 5: "Fritz Kreisler . . . created somewhat of a sensation among Hawaiian enthusiasts when he asserted that 'Aloha Oe' was not a Hawaiian song but really an old Austrian folk song."

The Hawaiians were understandably crestfallen, for their charming islands have been internationally popularized by the ingratiating tune of "Aloha Oe."

Fritz chuckled when reminded of the incident. "What had happened was this," he volunteered. "A German-born violin teacher of San Francisco went to Honolulu frequently and somehow became acquainted with the last reigning queen of Hawaii, Liliuokalani, who commissioned him to write a national anthem.

"I suppose the easy-going fiddler figured, 'Austria is far away from Hawaii.' So he took the Viennese ditty, 'Jetzt geh'n wir gleich nach Nussdorf 'raus' (We'll go to Nussdorf right away), and offered it with certain adaptations to Her Majesty as the music for Hawaii's national anthem." (Nussdorf is a popular suburb of Vienna.) "He was knighted by Queen Liliuokalani for his feat of providing Hawaii with its most popular song!" *

For weeks before the arrival of the Kreisler party, consisting of Harriet and Fritz, as well as of "Gretchen" (Helen) and Carl Lamson, the Australian newspapers and musical magazines carried stories about the "wizard of the violin," emphasizing his unique stature in the music world, pointing out that he was the first ex-enemy to perform in Australia and New Zealand, and stressing the great value to students and lovers of music of having two celebrities in their various fields like Kreisler and Chaliapin (who, they said, was to come the following year) to give authoritative interpretations of the great masters. The phonograph companies published expensive advertisements listing the Kreisler recordings. Photographs of the violinist and his beautiful wife appearing frequently in the dailies and weeklies made Harriet's and Fritz's faces familiar to the Australians and New Zealanders long before their arrival.

The party sailed from Honolulu on the *Aorangi*. They were greeted in Sydney on May 1 by the Australian concert manager McCrae, a man sporting a goatee and expressing himself in cockney. "I 'ope these concerts goes without 'itch," he commented.

"Why have you been so long coming?" Kreisler was asked by the Sydney press.

"You are a long way off," he replied. "But the delay is all the better, for then one comes to you with riper experience."

Asked for a formula for achieving eminence in art, he said he had none. He added, however:

> "When one walks out on the platform and plays, one becomes absorbed in one's music. That absorption is something within oneself over which one has no control. What it is we do not know. Just as the orator communicates with his audiences without being able to explain how he casts his spell, so the musician communicates with his. There are circumstances beyond our control which influence our playing. A new audience, a different hall, altered climatic conditions—all these affect an artist's work."

* Queen Liliuokalani, were she alive, would probably take issue with this statement. She claimed to be the composer and had "Aloha Oe" copyrighted as her work in 1884. In 1892, the Pacific Music Company of San Francisco published the song with Hawaiian, English, and German texts and the statement, "Composed by Her Royal Highness, Princess Liliuokalani of Honolulu, Oahu, H. I."

The first concert did not take place until May 9. On May 4, however, there was a civic reception.

"It was a very formal occasion," Carl Lamson remembers. "The acting mayor delivered a eulogy proclaiming the guest of honor the greatest living violinist, but before coming to the climax that was to end in the pronunciation of Fritz's name, he turned to someone near him and whispered in an aside, 'What's his name, anyway?'

"Fritz delivered the first long speech in his life. It was excellent. He stressed the value of music in binding peoples together. He pleaded for peace and harmony. I remember only one other occasion when Fritz spoke. That was in San Francisco. It was quite an effort for him, and he meant it when he told the audience, 'I now realize how easy it is to play the violin.'

"When Fritz finished his address in Sydney, the whole audience sang, 'For he's a jolly good fellow.' "

One should not be too hard on the acting mayor for delivering a speech without apparently knowing whom he was talking about. It was the deputy mayor and not His Honor himself who acted as host. The Lord Mayor had suddenly been called out of town on official business, and had left the prepared speech of welcome behind.

The Sydney *Morning Herald* quoted only a line or two of what Carl Lamson remembers as an "excellent" speech, but even these lines reveal Kreisler's imaginative mind. "The artist is like the honeybee," he said. "He gathers the pollen and travels from country to country sowing the seed of understanding. His is the message of friendship and goodwill."

Another speaker was W. Arundel Orchard, director of the Sydney Conservatorium. The burden of his remarks was that the benefit to Australian students of hearing Kreisler would be tantamount to their going overseas for study.

On the day of the first recital the Sydney *Morning Herald* published a brief interview on modern music. Kreisler reasoned that "these developments may lead somewhere—we can't say as yet. Whether they will open a new pathway for us, or peter out in a blind alley, it is too early to say. But I am inclined to think that they will peter out. . . . The real test in all these things is sincerity."

More than five thousand people attended the first Kreisler concert in the huge Sydney Town Hall with its imposing pipe organ in the center of the stage. The *Morning Herald* observed: "Fritz Kreisler held the great audience under a spell at Town Hall. It was one of the most remarkable first nights in the history of music in this city. The artist was greeted with protracted cheering." At the end of the first movement of the Handel Sonata in A, the paper stated, Kreisler had to interrupt his playing to accept a huge wreath. After the Bach Suite in E "the house rose to him and he was many times recalled. His subjugation of the audience was now complete."

Among the notables present were Viceroy Lord Foster and Lady Foster, as well as Governor Sir Dudley and Lady de Chair. Kreisler "closed the concert by playing the national anthem."

It would be carrying coals to Newcastle to repeat the superlatives that were applied day after day to Fritz Kreisler's Australian performances. Suffice it to say that at the end of the Sydney series the *Morning Herald* summed up the impressions of Sydney music lovers in an editorial:

> In these days, when so many of the modern composers are crowding their scores with fantastic dissonances, quarter-tones, and similar eccentricities, and calling the result music, it is a relief to find a sane interpreter who goes serenely on, showing us not only that the works of the old masters are fresh and beautiful, but that within their pages are many qualities we ought to study far more keenly before being led off into dubious pathways in the name of art.

Had the Kreisler party been so minded, a continuous round of social events could have made Sydney's socialites very happy, but would probably have exhausted the artist and his accompanist. Harriet, however, put a taboo on social engagements. "Fritz must stay in form," she insisted. Fritz later commented to me, characteristically, "and she was right." She would even frown on his conversing animatedly after concerts with the people who flocked into the artist's room. Half banteringly, half in earnest she would say to "Gretchen" Lamson: "Look at that Fritz. Why, he's a regular show-off."

One incident stands out in the Kreislers' mind particularly. A British colonel very late one afternoon knocked at the door of their hotel suite despite the sign, "Do not disturb." He explained, apologetically, that he was the aide-de-camp to an Indian maharajah who happened to be in Australia on a visit and who, because of his rank, was accustomed to sit in the front row, at any performance he had attended. He had been unable, however, to procure the desired tickets. Could Mr. Kreisler do anything about it?

The situation was solved to the satisfaction of all parties concerned in that extra chairs were placed in the front of the concert hall, directly under the podium and ahead of the regular seats, for the maharajah and his party.

The Indian prince had a beautiful yacht to which he invited the Kreislers for a tour of the coastal environs of Sydney. On departing, he expressed himself graciously, if unusually: "I hope that when some day you come to India, your motor car will break down before my door, so that I may not only welcome you to my home but also present you to some of the other maharajahs of my country."

As is to be expected of an Indian prince, he was very picturesque indeed in his ceremonial robes, his jewels, and his turban.

On one occasion, the Lamsons recall, the Papal delegate called before the concert, blessed the concert hall and the piano, and then went into the artists' room to bless the violin and the performers.

Harriet, who naturally knew all of her husband's repertoire by heart, spent some of the concert evenings attending boxing and wrestling bouts. It was quite a relief from the formal functions which she has had to attend so frequently as an artist's wife.

Once the whole party went to the races. Fritz and Harriet quite unexpectedly there met the great Scotch comedian Sir Harry Lauder, and Helen Lamson met her classmate, the late Pauline Frederick, who was starred in *Spring Cleaning* during an all-Australian tour.

After Sydney came Melbourne for three public concerts and a private playing for one thousand Catholic nuns who were prohibited by the rules of their order from attending a public recital.

"The Melbourners won't take anything at Sydney's word," Carl Lamson remarked. "So we had first to prove ourselves in an initial concert attended by only seventy-five people. But the hall was filled for the remaining two recitals."

Brisbane and Adelaide followed, and then Kreisler, Lamson, and

Manager McCrae proceeded alone to New Zealand, Harriet and "Gretchen" returning to Sydney. "We had a terrible boat and a very bad crossing," Lamson recalls with a shudder. "We all got awfully sick." The two islands that make up New Zealand, it should be remembered, are one thousand miles from the eastern coast of Australia!

They had no cause to regret having gone to the big southern islands that are about the size of the States of New York, Connecticut, New Jersey, and Pennsylvania. The *New Zealand Herald* of Auckland, for instance, wrote:

> To hear Kreisler is to freely acknowledge that we are privileged to live in days when the pinnacle has been reached as far as sovereign mastery of violin technique is concerned. Yet added to this quality in the case of the distinguished visitor is an artistic enthusiasm, intellectual capacity, and fiery, yet never exaggerated temperament which would make even the feeblest composition glow with an importance it never possessed.

On June 9 Fritz Kreisler and Carl Lamson were tendered a reception by members of the Wellington Society of Musicians at the Pioneer Club. Again Fritz was called upon to speak. He responded by stating that he considered himself "one of art's messengers of understanding and sympathy."

Of one of his concerts in Wellington, the *New Zealand Evening Post* of that city wrote:

> Like a sheaf in a gale, Kreisler bowed and bowed before the storm of applause at the close of his performance. . . . Personally, Kreisler appeared to make an irresistible appeal to his audience.

On their return to the mainland on June 19, Fritz Kreisler and Carl Lamson found that two more concerts had been arranged for Sydney, and that W. Arundel Orchard was eager for Kreisler to play the Beethoven Violin Concerto with the orchestra of the conservatory. Also, one more concert had been scheduled for Melbourne.

To the interviewing journalists Fritz likened Australia to a "smaller America, in an early stage of development." He pointed out that "America is now a great center of art, and as you develop you will occupy a like position."

In the last recital on June 26, the lights failed during the last number, Kreisler's arrangement of several of Brahms's "Hungarian Dances." "But," remarked the Sydney *Morning Herald*, "the two continued in the grey light of the fading day. They and their audience looked like wraiths."

Just before the recital Kreisler had received a wireless message from Admiral S. S. Robinson, USN: "The privilege of again hearing you will add much to the pleasure of our visit." He was on his way with his flotilla for an official visit to Australia. The Governor of New South Wales, Sir Dudley de Chair, and Lady de Chair also attended, as they had on the opening night.

After the concert with the conservatory orchestra under Orchard's baton, Kreisler complimented his Australian fellow artists with these generous words which were long gratefully remembered: "The players did very well. I was certainly pleased with the general results. The orchestra is already in fine shape and will in due course bring credit to Sydney."

The press reported the next morning that the applause was so prolonged that Kreisler finally led Orchard out to intone the national anthem, with his beautiful Guarnerius soaring high above the other instruments.

Before departing from "down under" with his small party, Fritz addressed a farewell message to the *Australian Musical News*:

> It is easy enough for an artist who has given so many concerts in each Australian city he has visited to declare that Australians are a most musical people, but I felt that at the very beginning of my work here. I felt an immediate responsiveness to whatever message of the spirit I had brought to them. I felt it in the great music as well as in the little things.
>
> And my message was as great a one as a man could bring, for I feel as an Austrian and the first artist of a former enemy country to come and play to you, that I have made the way a little easier for the restoration of good will. Music is the tongue that speaks to all civilized humanity.
>
> (Signed) *Fritz Kreisler.*

CHAPTER TWENTY-TWO

THE WORLD AT HIS FEET

[1925-1932]

FRITZ KREISLER was now fifty years old. The music world lay at his feet. Criticism of an adverse nature was as scarce as gossip of marital infidelity.

How did Fritz Kreisler appear physically during his fifties? H. T. Parker drew this picture: *

What an ingratiating and stimulating figure Mr. Kreisler is . . . this plain man without a trick of manner, without a touch of affectation, without a hint of self-assertion! In his springy stride, which seems to halt only because there is an edge to the stage, speaks his elasticity of spirit; his quiet pose suggests its concentration; his clear glance its poise and its faculty of illumination. . . . He does not consult the ceiling; knit or relax his brows, or weave back and forth after the manner of elephants in chains.

As to the quality of his musicianship at the fiftieth milestone, Adolf Weissmann, one of the most feared of Berlin music critics, who made and unmade artistic careers by a few strokes of his pen, wrote in 1925:

Fritz Kreisler has . . . developed a new type of virtuosity to highest perfection. He . . . has imbued his playing with a human feeling that nobody else attains. . . . We have, then, here a case of a violin virtuoso who rose to the top as a representative of bourgeois, human art but who at the same time has remained the virtuoso who wins the masses over to music through his fine sensitivity and his truly human method of expression.

For full measure, this tribute from Mrs. Channing Ward, writing in the Richmond, Virginia, *News Leader* for February 10, 1927 under

* Reprinted by permission of Dodd, Mead & Company from *Eighth Notes, Voices and Figures of Music and the Dance* by H. T. Parker, copyright, 1922, by Dodd, Mead & Company, Inc.

her pen name, Helen de Motte, may be added:

> We—all of us who come under his spell—are the merest star gazers, who are lifted for a brief period into the rare atmosphere of unfrequented spaces. He travels a celestial orbit the vibrations of which hold all the joys and all the sorrows of this old world, but in which all dross is transmuted into prismatic radiance.

The years under discussion (1925-1932) brought Kreisler honors he never dreamed of in his youth. The greatest of these was the receipt of the honorary degree of Doctor of Laws from Glasgow University on June 19, 1929.

The Glasgow dailies carried vivid descriptions of a ceremony that must indeed have been unique. They have been combined here in one composite and abridged but textually unchanged account, the major share taken from the *Daily Record:*

> Varied interests were represented at an important graduation ceremony in Bute Hall today, a number of distinguished personalities receiving honorary degrees. Among the LLD's were Kreisler, the famous violinist, and Mme. Marie Curie.
>
> It was Kreisler's special wish that he should be allowed to play to the students of the University that had honored his art.
>
> The scenes at Bute Hall, where the recital took place, were remarkable. An hour before the doors were opened to ticket holders, huge crowds of students assembled; their "Ygorras" penetrated to the official luncheon then proceeding. In the rush for seats when the hall was thrown open earlier than arranged, women students lost their "chubbies," gloves and trinkets, and at least one wristlet watch was picked up by the janitors as part of the "casualties."
>
> Violin and bow in hand, and wearing the scarlet which indicated the honor conferred less than an hour before, Kreisler was glimpsed in the doorway leading from Randolph Hall to Bute Hall. Men and girls sprang to their feet, waving handkerchiefs and arms in demonstration of their enthusiasm.
>
> Stepping forward to the open piano Mr. Henderson, organist to the university, struck the appropriate note—the Glasgow students' slogan "Ygorra." Old and young took up the challenge, Kreisler by this time on the dais, glancing about him with a slight air of bewilderment, yet obviously charmed at the spontaneity and exuberance of the tribute.
>
> Silence was long in being restored. In the first lull, Kreisler left the little platform and threw off his gown as became a workman who wished to do his

job unhampered. Then, with Mr. Charles Keith as accompanist, he embarked on a program which revealed the musician as master of many moods.

If the audience was grateful, the performer was no less appreciative of the compliment their approval signified, for instinctively he lowered the violin and murmured, "Thank you very much."

"Speech," resounded from all parts of the hall when the recital, which had lasted over half an hour, came to what everybody regarded as an untimely end.

Reluctantly, because he is a modest man, Kreisler made his way back to the dais hoping—in vain it proved—that by bowing again and again he might appease those who wished him to say a word.

"I had been given to understand," he said, when the echoes died away, "that I was not expected to speak. So I am entirely unprepared. However, let me tell you how proud and happy I am today. When it became known that the Senate of the University of Glasgow graciously had invited me amongst distinguished recipients of this high degree, I received very many messages from all over the world that left no doubt, at any rate in my mind, that almost every violinist and every Austrian felt that the honor which has been conferred upon me today was in some slight measure conferred upon every one of them.

"I feel that, therefore, I am standing beholden today to the University of Glasgow in a threefold capacity—as the exponent of my art, as the representative of my country, and as an individual. My gratitude is immense, but alas, so also is my knowledge of the inadequacy of my linguistic abilities to express it. I have been permitted, however, to thank you through the four strings of my violin. You have been able to gauge by it the depth of my feeling and the quality of my gratitude."

As the storm of cheering broke out afresh, the musician, smiling and bowing, backed away. Sir Donald MacAlister then rose in his place at one of the stalls and said: "Allow me, a senior student of the University, to voice our gratitude to Dr. Kreisler for the charm and beauty of his performance for the benefit of us students. I have often to take around the university distinguished visitors from foreign lands and from our own country, and I take them to the Bute Hall as a private duty. But in future I shall have to tell them all—as I shall—that this is the hall in which Kreisler played to the students of Glasgow."

This account lacks one detail which Fritz Kreisler remembers vividly to the present day: he had none of his priceless instruments with him and had to play on a borrowed fiddle.*

Other honors were showered upon Fritz Kreisler and his wife during these eight years. On December 18, 1926, Fritz was presented with

* Almost three years before this impressive ceremony, Kreisler nearly came to grief as he was on his way to Glasgow. The Channel steamer at Belfast, Ireland, had been held to permit him to finish his concert and to proceed to Glasgow, but the taxi rushing to the quay crashed into another vehicle. The taxi was wrecked completely but Kreisler remained unhurt and caught the boat.

an artistic medal by Dr. Felix Frank, Austrian minister to Germany, in recognition of his benefactions to starving Austrian children. The medal, designed by Artur Löwenthal, a Berlin sculptor, bore Kreisler's likeness on one side and an allegorical figure of music on the other. A copy was acquired by the Kaiser Friedrich Museum of Berlin.

Kreisler utilized the occasion of his brief stay in Berlin to start a fund for the support of needy students at the University of Berlin.

Two months later, in New York, Harriet received the Golden Cross of Honor of Austria, bestowed by order of the Austrian President through the consul general in New York, in recognition of her work for the Vienna Children's Milk Fund. There was a jeweled cross worth $200 on the decoration. Characteristically, Harriet said after the ceremony, and after the consul general had left, "To hell with decorations!" and promptly sold the cross for charity.

At about this time Fritz was also honored by the Portuguese Government with a decoration consisting of a cross in the center and jewels and hammered leaves on the sides, on which were entered the words "*Scientias e Letras e Artes.*" In telling about it he said, "Harriet immediately took the jewels and the cross and sold them for charity."

His own attitude was: "I never wore decorations if I could help it. I think it lowers one to show them off by public display. Once or twice, of course, I could not get out of it without being absolutely rude."

On one occasion the violinist almost failed to receive a high decoration. The Scandinavian tour of December, 1926, was a strenuous one, and when Fritz and his accompanist reached his Stockholm hotel after three concerts in four days, he felt very tired and asked Harriet to see to it that nobody disturbed him with telephone calls or visitors, as he felt the need of a rest before that night's concert.

Suddenly there was a knock at the door despite the sign. Harriet, thinking it was an autograph hunter, refused to admit the intruder. The caller then went to the hotel manager and insisted that he simply must deliver a royal message, whereupon, with many apologies for the disturbance, the king's aide—for such he proved to be—presented a letter advising Fritz that His Majesty King Gustavus V had awarded him the Commander's Cross of the Royal Order of Vasa! He added that the royal family would attend the concert that night. That meant, of course, that Fritz had to hang the Commander's Cross around his neck throughout the performance, even though, as his accompanist Arpad Sandor put it, "he felt decidedly uncomfortable as it dangled over his boiled shirt and vest."

Kreisler's constant concern for unknown composers manifested itself in the case of another accompanist who made a tour of Scandinavia with him during this period: Ernö Balogh. He took this accompanist's two compositions, "Caprice antique" and "Dirge of the North," transcribed them for the violin, and placed them in his repertoire. He also, in 1927, placed compositions by two fellow violinists, Eugène Ysaÿe and Paul Kochansky, on his programs.

An incident of a slightly different kind, also of assistance to a fellow musician, occurred in Dublin, Ireland, in 1932. While on his way to the theater, Kreisler heard the strains of a violin. He left his car and found a poorly dressed girl playing the violin by the curb. He was especially attracted by her beautiful execution of double stops. He asked her to come to his hotel apartment for an audition. As a result Lillian Mack of County Westmeath obtained a concert engagement in Dublin for the following week.

During the same tour of the British Isles, an unnamed British passport officer wrote in the *White Star Magazine* of August 21, 1932:

> The great Kreisler arrived one day at the port where I was stationed. He missed the train and had to wait another hour in the cold and cheerless station. An official laughingly suggested that the famous master while away the time by giving a short recital to the officers. With a little laugh, Kreisler took out his violin and there, to a spell-bound audience of passport and customs officers, railway men and dockers, the world's greatest violinist played as only he can play.
>
> "I hope you enjoyed it," he said shyly when he had finished. That night people paid fantastic prices to hear him in London.

Charities, it goes without saying, occupied an important place in the Kreislers' minds during the years under discussion. The battle against cancer also became their fight, all the more so as both of Harriet's parents had fallen prey to this disease. On February 28, 1927, Harriet addressed a letter to Dr. George A. Soper, managing director of the American Society for the Control of Cancer, offering to the

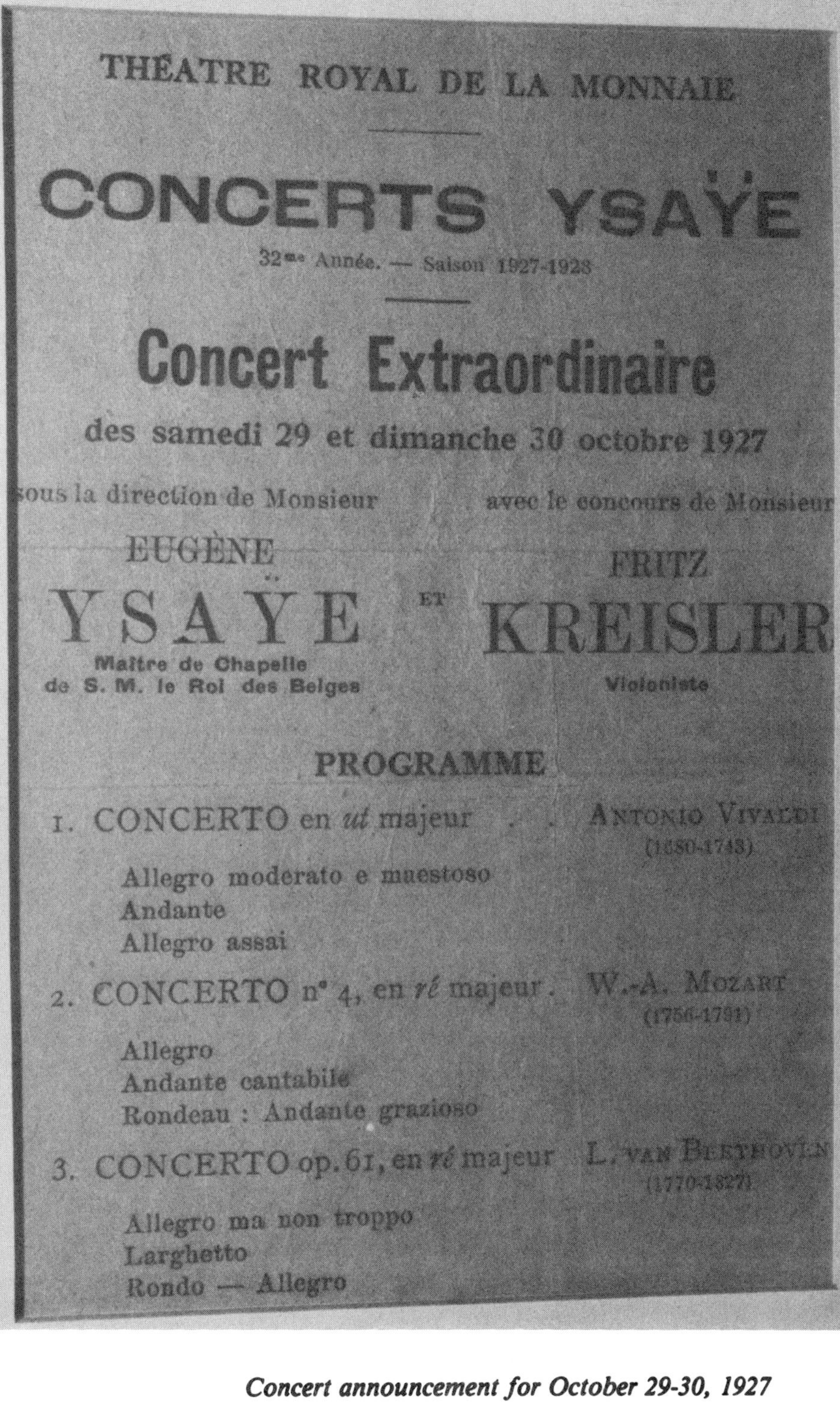

THÉATRE ROYAL DE LA MONNAIE

CONCERTS YSAŸE

32me Année. — Saison 1927-1928

Concert Extraordinaire

des samedi 29 et dimanche 30 octobre 1927

sous la direction de Monsieur

EUGÈNE

YSAŸE

Maître de Chapelle
de S. M. le Roi des Belges

ET

avec le concours de Monsieur

FRITZ

KREISLER

Violoniste

PROGRAMME

1. CONCERTO en *ut* majeur . . . ANTONIO VIVALDI (1680-1743)

Allegro moderato e maestoso
Andante
Allegro assai

2. CONCERTO nº 4, en *ré* majeur . W.-A. MOZART (1756-1791)

Allegro
Andante cantabile
Rondeau : Andante grazioso

3. CONCERTO op. 61, en *ré* majeur L. VAN BEETHOVEN (1770-1827)

Allegro ma non troppo
Larghetto
Rondo — Allegro

Concert announcement for October 29-30, 1927

Sir Landon Ronald with Kreisler in England

society "the entire proceeds of a concert which Mr. Kreisler will give on Sunday, March 27, in the Metropolitan Opera House." Fritz, who was on tour, knew nothing of this arrangement until his manager, Charles Foley, wired him that Harriet had hired the Metropolitan. "I thought it was one of Harriet's jokes," Fritz said.

The concert netted $26,000—almost nine times the $3,000 recital fee to which Kreisler was at that time accustomed as the highest-paid violinist! With the aid of pledge blanks in ensuing recital programs, over $6,000 additional was raised.

A few months previously Fritz and Harriet Kreisler had been in Vienna to close out Harriet's relief work there. She had collected almost $500,000 in America and thus saved many Austrian babies' lives. She distributed the balance of $64,000 among the charitable societies of Vienna.

Passing through Berlin, Fritz gave his only concert of the season for the benefit of the German capital's needy children.

In 1927, during his annual tour to the British Isles, Kreisler, as the Court Circular pointed out, gave a concert in aid of Queen Mary's Hospital Fund for the East End, Stratford, at the Royal Albert Hall. The king and queen, Prince Henry (president of the hospital), the lord mayor and lady mayoress, and the sheriffs of the City of London attended.

He also gave a benefit performance for the Foundation Fund of the Royal Philharmonic Society, "a generous offer in the year of the Beethoven centenary," as the London *Times* put it. Sir Landon Ronald conducted.

One other charitable undertaking deserves mention: the establishment, in November, 1930, of a Fritz Kreisler prize to be awarded annually to the most gifted violinist to be found in Belgium. It was to be open to foreigners as well as natives, but all competitors must have pursued their studies in Belgium and be under twenty-six years of age on January 1 of each year's competition.

It is characteristic of Kreisler's popularity at this time that Deems Taylor in 1925 called attention to the fact that Charles Foley "never advertises in advance what the program is—he knows it is sufficient to say Kreisler will play." He continued:

For once I am inclined to side with a public that puts the interpreter first and the music second. For I know of no virtuoso whose playing gives one to such a degree the feeling of being in close communion with a great and rare spirit.

A violinist of note who chanced to meet or hear Fritz for the first time in the late twenties has supplied interesting recollections of his first impressions. Nathan Milstein said: "I heard Kreisler play in 1926 in Paris, with Philip Gaubert conducting. It was divine! Bach's E Major, Beethoven's, Mendelssohn's, and Viotti's No. 22 concertos—what more could I want?! It was the realization of my dreams. I had first become acquainted with Kreisler's art through his recordings. Over in Russia I had bought everything by him that I could lay my hands upon. I specialized in recordings by Kreisler, Casals, and Chaliapin."

Personal grief came to Kreisler on March 26, 1926, when he received the news that Franz Kneisel, first violinist of the celebrated Kneisel String Quartet, had died. He was asked to be one of the pallbearers. The tears streamed down his face as they carried the coffin out. He played the Adagio from Bach's Double Concerto in E Major with Gaston Déthier as a final tribute to his friend.

The great depression in the United States in 1929 made Kreisler prouder of America, his "second fatherland," than ever before. For it was then that men and women who overnight became penniless showed what stuff they were made of. He is fond of telling how the daughter of a family of formerly wealthy people walked from office to office unashamed and unafraid; how the daughter of a banker came home flushed with excitement because she had secured a job in a department store. "I never admired the United States more than during the depression," he said.

Harriet was discovered by a reporter to have temporarily taken the place of some jobless veteran who, like thousands of others, was selling apples during the depression. She took charge of his stand so that he might go off to a good lunch for which she provided the wherewithal.

During the depression Fritz, in December, 1929, in a Carnegie Hall recital, played the E Major Suite for violin by Carl Goldmark, with the Russian composer Glazounoff as an interested listener. The rendition provoked an unusual criticism in the New York *Times* of December 14:

> The atmosphere was a paradoxical anachronism. Actually Carnegie Hall in New York City was the scene; virtually Stephansplatz [St. Stephen's Square] and the quaint *Gassen* [lanes] leading up to it from all sides in Vienna was where the hearers were transported by the wand of the player. Even the time was changed to a few decades back.
>
> Mr. Kreisler's playing was more than usually wistful and reminiscent. Perhaps the inclusion of Goldmark's work was a tribute to an old friend. The little shifts connecting his notes, the serpentine *staccato*, the characteristic *rubato* and lift at the end of a short phrase, and especially the celestial *flageolets*, were again in evidence.

One of the most amazing episodes of these history-laden eight years was an offer that came from the Soviet Government in 1930 for Kreisler to play two concerts in Moscow, one in Kiev and one in Leningrad, and Kreisler's rejection of the offer. Gershon Swet, former foreign correspondent in Berlin and now in New York, relates the facts as follows:

"An American agronomist, Dr. Josef Rosen, was living in Russia as the representative of the American Joint Distribution Committee. He was very fond of music and a regular attendant at Carnegie Hall recitals.

"At that time there were virtually no concerts by outstanding foreign artists in Russia. There was a strict embargo on the exportation of Russian money. Such artists from abroad as happened to visit the Soviet Union were permitted to acquire and take with them pictures, antiques, or furs, but not currency. The result was that none of the really famous virtuosi cared to go to Russia.

"Dr. Rosen was on friendly terms with Kalinin, who 'fronted' as president of Russia. One day Rosen complained to Kalinin that he never had an opportunity to hear great violinists or pianists such as he was wont to hear in America. Kalinin then asked him whom he'd like to hear.

"Rosen replied, 'First of all, of course, Kreisler.'

" 'Would he come if invited?' Kalinin queried.

" 'If he's paid in foreign exchange,' was Rosen's answer.

"Kalinin then told Rosen that he was ready to pay Kreisler $10,000 for four concerts—two in Moscow, one each in Leningrad and Kiev—and that he was prepared to deposit this amount for Kreisler in advance in Berlin.

"This was an unheard-of offer, such as had been made to no other foreign artist. Rosen came to Berlin early in January, 1931, and requested me to be the intermediary. I contacted the concert agency Wolff & Sachs, who arranged for me to meet Fritz Kreisler on a certain Saturday morning in his home in the Bismarckallee.

"I remained for several hours. For Kreisler told me about his numerous trips to Russia—how he had visited it for the first time in 1896 to give a concert in St. Petersburg (Leningrad); how he had later traveled there almost every year and played in Moscow, St. Petersburg, Kiev, Kharkov, and Odessa; how he met Borodin, Rimsky-Korsakoff, César Cui, Liadov, and Ziloty, and was especially intimate with Rachmaninoff and Koussevitzky.

"But what really surprised me was that, in the first place, he manifested a decided interest in Russian culture and art, and in the second, that he knew a great deal about Russian history. He mentioned among other things that Mozart was but little understood in Russia because his style simply did not suit the Russian mentality and emotion. He explained their lack of appreciation of the rococo style in music on the grounds that the Russians were more Asiatic than they were European.

"Our conversation turned to the Slavophiles of the Chomiakoff school, who are of the opinion that Peter the Great rendered a poor service to Russia in turning to the West, thereby pouring water into Russia's unadulterated Slavic wine. Their movement led to the formation in Russia, and especially among the emigrants in Berlin and Paris, during the first years after World War I, of a sort of countermovement called Eurasia. The essence of its philosophy was that, since Russia was half European and half Asiatic, a fusion of the European with the Asiatic should be achieved.

"One of the apostles of the Eurasian theory, Peter Suvchinsky, was a music critic by profession and lived in Berlin, where he published articles in German weeklies.

"It was amazing to me to learn that Fritz Kreisler knew all this and was in sympathy with the Eurasian philosophy.

"Kreisler did not accept the Soviet proposal. He said he was tired and loved his new home and did not care to go on tour.

"Before I took my leave the name Heifetz fell in the discussion. Kreisler then said: 'I'm told that I don't play the Mendelssohn Violin Concerto exactly badly. And yet, the way I heard Jascha Heifetz play it the first time he came to Berlin, I don't think it has ever been played before and probably never again will be played so well.'"

When the Kalinin offer was recalled to Kreisler recently, he said: "My official reason for declining was that I was tired. But what really turned me against it was a conversation I had with Anatol Lunacharsky, the Soviet commissar for education, who, you will remember, visited Berlin that winter with his beautiful wife, a well known Russian actress.

"During an evening reception Lunacharsky attempted to persuade me to accept the invitation to play in the Soviet Union. He suggested, however, that in case I came, I should please not bring, say, violin strings to present to Russian colleagues.

" 'Why not?' I asked, surprised.

" 'Because that might make others who do not receive them envious,' the commissar replied.

" 'But your wife wears costly jewelry,' I challenged. She had come to the reception wearing wonderful pearls and an expensive gown. 'Doesn't that make the other Russians jealous?'

" 'Ah, that's something quite different,' Lunacharsky countered. 'When we go abroad we must represent the dignity of the Soviet State.'

"Lunacharsky claimed that Russian artists were much better off than ever: The Soviets protected art. They gave an artist three eggs per day instead of the regular ration of one per week. They took the Stradivari and other precious instruments out of the museums and permitted the artists to play their concerts on them.

"Then, however, came the 'joker.' Lunacharsky continued: 'The only stipulation to the artists is that they must fit themselves into our ideology. We must ask you, too, in case you come, not to play Mendelssohn or Tchaikovsky, because they do not fit into our scheme of things.'

" 'But how can you come to know a composer, let us say, like Bach, if you don't permit study of his works?' I pressed.

" 'Well, with the Catholic priest history begins with the Christian era,' the Russian dictator of culture responded. 'What went before was heathen. So with us, too, communism is a religion that begins with our seizure of power. We must insist that art, too, submit to our dogma. It is all right for a student to play scales and études for practice, but when he selects a solo piece, it must fit into our ideology.' "

Fritz concluded: "I could never work in Soviet Russia. I therefore declined the offer, even though Lunacharsky, later in the discussion, conceded that in my case no restrictions would be placed upon my programs."

As an afterthought he said with a chuckle: "They play my compositions all right in the Soviet Union, but they simply steal the music and I don't get a ruble of royalties."

Although Kreisler was "too tired" to go to Soviet Russia, he had just as extensive a schedule of appearances on the European continent during this period as he did in America and the British Isles. A letter from Michael Raucheisen, who accompanied him during these years, reveals what happened on these transcontinental tours:

> It was interesting for me to observe that in the countries of the more hot-blooded people, as for instance in Italy and Spain, the great masses of the people fanatically demanded Bach and Kreisler's own lyrical *cantilene* pieces, whereas in the Nordic countries the virtuoso Kreisler was more in demand. In Italy the public would gladly have sent the accompanist to Hades. The Italians were so intoxicated with the sound of Kreisler's notes that they did not want to hear any auxiliary noise.
>
> I shall never forget the storm that broke loose when I began on one occasion to play with the lid of the grand piano opened. So I merely touched the keys gently.
>
> It was much the same in Spain. Kreisler was given a greater ovation when he entered the bullfight arena than were the most famous matadors. The

Spaniards were too happy for words that the *maestro* had put in an appearance. Personally I know he suffered tortures and fairly had to be dragged there by the impresario.*

In one country—I believe it was in Greece—Kreisler at the last moment agreed to yield to the importunate entreaties of a prince to play a concert on an instrument he had never before seen. Some sort of wager was at stake. The prince won the bet easily; Kreisler played gloriously.

Mussolini took special delight in hearing Kreisler. The whole program played in the Augusteum had to be repeated in his private villa. He then personally turned the pages for me.

As in most countries, so also in Italy the concertmasters and virtuosi fairly pursued him. The well known Italian violinist Arrigo Serato traveled wherever Kreisler went in Italy, in order to learn from him.

When in Naples on one occasion we began with the Allegro by Pugnani in the Teatro San Carlo, Mt. Vesuvius rather than my left hand played the tremolo!

I should like to give you a few examples of Kreisler's unbelievable imperturbability while on tour: After a concert in Munich we had to catch the sleeper for Berlin. We had only a few minutes to grab a few sandwiches and a glass of beer in the station restaurant. It was 10:45 P.M.—and the train was to leave at 10:50. I sat as if on hot coals, but Kreisler did not seem to be in a hurry. Exactly two minutes before the departure of the train he left the restaurant. His mathematical calculation proved exactly right—we just made the train.

On another occasion, when we arrived in Pisa, Italy, Kreisler wanted to see the Leaning Tower. According to the timetable, the train was to stop there for eighteen minutes. Kreisler set his watch exactly by the railway station clock, confident that nothing could happen now.

His calculations were right in this case also—only the train, which was already late, wanted to make up for lost time and therefore remained in Pisa for only fifteen instead of the scheduled eighteen minutes. I hadn't noticed the earlier departure because I became engrossed in a book I was reading in our compartment. When the train started I was alone and faithfully kept my eye on his violin and on our baggage and also on his hat and coat which he had left on his seat. It never occurred to me that Kreisler might not be on the train. I took it for granted that, as happened so frequently, he had met friends or acquaintances and gone directly into the diner.

After an hour I began to get worried. I couldn't find a trace of Kreisler any-

* An Associated Press dispatch from Barcelona, Spain, on Aug. 10, 1926, stated that Kreisler had contracted with the Palace of Music to appear in a single performance for the unheard-of fee (for Europe) of 25,000 pesetas—about $4,000. This, the A.P. commented, was "a record sum in Spain for any artist." Kreisler after 1929 repeatedly played for Casals's Camera de Musica in Barcelona.

where. I got quite excited, and already saw our Florence concert endangered. But oh no! Kreisler had immediately telephoned to Florence and assured the management he was coming with a car which he hired. He arrived practically at the same time as I. Only—it was I who had to submit to being most ceremoniously welcomed by a reception committee!

The episode did not have the slightest adverse effect on Kreisler's playing that evening. He simply refuses to get excited.

On one occasion in Florence, Italy, Fritz had become so engrossed at the bookstalls that he missed his train for Milan. While he was pondering what to do, an Italian dignitary came up to him and asked whether he was Fritz Kreisler.

"Yes," said Kreisler, "but how did you know?"

"Why, your picture is in all newspapers, showing you standing with Il Duce in Rome yesterday. Anything we can do for you?"

"Yes, indeed," Kreisler replied. "I have missed my train for Milan, where I must play this evening."

"*Momento,*" the dignitary said and disappeared.

A few minutes later a beautiful limousine took Kreisler to Milan, where he arrived ahead of the train.

When the Kreislers speak of the evenings at Mussolini's villa, they will tell you that the Fascist dictator always addressed Harriet as Sherlock Holmes. The reason was given by Fritz in these words to Bernard Smith for the May, 1931 issue of *Musical Observer:*

"When Mussolini greeted us Mrs. Kreisler said, 'You are a violinist, too.' 'No,' he said, 'that is ridiculous. I can't play the violin.' She looked at him closely. 'Then what are those marks on your neck?' she asked. 'I thought I had invited artists,' he said. 'I find I am harboring detectives. But you are wrong. Those marks are from my playing with, not as an artist upon, the violin.' "

Mussolini's reply prompted the interviewer to ask Kreisler who played the better—his friend Albert Einstein or Benito Mussolini? The account continues:

"Kreisler looked keenly for a moment, then lay back in his chair, slapped his knees and roared with laughter. 'That is a question! I would not answer it. I would, anyway, have to hear them together, and what an occasion that would be! A violin contest between Einstein and Mussolini! Superb! And this you would see: you would see those two men, each so serene, so supreme in his own field—you would see them trembling, with the sweat rolling down their brows.' "

During this period Fritz Kreisler found time only twice to engage in literary activity. *Le Quotidien* of Paris, on December 23, 1928, published his article, "L'Argent et les musiciens" (Money and the Musicians), from which the following is quoted:

> In the old days it was not the money earned by an artist but his reputation that counted. Now the favor of the public and not the opinion of the critics is the supreme arbiter. However, the admiration of the mass is instinctive and, on the whole, justified; very few artists have provoked an admiration that is not merited.
>
> It may not be good for an artist to earn too much. The artist is forever in need of a goad or spur. Consequently it is a good thing for his creative powers that he be subjected to the influence of sorrow, of anxiety, of love and of friendship. All that stimulates his nervous system and prevents his creative abilities from becoming atrophied.

For *Het Volk* of Amsterdam, Fritz Kreisler wrote, in January, 1932, in part:

> Very little worth while is being written for the violin anymore. People haven't any feeling anymore for this instrument, for its charm, its loveliness, its intonation, its wealth of possibilities in variegation. Beethoven wrote things held impossible of execution by his contemporaries. But he had a prophetic vision of the development of instrumental technique, which, besides, was merely a means to an end for him. At present technique has become the whole end. Music is written for the metronome.
>
> The technical talent of the youth of today is almost unbelievable. I know five "wonder children" in New York alone who play anything, no matter how difficult, as if it were nothing. But they all are *technical* "wonder children," just as a child now can put a radio or an automobile together. This can never remain the object of music. People will get away from it again.
>
> I don't think the general situation is so bad. Music has gone astray. Nevertheless it is, and always will be, what it has been through all the ages—a cultural necessity, a necessary medium for the refreshing of a person's soul and spirit, so that he can concentrate upon higher things.
>
> We haven't yet recovered from the effects of the fearful war. That was like a severe illness, the effect of which is felt for years afterward. We are still living in a sort of state of war. Although they don't use a cannon now, they are fighting with bills of exchange. And that is called an economic crisis. We are still living under the pressure of a spiritual blockade. The

world must overcome its miserable selfishness, and it doubtless will. Good music will help make men better. At least that's the way it affects me.

A man as well balanced as Kreisler does not, of course, work all the time, no matter how crowded his schedules may seem. The Kreislers, therefore, have many a pleasant memory of hospitality enjoyed during these eight years, of wonderful vacation trips undertaken, of music festivals attended, of glorious music made for the mere fun of playing.

In America the evenings spent at the Pittsburgh home of Victor Herbert still loom large in Fritz's memory. "We would often play or sing new things Victor had composed," Fritz said reminiscently. "I would often play the piano accompaniment. Many of his operettas were probably played then for the first time—during those evenings we had together.

"Once he dedicated a Serenade to me. I believe he originally wrote it for the cello, but it didn't quite go. Then he rewrote it for orchestra, and again there was something lacking. Then he tried it for the violin. I liked it very much.

"One night when I played under his baton in Carnegie Hall in Pittsburgh, there was considerable applause at the end of my number. I wanted to play the Serenade as an encore. I don't remember just what happened, but perhaps a string burst. At any rate, Victor suddenly took me by the arm, led me to the piano and asked me to play his Serenade as a piano solo. Perhaps, too, no accompanist was available, for it was an orchestra concert. Anyway, I played the Serenade as a piano solo instead of a violin solo."

Kreisler, who is fond of good eating, found the exquisite Viennese cuisine of Victor Herbert's wife, the former Austrian prima donna Therese Förster, as tempting as he did the opportunity for a musical "bull session."

In Europe the Kreislers often went on automobile tours with Josef Hofmann, especially along the slope of Mt. Salève near Geneva. Frequently, too, they stopped with the Ernest Schellings at Céligny, where Paderewski also was a much appreciated guest.

One afternoon Fritz had played chess with another house guest for hours, until only two figures were left on either side. He then left

Victor Herbert

ef Hofmann with Alexander Lambert, 1862-1929

Ignace Jan Paderewski, 1860-1941

Bulldog watching Kreisler and Schelling play chess

to dress for dinner. When the guests walked into the social hall after the evening meal, they found that Paderewski had meanwhile converted the floor into a huge chessboard. Human figures, beautifully costumed in the garb that befitted their roles on the chessboard, stood there in the spaces in which their inanimate predecessors had been before dinner, to be moved around at the behest of Kreisler and his chess opponent.

"We were asked to finish the game, to the amusement of everybody present," Fritz recalled. "By that time our party had become so hilarious that I didn't know what moves I directed to be made."

There is an amusing photograph extant of Fritz Kreisler and Ernest Schelling playing chess, with a huge white bulldog sitting on a chair between them and solemnly watching the proceedings.*

Michael Raucheisen wrote concerning Kreisler's ability as a chess player:

> For years I had been occupying myself seriously with chess and had analyzed almost all games of famous masters. Kreisler once saw me quite accidentally as I was playing on an ocean liner. He challenged me to a game, but urged lenience on my part since he had not had a chess figure in his hands in years. I was so certain of my superiority that it was rather painful for me to match my skill against his, for my reverence for Kreisler then was such that it would have interfered with my peace of mind to see him lose. After a few moves, however, I revised my opinion. He made one surprise move after another—and already I was checkmate! †

In Germany, Kreisler during these years attended many music festivals, such as the Rhenish, the Meiningen, the Brahms. Even though he often appeared in these as soloist, they are here recorded under

* It is characteristic of the intimacy with the late Ernest Schelling that Fritz on the occasion of his friend Ernest's birthday in 1936 presented him with a baton made of one of his violin bows, at the end of which was a silver handle engraved with the dedication, "To Ernest from Fritz," the date of Schelling's birthday, July 26, 1936, and the opening bars of "Caprice viennois."

† I tried to elicit a "professional" opinion concerning Fritz's prowess as a chess player from his eminent violinistic colleague Louis Persinger, who ranks among America's greatest chess experts. Persinger, to his regret, could not accommodate me as he had unfortunately never played with Fritz. "We once tried to play together in San Francisco," he said, "but something or other intervened."

relaxation because Fritz derived so much pleasure from them, as he did also from attending the Bayreuth Festival performances.

Mention of Bayreuth prompted the question why Fritz Kreisler never made any Wagner transcriptions. Was he, perchance, fundamentally anti-Wagner?

"By no means," was his firm reply. "My answer is quite simple: August Wilhelmj, Wagner's first concertmaster, has not only done all this capably and excellently, but with the approval of Wagner. If I, who had no personal connection with the Master of Bayreuth, had then come along and also made transcriptions, the critics would rightly have objected and asked whence I derived my authority.

"Besides, don't forget that Wagner's music is often unthinkable without the human voice. Only few things of his lend themselves to violin treatment. And finally, on the whole it is not good practice to come from something bigger and greater to something smaller. Most of Wagner's music is written with a great orchestra in mind. To bring it down to a violin solo in most cases would seem to belittle it."

The end of this eight-year period brought Kreisler a cherished triumph: his second comic opera, *Sissy*, proved an outstanding success. Its première was given in Vienna Friday, December 23, 1932.

The *Vossische Zeitung* of Berlin published an item by its Vienna music critic, according to which "the night almost wasn't long enough for the society and star success which Fritz Kreisler achieved with his old-Austrian festival operetta, *Sissy, the Rose from Bavaria-Land*." The London *Times* correspondent cabled that "much entertainment was derived from the contrast between the unceremonial life in the petty ducal home and that of the powerful emperor even in his summer villa at Ischl. Fritz Kreisler was present and enthusiastically applauded."

Arriving in New York late in October of the following year, Fritz Kreisler could tell the reporters that *Sissy* had by then been given two hundred times in Vienna, and was running in Amsterdam, Munich, and Basle, in addition to a number of smaller cities on the Continent. "I conducted a few rehearsals of *Sissy*," he added, "but only to show the cast what my conception and interpretation was."

The libretto for *Sissy* was written by two very popular Viennese lyrics writers, Ernst and Hubert Marischka. The music is exclusively Fritz Kreisler's. The cast of characters is:

Francis Joseph, Emperor of Austria
Grand Duchess Sophie, his Mother
Duke Max of Bavaria
Ludovika, called Louise, his Wife
Helene, called Nené
Elisabeth, called Sissy
Karl Theodor, called Gackl
Sophie, called Spatz (Sparrow)
Rupert
Annemarie
Maximilian
Field Marshal Count Radetzky
Prince of Thurn-Taxis
Baron Hrdlicka, Master of Ceremonies
Count Greneville, Adjutant
Von Kempen, Colonel of the *Gendarmerie*
Prince Menschikov, Envoy of the Czar
Ilona Varady, Ballet Dancer
The Ballet Master of the Vienna Court Opera
Petzelberger, Keeper of the Tavern "To the Golden Ox"
Zenzi, Bar Maid
Peter, the Butler
A Watchman, a Sergeant of the Guards, Lady's Maid, Coachman, Ballet Girls, Officers, Life Guards, Ladies in Waiting, Lackeys, Peasants, Singers, Soldiers, Servants, People

The Time: August 15–17, 1853

Act I takes place in Posenhofen Castle on Lake Starnberg, Bavaria. The remaining scenes are laid in Ischl, the second and fourth in the emperor's villa, the third in the tavern, "To the Golden Ox."

The story is briefly as follows:

Duke Max of Bavaria has two daughters—Nené, aged eighteen, a rather demure and pretty lass, and Sissy, aged sixteen, a tomboy and in many respects like her father, who cares nothing for court ceremony.

The duke's wife Louise has hopes of marrying Nené off to her nephew Francis Joseph, the twenty-three-year-old Austrian emperor, and has negotiated with her sister, Grand Duchess Sophie, about it. But nothing happens.

The Prince of Thurn-Taxis arrives to ask for Nené's hand. The two are ardently in love with each other. Hardly has Louise given her reluctant consent, when a messenger from Sophie brings a formal invitation to Louise and Nené only, to come to Ischl for the emperor's birthday celebration.

Sissy promises Nené to help prevent "coupling" with Francis Joseph. She instigates her father, Duke Max, to follow Louise and Nené to prevent the match. Max takes Sissy and several others of his children along.

The unwonted guests arrive unannounced and incognito. Sissy picks an armful of the special roses reserved for His Majesty, is arrested and taken before the emperor. As he has never seen his pretty cousin, she pretends to be a simple tailor's apprentice who has come to bring a dress for Nené.

The inevitable happens: the two fall in love with each other. Sophie, who has hitherto always had her way with her son, is amazed to find that he remains ostentatiously cool to Nené.

After a series of rollicking scenes the misunderstanding concerning Sissy's lineage is cleared up and Francis Joseph asks Duke Max for his daughter's hand. Nené is free to marry her Prince Thurn-Taxis.

The world première in Vienna was given added luster by the fact that one of the most popular actresses on the German-speaking stage, Paula Wessely, sang and acted the title role, and Hans Jaray, the equally important role of Emperor Francis Joseph. Paul Henried, now a famous movie star, was Jaray's understudy.

One fetching tune in *Sissy*, "Stars in My Eyes," has become familiar to American movie fans in that it was used in the film *The King Steps Out*.

Sissy began a new run in Vienna in 1948.

CHAPTER TWENTY-THREE

KREISLER RECORDINGS

FRITZ KREISLER, as already noted, began recording when the gramophone industry was in its very infancy. In 1925, shortly after his return from "down under," he signed a contract for five more years with the Victor Talking Machine Company, for whom he had already been recording regularly since 1910. The contract was later extended automatically year after year.

"I was at first afraid of recording," he confessed. "I feared it would interfere with the attendance at concerts. But Harriet was right—it helped." He maintained, however, that he never was completely satisfied; that no matter how perfect the recording, there was something mechanical about it. Nevertheless, he said, "in the big, over-all picture recording certainly is a wonderful thing.

"It has made it possible for people to prepare themselves for classical concerts by first hearing the program numbers on their talking machines. Many students of music, too, have been aided in understanding the intentions of composers, because the writers of music themselves played their works for the recording machine. Just think what it would mean to a violinist today to know just how Paganini interpreted and played his own compositions!

"Many a time I take up a Caruso record, and chills run down my spine as I hear the voice of the great artist who has passed from us. The phonograph, I believe, is a distinct aid to musical development."

The Victor executives have found Kreisler one of the most congenial people to work with. He was "always a good comrade," they said. He was the envy of Casals and Rachmaninoff, F. W. Gaisberg, chief recorder for the Gramophone Company (His Master's Voice), tells us, because of the ease with which he took recording in his stride. The microphone did not bother him in the least, as it does some less experienced artists.

Charles O'Connell, once a Victor executive, claims that Kreisler was the only famous musician who never complained.

Kreisler went into the recording studio in the same spirit in which he walked onto the platforms of the world's greatest concert halls: he played for the joy of playing, and not to fret or worry how this or that passage might turn out. He was thus the very antithesis of a perfectionist like his intimate friend Sergei Rachmaninoff. Geraldine Farrar remembers how, at the time when Kreisler and Rachmaninoff were recording Schubert's Sonata in A Major (it may also have been Grieg's Sonata in C Minor), Kreisler would come out of the studio in high glee, still aglow with the beautiful music which he had helped to create. Rachmaninoff, on the other hand, emerged with his sad face, worried about this or that phrase which he thought had not quite come out as it should. He would continue to brood over the situation for days and finally decide that another recording ought to be made. His friend Fritz, however, thought only of the beauties of their ensemble effort and artfully dodged the issue of doing the whole thing over again. As Rachmaninoff put it to Miss Farrar in his slow, deliberate way: "Fritz—he is like a flea; one just can't put a finger on him." This fundamental difference in viewpoint did no harm to the Kreisler-Rachmaninoff friendship. Charles O'Connell, in fact, tells us:*

> With his friend Kreisler and their friend and manager Charles Foley, I have spent many an hour over spaghetti and red wine in some obscure Italian restaurant, and at such times it seemed to me Rachmaninoff would lose his customary appearance of a deflated Buddha.

* Reprinted from *The Other Side of the Record* by Charles O'Connell, by permission of Alfred A. Knopf, Incorporated, copyright, 1947, by Charles O'Connell.

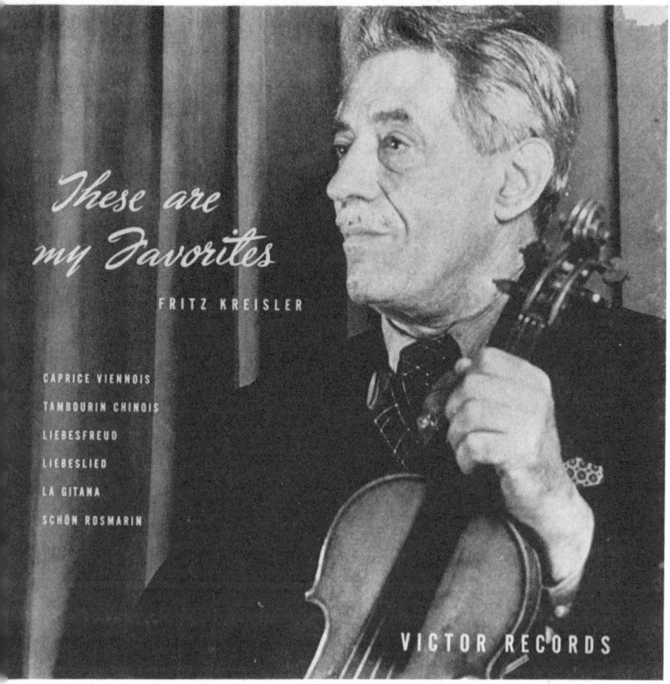

Jackets of Kreisler's Victor record albums

New

VICTOR RECORDS

ORTHOPHONIC RECORDING

FEBRUARY 1930

RACHMANINOFF AND KREISLER RECORD A BEETHOVEN SONATA

RACHMANINOFF

It is seldom that music-lovers in this country have the opportunity of hearing these two famous artists in a joint concert. Hence, this new Victor recording (Nos. 8163-8164) will be of peculiar interest. The G Major Sonata of Beethoven (Opus 30, No. 3) for piano and violin is in three movements. The [illegible] of these is lively. Violin and [illegible] First heard in beautifully blended ensemble. In the second movement the tempo is slower and the melody more warmly lyric. The exquisite tone of Kreisler's violin lends super-loveliness to this movement, even as the crystal clarity of Rachmaninoff's notes. The final movement flashes a sparkling *allegro vivace*, smoothly mastered by the genius of these two titans, and brings this

KREISLER

Announcement of a Rachmaninoff-Kreisler recording

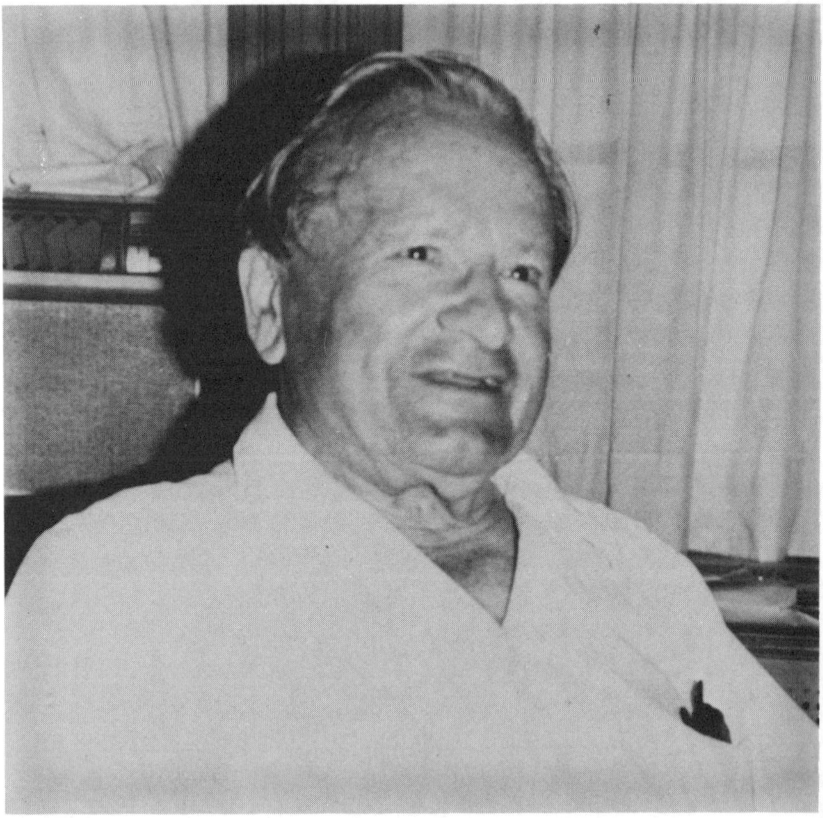

Franz Rupp, one of Kreisler's accompanists

And Oskar von Riesemann, Rachmaninoff's biographer, informs us concerning a series of songs, set to music by Rachmaninoff, which were gleaned from Russian lyric poets: *

Each of these songs is a small masterpiece, but the one called *Daisies*, that concludes with the melting trill of the nightingale, is perhaps best known through Kreisler's arrangement for the violin.

It is no wonder that the efforts of the Victor management to get the Austrian and the Russian to record the entire series of Beethoven sonatas together did not materialize, even though their recording of the G Major, Op. 30, No. 3, sonata is regarded as a magnificent interpretation. Close friends that they were, they were nevertheless not temperamentally mated for that sort of a continuing ensemble task. Kreisler did, however, record all of Beethoven's sonatas for violin and piano for the Beethoven Society of London. He chose as his partner a young Munich pianist who was just beginning to make a name for himself: Franz Rupp, now the accompanist of the contralto Marian Anderson.

Franz Rupp told the story in these words: "The recordings were begun in 1935. Fritz Kreisler generously suggested me as his piano partner. The Londoners did not think I was big enough, but Kreisler insisted that I be given an opportunity. A sample recording of the 'Frühlingssonate' was therefore made at Berlin. It found favor. I was in heaven. What an honor to be associated with Fritz Kreisler! Whenever in the years following, Kreisler went over to London for an extended period, I would join him to work on the recordings. These were done very carefully. Now, many years later, I am very critical of my effort, but I still believe that from a mechanical standpoint, especially as far as the tone is concerned, the recordings are the best that was ever done on the Beethoven violin sonatas by Master's Voice or any other concern."

Kreisler commented on the Beethoven series: "Rupp is the born pianist. You just have to be born to it or you haven't got it. The

* Reprinted from *Rachmaninoff's Recollections* by Oskar von Riesemann, by permission of George Allen & Unwin Ltd., London and The Macmillan Company, New York, copyright, 1934, by George Allen & Unwin, Ltd. and The Macmillan Company.

Beethoven sonata recordings which I did with him are indeed worth while."

In 1935 Kreisler also made a recording of his Quartet in A Minor in London. He as the composer was at the first violin desk, the late Thomas Petrie at the second; William Primrose played the viola, and Laurie Kennedy the cello. The beautiful record is now a rarity for which record collectors pay high prices. Kreisler himself is searching for this record at the present writing, since he wishes now, after an interval of fifteen years, to hear how he and his fellow artists performed it then.

The most interesting thing about this recording is something not connected with Kreisler's Quartet but with Kreisler himself, as F. W. Gaisberg has revealed: *

> Harriet and Fritz arrived in London in 1935 to record the Mendelssohn *Concerto* and his *Quartet in A Major*. Harriet attended the rehearsals and acted as floor manager. When she could not come she would ring up from her hotel every half-hour, and Fritz would have to report on the progress of each record.
>
> The Quartet in question was only long enough to cover seven sides, or three and a half discs. The gap would have stumped most musicians, but not Kreisler. Remembering his "Dittersdorf Scherzo," he then and there started adapting it for the Quartet, completing his task during intervals between recordings. When they came to play the fourth record not a single note of it had to be altered. He dedicated this impromptu work to me and presented me with the manuscript.

During the recording of the Mendelssohn Concerto the Victor executives were impressed anew with the camaraderie which Kreisler always showed members of the orchestra, with whom he liked to chat during pauses. There was nothing of the prima donna about him!

Once as Kreisler was recording in Camden, New Jersey, for RCA-Victor, his friend John McCormack was at work in another studio on the premises. When the two met, McCormack told Kreisler that he was just doing Rachmaninoff's "Song of Georgia," but was not quite sure whether he was singing it exactly in the tempo desired by the composer.

* Reprinted from *The Music Goes Round* by F. W. Gaisberg, by permission of The Macmillan Co., copyright, 1942, by The Macmillan Co.

Kreisler at a recording session

The London String Quartet in 1935
(Fritz Kreisler, William Primrose, Lauri Kennedy, Thomas Petrie)

MARCH RED SEAL RECORDS

Kreisler and Zimbalist Listening to the Double Concerto

Kreisler and Zimbalist Play Bach's Famous Double Concerto

Fritz Kreisler—Efrem Zimbalist

(Accompanied by String Quartet) Twelve-inch, $2.00 each

76028 Concerto for Two Violins *(In D Minor) First Movement, Vivace* **Bach**
76029 Concerto for Two Violins *(In D Minor) Second Movement, Largo* **Bach**
76030 Concerto for Two Violins *(In D Minor) Third Movement, Allegro* **Bach**

A highly interesting novelty offered this month is a complete presentation of the well-known concerto in D Minor for two violins. Although this composition does not contain any of the complexities of the *Chaconne* it is very difficult nevertheless, especially the first and last movements. The slow movement is a beautiful one, and to the average hearer perhaps the most attractive.

This fascinating composition, in which the instruments seem to carry on a musical conversation, is admirably played by these two artists, and the contrast between the spirited *Vivace*, the lovely *Largo* and the dashing finale is highly interesting.

12

Announcement for Kreisler-Zimbalist recording, 1915

"I walked with him to his studio, looked at the score, and said to the accompanist: 'If you want to play it like Rachmaninoff, you must be a little more ebullient. Let's see how it then sounds.'

"So he played and John sang, and I took up my fiddle and improvised a sort of obbligato. When we finished, I was told to my utter surprise that a recording had just been made and that the radio company felt it could go out like that, without further tests."

On another occasion Kreisler was to do some recordings with Geraldine Farrar. "Out of a clear sky she suddenly suggested that I improvise an obbligato for 'Mighty lak' a Rose.' Well, what could I do but oblige her? So I made up something or other, and the record went out in that form."

In 1920 John McCormack made a bet that his friend, William T. Tilden, 2nd, would win a certain match. "I'll do anything you want if you win," John told Big Bill. "Anything. Just ask me."

"Sing me Rachmaninoff's 'When Night Descends,' " the tennis champion bargained.

When Tilden later received the recording, he was more than pleased that there was a violin obbligato with it. "I thought you'd like Fritz to play the obbligato," McCormack explained. "So I asked him and he did."

Asked years ago which of his recordings he liked best (this was long before the Beethoven series), Kreisler replied: "Of the many records I have made, my favorite ones are Bach's Double Concerto for Two Violins with Efrem Zimbalist, the Russian violinist; the 'Caprice viennois,' Dvořák's 'Humoresque' . . . and most Viennese melodies. Another of my favorites is Heuberger's 'Midnight Bells.' "

It is interesting to note that the only time Kreisler offered a longer explanation concerning one of his compositions or arrangements was when he wrote the following for the *Victor Record Catalog* concerning his Rondino on a Theme by Beethoven:

This theme consists of only eight measures, which occur in a very early and unimportant composition by Beethoven, now quite forgotten. The little theme itself is of indescribable charm and its rhythm is of such alluring piquancy that it grows by every repetition. In order to set this peculiarity off to advantage, I conceived the idea of writing a *rondo* around it, the *rondo* being a form of composition where a short tune returns obstinately in more or less regular intervals. *Rondino* means "little *rondo.*" I have tried to keep the old classic style throughout the little piece, and I hope I have succeeded.

The Rondino on a Theme by Beethoven was dedicated to Kreisler's colleague Mischa Elman. Thereby hangs a tale:

"I happened to be with Elman and Leopold Godowsky just after I had blocked out the Rondino," Fritz revealed, "but of course it was only in sketch form. Elman took it and began to play it. Then Godowsky chimed in on the piano, and the two did a clowning act of stamping with their feet and caricaturing my composition. So I punished Mischa by dedicating it to him."

Helena Huntington Smith, in her "Profile of A Gentleman from Vienna" in the *New Yorker*, claims that Kreisler was the first to record a full violin concerto for the phonograph. His recordings of the Beethoven, Brahms, Mendelssohn, Paganini, and two Mozart concertos are things of rare beauty.

The big financial returns came, however, not from these long works, but from his short, one-disc pieces. Authoritative figures on the sales of Kreisler records were unavailable, but a press item appeared to the effect that one year they exceeded those of Enrico Caruso, "whose royalties were $125,000 per annum." The reader may conjecture by analogy what the Kreisler records may have brought in the course of years. When Fritz reached Rio de Janeiro on his 1935 Zeppelin trip, he was told again and again that his records were best sellers in South America.

The lengths to which students of music went to fathom the secrets of Fritz Kreisler's art are illustrated by an experiment conducted by Eugene Riviere Redervill, who dissected, as it were, a Kreisler recording. Redervill in December, 1916 wrote about his experiment in *The Violinist*:

> Secrets are sometimes detected under the magnifying glass. The magnifying glass used in this criticism is a little Victrola and the artist Fritz Kreisler. The composition is Kreisler's own *Tambourin Chinois*.
>
> In striking B-flat on a piano, or any other instrument of international pitch, and regulating the Victrola so that the opening measures of the piece correspond in pitch, we get the exact tempo used by Kreisler. This artist uses great

Mischa Elman, 1891-1967

Fritz Kreisler and Franz Rupp in 1935

Kreisler in the 1930's

speed, and his changes from *staccato* to *legato* are made with such quick change that a violinist does not fully appreciate his terrific tempos until he attempts to play along with the record. . . .

In the first few measures we realize that Kreisler is a student of psychology in music; he knows all the means of contrast in tone shading and accentuation. . . . This is the secret of Kreisler's crispness of playing. . . . His phrasing is marked with strong accents, *spiccato* and *staccato* notes. No sleepy or drawn-out musicianship is Kreisler's.

His trill is like lightning.*

In the *Lento* movement . . . the simultaneous bow and finger attack in the Kreisler trill is crisp in effect and hardly equalled by other artists. . . .

Kreisler's rapid *vibrato* is quite audible in cutting the Victrola down to one-third speed. His *vibrato* and trill seem to be nearly double the speed of most other artists. The secret of his trill seems to be the simultaneous attack of the bow and deft finger of the left hand. Most of his trills are made a whole tone above the written note notwithstanding the signature of the composition.

In studying Kreisler's *vibrato* with the aid of the Victrola at one-third speed, it is apparent from the wavering pitch even in the rapid passages that this great artist gives life to his tone by using the rapid *vibrato* continuously.

Discussion of recordings led to the question whether Kreisler had ever wanted to write a symphony and have it recorded. He replied in the negative, then added that he had wanted to write an opera. "I even had a libretto for an opera," he said, "but somehow I never got around to writing it. Nor were violin concertos wanted in those days of the record boom, whereas anything I composed in the way of one-disc things was seized eagerly. I was, frankly, making money for Harriet's many charities, and there was more cash in those little things."

Most of his short pieces, he said, were composed in one day. "My stimuli came from the violin. If I wrote a song, however, it was the deep emotion, say, of an Eichendorff poem, which stirred me to composing. I usually received my musical inspirations while walking, especially while hiking in the mountains with my *Rucksack* (knapsack). Nature has so many beautiful sounds—the nightingale, the thrush, the cuckoo, the murmuring brook, the buzzing of myriads of insects. Many of the greatest masterpieces have, after all, simple melo-

* When Kreisler read this sentence in my manuscript, he laughed merrily and said, with a twinkle, "The noted musicologist apparently has never heard Heifetz and the followers of his school of technique. If he thinks my trill is like lightning, what shall we say of the much faster one of Heifetz?"

dies." (By way of illustration he here hummed the initial bars of Beethoven's Fifth Symphony.)

"Traveling in a train, too, often inspired me with the rhythm of the moving vehicle. I remember reading that ideas came to Machiavelli as he walked among people. Leonardo da Vinci got his inspiration from seeing rifts in walls. We all have some equalization space (*Ausgleichsraum*) in our brain—some place where ideas are coordinated, are translated from experience or impression into expression."

His attention was called to a passage in *Music Comes to America:* *

> Before 1920 people who bought records generally emphasized the importance of the interpreter over the music itself. Today, it is the music and not the artist that sells the records. People demand, first of all, a specific work; then, and only then, are they interested in the performer. . . . Twenty years ago or so the best Kreisler sellers were his Viennese bonbons—*Liebesfreud, Liebesleid, Schoen Rosmarin.* Today these Viennese morsels are fabulously outsold by his interpretations of the concertos of Beethoven, Brahms, and Mendelssohn.

"That marks great progress," Fritz commented. "The music listener has entered the selective stage—that's what that indicates. In the case of Bing Crosby, for instance, who is a newcomer at recording compared with us oldsters, people still simply ask for 'something' by him. Some years later they will want this or that best record of his and ask for the piece first, and for Crosby second."

Although most of Kreisler's recordings were made in the studios of the Gramophone Company, Limited, of London and of RCA-Victor of New York, some were done in Berlin with the German affiliate, the Electrola-Gesellschaft. Its chief director, Max Ittenbach, wrote on November 25, 1949, with reference to the fate of Kreisler recordings during and after the Nazi regime:

> Despite my efforts to retain these wonderful recordings in the Electrola Catalog my plea was rejected by the (Nazi) Propaganda Ministry about the middle of the past decade.
>
> Disregarding an order to the contrary, we kept all matrixes in the hope that we might be able to use them some day after all. They survived the war, but after the Battle of Berlin on May 7, 1945, were lost together with all other

* Reprinted from *Music Comes to America* by David Ewen, by permission of David Ewen, Revised Edition, Allen, Towne & Heath, Inc., copyright, 1947, by David Ewen.

stored matrixes. It is an irony of fate that this happened to them after having withstood the war.

During the same year in which he signed a long-term contract with Victor, that is, in 1925, concertgoers rubbed their eyes in wonderment at an advertisement in many programs of which the following, taken from a Washington recital under the management of Mrs. Wilson-Greene on February 24, 1925, is a sample:

Do you know
that KREISLER Plays the Piano?
Unless he should happen to play for you
in person,
there is *but one way*
in which Kreisler can be heard
and that is by means of
THE AMPICO
for which he records his remarkably
beautiful piano playing exclusively.

Kreisler's piano playing is as fascinating, alluring and brilliant as the violin playing which has brought him the great renown which he enjoys. You should hear these amazing recordings if only to satisfy your curiosity as to what they are like.

Ask especially for the "Caprice viennois," the old Viennese Dance Melodies, and others of his own compositions in delightful arrangements for the piano. These beautiful works reveal Kreisler at his best, both as pianist and composer.

Another Ampico advertisement emphasized:

You cannot hear him play the piano in concert. But in the quiet seclusion of your home *Kreisler will play the piano for you.* . . . Kreisler the violinist and Kreisler the pianist are equally great. To hear one is the privilege of the whole concert-going world. To hear the other is the exclusive privilege of the owner of an AMPICO.

Kreisler made player-piano recordings of the following of his own compositions: "Liebesfreud," "Liebesleid," "Schön Rosmarin," "Caprice viennois," "The Old Refrain," "Polichinelle," "Tambourin chinois," and "Toy Soldier's March." Also, he recorded A. Walter Kramer's Entr'acte, Op. 46, No. 2, as transcribed by himself.

Some recordings were also made by Ampico of accompaniments

only, with the idea that a violinist lacking a steady piano partner might turn on his player piano and have a well known accompanist work for him. Among such records there was Carl Lamson's version of the piano accompaniment to Kreisler's "Tambourin chinois."

When Fritz Kreisler's attention was called to the Ampico advertisements, he commented:

"That was at a time when a lot of experimenting was going on with player pianos. Leopold Godowsky and other pianists had tried their hands at this sort of thing, and they challenged me to do likewise. In those gay days a cocktail was often enough to start anyone of us off. So I sat down to experiment. I certainly never dreamed I was doing it 'professionally.' But somehow my playing went over and Ampico included my numbers with the recordings offered for sale. That's the way things sometimes happen. They were in the business and wanted to make money. But the player piano is now almost obsolete."

The Ampico recordings led an inquisitive musicologist, John Tasker Howard, to try to discover the reason for Fritz Kreisler's unique appeal by analyzing one of the piano records—the "Old Refrain." Howard observed in the September, 1925 issue of *The Musician* that Kreisler's "command of the piano is such that he can bring to the keyboard the same individuality he employs with the bow." Analyzing the "Old Refrain," he continued:

> Repeated hearings of the piece, and careful attention to detail, demonstrate one of Kreisler's favorite tricks—an occasional sudden dropping of inflection on the final note of a phrase, or at some other point equally unexpected. An artist of Mr. Kreisler's taste naturally uses such a device sparingly, so that when it occurs, its effect is indeed telling. Nor is the effect exaggerated, sometimes it is almost imperceptible.
>
> Equally unexpected is the sudden *piano* at certain points.
>
> It may be that such well placed nuances form one of the secrets behind Mr. Kreisler's tremendous appeal. His playing of the entire piece is marked by elasticity of rhythm and dynamics. He achieves a variety of tone and style that many a student would give his choicest possession to attain.

Frequent efforts were made by the large broadcasting systems to get Fritz Kreisler to use the radio to carry his message to the four corners of the earth. But he always declined. His position was explained to Richard Matthews Hallet of the *Christian Science Monitor* in 1940 in these words: *

"I avoid the radio because I do not like the idea of being turned on and off like an electric light or hot water. I remember an afternoon when eight or ten of my friends, all excellent musicians, came together in San Francisco to play bridge. As Toscanini was broadcasting at the same time, I sat at first listening to him. I was disturbed when I heard one of my confrères say, 'Two spades,' another, 'Three diamonds.' I said, 'Here is Toscanini on the air,' but in a few moments someone yelled, 'Shut that thing off,' and that, to my great regret, was the end of Beethoven's Ninth Symphony.

"Radio must be an immense consolation to the sightless, but it can't give untrammeled, unstinted pleasure to the ear. It's not clear, it's not perfectly pure, and it's too easy. If you go to a concert hall, for one thing, you exert yourself. You buy a ticket, you select your particular master, you contribute your eager receptivity—and you put a dent in your pocketbook. In short, you suffer something, and then you are ready to listen. Certainly you differ from the impersonal unseen millions who sniff and away.

"Why are radio and movie stars so short-lived in their reputation? Paderewski was before the public for sixty-five years, and still people crowded to hear him. It was so with Patti and Bernhardt. These artists played and sang and acted for exactly the chosen ones who had been truly captivated by their art. Visible audiences make the artist's longevity. Screen artists play for the world, and the world is a great child and tires easily. You cannot make friends for long with all the world."

Marks Levine, director of the Concerts Division of the National Concert and Artists Corporation, who has handled Kreisler concerts for eighteen years, added that further reasons, in his opinion, for Fritz Kreisler's hesitancy to appear on the air were, first, his dislike of cheapening commercials ("Beethoven and some laxative!"); second, his objection that radio programs are so short that one cannot play any one large, standard work through; and third, that one cannot control flaws which are multiplied indefinitely, especially if recordings of broadcasts are made. In phonograph recordings the artist can repeat and repeat until a disc comes out which the artist is willing to let stand

* Reprinted from "Fritz Kreisler, and What's In Him" by Richard Matthews Hallet, from an article in the December 7, 1940, issue of *The Christian Science Monitor*, by permission of *The Christian Science Monitor*, copyright, 1940, by *The Christian Science Monitor*.

as the best that can be done mechanically. Not so with a radio recording. Fritz agreed when told of Levine's opinion as expressed to me.

Kreisler held consistently to the theory that neither radio nor the talkies could replace the personal appearance. As far back as October 5, 1929 he told the New York *Times*:

"I believe people will turn out to see and hear the artist in person after attending the talkies, just as they turn out to see movie stars in person. The concert, after all, will be the only means of getting the artist's personality in his creations."

Then followed a suggestion that, if radio and talkies improved sufficiently, he might yet change his mind. For, he continued:

"Frankly, I hope both the radio and the talking pictures will develop. I should like to use them. Any serious artist would. The artist's vocation is to address himself to the masses. What good would an artist be, except philosophically, if he did not show his art to the masses?"

The story of what changed Kreisler's mind in 1944 and persuaded him to go on the air in his seventieth year will be told in its proper chronological place.

CHAPTER TWENTY-FOUR

KULTUR IN HIGH BOOTS AND SPURS

[1933-1938]

A DISTRESSING period for German art began with Adolf Hitler's accession to power on January 30, 1933. "Artists, too, who have hitherto subscribed to the principle 'Art for Art's sake,' must realize that art cannot live unto itself but must be fitted into our ideology," Hans Hinkel, Nazi commissioner for cultural affairs in Prussia, said. "It follows that the artist, like everyone else, must be *gleichgeschaltet*" (molded in the same cast).

As he said this, an American who happened to attend the meeting of musicians, painters, sculptors, actors, and writers whom Hinkel addressed, said to the man next to him, a judge of the supreme German disciplinary court, "Can you imagine a Beethoven submitting to *Gleichschaltung*?" To which the learned justice replied resignedly, "Well, then, we'll have to get along without a Beethoven."

Nazi Germany had soon to learn that it would have to get along without Fritz Kreisler. As early as 1920 he had said to the now defunct *Literary Digest*:

> "My message is a purely artistic one and always will be in every country under every circumstance. I will never stand for any inclusion of the nationalistic element in art. I would quickly oppose any attempt in Vienna to agitate against French music. The higher art goes, the less it has to do with terrestrial things. It is like religion and philosophy. Music is no more confined to nationalities than religion is for one favored people alone. Personally, I consider myself a humble servant of humanity as an artist."

Kreisler had already shown by his reactions to Soviet Commissar Lunacharsky's attempt to prescribe an ideological course for him should he come to Soviet Russia to play, how impossible it was for him to mix art and politics. Mussolini had made no such stipulation, and Kreisler had continued to play in Italy as he did in monarchies, republics, democracies, socialist and capitalist states everywhere, unconcerned about the form of government or the type of man who chanced to head a given state.

The Nazi régime, it must be remembered, did not reveal itself immediately. It seized control of German life gradually. Hitler solemnly promised the Protestant and Catholic faiths, for instance, in his very first Reichstag speech that they would be unmolested. His out-and-out fight on religion came years later. Hinkel's speech, too, was not delivered until months of Nazi domination had passed.

Kreisler's American concert season was on as usual early in 1933. He not only played his usual recitals but gave a benefit for the endowment fund of Town Hall, New York, on March 3, and agreed to be a soloist at one of the five festival concerts arranged by Walter Damrosch in Madison Square Garden for the benefit of the Musicians' Emergency Aid Fund.

Once again a word picture can be drawn of Kreisler's physical appearance at the beginning of the Hitler régime. Helen L. Kaufmann and Eva vb. Hansl described him in 1933 in these terms: *

> As Kreisler, king of violinists, stands upon the stage, his keen dark eyes gazing with a faraway look over the heads of his audience, one hand grasps his coat lapel, while, from the other at his side, dangles his Guarnerius, which he holds by the neck. Magnificently erect, shoulders squared, he awaits his cue—then jerking back the leonine head, he tucks the fiddle under his collar and plays as only he can, with a noble Viennese grace and virile strength, unmistakably Kreisler.

When Kreisler returned to his Berlin home for the summer holidays, he realized that the Nazis were determined to suppress artistic freedom as they suppressed every other freedom. They were, however, by no means very sure of themselves as yet, and therefore cast about eagerly for big names which they hoped to identify with their

* Reprinted from *Artists in Music Today* by Helen L. Kaufmann and Eva vb. Hansl, by permission of Grosset & Dunlap, Inc., New York, copyright, 1933, Grosset & Dunlap, Inc.

cause—men like Gerhart Hauptmann, Richard Strauss, and Fritz Kreisler, with world-wide reputations. Wilhelm Furtwängler, who was doing his utmost to save what could be saved of musical culture in a political régime that tried to promote *Kultur in Schaftstiefeln und Sporen* (Culture in High Boots and Spurs), invited Fritz to appear as soloist of the Philharmonic Orchestra series during the season of 1933–1934.

Kreisler's reply to Furtwängler upset their calculations. Under date of July 1, 1933, he wrote in part:

Dear Dr. Furtwängler:

Thank you sincerely for the invitation to appear in a Philharmonic concert under your conducting and especially for the honor implied in your solicitation, viz., of being, as it were, the first artist called upon to re-tie the strings that have been rent asunder.

To be that sort of a leader would fill me with pride if I could consider myself as fulfilling the preconditions for such a mission. That is, however, not the case. . . .

I believe that nothing but the recall of artists like Bruno Walter, Klemperer, Busch, etc. could demonstrably further and clarify at home and abroad the cause which is as dear to me as it is to you, whereas in my case the idea of a compromise solution could easily arise.

I am therefore firmly determined to postpone my appearance in Germany until such time when the right of all artists, irrespective of origin, religion or nationality, to practice their art in Germany shall have become an irrevocable fact. I trust that I may soon have the good fortune of making music with you.

With hearty greetings,

Very respectfully yours,

[Signed] *Fritz Kreisler.*

Even then the Nazis did not desist in their efforts to use Kreisler's unheard-of popularity for their purposes. Prussian State Commissioner Hinkel three weeks later issued a pronouncement to the effect that the free artistic activities of foreigners and non-Nazis were in no wise to be hindered.

When Kreisler was asked to comment, he declared:

"I appreciate Commissioner Hinkel's announcement, but before I appear I must see it established beyond peradventure of doubt that all my colleagues in the musical world, irrespective of nationality, race or creed are not only tolerated but actually welcomed. I would rather appear, if at all, at the end of the season after having seen it demonstrated that Commissioner Hinkel's words have been translated into action. Art is international and I oppose chauvinism in art wherever I encounter it."

This statement was much bolder than appears on the surface. By that time it had almost become sacrilege publicly to doubt the word of any Nazi leader. Although Kreisler was an Austrian citizen and therefore not subject to seizure and delivery into a concentration camp as German nationals were, yet he had his beautiful home and parklike estate in the Grunewald section of Berlin. He might have been submitted to various forms of chicanery.

Even more serious was the fact that all of Kreisler's compositions, transcriptions, and arrangements were published for the European continent, the British Empire, except Canada, and for South America, by B. Schott's Söhne, music publishers of Mainz, Germany. The royalties involved were considerable. It was not long before the Nazis forbade the sale of any Kreisler music in Germany and banned all such music from the radio.

For Wilhelm Furtwängler, it must be said that he tried to fulfill Kreisler's stipulation of equal treatment for all artists. He managed to persuade someone in the Reich's Chancellery to permit him to address invitations to play under his conductorship to the following artists: Pablo Casals, Alfred Cortot, Josef Hofmann, Yehudi Menuhin, Gregor Piatigorsky, Artur Schnabel, and Jacques Thibaud.

The year 1934 began favorably enough. His American tour was successful as usual, and showed that his letter to Furtwängler was understood as in keeping with his creed of divorcing art from political ideology.

Arriving in England after his American engagements, Kreisler was particularly happy to be able once again to play the Elgar Concerto in London for the benefit of the Musicians' Benevolent Fund under the baton of Sir Landon Ronald. The Princess Royal and Princess Beatrice attended, and the private secretary to King George sent him a telegram, dated June 3, 1934, conveying "His Majesty's appreciation of his playing at the Elgar Memorial Concert in Albert Hall on the occasion of his birthday."

After a brief stay in his Berlin home, Kreisler that summer went on

Wilhelm Furtwängler, 1886-1954

Fritz Kreisler in the 1940's

Fritz Kreisler in the 1930's

to Italy and France for his vacation. In Rome the appalling news reached him early in August that a dear Austrian friend, Chancellor Engelbert Dollfuss, had been murdered by Nazi sympathizers.

"I was deeply depressed," Kreisler said. "A few days later we were in Paris. At a luncheon a French senator from Savoie sat next to me. He asked me why I was so gloomy. I told him my friend Dollfuss had been killed by Nazis; this meant that, sooner or later, Austria would be drawn into the Nazi orbit, and I might have to face the possibility of having to become a Nazi subject. That was something I did not want to see happen.

" 'And you won't have to,' the senator said.

"But it takes five years to become an American citizen and three to four to become a Frenchman," I countered.

" 'Wait a minute,' he reflected. 'There's a law from the time of Napoleon to the effect that anyone who renders a special service to the French nation can be made a citizen directly. I'll go to Georges Bonnet and arrange it. You can become a Frenchman overnight.' A few days later the senator came to tell me I could acquire a French passport at any time. All I'd need to do was to ask for it; everything had been arranged."

This was certainly quick action, but Kreisler could not persuade himself immediately to cancel his Austrian citizenship, to which he was so devotedly attached that one could not visit his home without noticing a framed certificate prominently displayed, testifying to his being an Austrian.

I shall here interrupt the chronological story of Kreisler's life to carry the account of his becoming a French citizen to its ultimate conclusion. Only after the Nazis in 1938 had taken control of Austria, integrated the unhappy little country into the Greater German Reich, and asked all of the little republic's citizens to turn in their passports and apply for German passports did Fritz avail himself of this unusual act of French hospitality.

Meanwhile, the French Government had taken the further step of showing its esteem of Kreisler by making him a Commander of the Legion of Honor in May, 1938, soon after the "Anschluss," in "recognition of his art." It was a rare honor.

To avoid possible embarrassment, Kreisler had taken up residence in southern France, near Monte Carlo, when the annexation of Austria by Hitler appeared imminent. He was now ready to accept the generous French offer.

A solemn ceremony ensued. Kreisler was received by the French Minister of Fine Arts in the presence of a number of members of the French Parliament.

The minister delivered an address, emphasizing the thought that art is destined to mediate between conflicting political ideologies. Kreisler, he said, in view of his international standing, was destined to bring nations more closely together and to become the connecting link between Germany and France.

Fritz, visibly moved, replied with a brief speech:

> "In a world carried away by the folly of men, France still represents a stronghold in which are intact all ideas which make up human dignity: honor, liberty and the love of art. If the pleasantness of living has lost, in the last several years, a little of its reputation, on the other hand it seems accompanied by ancient virtues: courage, energy and patience. These are the virtues which appeal to my heart."

When the news of Kreisler's change of citizenship reached America, the New York *Times* editorialized on May 2, 1939:

> It would have been pleasant if our "war" with Mr. Kreisler could have been ended by his becoming an American citizen. He has done the next best thing by taking out naturalization papers in another country which he happily praises a "stronghold . . . of art." His American public will want him to know that such ideas will never be alien here, either, and that we shall not entirely surrender him to France. In a sense his homeland is what it always was, for, whenever and wherever he plays, there is the Vienna of his youth, unconquered and immortal.

The whole matter became official and public when on May 21, 1939, the *Journal Officiel*, a publication of government notices, stated that "Fritz Kreisler, musician and commander of the Legion of Honor, born February 2, 1875, and living at Roquebrune-Cap-Martin (Maritime Alps) has become a French citizen," and that the certificate of naturalization "was brought him by a French friend, and was issued in the name of President Le Brun. It bore the date of May 13, 1939.

M. Kreisler had become a Chevalier of the Legion in 1914 through the efforts of Vincent d'Indy, with whom he had been at the Conservatoire."

Foreign Minister Joachim von Ribbentrop at first refused to recognize the validity of Kreisler's French citizenship. His legal experts, however, found that there was a law on the Austrian statute books by which citizens of Vienna, through some arrangement effected by Napoleon, were authorized to accept French citizenship.

But to return to the events of 1934:

Soon after his 1934 luncheon with the French senator who had solved his citizenship problem, Kreisler, accompanied by his wife, started for the United States again. On the ship he put in much time revising and editing a Paganini violin concerto—a revision which the critics in St. Louis, where he played it for the first time, acclaimed as a distinct improvement over Paganini's own arrangement.

From America, Kreisler went, as so often in the past, to England. It was now January, 1935. One day there was to be a bridge party at the home of Sir Louis and Lady Sterling. Some guests were already seated at the card tables impatiently waiting for the others. But in another room Kreisler, Artur Schnabel, Lauritz Melchior, and ex-Mayor "Jimmy" Walker of New York became involved in a discussion about Nazi Germany. The theme seemed inexhaustible; there was no stopping the four. The card party was a failure, the political discussion a brilliant success.

On February 2, 1935, Fritz Kreisler was sixty years old. All over the world, radio networks devoted a full program to Kreisler compositions. Artists appearing during February made it a point to pay tribute to the Austrian master by playing one or more of his ingratiating pieces.

Only in Nazi Germany did a blanket of silence enshroud the name of Kreisler. A mere handful of devoted friends came to the beautiful Grunewald mansion for a quiet birthday celebration. It was obvious to us, sitting around the festive table artistically decorated with choice flowers from the Kreisler conservatory, that someone ought to deliver the joint felicitations and propose a toast in a more or less formal speech. The men furtively looked at each other, wondering who could do justice to the occasion. Before they could make up their minds, up rose the witty, accomplished lady on Fritz's right—Katharina von Oheimb-Kardorff, a brilliant member of the Weimar Republic's Reichstag and a political adviser to the late President Friedrich Ebert.

In a touching little address she referred to her feeling of shame that her own country, alone, failed to pay any attention to the anniversary, then continued by pointing out that the dozen friends present were symbolical of millions in the world who at this time were thinking of Fritz and who loved him even more, if that were possible, now that he was being ignored in the very city to which he had for years given such generous aid.

Frau von Oheimb-Kardorff was right: other countries seemed eager to do what the Nazis had failed to do. A South American tour was being arranged; Greek music circles, with the hearty support of their King George, initiated a movement to have Kreisler make a tour of Greece, Bulgaria, and Yugoslavia late in 1935 or early in 1936; forty-eight concerts for that year were scheduled in the United States; Vienna invited her illustrious son for a special ceremony.

Four days after his birthday anniversary, Kreisler stood in the lord mayor's room in Vienna, surrounded by the vice mayor, the president of the Academy of Music, the director-general of the opera and their wives, and other dignitaries. Lord Mayor Richard Schmitz presented him with the *Ehrenring* (Ring of Honor) of his native city, and paid a glowing tribute to the sexagenarian for the glory he had shed upon Vienna, throughout his career, by his artistic and philanthropic work.

While in Vienna, an inquiry from Olin Downes in New York elicited the confession about the origin of his compositions by "old masters" which will be discussed in full in the ensuing chapter.

It was now time for him to rest before beginning his South American tour. Kreisler therefore went to charming Kitzbühl, in the Austrian Alps. There was much excitement when he arrived there, for the Prince of Wales had just come to the popular winter resort for an extended stay.

The tour of South America in May, 1935, was unique in more than one respect. It was the first time that an artist had used a Zeppelin lighter-than-air craft to travel from Europe to South America. Kreisler even managed to crowd in a concert at Pernambuco between refueling stops of the gigantic dirigible.

The tour almost failed to materialize, for Fritz Kreisler's long-time friend and manager, Charles Foley, who had come to Europe to talk over the details of the unusual air voyage, fell ill in Paris on his way back to New York, from where he was to proceed to Brazil in advance of Fritz. With characteristic loyalty Kreisler announced that he would cancel the tour if Foley were prevented by his illness from going to South America.

The Zeppelin cruise was one of the high points in Kreisler's rich life. "A glass of water," Fritz said, "was put in a certain place on the Zeppelin as we started; when we reached Brazil, not a drop had been spilled." The ease with which it sped on its course and the comfort of travel were such that Fritz keenly regrets that Dr. Hugo Eckener's dream found an untimely end.

For this tour Kreisler took Franz Rupp with him as accompanist. Rupp kept notes which enabled him to convey an accurate description of what happened.

"Fritz Kreisler arrived by plane from Berlin at Friedrichshafen on May 4 toward evening," Rupp reported. "The following morning, when we were about to take off, we almost had a bad accident. A sudden squall arose which nearly dashed the *Graf Zeppelin* to the ground. We flew by way of Basle and the Cape Verde Islands to Pernambuco, where we arrived too early for the landing crews. So, for several hours our dirigible cruised about on what might be called a sight-seeing trip. The coral reefs were especially interesting.

"It was frightfully hot when we finally landed between 5:00 and 6:00 P.M.—somewhere around 104 degrees. At nine o'clock that night, while the *Graf* was refueling, we gave the scheduled concert and then returned to the hotel, hoping to get a few hours of sleep. Alas, all the roosters of the world, so it seemed to us, had united in crowing at all hours of the night, as though there were a world convention of them, with each sounding off at the accustomed hour of the time zone from which he came.

"Early the next morning we started for Rio de Janeiro, where Charles Foley and Herr Schramme, the manager in charge of the Argentine concerts, awaited us. We registered at the Globe Hotel and asked for permission to practice in the social hall in which there was a piano. It was so hot that Kreisler took off his coat. He was politely told that etiquette forbade this! So we did without a rehearsal. The first two Rio concerts took place in the Teatro Municipale on May 10 and 12."

The Federal District Civil Police presented Kreisler with an identification card stating that he was registered as No. 1324 in the "Chamber of Artists, Profession: Violinist."

For weeks preceding Kreisler's arrival in Rio there had been stories about him, about the uniqueness of his playing, about his violins. The critic for the *Correio da Manhã* even boasted that he "had succeeded in discovering a slight act of forgery" on the part of Kreisler. He referred to Kreisler's ascribing certain of his own compositions to old masters. It is hard to imagine that the Brazilian music expert succeeded in "discovering" what uncounted musicologists had for four decades failed to notice! He had obviously read the most recent American and British newspaper accounts of the "confession" already referred to.

On the afternoon after his arrival Kreisler, described by *O Globo* as "the most modest celebrity in the world," received the Brazilian press at a cocktail party. He immediately captivated his interviewers by his honest enthusiasm for the beauties of Rio. "An absolutely fascinating panorama," he exclaimed. "Your mountains, your skyscrapers —all this viewed from above—it is something one cannot forget." He made everybody laugh when he answered a press photographer's request for permission to take a picture with "Yes, but painless, please."

As everywhere else in the world, the Rio criticisms of his concerts were replete with fulsome praise. The *Correio da Manhã* stated:

> Fritz Kreisler has conquered us Cariocas triumphantly. . . . He is a sorcerer of sounds, and his unusual qualities can perhaps be explained only by some occult power that radiates some particular magic.

Rupp and Kreisler in Rio de Janeiro, June 1935

Kreisler in São Paulo

During their Rio stay, Rupp informs us, he and Kreisler "went by motorboat to the famous Island of Love; also, we made a tour of the wonderful harbor. We also visited a snake farm." They were so besieged with invitations to social affairs that Kreisler had to appeal through the Empresa Artistica Teatral Ltda. to spare him such attentions, as he was unable to accept them.

After a second concert the Kreisler party left by rail for two concerts in São Paulo. All São Paulo papers stressed that Kreisler was popular in Brazil long before his arrival there, because of his gramophone recordings.

"Back to Rio we went," Franz Rupp resumed, "for a popular concert to enable the rank and file of the people to attend; after that by airplane to Buenos Aires by way of Rio Grande. We got into a bad storm and I felt so miserable that I suggested Kreisler go alone to Buenos Aires. Why, during our bumpy flight Kreisler's violin even fell on his head because of the sudden lurching of our plane.

"In Argentina we found ourselves constantly placarded as 'Fritz y Franz.' Kreisler gave six sold-out concerts in the Teatro Colón of Buenos Aires alone. People would run after him in the streets, so popular was he. But not only in Argentina, also in Brazil and Uruguay he never went to any affair unless he was assured it was a stag party; that's how faithful he was to his wife."

The Argentine capital was in a high state of excitement the day Kreisler gave his first concert, May 23. Dr. Getulio Vargas, President of the United States of Brazil, was in Buenos Aires to visit his colleague, Argentine President General Augustín P. Justo. But the festive mood of the city, far from interfering with the first appearance of the long-awaited Austrian virtuoso, injected itself also into the Teatro Colón. There ensued, according to the Buenos Aires *Herald*, "A remarkable scene as he (Kreisler) stood smiling and bowing."

This paper obtained an interview with Kreisler on May 30. Its reporter was especially impressed with the deep humility of the artist:

> I was in the presence of the most human of beings that one could wish to meet. He is just the most simple of God's creatures, an ardent lover of things beautiful. . . . "Art," he explained, "is a tremendous whole and we who

are its servants are only little insignificant atoms of this great whole. I love playing. Concerts are a pleasure."

Fritz Kreisler, despite his six concerts in fourteen days, attended a gala performance of *Carmen*. His warm praise of the orchestra under Hector Panizza was naturally deeply appreciated.

After his last recital on June 4 the Buenos Aires *Herald* wrote:

> The great violinist has endeared himself to the hearts of many thousands during his visit. There is a note of sadness in his departure, but his public is the richer for what he has left behind.

Franz Rupp continued his story: "From Buenos Aires we went by rail to Rosário. There, too, the concert was sold out. Many persons of German extraction attended. Charles Foley especially regretted that there were no races; so did the rest of us.

"On June 5 we flew to Montevideo at the invitation of the president of Uruguay. We did not go to the hotel that night to sleep, since our plane was to leave at five the next morning. It was now winter and quite dark. The weather again was so bad that we had to make one unscheduled landing. It was eight o'clock at night when we finally arrived in Rio. We had had no sleep the night before; we had been en route for fifteen hours—and an hour later our farewell concert was to begin in Rio! We just had time to go to the Gloria Hotel, change clothes and walk onto the platform.

"For both of us the floor seemed constantly to sway under us as we played. Worse than that, neither could hear the other as we were virtually deaf from the noise of the motors. During the pause I had to ask Foley, 'Can you hear us?' To our joy Kreisler's old friend Jacques Thibaud was present and greeted us.

"Immediately after the concert we had to board a mail plane for Pernambuco, where the *Graf Zeppelin* obligingly delayed its departure for four hours to make it possible for us to return to Europe on it. Frederic Lamond was on the flying field to greet us. Charles Foley flew back to Europe with us.

"It must have cost the Zeppelin a pretty penny to wait for us, for the changed schedule meant that we arrived at Friedrichshafen at noon instead of early in the morning. Not that we minded, for Cap-

Franz Rupp's photograph of the Graf Zeppelin

Franz Rupp at the piano

View of Athens in the 1930's

tain Hans von Schiller, in charge of the dirigible, took us on a four-hour beautiful cruise over the Swiss Alps until it was late enough in the afternoon to make a landing possible. Meanwhile we managed to empty what was left of the *Graf's* wine cellar.

"Again a dear friend of Kreisler's was on hand to greet him: Sergei Rachmaninoff. That ended our tour, but I am happy to say that I recently received word to the effect that the Beethoven sonatas for violin and piano which we recorded together in London are in constant demand in South America."

The busy 1935–1936 season of forty-eight concerts in America detained Fritz Kreisler in the States until December 27, 1935, so that, for the first time in years, he could not participate in his annual Christmas party for the poor children of Berlin.

During the following February, Fritz Kreisler went on his tour of Greece, Bulgaria, and Yugoslavia, adding three more countries to the great number in which his name has become a household word.

From various quarters more high decorations were showered upon him during this and ensuing years. The Greek Government showed its appreciation of his coming to Athens by having A. Rizo-Rangabé, the Greek minister in Berlin, present him with the Grand Commander's Cross of the Order of George I, a decoration so high that Dr. Leodegar Petrin, chief of the education section of the Austrian cabinet, wrote him a special letter congratulating him upon this unusual honor.

The Royal Academy of St. Cecilia of Rome apprised him in a letter signed by its president, the Duke of San Martino, a relative of the king, that he had been made an honorary member of this ancient musical institution.

King Leopold III of Belgium on April 28, 1937, sent him word that he had been made a Grand Officer of the Order of Leopold II, and his ambassador to Berlin Count Jacques Davignon, somewhat later presented him with the plaque of a Grand Officer.

Besides making a successful tour of the Near East, Kreisler during 1936 gave nine recitals in the Scandinavian countries and also appeared in Paris. The French critic Émile Vuillermoz summed up his impressions of the Austrian artist in these words:

Not only will this modern Paganini leave an indelible imprint in the history of the violin, but for all who still have respect for the dignity and generosity of art Fritz Kreisler today represents an exalted factor of morality and a wonderful example.

In the autumn Kreisler came to America for a schedule of forty concerts, at many of which he offered his painstaking revision of Schumann's Fantasie in C Major.

Just before returning to Berlin for Christmas, he learned that his intimate friends Lucie and Ernest Schelling were both very ill in their summer abode at Céligny, Switzerland. Fritz sat down immediately in his Berlin home and penned a letter in longhand which again bears testimony to his loving character. It read in part:

Jan. 2, 1937

Dear Ernest,

Shortly before we sailed for Europe we heard from the Mitchells what a series of misfortunes had befallen you. I cannot tell you how deeply we feel with you. We only pray and hope, that in the meanwhile there has been a turn for the better both in Lucie's and your own state of health. We would be grateful if you could give us news about it. Of course we realize that writing might still strain your eyes but please send us a postcard or have one written by the nurse. . . .

In your misfortune it must have been some solace to you both to realize in what deep affection you are held by friends, colleagues, and the public at large. I only spent a few days in New York after completion of my tour before our departure, but wherever we went, we heard utterances of deepest sympathy and fervent hopes for the complete and speedy recovery of you both.

Barbirolli and Ganz behaved splendidly, as true and steadfast colleagues, and when you come back to New York after a year's absence, you will find a great welcome and a warmer place, if possible, in the hearts of friends, colleagues, and public.

Yours always

Affectionately

[Signed] *Fritz* *

Much of the summer of 1937 was spent on the Riviera. His friends the Pistors visited there. Mrs. Pistor wrote enthusiastically:

We had a wonderful time at Cap Martin. It was an eye opener for us to note how Fritz was held in esteem by the international world. Everybody gath-

* From the Ernest Schelling Collection.

ered around a table in the evening, and then all sorts of persons came to ask for the honor of being introduced to him. Since he is such an extremely modest character, however, it was always embarrassing to him to have such a fuss made over him.

The annual American tour which followed was uneventful except for the fact that at Ann Arbor someone for some inexplicable reason dropped a tear-gas bomb just after Kreisler had finished playing a Bach concerto to five thousand students and professors of the University of Michigan. The imperturbable Fritz took the interruption of five minutes good-humoredly. Many left in a panic, but not he!

However sad and heart-rending the year 1938 was for Kreisler, when Austria was incorporated into the "Thousand-Year German Reich," he might have converted it into a year of rare triumphs for himself in America had he been so minded.

Fifty years had elapsed since he made his début in Boston, New York, Philadelphia, Chicago, St. Louis, New Orleans, and other American cities as a lad of thirteen in knee breeches. The golden anniversary as performing pianist of his friend Josef Hofmann had just been observed with imposing exercises. Kreisler's innumerable friends and admirers were eager for the opportunity to demonstrate their love for him. But Fritz would have none of it.

His annual Carnegie Hall concert in New York was not even placarded, yet hundreds had to be denied admission. *Time* magazine called the event an "Unannounced Anniversary." It contrasted this modest jubilee with that of Moriz Rosenthal, who, it will be recalled was responsible for Kreisler's American début in 1888. Rosenthal, *Time* pointed out, celebrated the fiftieth anniversary of his first appearance in America by "playing on a special gold-lacquered piano in Manhattan's Carnegie Hall."

Going next to Philadelphia, where he was as well known and beloved as in New York, Kreisler again forbade all demonstrations and played for the pension fund of the Philadelphia Symphony Orchestra under the direction of Eugene Ormandy.

He had selected the Brahms Violin Concerto for the occasion. When Marcel Tabuteau, Philadelphia's famous oboist, played his beautiful solo at the beginning of the second movement, Kreisler turned his back to the audience and listened intently, deeply moved. Then, as his turn came to take up the melody, he intoned in a manner that clearly supported the oboist's conception of the air. Afterward he remarked reverently, "Brahms has been talking to us."

The season of 1938–1939 was the last for Kreisler to appear as an Austrian artist. Gone was even his fatherland's name; it was now the "Ostmark" of Hitler's Greater Germany.

When he returned to America in the autumn of 1939, he was a French citizen and a refugee from World War II, which had started only nineteen days previously. He has not been in Europe since.

CHAPTER TWENTY-FIVE

CONFESSION OF AN OLD HOAX

[1935]

FRITZ KREISLER always knew that at some time or other he would have to confess publicly that he had fooled the world for many years by crediting a dozen of his most popular pieces to such seventeenth and eighteenth century masters as Jean Baptiste Cartier, Louis Couperin, Karl von Dittersdorf, François Francœur, Padre Martini, Niccolò Porpora, Gaetano Pugnani, Johann Stamitz, and Antonio Vivaldi.

What genuinely surprised him was the fact that it took thirty-odd years for the proper occasion for unburdening his mind to present itself. He had to become sixty years old before he stood revealed as a paragon of modesty, a genius with a sense of humor who played a "magnificent joke," an unethical imposter, a conscienceless forger—depending upon what view one took of his unintended hoax.

As a young man of thirty-five, he had tried in vain to set musicologists on the scent of his "forgeries." On one of the recital programs in Berlin he had presented his "Liebesfreud" and "Liebesleid" as transcriptions of posthumous waltzes by Joseph Lanner, whereas he ascribed his "Caprice viennois" to himself as composer. Thereupon the noted critic Dr. Leopold Schmidt of the Berliner *Tageblatt* gave him a verbal reprimand for daring to include his own "insignificant" composition in the same group with "Lanner" gems. Schmidt wrote:

A feeling slightly akin to bad taste was engendered by the somewhat daring juxtaposition of Kreisler's "Caprice viennois"—to be sure a charming offering —and the dances of Lanner, these delightful genre creations filled with Schubertian melos and reflecting the good old Vienna days, for which encores were enthusiastically demanded.

Kreisler retorted that the "Lanner" dances weren't by Lanner at all but flowed from the same pen that had written the "Caprice."

"Depressed over this injustice," he said, "I decided then and there to confess authorship to these dances, which were later also published under my name. But even this confession, which certainly offered a clue, did not point the way for the learned experts. To the present day I am unable to explain why they did not stumble upon the truth immediately."

Kreisler then dropped the matter and waited for a more auspicious moment to confess and explain his action.

In 1923, an incident occurred which made him think his hoax had at last been discovered. His friend, the composer Vincent d'Indy, sat in the front row during his Opéra concert and, as he played the Praeludium and Allegro ascribed to Pugnani, pointed an accusing finger at him. After the recital, however, D'Indy came to the artist's room, again pointed his finger, and said, "Pugnani would not have played the Allegro in that tempo." That was all. Even D'Indy accepted the composition as a genuine Pugnani!

From time to time Kreisler took fellow musicians into his confidence. Efrem Zimbalist was one of the earliest to know. He kept quiet, however, for as he explained when the dénouement finally came in February, 1935:

"The violin repertory has been wonderfully enriched by these compositions, and as Kreisler did not think it advisable to say they were his when he wrote them, he had a perfect right to attribute them to anyone he pleased. Any composer, living or dead, should be proud to claim them as his own. However, anyone who is really familiar with Kreisler's style of writing would recognize the infallible signs of the actual composer of these works."

Others who apparently knew for years were Albert Spalding, Jascha Heifetz, Georges Enesco, Louis Persinger, and Franz Rupp. Carl Lamson remembers how on one occasion William Chase, New York *Times* critic, asked him for the name of an encore which Kreisler had played. When Lamson said, "La Chasse by Cartier-Kreisler," Chase, "with a roguish wink, crossed out the word Cartier."

Vincent d'Indy, 1851-1931

Efrem Zimbalist, about 1935

Yehudi Menuhin in the San Francisco studio of Louis Persinger, 1887-196

Georges Enesco in drawing by Fortuna Brulez-Mavromati

Enesco urged his pupils, including Yehudi Menuhin, to "buy all of Kreisler's work, irrespective of the strange names connected with some of them." He admonished Menuhin to "study them, because they are excellent works."

Tired of waiting for musical experts to extract his "confession," Kreisler, during a visit to New York in December, 1934, requested his American publishers, Carl Fischer, Inc., to announce the twelve compositions hitherto listed as "Classic Manuscripts" as his original works in the catalog for 1935. In other words, the hoax would have been revealed early in 1935 anyway, and would probably have drawn but little comment.

It so chanced, however, that Olin Downes, chief music critic of the New York *Times*, stumbled upon the facts in the case shortly before the Fischer catalog was sent out. His story follows: *

The events which led to the revelation of Mr. Kreisler's authorship were very simple, and may be cited here merely to show how unpremeditated the disclosure was on the part of those who had the secret in keeping. This writer had been engaged by the Brooklyn Institute of Arts and Sciences to give a lecture-recital with Yehudi Menuhin on certain aspects of violin music. After many compositions had been considered with a view to illustration, it was decided to begin with what was then known as the Kreisler transcription of the "Praeludium and Allegro" of Pugnani.

It, therefore, became the business of the lecturer to find out what the differences were between the supposedly original composition and its arrangement by Kreisler. Was Pugnani's score available, either in print or in manuscript, in this country? Intensive search in New York and in the Library of Congress † failed to reveal a note of Pugnani which suggested the material of the professed transcription. The investigator then asked the Carl Fischer house for information on the subject. It was promptly given him by word of mouth and in the printed form of the new Fischer catalog. His inquiry was made easy and simple, as it happened to coincide with Mr. Kreisler's decision to make known his authorship.

There was no pursuing Mr. Kreisler to his lair and forcing from him an unwilling acknowledgment of his culpability in the matter. Asked by cable

* Reprinted from *Kreisler's 'Classics'* by Olin Downes in the March 3, 1935 issue of the New York *Times*, by permission of the New York *Times*.

† Harold Spivacke, now Chief of the Music Division of the Library of Congress, was engaged especially by Mr. Downes to do the detailed research work.

if he would verify the information the *Times* had secured, he answered promptly, under date of February 6: "Your statement absolutely correct. The entire series labelled *Classical Manuscripts* are my original compositions with the sole exception of the first eight bars of the Couperin *Chanson Louis XIII*, taken from a traditional melody. Necessity forced this course upon me thirty years ago when I was desirous of enlarging my programs. I found it impudent and tactless to repeat my name endlessly on the programs."

His explanation was simple and frank, and it gave his reasons for concealing for some thirty years his creative identity. The reasons seem to us quite logical and in no sense such as to reflect discreditably upon Mr. Kreisler. . . .

It was undoubtedly to the great advantage of the compositions that they did not bear his name as composer. For it is unfortunately true that there is a great deal in a name. Neither the public, nor the press, nor Mr. Kreisler's colleagues would have taken as kindly to these compositions had they been designated as being merely the creations of a living violinist.

Neither Fritz Kreisler nor Olin Downes could know that their friendly exchange of messages and the *Times's* revelation of the hoax would lead to a literary feud between Kreisler and Ernest Newman, chief music critic of the London *Times*, author of books on Mozart and Wagner and an ardent admirer of Kreisler's art. The case of the authorship of the "Classical Manuscripts" and the ethics involved thus became a *cause célèbre*. A biography of Fritz Kreisler would not be complete without the inclusion of salient passages from Newman's attack, Kreisler's rejoinder, Newman's reply, and Kreisler's final word.

Ernest Newman wrote in part in the *Sunday Times* for February 24, 1935, under the title "The Kreisler Revelations—Debit and Credit":

I do not know if any comment has been made in the press on Kreisler's recent admission that certain works long regarded as being merely arranged by him are his own compositions. . . .

Now if this news is true, the revelation is both welcome and regrettable. It is welcome to show how easy it is, and always was, to write this kind of music. The average concert goer no doubt feels that those hateful fellows the critics have had their ignorance shown up and been made to look foolish. On the contrary, what is shown up is the falsity of current judgments upon certain types of old music and the absence of any really critical standard where music in general is concerned.

The simple truth is that a vast amount of seventeenth and eighteenth century music was merely the exploitation of formulae, the effective handling of which is within the scope of any ordinarily intelligent musician today. From one point of view Kreisler has not gone nearly far enough in the excellent work of clearing up the world's muddled thinking on these points: for my part I could wish he had "discovered" some Bach and Handel manuscripts as well. In so far as Bach and Handel merely sat down in perfectly cold blood and ground out their morning's ration of music according-to-the-recipe they merely produced well-sounding stuff that anyone of any intelligence today could turn out by the handful. . . . Take as an example the ouverture to "Acis and Galatea." Anyone with the least bit of music in him and the least knowledge of the period could produce this sort of thing any morning with the hand he did not require for shaving. The pattern is to be met with thousands of times in the music of the Bach-Handel epoch—a pompous opening gesture, followed by a few bars of bustling semiquavers over some consequential harmonies, the gesture again, and so *ad infinitum*. . . .

The average music of that period is as easy to imitate as the average political speech of today. Just as the latter says next to nothing in sonorous phrases about exploring avenues, leaving no stone unturned, taking immediate steps, and all the rest of it, so a great deal of music says next to nothing in phrases that reproduce again and again the same formulae of noble gesture, dignified attitude, airy grace and so on. The only difference between the mental operations involved in the two cases and the results obtained comes from the fact that sounds have of themselves a charm that words of themselves have not. . . .

There is thus ample scope for the talent of any ordinarily good musician who likes to amuse himself with reproducing these old patterns and formulae of expression whether he chooses to give his word to the world "in the style of" So-and-So or prefers to affix to it the name of some actual composer of the past.

When music becomes a less generalized and formalized and more personal matter as it did in the nineteenth century, imitation becomes more difficult, because there is no formula to exploit. . . . It is easy to produce a Mozart *minuet* or a Handel *concerto grosso* or a Pugnani *prelude* that shall be as like the original as makes no matter, but far from easy to produce something on the lines of the famous Bach *aria* or Handel's *Ombra ma fu* or the first movement of Mozart's *G-minor* symphony; while the combined brains of all the best imitators of the present day would be unequal to the task of finishing *Turandot* from the point where Puccini left off or, supposing Berlioz to have died before he had completed the *Royal Hunt and Storm*, to the task of adding the final page.

As far as the merely musical point is concerned, then, there is nothing whatever in Kreisler's achievement. But what of the ethical aspect of the matter?

I am sure that Kreisler would have acted otherwise had he reflected upon all the consequences of what he has done; for what he has unintentionally done is to place all "arrangements" of old works under a certain suspicion. . . .

If some clever joker or other chooses to allege that a certain work in the programs is an arrangement from Handel, let us say, while all the time it is a work of his own, who is to gainsay him? Only the Handel specialist can be intimately acquainted with the whole of Handel's now forgotten works, including the operas; and even if the listener suspects that the "arranger" is playing a joke on him, what can he do about it? To verify his suspicions he would have to go to the British Museum and work his way through the whole of the ninety-seven volumes of the Handel Society's complete edition. . . .

A great deal of this old music still exists only in manuscript in Continental libraries. We can only rely, therefore, on the word of the alleged discoverer of the manuscript that he really has done what he professes to have done. . . .

And perhaps the matter has another aspect. In the case of paintings, a purchaser can proceed at law against anyone who sells him a picture which is not by the artist to whom it is attributed; at the present moment the grandson of a distinguished French painter is being sued in the Paris courts in connection with pictures of his own to which, it is said, he had the bright idea of affixing his grandfather's signature.

It would be interesting to see what would happen if someone were to claim damages from Kreisler and his publishers on the ground that he had been induced to purchase the score of a certain concerto on the representation that it was by Vivaldi, whereas Vivaldi on Kreisler's own admission had nothing whatever to do with it. Presumably he would at least be entitled to have his money back! *

Kreisler's rejoinder, addressed "To the Editor of the *Sunday Times*," from Berlin, appeared in that publication on March 10, 1935. It reads substantially as follows:

When, a few weeks ago, the *New York Times* disclosed the fact that a series of violin compositions published thirty years ago as my transcriptions of twelve various Italian, French and German composers of the seventeenth and eighteenth centuries were in reality my own works, it was followed in the world's press by such favorable comment as to fill me with pride.

The English musical critics accepted the disclosure with delightful good humour and splendid sportsmanship. Only that inveterate grumbler Mr.

* Carl Fischer, Inc., American distributors of Kreisler's published works, accepted Newman's challenge and offered to refund the money to anybody who felt he was cheated in music that he purchased under the impression that it was the transcription of an old master by Kreisler. Nobody asked for a refund. On the contrary, there was a sudden extra demand by music lovers for printings of the old edition as souvenirs!

Ernest Newman in an article in the *Sunday Times* of February 24 took up the gauntlets against me, ostensibly on behalf of musical ethics, but in reality in his own defence. He is hard put to explain why he, the musical augur *par excellence*, failed to nail down my transcriptions for the *pastiches* they were. There was really no necessity for Mr. Newman to worry, for the prestige of a critic with a sense of musical values is not in the least endangered because a piece, which he pronounced good, is found to have been written by another person than he thought. The name changes, the value remains.

But Mr. Newman's pique is aroused. . . . He proceeds to tell an astonished world that there is a formula by which any ordinary intelligent modern musician can write in the style of any composer of the seventeenth or eighteenth century he chooses. . . .

Of course, there is no such formula, as the eminent critic knows very well. Nor is there the slightest evidence in my work of any desire to imitate closely any style, for did I not endure all these years the vituperation of the Newmans of the world, for having modernized the pure form of the old classics and kreislerized their work for my own selfish needs as a virtuoso? Indeed, *difficile risum tenere*!

But is it admissible that the gigantic musical achievements of two centuries may be thus maligned and degraded and in a measure even Bach and Handel brought down to the level of any ordinary intelligent musician . . . ?

But why this spite of Mr. Newman? Did I not do my best to save him from his present discomfiture? Did not every copy of my incriminated transcriptions since their publication thirty years ago bear a notice in three languages, covering a full page, warning Mr. Newman that they (the transcriptions) are moreover so freely treated that they constitute, in fact, original works? . . .

As for the ethics of the case, so sternly invoked by their relentless defender, I beg to assure Mr. Newman that no hoax was ever intended, either for him or for anyone else. I did not write the pieces in question as a young man of twenty-five in the hope of tripping up the eminent critic thirty-five years later. I simply wrote them in order to enlarge my programs, where they figured modestly in the style of Pugnani, Cartier, etc., etc.

A few colleagues borrowed copies, but they soon fell into the habit of first dropping the "in the style of" and finally omitting my own name as well. Thinking that my colleagues rather exaggerated my modesty, I recalled the outstanding copies and henceforth used the transcriptions exclusively for myself. But I had reckoned without the "Newmans" of the day who clamoured in unison with my colleagues that I had no right to monopolize a valuable literature (so they claimed) for myself and sternly demanded publication in the name of musical ethics. . . .

Yielding finally to the pressure I consented to the publication with the proviso of the above-mentioned notice. . . .

Ernest Newman's ire was apparently aroused by Fritz Kreisler's rejoinder, for he now replied in much more caustic language in the *Sunday Times* for March 17, 1935:

Any one would think, to read your letter, that after having given years to the critical study of your "transcriptions" I had still failed to detect that they were—impersonations, shall I call them? You at once deceive yourself and flatter yourself. I know practically nothing of these works of yours; I doubt whether in all my life I have heard more than two or three of them; if I have, I have taken no particular notice of them; and I doubt whether what I have scribbled about them in the course of my concert-going during the last twenty-five years or so would occupy, in all, ten lines of the column.*

I am concerned with nothing in connection with them but the fact that for many years both violinists and listeners have accepted them, on the strength of your word, as genuine. In one sense I ought to be grateful to you for your revelations, for you have unwittingly played into my hands. . . . You yourself have proved my thesis for me: you have demonstrated convincingly that any ordinarily good musician, no matter how modest his endowment for original composition may be, can turn out with perfect ease a manufactured modern article so like the ancient thing it purports to be that listeners everywhere will unquestioningly accept it as genuine.

It is not the hated "critics" alone who are without sure criteria in these matters, but the whole body of scholars—and that for the simple reason that in the secondary and tertiary work of past epochs a formula or manner general to the epoch so far prevails over individual thinking that the greatest scholars have again and again been at fault. Scores, perhaps hundreds, of compositions have been ascribed to the wrong composers. . . .

The practice hitherto has been to assume that when an "editor" claimed to have in his possession an original manuscript of the work he was speaking the truth. You have unfortunately shown us that in this connection words do not always, or entirely, mean what they say.

You seem to think you have saved *your* face by saying that every copy of your transcriptions bore the words, "They are, moreover, so freely treated that they constitute, in fact, original works." You know as well as I do that the musical world regards that simply as a formula to ensure copyright. . . .† All this has nothing whatever to do with the ethical point at issue—that *you* gave the public to understand that what you had done was to operate upon

* This statement is difficult to believe. As every concertgoer knows, Kreisler invariably filled the third part of his program almost exclusively with his own compositions, many of which before 1935 were ascribed to classical masters. Newman must have heard them dozens of times. On the night of Kreisler's "comeback" in London in 1921, Newman was present and wrote, "There is not a violinist in the world who can approach him." On that night Kreisler played, *inter alia*, the "Vivaldi" concerto!

† This statement, too, is difficult to believe.

an *original manuscript* by some famous composer or other when as a matter of fact *there was no such manuscript*. Even to say, as you do, that "they are so freely treated as to . . . ," etc., is equivalent to affirming that there *was* an original to be so treated. . . .

But why did you not adopt a *fictitious* name or names for your compositions? Why use the names of well known composers of the past? Surely the other perfectly legitimate device would have equally well secured the modest end you had in view? . . .

"Necessity forced this course on me thirty years ago when I was desirous of enlarging my programs." I can understand a composer wishing certain works of his to appear under another name than his own. But what is this "necessity"—more dire, surely, than anything ever conceived by the imagination of a Greek tragedian!—that compels him to choose, out of the million possible names offered to him by Europe and America, the names of Vivaldi, Pugnani, Porpora, Martini, Couperin, Cartier, Dittersdorf, Francœur, and Stamitz? . . .

The more you try to explain, the more difficulties you make for yourself. . . .

Kreisler had the final word in the controversy in a letter dated from Stockholm, Sweden, and published in the *Sunday Times* for March 31, 1935, which reads in part as follows:

I suggest that Mr. Newman be taken at his word and compelled to prove his simple-formula theory, by turning out *in clausura* a specified piece in antique style. (If, as an alleged second-grade product by Bach or Handel, this piece succeeds in getting by the caretaker of Queen's Hall, I am prepared to make humble apologies.) Or are we expected to believe that this grandiloquent censor, who for years has been lecturing eminent composers, instrumentalists and singers on their respective art, may in the end not be able to qualify as an "ordinary intelligent musician," according to the standard set up by himself?

Equally false is Mr. Newman's assertion that I had adopted "well-known" old names for my compositions, the sly contention being obviously that I profited by their renown. The names I carefully selected were, for the most part, strictly unknown. Who ever had heard a work by Pugnani, Cartier, Francœur, Porpora, Louis Couperin, Padre Martini or Stamitz before I began to compose in their names? They lived exclusively as paragraphs in musical reference books, and their work, when existing and authenticated, lay mouldering in monasteries and old libraries. Their names were no more than empty shells, dusty old, forgotten cloaks, which I borrowed to hide my identity. . . .

Let me make myself perfectly clear. I am in no way concerned with Mr. Newman's critical opinions. His right to emit them is incontestably vouchsafed by the confidence of his editor. . . .

Had he kept his attack within the decent bounds of his prerogative as a critic, he would never have drawn a word of reply from me.

Mr. Newman is a scholar, a musical writer of great experience, a meritorious compiler of data from musical reference books. Beyond that he may be conceded to be valuable as a healthy antidote against the growth of artistic incompetence and as a beneficial irritant, a sort of gadfly that stings artists into better and higher things.

But when he arrogates to himself the office of a musical Cato in England, interrogates these artists in public, impugns their motives and questions their musical ethics, then it is time to call a halt.*

The various "Classical Manuscripts" of which Kreisler confessed himself to be the author and the composers with which he linked their names for thirty-five years are:

Concerto in C Major	Vivaldi
Allegretto in G Minor	Porpora
Andantino	Padre Martini
"Aubade Provençale"	Couperin
"La Chasse"	Cartier
Menuet	Porpora
Praeludium and Allegro	Pugnani
"La Précieuse"	Couperin
Scherzo	Dittersdorf
Sicilienne et Rigaudon	Francœur
Study on a Chorale	Stamitz
Tempo di Minuetto	Pugnani
Preghiera	Padre Martini
Chanson Louis XIII and Pavane	Couperin

In England, Basil Maine took sides with Ernest Newman, declaring that "such deception amounts to a confession that, in the hoaxer's opinion, his supporters are fools." †

The issue is not Kreisler or his fortunes. It resolves itself rather into one of honesty of authorship and the possible influence on others of so curious a course by an artist of Kreisler's high standing and wide acclaim. . . .

* When Kreisler recently reread the heated words exchanged between himself and Newman, he said with a twinkle in his eye: "It was a tempest in a teapot as far as I am concerned. My indignation lasted for only a few months. I still like to read and reread Newman's books on Wagner and Mozart, and my respect for him remains undiminished. His work on Wagner is truly monumental."

† Reprinted from *Maine on Music* by Basil Maine, by permission to use extracts from copyright material from John Westhouse (Publishers) Limited, London, copyright, 1945, by John Westhouse (Publishers) Limited.

On the whole, however, the British musical world took the matter as a joke on the critics. Its affection for their idol of three decades remained undiminished.

In the United States, too, musical opinion was overwhelmingly on Fritz Kreisler's side.

Dissenters were *Musical America*, which observed: "A departed musician who cannot speak for himself is being made a party to a deception and is being given a false musical front before the world"; and Lawrence Gilman of the New York *Herald Tribune*, who said he was "a little saddened by Mr. Kreisler's curious mental attitude in the case," and who considered the Newman strictures "a dialectical masterpiece."

Olin Downes, however, whose news story on Kreisler's "confession" had started Ernest Newman on his tirade, laughed the whole thing off. In the *Times* article on *Kreisler's 'Classics,'* already alluded to, he said:

> Let us admit that Mr. Kreisler has hoaxed us rather handsomely. Has not the principal harm, if any, been done to the feelings of the hoaxed? Nothing has been taken from the reputations of composers of the past, nearly all of them minor figures of certain epochs. No one of them lost royalties or reputation by a device which has again and again been employed in the history of art, and nowhere more harmlessly than in the present instance. . . .
>
> Mr. Kreisler has added to the gayety of nations and the violinist's repertory. Shall we begrudge him that? Should the man who kissed the wrong girl in the dark condemn the practice of kissing?"

David Ewen wrote: *

> It was to be expected that musicians should greet the hoax as if it were a personal offense, with grumbles of anger, and bitter accusation of artistic dishonesty. . . .
>
> It is very doubtful, however, if Kreisler's confession will diminish to any perceptible degree his enormous stature in the eyes of his audiences. . . .

Probably most amusing of all, when one considers Ernest Newman's high moral indignation, is the fact that a writer in the *Journal of*

* Reprinted from *L'Amico Fritz* by David Ewen, in the August, 1935 issue of *Esquire*, by permission of *Esquire* and David Ewen. copyright, 1935, by *Esquire*.

Religion for October, 1940, pointed to Kreisler's hoax as "an illustration of the modern and honorable use of pseudonymity"!

One may wonder, indeed, why of all persons a man of the stature of Newman should have become so exasperated with Kreisler. As a student of musical history he must have known that none of Kreisler's predecessors in the art of fooling his contemporaries and musicologists were indicted for moral turpitude.

Hector Berlioz was not castigated when he wrote a piece of sacred music in the old classical style and produced it as the work of an unknown chapel master. The famous Hungarian folk song, "Csak Egy Kis Lány," used in the "Gypsy Airs" by Pablo Sarasate, is either credited to Sarasate or is believed to be a Hungarian folk song in the public domain; yet the early European edition of "Gypsy Airs" contained the note, "Composed by Szentirmai Elemér" (in reality János Német). The publishers later dropped the reference, "Composed by—" just as Kreisler's publishers in due time dropped "In the style of—."

The noted Los Angeles musicologist and teacher of George Gershwin, Edward Kilenyi, Sr., has unearthed a case of a mistaken claim of authorship by no less a person than Johannes Brahms. Kilenyi writes:

> In my student days in Germany, I bought a collection of various compositions arranged for piano and violin. Two of these compositions contained the name of Keler Bela. But—the name of the composer was printed on a tiny piece of paper *pasted* on the page.
>
> Curiosity and interest made me cut off the glued-on small piece of paper, and to my surprise under it I found printed the name of Johannes Brahms. After some research I found that Keler Bela had sued Brahms in the Hungarian courts for having used and printed under his own name two Hungarian dances composed by Keler Bela. Strange to say, the compositions in question were the two best known of Brahms's "Hungarian Dances"—Nos. 5 and 6.
>
> Brahms appeared in court and stated that no higher compliment could be paid to the talent of a young composer than to find his melodies used by the illiterate country folk far away from the cities living in the mountains or on the plains. He, Brahms, in his search for old original Hungarian folk songs had gone around among Hungarian peasants, and among the many songs and dances he listened to and wrote down were the two dances which Keler Bela was suing him for.
>
> The name of Keler Bela printed and pasted over the name of Brahms in the

edition which I acquired was evident proof of the publisher's and Brahms' best intention to give Keler Bela proper credit. Probably later, when the Brahms dances were re-published, the editors neglected to make the proper reference to Keler Bela, and we can surely take it for granted that Brahms must have protested in vain, just as the publisher omitted from the Kreisler compositions the words, "In the style of—."

Above all, Ernest Newman as a man steeped in the history of music should have remembered the celebrated case of the Westphalian schoolmaster Anton Wilhelm Florentin von Zuccalmaglio (1803–1869), who successfully passed off as ancient folk songs allegedly written by W. von Waldbühl or by Village Schoolmaster Wedel melodies which so intrigued Robert Schumann that he invited Zuccalmaglio to join his staff of collaborators on his *New Magazine* as specialist on folk songs.

Johannes Brahms, desirous of revivifying the German love for the folk song, published an edition of forty-nine of these alleged Waldbühl-Wedel songs, many of which he characterized as *altdeutsche Minnelieder* (Old German love songs). It remained for Max Friedländer to reveal that Brahms was the victim of a hoax similar to that perpetrated by Fritz Kreisler, in that many of the forty-nine folk songs and old love ditties did not stem from people long dead, but were the product of a contemporary. He wrote:

> Is it not a curious fact that all these songs [he had mentioned a whole series from the Brahms album] did not stem from the people, much less were "Old-German love songs," but had their origin at the writing desk of a poet-composer belonging to the educated classes? Brahms and Heine permitted themselves to be duped, and even as critical a researcher as Ludwig Erk overlooked the origin of these new melodies.

Professor Friedländer, far from blaming Zuccalmaglio as Newman lashed Kreisler, insisted that the Westphalian schoolmaster had no intention of playing a hoax on anybody.

Friedländer continued:

> He was well aware that nothing would be more damaging for the spread of folk songs than a note stating that they were arranged or freely transcribed by a contemporary poet and composer. . . . We owe some of our most beautiful and best known Lieder to him.

The parallel between Zuccalmaglio and Kreisler is indeed striking: the Westphalian schoolteacher wanted to enrich the literature of the German folk song; the Austrian violinist, the literature for his instrument. Both realized that a contemporary composer usually is envied and derogated by the critics of his time. Both therefore chose fictitious names for reasons of modesty and expediency rather than with malicious intent.

Zuccalmaglio found an ardent defender in the learned Dr. Max Friedländer. Fritz Kreisler has his in America's outstanding critic, Olin Downes.

CHAPTER TWENTY-SIX

WORLD WAR II

[1939-1945]

On September 19, 1939, less than three weeks after the bloodiest war in history had been unloosed, Fritz Kreisler arrived in New York on the *Washington* with his wife. Some 1,750 panic-stricken individuals, mostly Americans but also some refugees, crowded the ship. Some passengers had to sleep in the swimming pool. Harriet and Fritz had no stateroom to themselves, but each had to share a "cabin dormitory" with other travelers.

It was not panic but the usual concert season that brought the Kreislers to America at this time. One thing that Fritz certainly did not have to fear was that in due time he would again become a technical enemy of the United States, his second fatherland: he was now a French citizen.

His thoughts as he arrived were, however, not of himself. He told the ship reporters, with a sad shake of his head: "I am thinking of poor Paderewski, old and sick, with the dream of his life for a free Poland shattered. All the work of his life is toppling down around him now. It is a nightmare."

One pleasant task awaited him a fortnight after his arrival. Beman G. Dawes and his brother, former Vice President Charles G. Dawes, had in 1927 established an arboretum in Licking County, Ohio, at the spot where the Dawes ancestors had made their home as pioneers.

Every year since the founding of the Dawes Arboretum one or more trees had been planted by, and in honor of, some distinguished American or foreigner. A bronze tablet erected beside the newly planted tree in each case indicated the person thus honored.

Fritz Kreisler was invited by Charles G. Dawes to come to the arboretum on October 11, 1939, to plant a tree that was to bear his name. The general in a brief introductory speech hailed him as "a great artist, a brave soldier, a good and generous citizen, a friend to his fellow man." Kreisler in replying delivered a little speech which in a few words expressed his philosophy of life and at the same time added a touch to the ceremony which only a violinist could give. He said:

"General Dawes, I thank you with all my heart for the kind words you have said, although I cannot accept them in all their glowing terms.

"I am very happy to have been permitted to plant a tree here in the Arboretum. The planting of a tree is always of great, almost religious significance. Here we are face to face with one of the profoundest mysteries of nature. Every time a seedling grows into a tree we witness an act of God. The very annual rejuvenation of that tree and its eternal perpetuation is closely linked to the belief in the immortality of our own soul.

"To me the planting of this tree has an added significance because violins are made from trees. Who knows, but that from this very tree in the dim future a violin might be made that would sing the music of bygone ages to our children's children.

"I am proud to have my own name linked in this manner with those of the illustrious men who have already planted trees here, and I thank you with all my heart for the honor you have conferred on me."

The tablet at the Kreisler tree has the following wording:

FRITZ KREISLER
This tree planted October 11, 1939
By and Dedicated To
FRITZ KREISLER
Violinist and Composer
Captain, Austrian Army, World War 1914–15

Every time he returned for a few days to New York, where he now made his home, he more than missed his two dogs, the wirehaired fox terrier Rexie and the Airedale Jerry, whom he had left behind in Berlin when he started on his summer vacation. He therefore appealed to me, then still at my Berlin post for The Associated Press, to try to ship the two dogs, if possible, to Amsterdam, where a friend would send them to America by the first possible boat. Holland, it will be remembered, was not overrun by Hitler until the following May.

Fritz Kreisler, about 1940

Albert Spalding, about 1940

President Roosevelt's photo autographed to André Benoist

A Dutch journalist, Jan Stoffels, of the Amsterdam *Telegraaf*, was kind enough at my request to take them to Holland as their alleged owner. On November 5, 1939, Harriet Kreisler wrote this whimsical note:

It is impossible for us to thank you for your great kindness in arranging to get Rexie and Jerry through to us. Poor Fritz was in great anxiety about them. We had visions of their being ultimately sausage meat. They arrived on the Statendam early in the morning, but Fritz was there to meet them. Of course, they haven't been able to tell us about the rotten journey, but from their tiredness and lack of enthusiasm I fancy they did not enjoy the trip. But they are now pretty nearly normal.

I hope you and Hilde and the entire family are keeping well and fairly happy. How I wish we were all together again, drinking a fine bottle of wine. Will that time ever come again?

It was quite in keeping with their character that the Kreislers gave freely of their time and money to charitable undertakings during World War II. Together with his colleague Albert Spalding, Fritz performed the second and third movements of Bach's D Minor Concerto for Two Violins at a benefit, in 1940, for the Metropolitan Opera Association Fund, besides playing three compositions of his own. The concert netted $10,000 for the fund. He also played for the National Press Club at Washington on November 9, 1940, at a dinner in honor of President Roosevelt. Richard L. Wilson, president of the club, afterward wrote him:

As you could see, the whole Club was carried away by your superb playing, as indeed was the President. It seemed to me, as I sat by him, that he was completely relaxed in the enjoyment of your music as I have never seen him before on similar occasions.

Sometime later he played at the White House Correspondents' dinner, and again the representatives of the press and the President were vociferous in their praise and thanks.

To his "spiritual home," France, he sent a substantial sum early in 1940 for the purchase of books and sports gear for the French troops. At his wife's suggestion he assigned all royalties accruing in Great Britain during the war from his phonograph recordings to the Duke of Gloucester's Red Cross and St. John's Fund. The duke cabled on

February 22, 1941, "Please accept my heartfelt thanks for your most generous gift to the Red Cross."

Nor was the American Red Cross forgotten. This organization had requested him to say a few words of endorsement at one of its fund-raising meetings in 1943, but he replied he could do it only with his strings. Some three thousand persons rose in tribute as he walked onto the stage to open his benefit concert. One hundred Red Cross nurses' aides in their professional uniforms formed the background. The proceeds amounted to $10,200.

A special benefit for the Salvation Army on January 11, 1944, for which boxes and choice seats went at special prices, yielded, with donations that continued to come even after the concert, $105,000 of the $550,000 which this institution had set as its goal. During the intermission Walter Hoving, president of the Salvation Army Association, told of Fritz Kreisler's long interest in the association. In that connection he told a story of how the violinist one day in London gave a man who was down and out a one-pound note and advised him to call on the Salvation Army. Eight years later this man, Hoving said, now a rich and well known citizen, entertained Kreisler at his club.

Appearance in the Metropolitan Opera House for the benefit of the Salvation Army was as much of a surprise to Fritz as some of his previous charity concerts had been. He was on tour in California when the arrangements were made.

The way it happened was this:

Harriet had taken an interest in the Salvation Army for forty-five years. She became especially impressed by what this organization did during the First World War, when she could observe its workings at close range in Europe. Regardless of what any other organization may have done, she noted that the Salvation Army people were the only ones who minded neither hardship nor cold to be of service. No questions were ever asked. If a human being was in trouble, no matter what the cause, he was taken care of.

While her husband was on tour early in 1944, she happened to attend a reception at the home of Mr. and Mrs. Hoving. On the spur of the moment she took Hoving aside and said: "I think I'd like to do something for the Salvation Army. Supposing my husband gave a benefit concert. Would that make you happy?" When Hoving eagerly assented, Harriet stipulated as the sole condition that no mention be made of the proposed event until arrangements had been perfected.

Charles Foley gasped. What, fill the Metropolitan on short notice? But he yielded. "If you want me to engage the 'Met,' " he said to Harriet, "okay, I'll take it." The admissions alone totaled about $65,000.

Kreisler's sixty-fifth birthday in 1940 did not go as unnoticed as his sixtieth had been in Berlin. A number of papers paid tribute to him as a "legendary figure."

Two memorable published utterances by Fritz Kreisler stem from the year 1940. In the first, he describes himself as a mystic: *

> I am what might be called a mystic. I have no superstition in me, but all artists are mystics. How can one be a real musician and not a mystic? Music will be forever a matter of mysticism. Every form of music is linked to some form of thought; the drums of the jungle, savory love songs, Gregorian chants, modern jazz. They are alike, save for the association of the thoughts that go with them. African music and music in the United States, the music to which we dance is all the same, except for the thoughts that are linked with it. What becomes jazz in the United States was religious music to the Africans. Music is undefinable. It becomes something definite when it is associated with some thought. The nearest approach to the Infinite God available to any of us is through some form of music.

In the second he speaks of the creative impulses that guide him in his playing: †

> In the eight weeks I have been in Maine, I have not once taken my violin out of its case, except to clean it. If I played too frequently, I should rub the bloom off the musical imagination. I should drag my melodies like shackles. I prefer to be always thrilled by my interpretations of great music, and so it is well for me not to be always fiddling.

* Reprinted from *The Human Side of Greatness* by William Leroy Stidger, by permission of Harper & Brothers, copyright, 1940, by Harper & Brothers.

† Reprinted from "Fritz Kreisler and What's in Him" by Richard Matthews Hallet, from an article in the December 7, 1940 issue of *The Christian Science Monitor*, by permission of *The Christian Science Monitor*, copyright, 1940, by *The Christian Science Monitor*.

My craftsmanship loses nothing if I stop playing for a summer. It has been too long building. The intricate human machinery of playing is governed by a kind of directing ecstasy that takes its rise in the intellect and flies to the fingers. The fingers in time come to have little intellects in their tips perhaps. . . .

Let them have their vacation. In the fall, they will perhaps feel the impact of the strings a little more harshly, but then every melody will be new again, and the creative impulses will have more bloom.

These impulses are my directors. What rouses them it's hard to say. I may wander alone in the woods, when odors, colors, silences enthrall me—a splash of sunlight, the smell of forest mold. Or again my inspiration is the crowd. Success with the crowd must of course be the test of the professional artist. Many play marvellously for a few indulgent friends but fail dismally on a platform. Others can play well only the works of the greatest masters, and cannot catch the beauty of a melody by a lesser hand.

But the sincere artist will give 90 per cent of his best at any given time and in the least encouraging circumstances. He must be a master of mass moods, since his own force is re-enforced by the participating forces of his audience, those part-producers of musical effects. The public supplies receptiveness, resiliency.

The moment I appear before it, I can tell my chances of success by certain intangibles and imponderables. The atmosphere is charged or it is not; the expectancy, the receptivity of my hearers is there, or it is lacking. How keen, how keyed up are they? I will know at once.

But to begin with, I need only a receiving station here and there. A few ardent listeners may tinge the whole fluid mass. There is a kind of contagion to be reckoned with. You will see this in war. A platoon of 100 soldiers may have five heroes and the rest average men, but at the high pitch of things, they go forward as a unit. They are hammered into unit by the hammer of hard things. This directing ecstasy goes out from a few leaders only, but it fires the mass and produces exalted effects.

And this directing ecstasy is personal and immediate. It is in the air—but it can't be on the air. That is why I do not play radio programs. The radio audience cannot give me this reciprocal exchange of responses. It is not collected. A million stray hearers not in touch with each other have not the force of 100 hearers collected in a hall.

The year 1941 became one of the saddest in Kreisler's life. He had almost completed his "Viennese Rhapsodic Fantasietta." This composition is more than appears on the surface. It is not merely a piece replete with Viennese melos: in it Fritz Kreisler pours out his heart in grief over the fate that has befallen his native city, once so gay and proud and beloved by the world, now sad, debased, nazified, and lonely. It is written with his heart's blood. From time to time, after he has shown his grief in plaintive outpourings, he recalls the glories of the past, and there is conjured up the Vienna of the past, with its inimitable waltzes, its abandon, its ineffable grace and charm of yore.

On April 27, the world was startled by the news that Fritz Kreisler had met with an accident which fractured his skull, resulted in a serious concussion of the brain, and kept him in a state of coma for days, during which time he was heard to mumble Greek and Latin phrases.

Deep in thought, he was crossing Madison Avenue, New York, at East Fifty-seventh Street, within walking distance of his home, when he was struck by a delivery truck. He had failed to notice that the traffic lights had changed. For a while he lay there bleeding, unnoticed, and unrecognized. Young Melvin Spitalnik, a Postal Telegraph Company messenger, happened to come by, took the $16 camera he always carried with him, and photographed the bleeding, elderly man without the faintest notion that this snapshot would soon become famous as the "Picture of the Week."

Dr. Aldo Santiccioli of the Columbus Hospital passed by and had the unconscious traffic victim taken to Roosevelt Hospital. There it was discovered that none other than Fritz Kreisler had thus seriously been injured. There were frantic calls to locate Harriet Kreisler, who, like her husband, was on her way home for lunch. Howard Heck, his road manager for many years, on hearing the news over the radio, hurried to the hospital. Dr. James I. Russell, head surgeon of Roosevelt Hospital, rushed in from his home at Great Neck, Long Island, and soon issued the statement: "Mr. Kreisler has a severe head injury. His condition is satisfactory. His blood pressure and pulse are normal. It is probably a skull fracture."

From the moment that Harriet reached the hospital, she engaged a private room next to her husband's to be always near him and never left his side until he was out of danger.

For a week the bulletins which were issued by Roosevelt Hospital contained the laconic words, "Still in coma." Not until May 23 did the medical authorities pronounce Fritz Kreisler out of danger.

Charles Foley, his friend and manager since 1913, asked Dr. Samuel Burchell, famous brain surgeon, what was likely to happen. "Dr. Burchell told me," Foley recalls, "that he had never before handled the case of a genius. He pointed out, however, that certain events would in all likelihood be erased from Fritz's mind. As a matter of fact, it later developed that he remembers little of the years 1928–1930 and 1933–1936."

Howard Heck, who happened to visit soon after Fritz regained full consciousness, was pleasantly surprised to find that "Mr. Kreisler remembered the exact bar at which he had left off composing." Jascha Heifetz was happy to note that his older colleague knew him at once. Franz Rupp called, and Charles Foley told the patient who was calling. "Rupp?" asked Kreisler, "I don't know him." "Why," said Rupp with a sudden inspiration, "I was with you when you won $1,000 at Copacabana, Brazil."

Kreisler, who loves occasionally to take a fling at games of chance, then remembered, and there was no further difficulty. "Kreisler won so seldom when he played that I felt he would remember me by association with one of the rare times when he came out far ahead," Rupp commented laughingly.

Overshadowing all other anxieties regarding the extent of damage to his memory was this: Had the accident interfered with his remembrance of violin music? The doctors could not tell. But the ever practical Harriet had an idea.

One day late in May, when her husband was able to sit up again, she brought his precious Guarnerius to the hospital. "Fritz," she said, "there's a passage in the Mendelssohn Concerto which I simply can't remember. It's been bothering me all morning. Do you suppose you could play it for me? I mean the motif of the beautiful second movement."

"Of course," he said. He looked lovingly at the instrument, tuned it, picked up the bow, raised the violin to his chin—and unhesitatingly began to play. There was not a flaw in the execution, every note was remembered; but above all, the warmth and feeling and inimitable grace that is the characteristic of Kreisler's playing was there! One can imagine the infinite relief of Harriet and of the doctors who were anxiously watching the experiment.

"It was a test, but I didn't know it," Kreisler said later to Howard Taubman.* "I was not aware at that time of the possibility that the part of the brain which controls music—whatever part it is—might be injured. I could not understand why my wife wanted to hear Mendelssohn, but I wanted to be obliging. I didn't ask myself whether I could play; I took it for granted. . . . Since I was getting better, music would naturally follow in due course."

Harriet now felt her husband's recovery was assured and issued a public statement of thanks for the "overwhelmingly many tributes and well-wishes" showered upon her Fritz. Hundreds of persons had offered to donate blood. "It is a slow road from here on," she said, "but he is out of danger. I shall never be able to thank the country for its love of him. It was really this love that pulled him through. The great thing in his mind—the one thing he keeps harping on—is his love of music. All else at present has faded out." She added that her husband was now able to sit in his chair every day for five minutes, and that he often turned on the radio for orchestra programs.

On June 16, less than two months after it had seemed that Fritz would never emerge from his coma, he was able to walk from his hospital room to the car of Howard Heck, who drove him and Harriet to the home of friends on Long Island for final recuperation.

On the advice of his physicians he canceled his scheduled New York Stadium summer concerts, six appearances with the Philadelphia Symphony Orchestra, and twenty-seven other concerts. But by October he was well enough to attend the opening of the one hundredth season of the New York Philharmonic Orchestra as a keenly interested listener.

As yet no one could tell whether Fritz Kreisler was sufficiently strong to bear up under the strain that a professional concert involves. Recordings of some of his familiar pieces in the New York studios of

* Reprinted from *Grand Master of the Bow* by Howard Taubman, in the January 9, 1944 issue of the New York *Times*, by permission of the New York *Times*.

tne Radio Corporation of America in January, 1942, showed that his memory, his tone, and his technique could be depended upon. Samuel Applebaum has described the scene in *Violins and Violinists.**

> The musicians of the orchestra busily tuned their instruments and waited anxiously for the artist to appear. Then he walked out toward them from the wings. They ceased their tuning, and rose of one accord. Kreisler stopped for a moment; his steps faltered. Tears came to his eyes. He looked silently at them, seemed about to say something, but could not. His magnificent, his gentle face was glowing. Softly he asked, "May I have an A please?" Once more, before reverent onlookers, the great Kreisler tested his ever responsive A.

"I feel like my old self," he said after the recording.

During the same month Fritz Kreisler also tried himself out in his first public appearance, at Albany, New York, before three thousand enthusiastic listeners. It now seemed safe for him to sign up for the concert season of 1942–1943. How sure he felt of himself is indicated by the fact that his appearances were to include performances of the Bruch and Mendelssohn concertos with the Chicago Symphony Orchestra, and the Mendelssohn Concerto with the Philadelphia Symphony Orchestra.

The crucial public performance which would decide whether or not Fritz Kreisler was really his old self again was his Carnegie Hall recital in New York on October 31, 1942. Thousands of admirers, including hundreds seated on the stage, rose in tribute and applauded him. He opened with a concerto and a partita by Bach, continued with a concerto by Mozart, then played a number of shorter pieces, chiefly arrangements by himself, and finally offered as a novelty his "Viennese Rhapsodic Fantasietta," which he had practically completed when his accident befell him.

In the words of Oscar Thompson, music critic of the New York *Sun*, "The violinist answered every question that has been asked about his ability to resume his career."

* Reprinted from *With the Artists* by Samuel and Sada Applebaum, from an interview with Fritz Kreisler in the December, 1947 issue of *Violins and Violinists*, by permission of William Lewis & Son and Samuel Applebaum, copyright, 1947, by William Lewis & Son, Chicago. *With the Artists* will soon appear in book form and will be published by William Lewis & Son.

Sada and Samuel Applebaum in a 1953 photograph

Autographed "To Mr. & Mrs. Applebaum, Cordially, F. Kreisler, 1943"

Noel Straus commented in the New York *Times*: "It became obvious from the energetic sweep of the bow and the firm grip of the fingers on the strings that his enforced rest brought him back to his public with a new strength noticeable even in his physical appearance."

All critics agreed that his recovery was nothing short of "miraculous."

Elsewhere in the country, too, Kreisler proved to be the great attraction he had always been. At Dallas, Texas, for instance, the Junior League thought it took somewhat of a risk in engaging him for a concert intended to raise a large sum of money for its purpose. Yet after deducting all expenses and the artist's fee, the league had a surplus of $18,000 from the recital.

Once again a music critic with an eye for aetail has given us a picture of how Fritz Kreisler looked at this period of his life. The Milwaukee critic, Edward P. Halline, wrote in the Milwaukee *Sentinel* on November 4, 1943:

> Sixty-eight-year-old Fritz Kreisler, the good, gray romantic of the violin . . . stood there on the platform, straight and erect, darting defiant glances at some power above after every vigorous passage and then peering a little clumsily at the audience as they roared applause. He had a brief nod of appreciation which was as heart-felt as the lowest bow and you could see his lips moving.

In a discussion with Olin Downes shortly after his Carnegie Hall appearance, Fritz Kreisler showed that he was as eager as ever to fathom the secret of success in art in a spirit of great personal humility. He asked: *

> "What artist is sure when he has played his best? I am perpetually astonished by praise given performances of mine which I am certain were poor, and what seems to me a heart-breaking indifference, or reservation, on the part of the press or the public, in instances when I have finished and said to myself, 'Old fellow, you came somewhere near it today.' Of course, one only comes near it and then one is lucky. We work and we seek. It never comes just right, and we can never completely trust our conclusions. Today we think we have found something of the truth. Tomorrow we feel sadly disillusioned.

* Reprinted from *Talk with Kreisler* by Olin Downes in the November 8, 1942 issue of the New York *Times*, by permission of the New York *Times*.

But the search is the thing which leads and sustains and vitalizes us. But is the thing true of an art in one age true of the same art in the next? I sometimes wonder, and it frightens me."

Kreisler had not only recovered his old musical skill, but he retained his keen love of life, indeed, his joy of living. That fact is reflected in a series of candid camera pictures taken of him for *Life* magazine shortly after his reappearance on the concert stage. One of them shows Eugene Ormandy and the Philadelphia Symphony Orchestra rehearsing with Kreisler, who stands in his vest, beaming at the conductor in happy kinship of souls. Another depicts him in shirt sleeves and tuxedo vest playing a piano accompaniment for his younger colleague Nathan Milstein. Again he looks supremely happy.

This joy of life is also reflected in a song he composed for the University of Wisconsin in 1943, for which its late president, Clarence A. Dykstra, wrote the words. Dykstra had been prodded by a Hollywood lyrics writer and Wisconsin alumnus, Maxson F. Judell, to get Kreisler to write the tune for a new college song.

"After I went to Washington as Director of Selective Service," President Dykstra informed me, "I dropped a note to Fritz Kreisler, asking him if I could get a lyric for a Wisconsin song, would he put it to music for us. In a letter he indicated that he would be very happy to do so. . . . The next morning I had it typed and sent off to him. After a few weeks he sent me the music which is now attached to the lyrics which I wrote called 'Pioneers of Wisconsin.' "

The song was first performed at the home-coming football game of 1943.

Fritz then wrote a second song, "The Valiants of Wisconsin," this time with lyrics by Maxson Judell. Both are light, vigorous, joyful tunes, with no pretense of profundity. But they showed that an artist of sixty-eight can still have the youthful college spirit if he is a Fritz Kreisler!

What further buoyed Kreisler's spirits was the fact that on May 28, 1943, he could join twenty-three soldiers in American uniforms and ninety-six applicants of foreign extraction in swearing the oath of allegiance to the United States, thereby becoming an American citizen.

Kreisler in the 1940's

Kreisler with Charles Foley

Sergei Rachmaninoff

Nazi seizure of Austria had automatically ended his Austrian citizenship. The French Government had provided a generous interim solution by making him an honorary French citizen. It was not, however, a permanent solution, although conceived as such by the then French Government and accepted in the same spirit by Fritz. When the Vichy Government was formed in 1940 and called in all old passports, Kreisler found himself unable to accept a substitute passport from a regime of which he could not approve. As his wife was an American and his permanent home was now located in New York, with little likelihood of his ever traveling to Europe professionally again, he felt it no discourtesy to the France he loved, and no lack of appreciation of the magnificent act of the pre-Vichy Government, to become an American in his declining years.

From the citizenship ceremonies he went to the office of Charles Foley, there to give vent to his feelings in a number of improvisations on the piano. Asked by reporters how it felt to be an American, he said: "I have felt that way most of the time. I have been here so much."

Grief came to New York's musical colony when Sergei Rachmaninoff died on May 28, 1943. A memorial concert was arranged by the American Society of Composers, Authors, and Publishers (ASCAP) for June 1. Kreisler agreed without a moment's hesitation to play the violin obbligatos for three Rachmaninoff songs sung by James Melton. But he also became, at his own suggestion, the first concertmaster *pro tem.* of the New York Philharmonic Symphony Orchestra during its performance of the instrumental version of Rachmaninoff's "Vocalise." At his temporary first violin desk, he stood with all the others as the "Vocalise" was played. According to Olin Downes, "this moment was, on the whole, the most distinguished of the evening."

Rachmaninoff's death had one important consequence for hundreds of thousands, if not millions of music listeners who were acquainted with Kreisler recordings either through their phonographs or as radio fans, but who had never been able to hear him directly in what is known in radio language as a "live show." There had been a sort of pact between the two friends that each would not play for radio so long as the other was alive. Kreisler's reasons have already been stated.

Whatever may have been his inhibitions even after Rachmaninoff passed on, he bowed to Harriet's decision that the time had come for him to go on the air. On February 9, 1944, the New York *Times* stated in a two-column head: "Radio Finally Lures Kreisler and Violin; Will Give Five Recitals; Fee Put at $5,000 Each." The celebrated violinist would be heard during the Bell Telephone Company Hour over 118 stations of the National Broadcasting Company, it was announced.

Fritz said at that time: "Until the last few years, when I have been living in America, I never had time to broadcast because of heavy concert schedules. And I did not want to broadcast until I had time to learn the technique of the microphone. Now I have learned something about radio and I hope I am ready." He added that his reversal of his earlier position was based chiefly on "the many and increasing number of letters coming from the more isolated places of America, asking me to broadcast," and pointed to the fact that "now with wartime traveling so difficult, I have had to reduce the number of my concerts each season."

Many of his best friends among the violinists have regretted the decision to go on the air so late in life. They have pointed out that even his most excellent phonograph recordings could not communicate one factor that makes Kreisler who and what he is: the indescribable charm and magic of his personality. One must see him as he stands on the concert stage to have the full benefit of a Kreisler "experience," they all agree in saying. The radio multiplies many times the disadvantage that accrues from lack of personal touch between artist and listener.

"Fritz should go on playing in concert halls until the end of his days," one of his most ardent admirers among the younger generation of violinists remarked. "He will always have a message for his listeners there. His is a dignity, a natural superiority which age cannot destroy. But he is doing himself no service by using the impersonal medium of the microphone. He there lacks a third dimension."

The Kreisler radio début came on July 17, 1944. With Donald Voorhees conducting he played the first movement of the Mendelssohn

Violin Concerto, the Albeniz-Kreisler's Tango in D, and his own "Caprice viennois." As a delicate compliment to the beloved soloist, Voorhees chose as his opening number the overture to Mozart's *Marriage of Figaro*, a favorite of Kreisler's.

Seats in the small studio of the NBC were at a premium, and the artist was given an affectionate welcome when he appeared in his black full-dress suit, which contrasted effectively with the white garb of the orchestra and that of Mr. Voorhees. The entire broadcasting procedure seemed greatly to interest Fritz, as did the studio itself, at whose control room, microphones, and other gadgets he looked with curiosity.

Once again he ingratiated himself by one of those gestures of innate delicacy and modesty which are part and parcel of his nature: after his last number, instead of withdrawing, he lingered at one side of the orchestra, then walked up in front to join in playing "The Star-Spangled Banner," now also his national anthem.

His happiest moment as a radio artist came when, in November, 1949, he received word that Albert Schweitzer had heard him in faraway Lambaréné, Gabon, French Equatorial Africa, and that he had stated that his only regret about his visit to the United States to attend and speak at the Goethe Centennial was that he had not met Kreisler, whom he knew and esteemed from his Strasbourg days.

A month before his first appearance with NBC there had been another "first" in his life: he had played in one of the Lewisohn stadium open-air concerts which afford thousands of New Yorkers an opportunity every summer of hearing the world's greatest artists for little money. Some 16,500 people attended and rose in tribute to the white-haired artist.

On October 19, 1944, the press stated that he had completed an operetta, *Rhapsody*. Both he and Charles Foley deny participation in this ill fated undertaking which had a run of only two weeks, except that they good-naturedly permitted the use of some of his melodies. Fritz's version of the affair is this:

"A very rich lady who had once aspired to be a dancer wanted to produce an operetta. I wasn't enthusiastic about the idea, but she asked whether at least my airs might be used. She then got a librettist to build a story around Casanova and Maria Theresia. She made the mistake of wanting to manage everything, even the dancers, and sank $100,000 in the venture."

Charles Foley commented: "*Rhapsody* was never approved by Fritz. I refused to attend rehearsals after I had had one look at the affair. Fritz also had nothing to do with it except that, as a courtesy, he attended the opening night."

One critic, Lewis Nichols, explained in a few words what was the matter with the performance: "Where Kreisler's contributions called for gaiety, sparkle and charm, *Rhapsody* on the whole clumped along in hob-nailed heavy boots."

As the year 1944 came to a close, Kreisler played a benefit concert for French children. His last public performance before World War II ended was a benefit, on April 28, 1945, in New York for the Musicians' Emergency Fund. Critics described him as "in top form" and "at his best" as he played to an overcrowded house, with two hundred additional listeners on the platform.

CHAPTER TWENTY-SEVEN

KREISLER'S BEST FRIEND

Most of us, I believe, when we honestly examine our relations to our fellow men, realize that hundreds of those to whom we are wont to refer as "friends" are nothing more than frequently met acquaintances toward whom one has kindly feelings and who reciprocate these feelings. Real friendship connotes intimacy and a readiness to stand by the partner in this relationship in bad days as well as good, and especially in bad times. Measured by these standards, how many of those who have come into our lives can be depended upon as friends?

Kreisler has been fortunate since 1913 to have been associated with a quiet and self-effacing, though determined, man who has never failed him and, as he himself put it, has "never given Fritz away." That man is Charles Foley, technically his manager and his publisher, but in reality his confidant, buffer, counselor, and friend.

Charles Foley, Sr., his father, was the publisher of the librettos issued for performances of the Metropolitan Opera Company of New York. Charles, Jr., thus grew up in the atmosphere both of musical life and of music publishing.

The outstanding impresario in the days when young Foley grew up was Charles A. Ellis, manager of the Boston Symphony Orchestra and of three bright stars on the musical firmament: Ignace Jan Paderewski, Nellie Melba, and Geraldine Farrar. Ellis's business often brought him to New York, where he met Charles Foley, Jr. He offered him a position on his staff, which the ambitious young man gladly accepted.

Not much later an event took place which was destined to affect "Charley" Foley's future decisively. The manager who had looked after Fritz's concerts in the years following the turn of the century, in 1910 came to London to inform the Kreislers that he wished to put Fritz's American tour off for a year, as he had another big-name violinist to whose interests he wished to devote himself exclusively that year, especially as that artist would tolerate no gods other than himself.

Quick as a flash, Harriet told the manager, "Fritz's tour with you will be put off not only next year, but for all time. We're through with you."

Charles A. Ellis, on hearing of the break between artist and impresario, wired to Kreisler, asking if he would go on a concert tour with the Boston Symphony Orchestra and offering him $600 a concert.

It was a most flattering offer. Boston then stood at the very top in American musical culture. To be a soloist with the Boston Symphony was indeed an accolade. The organization had an ideal Maecenas in the person of Henry Lee Higginson, of the firm of Lee Higginson & Company, bankers, who implicitly trusted Ellis and gave him a free hand to raise the orchestra to hitherto unknown heights.

A shrewd business woman, Harriet cabled that her husband would gladly accept if one condition could be met; namely, that Fritz be engaged for two recitals at $800 each, in addition to the orchestra concerts. Ellis accepted.

"We arrived in December, 1910," the Kreislers recalled. "Charles Ellis was at the pier. A representative of our former manager was also there to greet us, but we thanked him curtly for this attention and then reminded him that in London the impresario had been told very definitely that we were through with him.

"The tour, which included Boston, New York, Brooklyn, Baltimore, Washington, and other cities, was a wonderful success. After the last concert Charles Ellis, who was a rather shy and retiring man, turned to Harriet and said, 'You don't look very happy. What's the matter?' "

Harriet, who knew that Ellis managed only three stars, made so bold as to ask, "Do you suppose you could accept Fritz as a fourth artist? Can't this year's temporary arrangement be put on a permanent basis?"

Ellis not only agreed but offered a fee of $800 per concert. No contract was signed. As Ellis gallantly put it, turning to Harriet: "I look into your blue eyes and need no contract." Until he gave up his concert management in 1919, there was never a contract between him and Fritz. Foley, who then assumed charge, also has never had a written understanding with the Kreislers. Their relationship is one of mutual trust.

By the time Fritz entered Foley's life, Ellis had already made him assistant road manager for his top artists. In this capacity "Charley" came to accompany Fritz on his tours for a period of years from 1913 on. At about the same time he was also assigned as road manager to Geraldine Farrar, Paderewski, and Nellie Melba. "I used to think of him as a sort of flying squirrel," Miss Farrar recalled, "for he seemed to be living on trains most of the time, jumping from place to place, trying to be a trouble shooter for each of us."

Foley proved so dependable, honest, industrious, and keenly businesslike that the aging Ellis in 1919 turned his concert agency over to his young assistant. Since then and throughout the years Foley has been Fritz's indispensable friend.

An outstanding quality of his is his discreetness. "You have to pull every word out of him," Harriet Kreisler, who is extremely fond of Charles, said to me. Another illuminating and wistful observation of hers was, "I am sure there are many facts and incidents in Fritz's life which only Charley knows, and which he will never divulge to anyone."

One of the early tasks Charles Foley found awaiting him when he became Kreisler's manager was the unconcern with which Fritz had disposed of his compositions. Violin students will probably have noticed that there are no opus numbers attached to Kreisler's works. He dashed off music without any thought of numbering his productions, and his financial arrangements in his earlier days were anything but businesslike. It was Charles Foley who brought order out of chaos, renegotiated many copyrights and, somewhat later in his career, when Dame Melba was no longer active and Sergei Rachmaninoff, on Harriet Kreisler's recommendation, had become one of his trio of stars, in 1926 founded a publishing house for the Kreisler and Rachmaninoff compositions, with Carl Fisher, Inc., as distributing agent.

Foley soon became known as one of the shrewdest managers of artists in the business. His advance guesses on box-office receipts were uncanny and made him the envy of impresarios. Knowing the worth of his three outstanding artists, he insisted upon fees that these performers themselves would perhaps never have dreamed of asking.

Marks Levine, who on behalf of the National Concert and Artists' Corporation (NCAC) became the agent for the Kreisler concerts in 1930, whereas Foley devoted himself to publishing and merely supervising the concert work as manager, told an amusing story illustrating Foley's shrewdness:

"I happened to be in California at the time when Foley suggested that the concert division of the National Broadcasting Company (predecessor of NCAC) take over his artists. He sold my associate, who was no match for the shrewd Charles, a bill of goods by which we agreed to book each of Foley's three artists for forty dates per season, at an average fee of $3,000 per date. My associate just had not figured out the financial responsibilities involved, but relied implicitly on the drawing power of the big-name artists to bring in the sums involved. That first year we ended in the red, but Foley was reasonable and made certain readjustments."

Another problem of Foley's arose from the fact that his friend Fritz's programs were more catholic in their make-up than was customary, in that each of them ranged all the way from unaccompanied Bach suites and sonatas to such music in a lighter vein as his own Liebesleid and Liebesfreud.

"I feared that prospective listeners with only a moderate knowledge of music might be scared away if they saw, say, the Chaconne by Bach advertised," Foley once explained to me, "and that, on the other hand, musicians with a classical bent might turn up their noses at the third part of Fritz's programs and stay away because of them. So I merely advertised that Kreisler would play in such-and-such hall on such-and-such date, and refused to give out the programs in advance. It worked."

It is doubtful if many impresarios could have done this with their artists! The name Kreisler was one to conjure with.

For the wife of an artist, no matter how exquisite his music, it is not always easy to have to listen hour after hour to rehearsals and practicing. To alleviate such a situation for Harriet, Charles Foley quietly had a Steinway Grand placed in his office, and it is there that Fritz, before starting out on his American tours, then rehearsed with Carl Lamson.

Near Foley's office on West Forty-fourth Street, New York, is the Italian restaurant—Del Pezzo's—in which Fritz often used to meet his friend Enrico Caruso for lunch. It is still one of Fritz's favorite haunts. He feels relaxed and at home in its intimate atmosphere, where every waiter as well as the proprietor greet him with affection. It is characteristic of Foley's standing with both Harriet and Fritz that the former implicitly trusts Charles to assume her role of dietitian to her husband. Usually once a week Fritz and Charley lunch there, enjoy their Zabboni wine, swap stories, and plan for the future. Recently one of their chief topics for business discussions has been the prolongation of expiring copyrights and the revision of some of Fritz's compositions, especially certain cadenzas. Fritz spends many an hour at the Foley office to work on, and go over, these revisions.

Near Foley's office, there is another place, on West Forty-second Street, which interests Fritz so much that he forgets everything else: the violin shop of Rembert Wurlitzer on the second floor of the big Rudolph Wurlitzer Building and sales rooms. For one thing, fiddlers from all over the world go there to have their violins conditioned or to try out various beautiful instruments. Rembert Wurlitzer has rare understanding for artists and their often unaccountable temperaments and has succeeded in making them feel so much at home that his suite of offices has become known as the "Violinists' Club." Fritz is naturally happy to run into old colleagues and exchange experiences and jokes with them.

But he is especially attracted to the workshop half a flight below, in which a corps of expert violin makers, headed by Roman Klier, do every form of violinistic repair known to the artists and the trade. Here he loves to chat with the craftsmen to whom great masters of the bow entrust priceless instruments for overhauling. To him they are artists, too, whose skill he values highly.

Kreisler then becomes forgetful of time and of the punctuality which his wife has always insisted upon.

Foley and Wurlitzer between them worked up a code of behavior for this rather delicate situation of letting Fritz have his fun on the one hand and meeting requests for information as to his whereabouts on the other. Somehow, it seems, Fritz on such occasions has left the one place without as yet having reached the other! He is informed that a call from home has come only when the two conspirators decide he has had his relaxation and fun in the "Violinists' Club."

One inestimable service which Foley has rendered his friend has been that of going over such public statements as he made, and of counseling regarding the numerous requests for appearances on behalf of causes. When one looks back in this book to see on what organizations Harriet and Fritz lavished a large part of Fritz's income as artist, one will readily agree that they were all worth while and deserving. Foley's keen judgment in separating the wheat from the chaff undoubtedly had something to do with the selection of causes.

On the purely personal side, a few occurrences from recent times may be cited to show why Charles Foley can claim to be Fritz's best friend.

When Fritz was run over by a truck in 1942 and for many weeks his life hung in the balance, it was Charles Foley who was admitted by Harriet to the bedside long before others could be permitted to see the convalescing patient. When the priceless Kreisler library of incunabula, first editions, and rare prints was auctioned off, it was Charles Foley who attended as Fritz's representative and after the sale declined my invitation to a drink because he had "promised Fritz and Harriet to come to their house for a late evening snack to tell them all about the auction." When in the course of the preparation of this book there were divergences of opinion on the method of treating certain situations, as well as on certain events of years ago, it was Charles

Autographed "To André Benoist in kind remembrance of an old friend, Fritz Kreisler, Dec. 16, 1940"

Charles Foley and Kreisler in their later years

Foley who was called upon to act as arbiter, and to whose judgment all concerned bowed. Reciprocally, when in 1935 Foley fell ill in Paris shortly before Fritz was to start for South America, the press was told by Fritz that the tour would be called off if Foley did not recover in time.

Yet although Charles Foley has been Fritz's most intimate chum, few people in the Kreislers' circle of friends and acquaintances, except those who must deal with him professionally, know him. He is self-effacing and finds fulfillment of his purpose in life in advancing the interests of the artists whose careers he has undertaken to guide. Of these, only Kreisler is still active as composer and occasional performer.

Even in his private life Charles Foley is more or less of a recluse. With advancing years and with the training of an efficient, able office staff, the necessity of his being in New York daily has disappeared, and he endeavors to attend to business requiring his personal attention on the days when he and Fritz lunch together, and when he must serve on the Board of Appeals of the ASCAP (American Society of Composers, Artists, and Publishers), of which he has for many years been a highly respected member and official.

Instead, he starts out from his home on Long Island for a certain pier off which his motor yacht is anchored. Fond as he is of dogs, he is always accompanied by these pets of his. The greatest hobby of the white-haired and blue-eyed manager of great artists is that of taking off for Great South Bay and the Atlantic Ocean through Fire Island Inlet, where he can be with Nature, far away from the din and noise of what his friend Fritz has aptly dubbed Babylon-on-the-Hudson.

CHAPTER TWENTY-EIGHT

KREISLER AND HIS ACCOMPANISTS

THE greatest of artists, no matter how sure he may be of himself, can be driven to the point of distraction if he must put up with an accompanist who is not sympathetic to his intentions, who does not understand what the soloist is trying to do, and who therefore fails to support him properly.

Conversely, the good accompanist, while willing and ready to subordinate himself to the soloist, will feel frustrated and hence incapable of giving his best support if the soloist insists querulously upon his own interpretation even in those passages in which the piano alone is heard, and will not permit the accompanist to add his own creative impulses to those of the soloist.

The relationship between soloist and accompanist is necessarily an intimate one. They must travel together. They usually take their meals together when on tour. They practice together. They are both subject to the same impersonal appraisal by exacting music critics. But however close the relationship is, the accompanist, after all, has been selected and hired by the soloist and is thus to a degree subordinate. If, therefore, the soloist is the selfish prima donna type and not a true comrade and fellow artist, he can make life miserable for his accompanist.

From the accompanist's viewpoint, Kreisler has always been the ideal colleague, comrade, employer, and friend. As one of his outstanding characteristics is that of loyalty, he kept his accompanists

André Benoist in photograph taken in 1917

Josef Hofmann and Fritz Kreisler

Andre Benoist at the Piano

1. Sonata, Two Movements . . . *Cesar Fra*

Allegro ben moderato — Allegro —

MESSRS. HOFMANN AND KREISLER

2. a. Air . . . . *Goldm*
b. Tambourin . . . . *Rameau* (1633-17
c. Menueite . . . . . *Porpora* (1636-17
d. Humoresque (by request) . . . *Dvo*

FRITZ KREISLER

3. a. Ballade, F-sharp major . . . . *Cho*
b. Mazourka . . . . *Hofm*
c. Rhapsodie No. 11. . . . . . *L*

JOSEF HOFMANN

4. Sonata Op. 47, "Kreutzer" . . . *Beetho*

Adagio sostenuto, Presto, Andante con Variazioni, Finale Presto

MESSRS. HOFMANN AND KREISLER

5. a. Dance Slave . . . . . . *Dvo*
b. Scene de Czarda . . . . . . *Hu*

FRITZ KREISLER

6. a. Two songs without words . . . . *Mendelss*
1. Duetto A-flat major
Spinning song
b. Overture "Tannhaeuser" (by general request) *Wagner-L*

JOSEF HOFMANN

Program for which Benoist was the accompanist

for many years, if possible. Others merely served as substitutes when the regular accompanist in England, America, or the Continent happened not to be available. Some of those who, in the course of sixty years, played for him have already passed on. But among those still living, the men within my reach readily offered their impressions and some of their experiences. Whether an accompanist was with Kreisler for years or only for a season, each had a fascinating story to tell, and each had a different approach. Yet all agreed in testifying to the ideal relationship that existed between them and Fritz Kreisler.

The accompanists associated with Kreisler during his long platform career include, for America, Dr. Bernhard Pollak for his "Wunderkind" and early manhood days, André Benoist in the early 1900's when Kreisler and Josef Hofmann were often billed together, and Carl Lamson ever since; for Germany and the European continent, Michael Raucheisen, Franz Rupp, Ernö Balogh, Hubert Giesen, Arpad Sandor, and Otto Schulhoff; for the British Isles, Señor Zulueta, Sir Hamilton Harty, Haddon Squire, and Charleton Keith.

Outdistancing all others by far in length of professional association with Kreisler is white-haired, gentle, lovable Carl Lamson. Like Ruth and Naomi of the Scriptures, Carl and Fritz appear to have an understanding that naught but death shall part them. Lamson has been Kreisler's accompanist on the North American continent and for Australia since 1912, which is probably an all-time record.

Richard S. David, the Milwaukee *Journal* critic, hearing the then sixty-five-year-old Fritz Kreisler and his accompanist, wrote on October 24, 1940:

> The reporter heard a part of the recital from the gallery, peering through one of those apertures in the top bulwarks. Thus the stage was set apart in a sort of frame and in this frame were set the two companions who were playing—Fritz Kreisler of the violin and Carl Lamson of the piano. It was a picture never to be forgotten, a portrait to be called, for lack of a better name, "Devotion."

Beverly Smith has observed:

> Anyone who has seen them together on the platform can sense the deep understanding between the two men. Whenever Kreisler has played a par-

ticularly difficult piece he turns to Lamson and pats him on the shoulder, as much as to say, "Good man, you certainly helped me out." *

Carl Lamson told his story in the idyllic quietude of Lake Placid, New York, where he and his wife and a group of her voice students spend every summer:

"In 1912 Charles Ellis, the impresario, engaged Fritz Kreisler to play twenty concerts with the Boston Symphony Orchestra. Suddenly he suggested, 'Why not put on a number of recitals also?' Fritz replied, 'But I have no accompanist.' Philip Hale, the noted critic, suggested my name. I had studied in Boston and at Amherst College, and had then gone to Berlin to study with Teresa Carreño.

"Fritz sent me the accompaniments for his first recital and asked me to come to the Hotel Bond at 3:00 P.M. for a rehearsal before we started for Northampton, Massachusetts. I asked for him at the hotel. He was not there. He had gone out for a walk. He finally arrived some minutes after four o'clock, just in time for us to catch our train. He said calmly, 'You know those pieces; I'm sure they'll go all right.' I was in a daze. We managed, however, to get in a short rehearsal at Northampton.

"Fritz was always most considerate. One simply cannot quarrel with him. When he differs with your interpretation, the wonderful thing is that he then sits down at the piano and shows you just how he wants it. All theorizing and explaining is nothing compared with his demonstrating to the accompanist exactly what he means. On one occasion I had to play from a pencil-written transcription of a Chaminade piece. At the end of the page a change of key was indicated, but I failed to notice it. A temperamental artist would probably have gone into a tantrum. Fritz merely said quietly, 'You overlooked the F-sharp.'

"He never expected me to accompany him without notes. 'Something might happen,' he would say. 'Your mind or mine might wander; one of us should therefore have the music before him.'

"It always proved difficult to get Fritz to practice the pieces before the next recital, but he did like to rehearse numbers scheduled four

* Reprinted from *He Plays on the World's Heartstrings* by Beverly Smith, in the February, 1931 issue of the *American Magazine*, by permission of Beverly Smith and the Crowell-Collier Publishing Company, copyright, 1931, by *American Magazine*.

Kreisler with accompanist Carl Lamson

The Boston Symphony Orchestra, about 1912

Carl Lamson

Kreisler in New York City, late in his life

or more weeks ahead. We usually rehearsed about three-fourths of a future program, stressing especially the new numbers.

"Nobody will ever know how much he improved compositions which he decided to play.

"Often he did not know himself what he should play as an encore, and only made up his mind on the spur of the moment.

"When we were on tour, Fritz often composed at the piano. The Steinways would deliver an instrument to his hotel room. I would then listen at the door and could always tell when a new composition was in the making. Soon thereafter it would make its appearance.

"Fritz hates to wait for anything. He arrives at the concert hall only three to fifteen minutes before the curtain goes up. He then tunes up before going on the stage. When we travel he is never at the train except just in time to catch it.

"When in a town he walks much to avoid pests and auditions. Sometimes people nevertheless recognize him and accost him on the street. He then calmly says to them, 'I'm often mistaken for Kreisler. No, I'm not Fritz Kreisler.' Often he goes to local symphony concerts to encourage the players. As he meets concert managers in various cities, he often puts in a good word for younger men and recommends them to these impresarios.

"He likes good fellowship and loves to hear good stories. As a story-teller he himself is unsurpassed.

"The fact that Fritz is so fond of the classics and philosophy no doubt had something to do with bringing us so close together. I was a classical scholar at Amherst and studied Greek and Latin.

"One day we were in Nashville, Tennessee, for a concert. Fritz, as you know, does not eat before his recitals. After the concert all places were closed except a Greek restaurant. As we were waiting for our meal, we saw a Greek newspaper and began to decipher the modern Greek phrases. The proprietor, greatly pleased that any non-Greek could read his native language, joined us. Somehow the story got around, and all over the country we were represented as 'conversing fluently in Greek with each other.' My name was even changed in the dispatches to Carlos Lamsonos.

"A classmate living on the Pacific Coast, where the story was also published, promptly debunked me. I received a card from him which read approximately as follows: 'If you don't know any more Greek today than you knew at Amherst, I don't see that you could do much with that newspaper in the Greek restaurant—you're a phony.'

"People in all walks of life always seemed to feel at home with Fritz. Once an old Civil War veteran came up to him in a restaurant. 'You handle the fiddle, don't you?' he asked quite familiarly. Fritz nodded. 'Well,' continued the old soldier, 'I used to handle the fife.'

"Among the many incidents that stick in my mind is a conversation between Rachmaninoff and Fritz. They were discussing Stravinsky. Fritz generously said, '*Petrushka* is a fine piece.' 'Yes,' replied the monosyllabic Rachmaninoff. '*Firebird* also,' Fritz continued, earnestly endeavoring to speak approvingly of a fellow composer. 'Yes,' was again the sole comment. Fritz tried a third time: 'And then there's *The Rites of Spring*.' 'That's already worse,' quoth Rachmaninoff. Fritz gave up.

"The two were devoted friends. One day after Fritz's accident I traveled in a car which Rachmaninoff had also boarded. To attract my attention, he whistled the 'Londonderry Air.' He then said with deep concern: 'What is the condition of Fritz? I am so worried about him.' He had his hand in his little muff that he always wore when it was cold.

"As far as I am concerned, it's the spirit inside that makes Fritz. Nothing else."

Michael Raucheisen of Munich, Germany, accompanied Fritz Kreisler from 1919 to 1931, with but minor exceptions; namely, in 1923, when Ernö Balogh played; in 1926, when Arpad Sandor played; and in 1931 when Hubert Giesen substituted part of the time. Raucheisen's observations are especially interesting because he was a professional violinist before he became a pianist. He wrote:

I had my first recital with Fritz Kreisler in Munich around 1919. On the day before the concert it was Kreisler himself and not, as was the custom, the concert agency, who called me on the telephone. "My dear friend," he said, "I'd like to ask you to rehearse with me. When would it suit you, and may I come to your place?" I remember distinctly how I turned from the

Sergei Rachmaninoff with gloves and heating pad

Igor Stravinsky, 1882-1971

telephone to my parents to express my surprise. The manner of approach was so different from that of most artists. Usually the concert agency called to say, "*Kammersänger* So-and-So desires a rehearsal at his hotel at x-o'clock." My very first talk with Kreisler, therefore, speaks eloquently for his modesty. You must remember that I lived in feverish anticipation in those days of meeting a man I revered. This first impression naturally had a tremendous psychological effect upon me.

Every rehearsal with Kreisler was a festive occasion for me. It depended solely upon the accompanist as to how many rehearsals were necessary. When playing sonatas one always had the feeling of being permitted to be his coequal partner. The thought of imposing one's own interpretation simply did not enter—at least that's the way it was in my case—, for a miracle world was unfolded before me, along the solitary peaks of which one was permitted to wander with him.

During the rehearsals one is in a trance. If as partner and accompanist one reacts toward him like a seismograph, one can rise above oneself and climb to the highest heights with him. He plays from memory, whether it be sonatas or solos. In the concert hall he also plays the sonatas by heart, but this is not due to vanity but rather to the fact that he is near-sighted, wherefore the score irritates him. Nevertheless he has the music on a stand before him, so as to give the impression of his reading the notes. He feels that, since he regards the accompanist as his equal-ranked partner in sonatas, it would not be right for him to seem to be playing from memory whereas the pianist does not.*

A partner of Kreisler is an important figure for the young generation of violinists. How often have I been asked by fiddlers how Kreisler interprets this or that episode, whether he executes it at the point, in the middle, or at the frog of the bow; whether he uses steel strings; how he tightens the bow; when he changes it; how he goes over the strings—whether *spiccato* or *détaché*, etc. (As a matter of fact Kreisler screws the bow so tight that no other violinist could play with it, but from that fact stems the purity of his tone, without any auxiliary noises.)

As I was a violinist and violist until I was twenty-two years old and played both in the Munich State Opera and the Munich Chamber Music Ensemble I have a certain right to discuss technical violin matters.

Shortly before a recital begins, he tunes his strings slightly higher than the tuning of the piano, in order that the flageolet tones and the open strings won't sound flat. I often admonish young violinists to tune their fiddles as sharp as possible, because gut strings always give when they become warm.

* Kreisler's attitude in this matter is that playing from notes always robs the performing artist of his freedom and hinders him from concentrating completely upon his interpretation of the work in hand.

The violin is now clear as a bell. As he stands there on the podium, Kreisler exudes repose and relaxation which are communicated not only to the listeners but also to the partner at the piano. Kreisler seizes the fiddle by the so-called scroll and lets it hang low from his left hand. There's a purpose behind this. If the violin, as is usually done, is held between arm and chest when not playing, the strings get warm and there's danger of their "flatting."

Now a word as to Kreisler's habits directly before and during concerts: Many a time he returned to the hotel dead tired only an hour or even half an hour before the recital. Concern for others (he is always concerned about his fellow men) or thirst for knowledge which detained him in the great state libraries made him forget the concert completely. In winter-time hot water poured over his hands made his fingers nimble. A few scales, a few octaves, a chromatic run—and already he stood like a statue on the platform. Sometimes he didn't have time even for this brief conditioning, for autograph hunters and poor musicians beset him to the very last moment. As his kindness is such that he cannot say "no" he sometimes had to be fairly shoved on to the stage before he could as much as play a scale. Arrived on the platform, however, he has sloughed off all the woes and worries of the world and he now stands there as the apostle of art.

During the intermission, when philologists, artists, natural scientists, mathematicians, or medicos came to express their enthusiasm to him he immediately changed the subject over to scientific problems. The concert is forgotten completely and only the bell reminds him that he hasn't finished his performance. He would then quickly ask, "What's next, anyway?"—and already he again faced the tumultuous crowd. Often he did not know until we were both on the platform what encore I had selected. He had meanwhile been besieged by lay enthusiasts, by artists and instrument dealers.

The psychological secret of Kreisler's imposing musicianship, his charm, personality, and freshness lies in the multiplicity of his intellectual interests. Playing the violin alone does not satisfy such a spirit. And precisely because he devotes himself to his calling only in the concert hall, his playing retains that entrancing youthful freshness with which he casts a spell over all the world.

Hubert Giesen of Stuttgart, who for two years (1929–1931) traveled with Yehudi Menuhin, stressed Kreisler's uncanny *sang-froid* in a letter which also affords a good insight into his rehearsal methods:

I was introduced to Fritz Kreisler in New York. Kreisler was interested in an accompanist for Europe and invited me to visit him in the Hotel Plaza to play with him.

I found him sitting at the piano and working on his operetta *Sissy*. He unpacked his violin and placed the piano scores of some of his well known pieces, "Liebesleid," Liebesfreud," "Schön Rosmarin," and so forth, before me.

Before sitting down to play I asked: "Am I always to *accompany* you, that is, shall I always be in the background and play very softly?" Immediately and for the first time I received the reply which I had always hoped to hear from a great artist: "Please make music. If you are a good musician, I shall also accompany you. Inspire me with your playing. I have played these pieces so often and am always very grateful when someone stimulates me to play them differently."

Soon Kreisler exchanged the violin for the piano and asked me: "What do you think of this little *chanson* from my operetta? Do you like it in this way? Or do you think I ought to change it?" My heart leaped within me. Never have I heard Viennese songs played on the piano in a more exquisite manner. Here, too, Kreisler had the same soft but saturated tone as on the violin. The right hand sang and his trills and grace notes were discreet yet at the same time compelling, while the left hand played a fetching, dancing rhythm that would not let one stand or sit quietly.

Our playing was then interrupted by a feminine voice from the adjoining room. When Kreisler returned from there, he said, slightly embarrassed, "My wife says I ought not to be playing the piano for you but should rehearse on the violin with you." We then did a few more pieces and Kreisler said I'd hear from him.

The evening of the first concert with myself as accompanist came. (We had had only a brief rehearsal.) When Kreisler took a look at the program in the artist's room he had a good scare. He had thought a different Bach solo sonata was to be the opening number. He had neither seen nor played the one printed on the program in years. He decided, however, he'd try it nevertheless. He did make a few mistakes, but only those who knew every note could tell. He simply went ahead composing on his own during the few minor lapses of memory, until he was back in the Bach groove.

That night I was terribly nervous and played badly. Other people and the newspapers told me so. Not, however, Kreisler. He said it had been quite good. I then experienced what a kindly and good man he was, who had full understanding for human weaknesses.

We had never discussed terms and I was simply astounded when he not only paid me well but added, "Or isn't it enough? Do I owe you more?" When it came to paying hotel bills and meals and other incidentals, he surprised me by saying that was his affair and part of the expenses he had to meet.

After a few more concerts there was a week's pause during which Kreisler traveled to Vienna to attend a rehearsal for the world première of his operetta. We were to meet again in Dresden, where a new program was to be played.

I importuned him to try the pieces once before he left. I couldn't persuade him. "I'll arrive in the morning on the sleeper from Vienna and we'll then have a short rehearsal," he said.

Well, he did not arrive on the sleeper; not even with the midday train. My heart sank down into my boots. When he finally arrived, two hours before the concert and I spoke of rehearsing, he said, "The best thing for you and me to do is to rest up."

I was afraid of playing things at first sight. That amused him and when the encores were due, he'd pick out of his bag things I'd never seen and ask me "Do you know this?" and when I'd answer "No," he'd say "Come along." With a broad grin he walked onto the stage, myself fearsomely following, and placed the piano score on my instrument. . . . I'd ask, "How fast?" and he'd say, "Just you start." In that way we played three or four encores with which I was completely unfamiliar.

On one occasion Kreisler and I were joined after the concert by his friend Richard Tauber, as well as by a married couple, also friends of his. A photographer came. Kreisler permitted him to take a picture only on condition that his friend's wife did not appear on it—because his own wife was not present!

Ernö Balogh, formerly Lotte Lehmann's accompanist, now a New York composer and pianist, played for Kreisler during the year 1923. He had no idea that he would be asked to travel with him when, two years previously, he had asked Erich Simon of the Konzertdirektion Wolff & Sachs for an opportunity at some time to play with Fritz Kreisler, whose renditions and interpretations had stirred him deeply. He wanted to play for the mere joy of making music with so thorough an artist. He said he was decidedly not looking for a job!

"Simon rang me up to say that Artur Schnabel had edited a piano score of the Brahms Concerto which Kreisler would like to try out," Balogh said. "So I went to Kreisler's home. After the first movement Kreisler suggested that I go with him on his tour of the Scandinavian countries in September and October, 1923.

" 'But,' I said to Kreisler, 'I had intended then to go to the United States to establish myself there as a composer and concert pianist.' Very modestly Kreisler interposed, 'I am rather well known in the United States and don't believe it will hurt you to go with me first.' Of his own accord, at the end of our tour, he sent letters to all managers in America whom he knew, warmly recommending me. I really owe my American career to that act of kindness of his. I found open doors everywhere. He also found me my first publisher and transcribed two of my compositions, "Caprice antique," and "Dirge of the North," for the violin in so beautiful and original a manner that I retranscribed some of his ideas into my originals.

"While we were on our tour Kreisler invariably gave tickets to his concerts to poor students who asked for them.

"To show you what a congenial person he is, let me recall the following: in Stockholm there was such a demand for him that he had to give four concerts instead of the scheduled two. This meant traveling every night to Copenhagen, Oslo, and other places and then returning for the extra concerts. Our schedule was so close that we had to play the César Franck sonata without previous rehearsal. After the recital Kreisler suggested that I had started the second movement out a bit too slow. 'But why didn't you speed it up when you took over?' I asked. 'That would have destroyed the unity of the ensemble,' he replied, 'and besides, it would have been indelicate for me to seem publicly to correct you; so I continued in the tempo you started with.'

"I asked him once why he refused the many invitations he received. He told me, with his quiet smile, that he did not care for pomp, ceremony, or society. He liked a man for what he was or what he did and not on account of his title. Ordinarily, kings of nations or kings of wealth meant very little to him. But he was always glad to meet the kings of science and art.

"There was quite a well known piano tuner named Fischer in Syracuse, New York, who died recently. Kreisler always declined social invitations when he came to Syracuse, but he always had time to have dinner or lunch with Fischer."

Arpad Sandor assisted Kreisler at the piano during the season of 1926–1927, when Raucheisen was on tour with the Philadelphia-born dramatic soprano Dusolina Giannini.

"I was thrilled and excited when the Konzertdirektion Wolff & Sachs in Berlin advised me in June of 1926 that I was to take Raucheisen's place," Sandor related. "Kreisler, I was told, would not return until September. So all summer I worked at all the standard sonatas, wondering which ones Kreisler would pick for us to perform.

"Then came the day when I could report for rehearsal in his study on the second floor of his beautiful Grunewald home. When I told Mr. Kreisler about what I had been doing all summer, he laughed and said, 'After all, I play only a limited number of sonatas on the concert platform, because a large part of the audience must, by constant repetition, be educated to an appreciation of the beauties of sonatas.'

"He then asked for suggestions. When I mentioned the Mozart Sonata in B Flat, he said, 'That's splendid; I've never played that one in my concerts.' Then we rehearsed. Kreisler is anything but tyrannical; he gives the assisting artist every opportunity for the expression of his individuality.

"Of our experiences, one in Lausanne, Switzerland, stands out especially. The unusual permission was granted to give the concert in the cathedral, since Lausanne had no large concert hall. There was one condition: in the house of worship there was to be no applauding.

"After the Mozart Concerto in A Major the audience could not restrain itself. It applauded. Thereupon the priest who sat in the first row arose to remind the people that one must not clap hands in a church.

"The next number was Chausson's *Poème*. What do you suppose happened? As Kreisler finished, the same priest forgot where he was and started the applause!

"One wonderful thing about being associated with Mr. Kreisler is that he is not at all problematical. When on tour he considers himself the host. He insists that his accompanist, for instance, precede him into the dining car."

Franz Rupp, now the accompanist of Marian Anderson, was associated with Kreisler from 1930 to 1938. His story of their trip to South America on the *Graf Zeppelin* has already been told in detail, as has his recording of all the Beethoven violin sonatas with Kreisler.

"Kreisler was not fond of rehearsals," he said, "but insisted that I understood him and knew my business, wherefore there was no reason to take up too much time rehearsing. He wanted always to come to his concert programs fresh.

"When we were on tour we often took long walks. If we heard music anywhere he would stop and listen, even if it was only a hurdy-gurdy man grinding out a Schubert song or what have you."

Besides these professional accompanists, the veteran music critic of the Richmond, Virginia, *Times-Dispatch,* George Harris, on one occasion found himself in the role of Kreisler's accompanist. "It was at Bar Harbor, Maine," George Harris wrote, "where Kreisler was to play in a private house. It was late in the summer and every other possible accompanist had gone away. This must have been in 1918, 1919, or 1920.

"I remember being a little perturbed, but being completely set at ease by Mr. Kreisler. In some way or other he made it all very easy for me, and I have thought of this often as an example of the fact that the great people do the logical and expected things and give out some sort of helpful warmth of personality rather than anything terrifying."

As every musician knows, the violinist of rank also often appears with orchestra. It is interesting to note that Kreisler, as soloist, was more concerned about the concertmaster than he was about the conductor. "He is telepathic in his understanding with the concertmaster," Harriet observed. "After that, nothing matters. The two always understood each other perfectly, no matter where Fritz played."

While Kreisler naturally has his preferences among conductors, he never has had any misunderstandings with any of them. His concern lest he keep an orchestra too long for rehearsals led him invariably to play only the opening and closing bars of his cadenzas.

The story of Kreisler's accompanists would not be complete if one failed to refer to the instruments upon which they played and to the family which produced them. A Kreisler recital in America is unthinkable without a Steinway Grand, as is a Kreisler biography without mention of three generations of Steinways.

A friend of both the Kreislers and the Steinways made the following observation: "There are only two parallels in musical history to the Kreisler-Steinway relationship—Frédéric Chopin and Camille Pleyel, Paris manufacturer of pianos, and Franz Liszt and Sébastien Érard, also a Paris piano maker. Chopin told all his troubles, even those with George Sand, to Pleyel; Liszt shared his joys and his sorrows, his triumphs and his disappointments with Érard. The fact that later, in Weimar, Liszt used a different make of instrument does not change the fact that Érard was his intimate and confidant. Similarly Kreisler throughout the years has considered the Steinways as among his best and most dependable friends."

Fritz had his first experience of Steinway friendship in the days of Charles and William Steinway, when he came over to America in 1888 as a child prodigy to be Moriz Rosenthal's supporting artist. It was the Steinway brothers of those days who took the boy under their protecting wing when his mother was too ill to move about much. He has never forgotten this act of kindness.

That friendship was carried over to the next generation—the third since the founding of the firm by Henry Engelhard Steinway (1797–1871)—when the present president of the firm, Theodore E., and the vice president and secretary, William R. Steinway, became cronies of Fritz. As to Theodore's children, four of whom hold positions in the family firm, they feel they have always known "Uncle Fritz."

When the Steinways still did business on Fourteenth Street, New York, a visit by Fritz and Harriet Kreisler usually ended in a jolly party at Lüchow's famous German restaurant. The Steinways and Kreislers were frequently joined by Ernest Urchs, their concert department manager, who was later succeeded by another man who equally revered Kreisler and his art—Alexander W. Greiner.

If it wasn't Lüchow's, it was Martin's, a French restaurant noted for its cooking. Or, they would meet at Mouquin's, noted for its choice wines.

Those were the days, too, when the Steinways were prominently identified with the Liederkranz Singing Society, in whose hall on East Fifty-eighth Street concerts were often given. Of course, Kreisler, too, often played there in his younger days.

Urchs had a clever daughter, Otonita, who made good use of her father's connection with practically every artist of note. She started a collection of musical autographs which by the time of her death had grown to three volumes, with 305 individual dedications—one of the finest in existence. It is now the property of the Music Division of the Library of Congress. The reason it is here mentioned is the fact that Kreisler, too, was naturally asked to inscribe a page. Now, as one goes through the three volumes, one cannot but notice that almost all musicians who also aspired to the role of composer adorned their pages with a few bars of their own works. Not so Fritz, although he had by December 19, 1912, when he contributed his autograph, written more music than most of the contributors. He contented himself with drawing about ten bars of the third movement of Beethoven's Violin Concerto! He thus inadvertently revealed his innate modesty.

Wherever in the days before the great depression of 1929 Kreisler went to give a concert, he would find a Steinway piano in his hotel suite. As Fritz usually writes a piano score of his composition first, the Steinways may well claim credit for having been instrumental in preserving this or that musical inspiration of Kreisler's for posterity. For, when a piano was readily at hand, Fritz would sit down at once, when the spirit moved him, to commit his musical thoughts to paper.

As was to be expected, other enterprising firms in the course of the years tried to wean Kreisler away from the friends whose pianos he had selected for his accompanists. The same personal loyalty and fidelity which characterized his human relations generally resulted in uncompromising rejection of such offers.

Nothing throughout the years marred a beautiful friendship between the House of Steinway and Harriet and Fritz Kreisler. It is a treasure with which neither will ever wish to part.

CHAPTER TWENTY-NINE

KREISLER'S VIOLINS

FRITZ KREISLER has said of the violin: *

After all, it is the player that produces the tone, not the violin. The melody is actually in the heart more than in the strings. A good instrument then may be defined as one that puts the least impediment in the way of expression. Bad instruments are obstructive, like shaky bridges or physical barriers that stand between you and your destination. It is the artist who does the journeying.

But for all that, a violin is not simply wood and catgut. It is a personality, and goes through the world looking for its rightful master. It has moods, and must be wooed. It selects, gives itself to one and withholds itself from another. At times its humors and whims must be combatted with everything at command.

Hardly a violin, even among the supreme specimens, that does not have a weak strain somewhere, and the master's task is to hide that strain, slur it over with his art. There are fiddles that are beautiful physically, and that reach great heights on occasion, and yet are not dependable. They are outlaws, rogues that love you one moment and betray you the next with some wolf-tone. This wolf-tone is moody, it rolls, is harsh, does not speak. Such a violin is like a horse that won't be ridden, or ridden only by certain masters and on certain days.

For sweetness of tone, Stradivarius is still king. He made about 1100 violins, of which perhaps 600 still exist. Some 20 or 30 of these are really very good, and five or six, better preserved, are supreme instruments. If they seem timeless, it is because of their destiny. To crush a "Strad" would be to kill an immortal.

* Reprinted from "Fritz Kreisler, and What's in Him" by Richard Matthews Hallet, from an article in the December 7, 1940 issue of *The Christian Science Monitor*, by permission of *The Christian Science Monitor*, copyright, 1940, by *The Christian Science Monitor*.

Yet violins are frail, and there must be good fairies at their birth if they are to survive for 200 years. They are full of adventure.

Here is my Guarnerius. It was brought from Spain by an English sailor, who had stolen it in some raid of the Napoleonic Spanish War. The sailor sold it for a guinea, though it was worth many thousands. But to the sailor it was just a fiddle, like any other. He might have destroyed it in a waterfront bout. Already it had come through one war, and perhaps another. My Guarnerius took plenty of chances of destruction in those wandering years, but it escaped everything.

The buyer sold it to a man named Twombley, the owner of a London pub. Quite by chance a good violinist took it down and discovered its tone. After that Twombley grew famous for his fiddle. The Guarnerius knew how to make its own way in life.

Word went round, "This is one of the world's great fiddles, and a rogue of a publican refuses to sell it." And so in time I heard of it. I was very young, but then I had been playing on a fiddle since the age of four. I played this Guarnerius mellowed by centuries. I loved its voice, but Twombley wouldn't sell it. "Come," I said to him, "this fiddle speaks for me. I am its fate. Sell it to me."

"There are other good men who come here and play," Twombley said. "How can I deprive them of the happiness? But come again. Come often."

I came often enough, and the fiddle knew its master, but still in the end it went back on its peg. There are nights when I woke in a bad dream of some fellow—like the sailor who had stolen it out of Spain—taking it from its peg behind that publican's bar.

Well, I do not have such dreams now. I have the fiddle. Old Twombley passed on at 90, and his two daughters sold it, perhaps to be rid of the need of running a pub.

And so I have my Guarnerius. It is robust. It has been to the wars, and so, for that matter, have I. We are companions. When we play together, it is as if I am in the Austrian army again. I see the charge. I receive again that thrust of a Don Cossack lance. But I go on playing. I think to myself, "Today is the day of the Guarnerius."

It is superb and pathetic, with its clouded destiny. There is no end to the music in it, if it is well kept. To whom will it finally appeal? But I know less of its future than of its past. I know only that for the present we are joined.

On another occasion Fritz Kreisler said about violins: "They are as sensitive as humans. They breathe and pulsate with a billion vibrations. They have a nervous system and an arterial system. They tire just like humans, and need a rest now and then. I always give my best instruments a rest of at least six months."

To the general lover of music who does not happen to play a violin it may be well to recall the words of the late critic, James Huneker:

Its lowest note is the G below the treble clef, and its top note a mere squeak; but it seems in a few octaves to have imprisoned within its wooden walls a miniature world of feeling; even in the hands of a clumsy amateur it has the formidable power of giving pain; while in the grasp of a master it is capable of rousing the soul. No other instrument has its ecstatic quality. . . . The angelic, demoniac, lovely, intense tones of the violin are without parallel in music or nature. It is as if this box with four strings across its varnished belly had a rarer nervous system than all other instruments.

Paul Bekker, the eminent German musicologist, reminds us of another interesting fact about the violin: *

Since the time of Amati and the later Stradivarius, the violin has remained unchanged and unchangeable, a miracle among human inventions, because improvement seemed to be neither possible, nor necessary, nor desirable.

Franz Farga adds the further touch: †

To no other instrument do there cling as many legends, unusual occurrences, dark tragedies, miraculous fates. Human kind never tires of hearing about old fiddles, of delving into their adventures, of brooding over their secrets.

However diversified instruments in the course of time became, there was one among them which from the very beginning was the favorite of man: the violin. For, its tones most nearly approached the human voice, its magic was almost that of a supernatural power. It seemed as though even the ignorant had a presentiment that something had here come into existence that reflected greatest honor upon man's inventive abilities.

A master violin is perfection personified, unique in the laws governing it, a technical miracle of clearest and most accomplished selection. No other instrument so appeals to the hearts of human beings, seems to them to be so unfathomable, and thus embodies all their unuttered yearnings.

The Austrian nineteenth century poet Franz Grillparzer has written a charming quatrain which in a few words sums up the secret of the violin:

* Reprinted from *The Story of the Orchestra* by Paul Bekker, by permission of W. W. Norton & Company, Inc., copyright, 1936, by W. W. Norton & Company, Inc.

† Reprinted from *Geigen und Geiger* by Franz Farga (3. Auflage, 1950), by permission of Albert Mueller Verlag, AG., Rüschlikon-Zürich, Switzerland, copyright, 1950, by Albert Mueller Verlag, AG.

Vier arme Saiten!—es klingt wie Scherz—
Für alle Wunder des Schalles!
Hat doch der Mensch nur ein einzig Herz
Und reicht doch hin für alles.

The story of Fritz Kreisler's life thus far has revealed that he began with a toy violin at the age of four, was presented with a half-size Thir at eight when a pupil at the Vienna Conservatory, was rewarded at ten with a three-quarter Amati for winning the Austrian First Prize, was given a shining red full-sized Gand-Bernadel at thirteen as the usual present of the Paris Conservatoire to a French Grand Prix winner, and received a beautiful Grancino upon his return to Vienna from his father. This instrument was Kreisler's associate for the next eight years.

Writing about his violins in 1908, Kreisler continued:

But the time came when it [the Grancino] was to be laid aside for a new love. The violinist should not be accused of inconstancy; he must follow the call of a siren voice—the voice of the magic piece of wood that dominates his destiny. It is a voice of an enchantress which he must obey. One morning I chanced to call upon an old friend in Vienna, an architect.

"Fritz," he said, "here is an old, battered violin that you can have, perhaps make some use of, by giving it away to someone who needs it. It is very much in my way. I took it from a poor man who owed me some money and could not pay it. If it is patched up it may yet be of service in the world."

I took it home with me, all unconscious of the great treasure in my grasp. Upon examination I found it to be a genuine Nicolò Gagliano, of entrancing tone and quality. It was shabby and battered, but it was in no wise injured. It became the best beloved of my violins until within three years ago. It traveled with me on my concert tours in almost every large city in Europe and America.

At one time only did I swerve in my devotion to my beautiful Gagliano. I bought a Stradivarius, for which I paid the sum of $4,000. After it was purchased and I had played upon it a while I found that I had made a costly error. For some reason it remained cold and lifeless under my most fervid appeals. I can only say it was antagonistic to me. A violinist cannot explain this attitude between himself and his instrument; he only knows that it "is," and that the condition is one of acute suffering. Within a short time I returned to my Gagliano and swore that I would remain faithful to it for the rest of my life.

Alas for the vows of a violinist! He is the slave of the Voice. When he hears it he must leave all and follow it until it is in his possession. Once more I foreswore my Gagliano, this time for a superb Joseph Guarnerius, which I bought for $10,000 from the celebrated dealer, Hart. "Now it is ended," I said; "this violin must be the last."

For one year I was in truth happy in the ownership of this truly superb instrument: then one day as I entered the rooms of Mr. Hart I heard a Voice, liquid, pure, penetrating, whose divine sweetness pierced my soul as a knife with the anguish of longing. I rushed into the room in a frenzy of emotion. "Whose is it? Where is it?" I cried. "At any cost it must be mine. What is its price? I will give my entire fortune, but I must possess it."

It was then the property of an English collector of wealth with a passion for collecting violins. That this divine Voice should be doomed to silence under the glass case of a collector was to me a tragedy that rent my heart. More than ever was I determined that I should endow it with life and the power to interpret the great messages of our music gods. From that day, with Mr. Hart as an abettor, I laid siege to the fortress which held the imprisoned Guarnerius. I gave no rest to its jailer, who, I must admit, was a gentleman of rare culture and attainments. For weeks and months I assailed him with my pleadings. Finally he took it from his case, saying, "Play." I played as one condemned to death would have played to obtain his ransom. When I had finished he said: "I have no right to it; keep it; it belongs to you. Go out into the world and let it be heard."

In this way I am the happy owner of what is considered to be the third most beautiful violin in the world in point of shape and decoration. In tone it is, as you say in this country, "not to be beaten." It is sweet, big, penetrating. It has, to be sure, a few cranky ways—its nasty moods; but never does it fail me in my most strenuous demands. Now that I have learned to understand its disposition it has become part of my being.

This time I shall be faithful until the end, for I do not delude myself that I shall ever hear a voice more beautiful than that of my last beloved, my "Hart" Guarnerius.

The "Hart" bears the date 1737 as the year of its manufacture. The English collector sold it to Kreisler in 1904 for only $10,000. In the opinion of London dealers the case alone was worth $1,000.

Despite his emphatic assertion, "This time I shall be faithful until the end," Kreisler later found a Guarnerius which he liked even better, and the acquisition of which led him in 1917 to dispose of the "Hart" Guarnerius to an American amateur player who sold it to the Rudolph Wurlitzer Company in 1925. It is now in foreign possession.

The Guarnerius which struck Kreisler's later fancy and which he

Efrem Zimbalist at the Rudolph Wurlitzer Company, about 1918

Kreisler's 1733 Joseph Guarnerius del Gesu

still owns today was made in 1733. "Hill, the London instrument dealer, claims it is the best violin Guarnerius ever made," he explained.

In fact, this 1733 Guarnerius is the subject of illustration in color in the work by three members of the Hill family, *The Violin Makers of the Guarneri Family*.

The firm of Hill & Sons, incidentally, seems to have profited by Kreisler's name in much the same manner in which the Bechstein piano firm profited by the fame of Franz von Liszt. Liszt was rather touched at the generosity of the Bechsteins in sending him a new grand piano every year. As a matter of fact, there was no "generosity" involved, for the Bechsteins were able to dispose of the year-olds at high prices because they could guarantee that each had been "Liszt's own instrument."

Similarly Kreisler recalls: "Hill offered me some fine instrument from time to time and suggested that I take it home and even use it for concert purposes. As I like to give my violins a rest, I gladly accepted the offer. No sooner had I used such an instrument in a public performance, however, than Hill was able to sell it for a much higher price because somehow the impression got around that I liked it so much that I even preferred it to my own violin."

Kreisler's judgment on the relative merits of the Stradivarius and the Guarnerius is: "The Strad is excellent for a small concert hall. At the time when Strads were built, only small halls were available for concerts. The Guarnerius has much more power. Recently a younger violinist bought a Strad. He wondered why, although it is such a marvelous instrument, he was not doing as well with the audiences as he used to do. The answer is simple: our concert halls today for the most part are too big for a Strad."

In 1930 he could apparently not yet make up his mind which he preferred—a Stradivarius or a Guarnerius. For he then said: "Can a man say that he prefers a blond beauty to a brunette beauty, and vice versa? One does not make a choice when face to face with beauty. My choice is a polygamous one as regards violins."

Fritz's 1908 story of his violins left off with his acquisition of the

"Hart" Guarnerius. He continued to collect and dispose of choice violins through the years.

There was, for instance, the "Greville" Stradivarius, brought to England from Cremona, Italy, in the early eighteenth century by an Englishman named Greville. After changing hands a number of times it came into Fritz Kreisler's possession in 1908, at which time Kempton Adams of New York, in whose family the instrument had been last, prepared a brochure telling the story of the violin and dedicated it to Kreisler. The dedication reads:

To Fritz Kreisler:

> The soul of music slumbers in the shell
> 'Til wakened and kindled by the master spell,
> And feeling hearts touch them but slightly,
> Pour a thousand melodies unheard before.
>
> SAMUEL ROGERS—*Human Life.*

Kreisler kept it for only two years, and in 1910 sold it to Lyon & Healy of Chicago.

In 1908 he also acquired a 1733 Stradivari which had been in the possession of a French family for generations. He sold it in 1934, and it was later acquired by Bronislaw Huberman.

At Hill's in London, one day in 1926, he found the "Lord Amherst of Hackney," a Stradivarius of 1734, which he sold in October, 1946 to Rudolph Wurlitzer. It soon became the property of the late Jacques Gordon, but Gordon was not to enjoy the priceless instrument long. On September 15, 1948, he died of a cerebral hemorrhage as he was returning to his home in Falls Village, from the summer home of Albert Spalding in Great Barrington, Massachusetts, where he, Fritz Kreisler, Albert Spalding, and several other musicians had spent an evening playing chamber music.

In the course of this sale to Rudolph Wurlitzer, Kreisler also disposed of the "Earl of Plymouth" Stradivarius, acquired from Hill in 1928 and purchased by Dorothea Powers; a Petrus Guarnerius of Mantua, which has since come into the hands of a private collector; and a Carlo Bergonzi, bought by Angel Reyes, a Cuban violinist.

The sale of the 235-year-old "Earl of Plymouth" Strad aroused world-wide interest. "Fritz sold it on my advice," Harriet said. "I

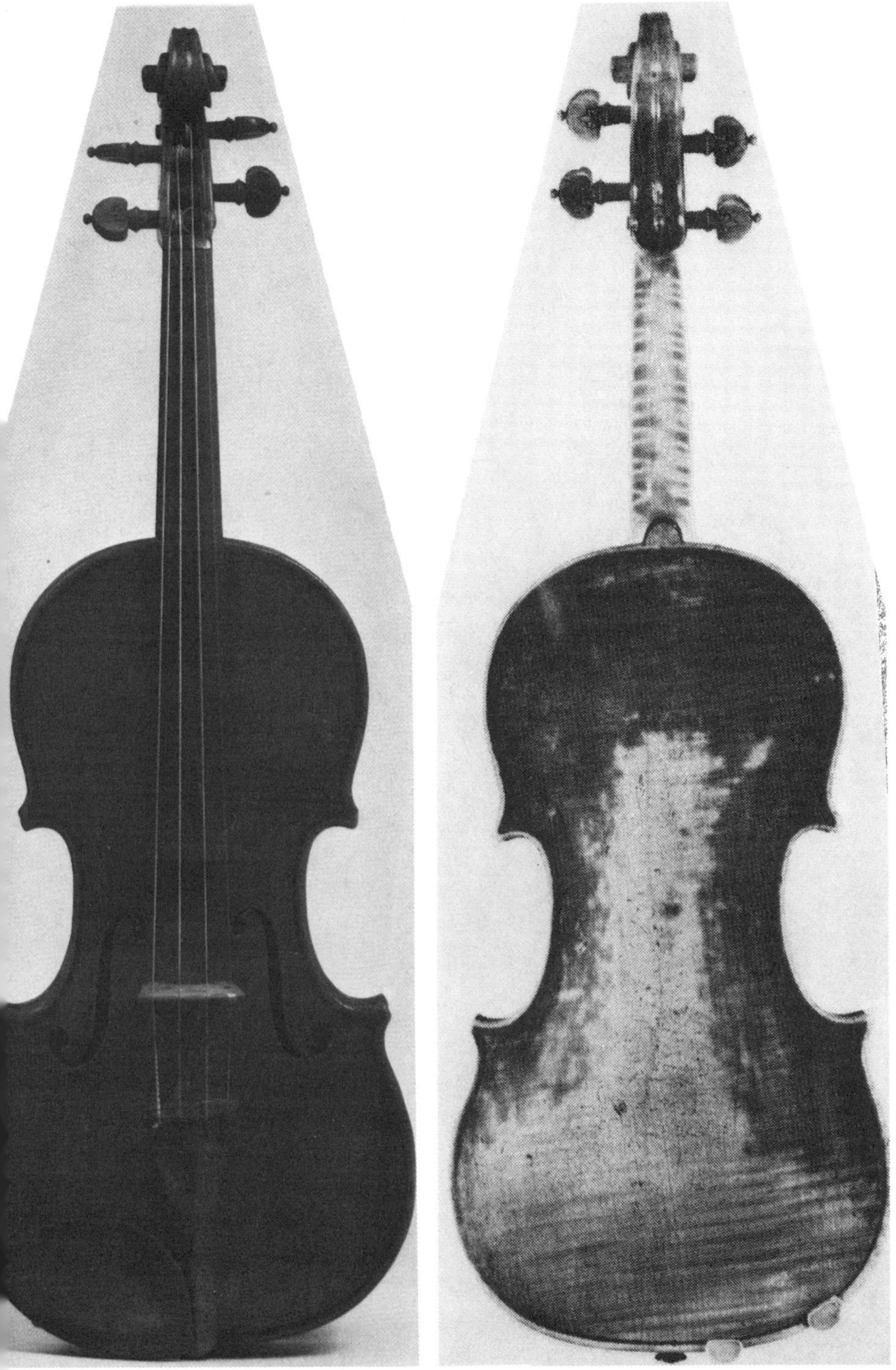

Kreisler's 1733 Stradivari, now known as "The Huberman"

Kreisler's 1722 Strad, "The Earl"

didn't want six fiddles hanging around when so many violinists need them."

This Stradivarius derives its name from the fact that in 1925 it was found in an old lumber room of the Earl of Plymouth. Experts proclaimed it to be on a par with the "Messiah" and the "Alard," both in English possession. No sales price was given.

For a while Fritz Kreisler owned a 1732 Guarnerius, formerly in the Thornley Collection, which he bought from the Hungarian violinist Tivadar Nachez and sold to Wurlitzer in 1925.

He frequently used a violin made in London about 1720 by Daniel Parker, one of the first English violin makers to copy Stradivarius. In 1948, however, he sold it to Wurlitzer. Also, as recently as at a New York Philharmonic-Symphony concert in 1946 he played on an unusually fine Guarneri copy made by Jean Baptiste Vuillaume, which he still possesses and of which he thinks very highly.

The Vuillaume copy was so excellent that Kreisler once tried it out on his colleague, Mischa Elman. As Elman tells the story: "I visited Kreisler one day in his Grunewald home, Berlin, when he took me upstairs to show me his precious collection of violins. He had me play on his 'Strad' and his Guarnerius, and then handed me another 'Guarnerius.' I played on it. It was fine.

" 'Do you see any difference in quality?' he asked. When I replied, 'No,' he said, 'This is really not a Guarnerius at all but a copy of a very famous one.' All of which goes to show that a skillful master with imagination can produce a beautiful instrument, and that you don't always need a big name to insure quality."

The story of his Vuillaume-Guarnerius is fascinating. "Paganini was the owner of two Vuillaume copies of his Guarnerius," Kreisler explained. "When he died, one of these was left to his natural heirs and is still in a museum in Genoa where, unfortunately, it is disintegrating rapidly. The other was left to his only pupil, the celebrated violinist Camillo Sivori. To make a long story short, in the course of time this second copy found its way to Hill & Sons. After much persuasion, I finally prevailed upon the London dealers to let me acquire it."

Rembert Wurlitzer, through whose hands virtually all the famous violins of the world have passed, pointed out that no artist of the bow has been less addicted to any particular instrument than Kreisler. "Some of the greatest players," he said, "feel they cannot play well unless their favorite violin is in their hands. Fritz can take any good violin and make it sound superb."

One might imagine that Kreisler would watch his priceless instruments most carefully while on tour. The contrary is true. He is serenely confident that so costly an instrument will turn up again, even if someone should steal it, as every instrument dealer in the world knows who the owners of the most famous fiddles are.

Michael Raucheisen wrote on this point:

> Just as Kreisler refuses to be slave to his art, so also he will not be a slave to his costly instruments. When we traveled he would with perfect peace of mind hand in his Stradivari at the hand-baggage checking counter of a railway station and in exchange for the costly violin take a 20-pfennig [about 5 cents] receipt. Thus relieved of ballast he would see the sights of a strange town, and he considered it self-evident that the clerk at the baggage counter would hand out the violin again.
>
> During my residence in America I called on him one day at the Wellington Hotel at noon of the day of his arrival from England. A Carnegie Hall performance was scheduled for that evening.
>
> After greetings were exchanged he opened his violin case. The violin had remained in there ever since his Albert Hall concert in London, and the case had not even been opened. With utmost composure he examined the instrument and noticed that the A and D strings had snapped during the ocean voyage. Any other violinist would have suffered tortures. I heard him in the evening and everything sounded as natural as ever. Kreisler, you see, always possessed tremendous reserves of nervous energy, because he simply would not get steamed up about trifles and always took everything as it came. Just stop to think how many artists use up their strength fretting if, for instance, they can't find a collar button! These small distractions then transmit themselves to the listeners.

Occasionally Fritz forgot one of his precious violins at a hotel or in a taxicab. Dame Ethel Smyth * recalls how when Kreisler once traveled from Rome to Naples with his wife, the train came to full

* Reprinted from *Impressions That Remained* by Ethel Smyth, by permission of Alfred A. Knopf, Incorporated, copyright, 1946, by Alfred A. Knopf, Incorporated.

stop because of a herd of bullocks blocking the road. It was then that Fritz suddenly noticed that he had left his "Strad" behind in the hotel. So he jumped out of his compartment, while Harriet pitched their bags, including a second instrument, out of the window. Fritz then caught Harriet as she jumped the four and a half feet to the ground.

The car, it appears, was largely filled with German tourists. Accustomed as they were to strict obedience to rules, they were scandalized. Why, they exclaimed, it is *strengstens verboten* (absolutely forbidden) to get out of a train between stations. To make matters worse, just as the engineer blew the whistle to start off again, Harriet discovered that her little handbag was missing. According to Dame Smyth:

> "Hand me down that bag on the middle seat, please—quick," said Kreisler. "I shall do nothing of the sort," replied one of the Germans and slammed the door. Whereupon Kreisler, swarming up to the side of the carriage, wrenched the door open, pushed past the German, and while the train was slowly getting into its stride jumped after the bag to the ground.

He recovered his Stradivarius at Rome without difficulty!

F. W. Gaisberg wrote that Kreisler usually left his expensive instrument in the recording studio when he went out, say for lunch, while other artists did not.

The New York *Times* reported on December 3, 1916:

> Kreisler, the citizen, soldier and patriot of Austria, but artist and violinist of the world, boarded an early morning train at Northampton where, the night before, he had played for the women of Smith College. He put his violin up on the coat rack, apparently not with the same loving care with which a woman would place her first born baby in its cradle, but casually, as a piece of hand baggage, whereupon a fellow traveler, getting aboard at the same town, exclaimed:
>
> "You ought not to throw that up there like that."
>
> "Why not?" asked Kreisler.
>
> "Because, after hearing you play last night, I should say that what is in that case is a sacred thing."
>
> Kreisler smiled graciously but did not seem to be much impressed. On the contrary, he began an eager reading of all the war news he could get in such newspapers as had found their way that far north so early in the morning.

Testing out his theory that instrument dealers know who owns famous fiddles caused Fritz Kreisler some trouble one day in Antwerp during the period before World War I, and made him miss his Channel boat. The story is genuine, though three versions of it differ slightly as to details. It became known for the first time in 1913. The following account comes nearest the facts as Fritz remembers them:

Kreisler happened to come upon a nondescript fiddle as he was browsing around in an old antique shop. Wondering what an instrument of this sort might sell for, he asked the aged owner of the shop the price. The reply must have intrigued him and, to find out whether this man really knew anything approaching expertness concerning violins, took his own instrument out of its case and asked whether the antique dealer was interested in buying it.

The old man looked at the instrument, handled it with a reverence that indicated familiarity with quality, and observed, "I'm not rich enough to pay what this violin is worth. But you are evidently a connoisseur. If you'll excuse me for a few minutes, I'll dash to my home and fetch an Amati which I have there and which you'll like to see."

He disappeared, but when he returned was accompanied, not by a violin but by a policeman. Pointing to the slightly bewildered customer, he cried out, "That man is a thief; he's stolen Fritz Kreisler's violin. Arrest him!"

Kreisler protested that he himself was indeed Fritz Kreisler. He could not prove his identity, because he had left his passport at the hotel. Then, however, he had a bright idea: clamping the priceless Guarnerius under his chin, he played "Schön Rosmarin."

The antique dealer's expression changed from incredulity to unfeigned wonderment, then to ardent appreciation. "There's no doubt about it," he finally said excitedly, as he regained speech. "The gentleman simply can't be anyone else but Fritz Kreisler. Nobody else can play 'Schön Rosmarin' like that."

The other versions substitute a Klotz fiddle for an Amati, and Kreisler's "Caprice viennois" for his equally famous "Schön Rosmarin." One of the versions of the incident adds that the "sadly humbled old man" presented the artist with an antique cameo ring to atone for his mistake in trying to have him arrested.

The story of Fritz Kreisler and his violins would not be complete without mention of the bows and strings he uses.

Kreisler was asked by a critic what bow he preferred. He replied, "I have a beautiful Tourte, a gift from Mr. Tubbs, which I use frequently." (Frank H. Tubbs was the editor of *Music Life*.) That was years ago. He later often used one of half a dozen Hill bows he owns, and at times a Pfretschner. Here, again, he was unlike most professional violinists who have one favorite bow without which they do not feel they can do justice to their task.

"Do you use any particular brand of strings?" Kreisler was asked by the same critic who wanted to know his preference in bows. "No," he answered, "I find very good ones wherever I happen to be. I am not a faddist." In later years, however, he has consistently used strings made by a friend in Chicago.

Violin makers find Fritz one of the most pleasant artists to work with. Roman Klier of the Wurlitzer establishment said to me: "As long as I have known him he has never ordered us to do this or that, or complained that the job was not well done. He merely tells us, in a gentle and friendly manner, what he would like to have done. But he never bosses us. 'You know how to make violins—that's your field; I only know how to fiddle,' he says. He is a man who is always concerned about others and never about himself. Some artists drive us nearly crazy by never being satisfied and by pretending they know better than we what should be done about their instruments. It is a great relief then to have Mr. Kreisler come and show by his whole attitude that he trusts us to know our job."

One story which Wurlitzer's men like to tell about Kreisler is the incident in a Florida town when during shaving he had failed to notice that some of the soap suds had landed on his violin bow. Imagine his surprise when, on reaching the concert platform and joining the symphony orchestra in playing our national anthem, his violin suddenly went dead whenever the middle of his bow was reached! Only then did he discover that the bow hair there was soapy.

He wanted to hurry off the stage immediately after the anthem to fetch a reserve bow, but the conductor had already begun the opening bars of the Paganini concerto that Fritz was to play as the first work.

Since he had to catch a train, the composition in which he figured had obligingly been placed at the head of the program.

Once again Kreisler performed one of those daring feats for which he is noted. He played the difficult piece without using the middle section of his bow! So perfect was his performance that one critic hailed him for having invented a new style of playing Paganini, playing only at the point and at the frog of his bow!

Kreisler showed his interest in the art of violin making publicly in October, 1942, when he attended the first national exhibit of national craftsmanship in New York. He spoke in appreciative terms of American-made violins and obligingly complied with a request by seven American violin makers to pose for a picture with them.

A closing observation regarding Kreisler and his violins: the diligent observer of his platform habits will have noticed that he never uses a cushion but places his violin directly on his shoulder. A cushion, he holds necessarily somewhat dampens the tone.

CHAPTER THIRTY

COLLEAGUES OF THE BOW

ARTISTS of the stage, it is quite commonly believed, are as jealous and envious as any professional group. It is indicative of the unique position which Fritz Kreisler has held now for sixty years among violinists that his most eminent colleagues have shown no hesitation in expressing their admiration and affection for the Nestor of their profession.

In a sense this is ironical. For Kreisler, though ever lavish in helping fellow artists and ever generous in praising them individually on occasion, has consistently declined to be drawn into any comparative evaluation of his colleagues. He has not hesitated to give his reasons. In the course of one interview * he said:

"I am a sincere admirer of certain artists, but after all, the judgment of one artist on another is subject to so many influences that one hesitates to express it. How is one to tell whether an artist is really great or really small? If an artist has confidence in his own ability and interpretations, if he believes honestly in the fineness of his own ideals, how can he honestly say that this artist or that artist, with whom he differs greatly, is right? An artist must be original, he must not be an imitator, and if every player is original, how can he help differing from his brother player?

"If, then, an artist believes in himself, how can he help being annoyed, irritated, when he hears a work played in a way of which his musical ideals will not allow him to approve? This spirit, not one of carping criticism, but rather an honest differing of artistic opinion, makes it impossible for one artist to understand, to a degree, any other artist. Suppose that I, believing in my own ideals, were to try to express my musical thoughts in a manner individual to another artist, could I be more than an imitator, could I be honest and sincere

* In the February 5, 1910 issue of *Musical America*.

with the public? In speaking of this I do not refer to technical equipment, for hundreds of artists have sufficient technic, and after all technic is only a means to an end, but to interpretation, to the re-creation of a work. And so we see violinists, pianists, singers, conductors even, who are apparently at daggers' points with other performers, but who really have the highest regard for their [colleagues'] real personal worth. . . . I keep my own counsel in these matters. There are many ways of playing beautifully, but only one way can appeal to each artist. I pursue my own ideals satisfied that I am right, otherwise I could have no faith in myself as an artist."

The violinists, whose personal views on their senior colleague are about to follow, are, in alphabetical order: Adolf Busch, Mischa Elman, Georges Enesco, Carl Flesch, Zino Francescatti, Jascha Heifetz, Yehudi Menuhin, Nathan Milstein, Albert Spalding, Joseph Szigeti, Jacques Thibaud, and Efrem Zimbalist. Further comments of an anecdotal or episodical character by some of them have appeared at appropriate points earlier in this book. Included also, as an ex-violinist, is Harold Bauer; and as an artist with especially close associations and affinities with Kreisler, the grand old man of the cello, Pablo Casals.

Jacques Thibaud, veteran French violinist who has known Kreisler since his eighteenth year, seemed especially mortified that some critics have tried to deny Kreisler his proper place as a composer merely because most of his pieces are not of concerto or sonata length.

"When people point out that Fritz's pieces are 'only' small," he said, "I remind them that Chopin, too, wrote many, many small pieces which are now part of the musical treasure of the world. Take Kreisler's 'Tambourin chinois,' for example. It is a real jewel. The musicianship! The writing of it! The way it sounds! Whatever he has touched is perfumed by his art and smells beautiful. I regard him as a marvelous composer.

"I find no fault for his writing things which he describes *à la manière de*. Take, for instance, the allegro in his 'Pugnani' concerto. It is a masterpiece.

"Fritz is a complete artist. Wagner, for instance, was a great opera composer, but when he tried himself at symphonies, he was not universal the way Beethoven and Mozart were. But Fritz is complete. To write his Beethoven cadenzas meant writing in an absolutely classic

Jacques Thibaud

Kreisler and Enesco

style, while at the same time employing the modern perfections of technique and of the instrument. What wonderful cadenzas they turned out to be! Fritz showed the greatest respect for Beethoven as he wrote them. I am sure if Beethoven were alive he would come up to Fritz and fervently shake his hands.

"Fritz is above all a personality—one of the great personalities of our time. His music is good for the soul. It is poetry. It is feeling. He is a real romanticist, who makes his tones ring. Fritz plays the violin as he is himself—a man full of generosity and heart. He plays with his fingers and his brains but first of all with his heart. He is never condescending. He is what Casals is on the cello."

Harold Bauer, who has known Fritz Kreisler since his debut in London in 1902 under the direction of Hans Richter and was frequently associated with him in ensemble work, also paid tribute to his colleague as a composer:

"I believe Fritz Kreisler has completely expressed himself in his so-called 'short' pieces. They represent a genre all their own and have supplied something that was badly needed in violin literature.

"No violinist has been looked upon for so long a time as a model as Fritz. He has been a model for the lightest things as well as the heaviest. Paganini's influence all had to come in the short span of ten years. Fritz's covers many more years. He is like a planet while Paganini was like a meteor."

On the humorous side Harold Bauer has added this anecdote about his friend:

"Mention of Fritz Kreisler reminds me of the sciatica from which I have suffered for many years. I was always happy to play with him, not only because he was a great artist, but because he gave me no trouble if I had a backache. Fritz has always acknowledged applause by an inclination of the head and, as far as I can recall, he has never bent over from the hips as Paderewski, for instance, was wont to do. Kreisler's attitude was very nice, indeed, when I had a stiff back and we took a bow together." *

Georges Enesco, whom Americans probably know best for his oft-

* Reprinted from *Harold Bauer: His Book* by Harold Bauer, by permission of W. W. Norton & Company, Inc., copyright, 1948, by W. W. Norton & Company, Inc.

played orchestral work, the *Rumanian Rhapsody* (for which, incidentally, he does not receive a penny of royalties, as he neglected to have it copyrighted), has followed Fritz Kreisler's career since 1903 not only as a friend, fellow composer, and violinistic colleague, but also as a music pedagogue. He had this to say:

"Fritz as a human being is good to the core of his heart. He is a total, complete, rounded-off artist and man. He is never malicious, always generous. We clicked from the beginning, partly, I suppose, because we both so intensely admired Eugène Ysaÿe.

"As to his compositions, I think Fritz's cadenza to Tartini's 'Devil's Trill' Sonata is one of the finest things he has written. Recently I heard his 'Viennese Rhapsodic Fantasietta' for the first time. Fritz played parts of it for me on the piano and then followed it up with a phonograph recording of which Harriet said it was poor, yet which showed me that as a composition this latest work is excellent. Fritz, like myself, was at first not careful about copyrights and royalties, so that, I believe, he is without income from his 'Caprice viennois.' That piece is played by everybody, whereas his string quartet is almost forgotten."

Enesco was disturbed to hear that Kreisler had stated he no longer composed as he felt his genre had outlived our times.

"Those things come in cycles," Enesco insisted. "When a thing is good, it should be written no matter what the present generation thinks of it. At present there is too much emphasis on mechanical perfection. But that will pass, just as the striving of atonalists now is back to tonality—witness Schönberg and Hindemith. No, Fritz should go on composing."

Pablo Casals from his retreat on the French side of the Pyrenees, from which he has vowed he will not return to his native Spain until the dictatorship is at an end, wrote me a beautiful, brief letter in French from which the following is quoted:

> As regards dear Kreisler, whom I haven't seen since his concert with my orchestra in Barcelona, I retain not only the most beautiful memories of his personality and of his art, but also the joy and honor associated with all the occasions which he afforded me for making music with him.

Pablo Casals, about 1973

Mischa Elman

Efrem Zimbalist

I salute in him the last crowned head of the Joachim-Sarasate-Ysaÿe dynasty.

Mischa Elman, one of the few persons to whom Kreisler dedicated one of his compositions (the Rondino on a Theme by Beethoven), thought he could best illustrate his regard for his colleague by narrating an unusual duplicity of cases of a lapse in memory.

"Some years ago," Elman recalled, "Fritz Kreisler was to play in Chicago and I happened to be in the city. Of course, I went to hear him. After a terrific program he played the Rondino as an encore. Now, there are various repetitions of the theme and each time it is slightly different. In the third repetition Kreisler's mind wandered, or something—at any rate he 'strayed off the reservation.' We all teased him afterward that, after having played a long and difficult program so well, he should have had a lapse in his own composition. He laughed heartily with the rest of us.

"Some months later I played in Carnegie Hall. I espied Fritz Kreisler among the listeners. So I, too, played his Rondino as an encore. Believe it or not—I got stuck at exactly the same point.

"I ask you: could I have paid him a greater compliment than that?"

Efrem Zimbalist, with whom Kreisler made one of his favorite recordings, the Bach Double Concerto for two violins, wrote this tribute:

I am grateful to be given this opportunity to say a few words about Fritz Kreisler. By good fortune I was on many occasions in a position to observe his genius at close range and my admiration for it is unbounded.

It is well for us indeed that Kreisler, the violinist, is also Kreisler, the composer. The incomparable charm, the warmth, the exquisite taste which he imparts both in his playing and composing, assures him, perhaps the only one of the performing artists of today, of a permanent place in the hearts of the future generations.

Adolf Busch, the most noted of his German colleagues, wrote from Switzerland:

When I first heard Fritz Kreisler, he was a young man and I was a boy. From his first note on his violin (he played the Mendelssohn Concerto) I was enchanted. It was his beautiful violin playing *and* his musicianship which I have enjoyed ever since then.

So I am one of his greatest and oldest admirers and I feel grateful to him for giving me so much joy and *Anregung* * through his great art of violin playing and music making.

Albert Spalding had this to say about his colleague and friend of many years standing:

"Fritz's commanding humanity makes you believe in magic when you hear him. His over-all conception, the curve of a phrase—all this is magical. What some of the youngsters do mechanically today is stupendous. But isn't it true that, no matter how perfect you may become mechanically, you can never equal the machine? The perfect thing in an artist's life should be his aspiration, not the fulfillment. For, if once you have fulfilled completely, you have set up a barrier to further progress. Fritz Kreisler keeps forever striving.

"Very rarely do you find in a performing artist a more happy balance between heart and mind than Fritz possesses. What an equilibrium is his! I suppose that's where, in part, his spell comes from.

"During the summer of 1948 an evening of music making took place in our summer home in the Berkshires, shortly after the conclusion of which Jacques Gordon died. Fritz was also vacationing in the Berkshires, but had not brought any violin with him. I offered him my Guarnerius but he declined to deprive me of it. So I brought out my Montagnana, known as the 'Mighty Venetian.' Now, Fritz had not drawn a bow for weeks, yet he soon played magnificently. Fact is, he drew on his inexhaustible reservoir and made bow and fingers obey his commands as usual."

In his published autobiography Spalding recalls a discussion by Kreisler of Sibelius which he describes as "one of the most searching appraisals that I have heard." His friend Fritz is there represented as saying: †

"One of the most significant and original qualities of Sibelius' music is its rather irregular use of rhythmical patterns, like different planes of perspective slightly out of focus. They make their entrances and exits at totally unexpected moments. The harmonic structure is simple, sometimes even conven-

* Stimulation.

† Reprinted from *Rise to Follow—An Autobiography* by Albert Spalding, by permission of Henry Holt and Company, Inc., copyright, 1943, by Albert Spalding.

Albert Spalding, autographed in 1920's

Joseph Szigeti, autographed "To Prof. Lev Ginsberg . . . 1962"

Jascha Heifetz

tional, but these architectural innovations produce an altogether new picture."

"El Greco achieves the same effect in painting—the distortion that is so fascinating," I suggested.

"Exactly," agreed Kreisler. "Before you is an altered world—a world with an added dimension."

Joseph Szigeti, for whom Fritz Kreisler smoothed the path in America by acting as his self-appointed advance agent in 1923, has closed his autobiography with so unique and spontaneous a tribute to his older colleague that no later requested expression could possibly improve upon it. Szigeti's book ends as follows: *

I recalled an incident at a Kreisler rehearsal in the Paris Opera one morning about ten years ago . . . Kreisler was playing a concerto by Mozart (that "supreme internationalist and equalitarian in art," as Olin Downes felicitously put it)—playing with that intense, human mellowness of his which speaks to all peoples, to all classes, to all ages. The conductor was Philippe Gaubert, and his face, as well as those of the musicians, reflected the joy of participating in an ineffably beautiful musical moment. At last Gaubert could not contain himself any longer, and—even while conducting—blurted out: "How that man plays! How beautifully. . . . *comme s'il était français!*"

The insularity of that praise—which was intended to be all-encompassing—shattered the enchantment of the moment, for me at least. But I quickly recovered what the well-meaning Frenchman had made me lose. Kreisler was still playing, and I silently corrected Gaubert's "*comme s'il était français*" by going beyond that, beyond even Goethe's "Good European," to the highest rung of praise: "He plays like . . . a citizen of the world!"

Jascha Heifetz's every word indicated his affection and reverence for the older master.

"At the beginning of my career I tried to imitate Kreisler," he said. "Coming out of Russia, it was a great experience for me to hear him as far back as 1912 in a concert in Berlin Philharmonic Hall.

"Since then, through the years, we have met frequently—at Efrem Zimbalist's, at the Schellings', at Paul Kochansky's, often alternating with other musicians at these musical parties. And of course you know about the dinner in Fritz's honor by the Bohemian Club, when Albert

* Reprinted from *With Strings Attached* by Joseph Szigeti, by permission of Alfred A. Knopf, Incorporated, copyright, 1947, by Alfred A. Knopf, Incorporated.

Spalding was made up like Kreisler and I played backstage, imitating Fritz's style.

"After his deplorable accident in 1941, his friends tried to get Fritz back into circulation socially. Mme. Kochansky one afternoon gave a cocktail party for old friends. We all tried carefully to avoid every reference to his accident. Somebody, however, inadvertently introduced the subject we tried to avoid, by asking him whether he had a good memory for numbers.

"Kreisler replied, 'I have never been good at numbers. On the other hand, I now remember all sorts of notes I used to forget.' We felt greatly relieved. He himself had broken the ice by referring to his mishap.

"Incidentally, we have the same birthday dates, and so at times I found our names signed in books on the same page. Once when I signed for the Queen of Norway, I found the names of Fritz Kreisler and Lord Kitchener under the same date."

Yehudi Menuhin's father took infinite pains to locate his son, who was concertizing in South America, in time to elicit an expression for this biography. Yehudi Menuhin wrote:

Fritz Kreisler is one of the best colleagues, one of the greatest gentlemen and most gentle characters I know. These characteristics have glowed through his music, and no public, during his long career, has been at a loss to recognize them. He is a human being whose every heartbeat is a feeling and a reality. He entertains no false ideas, bears no false pride, knows no vanity, has no false ambitions, and does not hide under any masks. When one meets him one knows him, and one will never be let down by assuming from the first his goodness, kindness, sympathy, and, let us never forget, his great ability. His tone, the favorite violin tone of all time, is beloved and admired by millions the world over. That tone expresses the man. No other violin tone, no matter how lush, how big, how vibrant, or how pure, has ever moved human beings in the same way. I would say no other tone has been produced by the same soul.

I first met Fritz Kreisler in Berlin when I made my debut in that capital of music, playing the three B's—Bach, Beethoven and Brahms concertos—with Bruno Walter. Since then, Fritz Kreisler has never changed, although I, of course, have changed a great deal as, at that time, I was but thirteen years old. Upon various occasions during these twenty years, we have met in various

Kreisler and a youthful Yehudi Menuhin

Zino R. Francescatti

Nathan Milstein

countries of Europe and New York, and I have always looked up to Fritz Kreisler as the most lovable and understanding of colleagues.

Zino R. Francescatti, arriving from a European tour just as this book went to the printer, expressed himself in these exuberant terms in a letter to me:

In every career, and particularly in that of the artist, you need to look at a bright sun to show you the difficult path, to help your earnest exertions. My sun has always been Fritz Kreisler. Since my first *balbutiements* * on my quarter-size violin he has been my artistic god.

One of the first "hits" and preferred pieces of mine was what we then called *Le Pugnani,* i.e., the Praeludium and Allegro in the style of Pugnani, one of his master pieces. My first His Master's Voice recordings 'way back in 1920 were Caprice Viennois, Liebesfreud, Liebesleid.

My father, who was my teacher, always said to me: you don't need to hear many violinists to have a kaleidoscopic view of the musical and technical violin inspiration—Kreisler has everything.

I shall always remember a Sunday in 1912, in the *Salle Prat* of Marseilles. Kreisler was playing Beethoven. I was just a kid, but my violin knowledge was far ahead of my age. I was in a state of ecstacy. My eyes stared at those heavenly fingers. And then came his own cadenza, which at that time had not yet been published. I must confess that those three minutes of miracle, bewilderment, wonder, surprise, and emotion are the greatest musical souvenir of my life.

We owe so much to that great artist. He has enriched the violin repertory more than any other composer. He has created the modern form of violin recital, and you could hardly make up a violin program without a Kreisler number.

His heroic stage presence, his dynamic rhythm, his pathetic and noble tone, the greatness of his musical enunciation, and his aristocratic way of approach to music are the canon of perfection every artist craves to realize. And for those who have the good fortune to know the man, his kindness, his simplicity, his sincerity, his smile, the universality of his ideas—you do not wonder why everybody loves and respects Fritz Kreisler.

The comment by Nathan Milstein, for whom Fritz Kreisler seems especially to enjoy playing piano accompaniments, has been placed last because certain of his observations were modestly challenged by Fritz when they happened to be introduced in the course of a chat

* Stammerings.

with me on violinistic progress through the centuries. Milstein said:

"The influence of Fritz Kreisler will be a lasting one. His arrangements point a new way, as do his cadenzas. He gave violin technique a new life.

"Take his way of writing double stops: Wieniawski and Sarasate also wrote things with double stops, but they were in parallels and for purposes of virtuosity. Kreisler often uses two themes, without, however, one killing the other, in double stop passages." Milstein went to the piano to illustrate his meaning from the Kreisler cadenza for the first movement of the Beethoven Concerto. "'That was epoch-making. He developed new violinistic thought.

"The artist should look not only after the content but also the texture of his playing. Joachim no doubt had the content. But it was probably all wool. With Fritz Kreisler there is wool, and silk, and cotton, and velvet.

"Kreisler injects a great personality. Whatever he does, there is still a great artist; the total impression is always that of someone who has a conception and a line. On the technical side Fritz Kreisler showed so many new things that we must all be grateful to him.

"His arrangements have been superb. They brought out things for the violin we never dreamed of.

"The violin was brought forward, advanced, by three persons—Bach, Paganini, and Kreisler.

"Personally, I love him. Nothing too nice can be said about him."

It was Milstein's reference to Bach, Paganini, and Kreisler as the trio to whom the violin owes its progress which drew a protest from the third mentioned.

"All artists have advanced their instrument," Fritz Kreisler insisted. "I learned an enormous lot from Ysaÿe. We also all learned from Wieniawski and Vieuxtemps. And then there was Joachim. He must be credited with colossal advancement of the violin. He dug up things by Mozart and Bach that we would never have heard of except for him. Then take Brahms—his use of the sixth was a distinct advancement, as was Schubert's use of the seventh, expressed in his famous String Quintet. Wagner used the quart. And so on. All helped

Eugène Ysaÿe

Joseph Joachim

Nicolo Paganini, 1782-1840

the advancement of the violin. And don't forget Joachim made the Mendelssohn Violin Concerto famous."

"Yes, but you made the Elgar Concerto famous," I reminded him.

"No," Fritz replied. "There you have one of those interesting situations in musical history. I certainly did everything I could to make it popular, but it is seldom played. Hence, I did *not* succeed as Joachim did with the Mendelssohn Concerto.

"Take Ernö Dohnányi: when he was still quite a young lad he composed a string sextet which is simply marvelous. Brahms as president of the Vienna Musikverein was enthusiastic about it and asked a group of us to play it. We did. Today, alas, it is almost forgotten.

"But to return to our friend Milstein: with all my affection for him, he is in error when he thinks that after Paganini nobody really advanced the violin until I came along."

Neither Kreisler nor Milstein were probably aware of the fact that the late Henry T. Finck, eminent music critic and essayist, as far back as 1916 had said:

> It has been said that there have been only three composers who could write in the best violin style—Bach, Paganini, and Kreisler. Paganini . . . exhausted the possibilities of technical display. Bach had a violin style of his own, in which "double stops" play a big role. In Kreisler's cadenzas . . . and in his own compositions, these harmonies resulting from "double stops" . . . assume such importance as to pen up a new era in violin music. When he plays, it often sounds as if two violinists were performing a duo—two Kreislers!

Everybody who has ever heard Kreisler, whether he be a professional musician or a layman, realizes that there is a unique appeal to his playing—a sweetness that is not effeminate; a gripping at the heartstrings which nobody can resist; a mastery of technique which enables him to stand above mechanical difficulties and concentrate exclusively upon the spiritual side of his art; above all, a warm-hearted, genuine humanity that exudes love for all mankind, and that casts a magic spell over all who see this unusual personality in action.

To the student of the violin, however, Kreisler's playing is also absorbing from a purely technical standpoint. How does he do it? is a question which many a young and aspiring fiddler has asked himself during and after a Kreisler concert.

Carl Flesch, one of Germany's greatest violin pedagogues and violinists and a friend of Kreisler's for many years, commented on the technical side of Fritz's art in his *Problems of Tone Production:* *

> The use of the *vibrato* during passages, mainly introduced by Kreisler, signifies one of the most important achievements of modern violinistic art. . . . Certain it is that the vibrato . . . is already valued as one of the indispensable parts of contemporary playing. Considered from a purely tonal point of view, it does away, above all, with that dry, etude-like character during *détaché* bowing which is apt to let passage work of this kind appear as foreign matter in the organization of the living art work.
>
> As regards bowing, here again, of course, the personality of the player will point the way. . . . Kreisler favors approach to the bridge with resulting stronger pressure and less bow strength.

We have seen what eminent colleagues of the bow have had to say about Fritz Kreisler, as a personality and concerning his technique. They all agree on the unique position which he has secured—a position which, he never fails to point out, he has achieved with the selfless, self-effacing help of his wife.

This outstanding exponent of his art has never placed himself apart from, or above, his fellow artists. Quite the contrary. He can become as enthusiastic as a young music student over an especially significant interpretation or an exceptionally beautiful tone drawn by the bow of a much younger and less experienced colleague.

"I always listen to street fiddlers," he once told me. "They may scratch and screech, poor fellows, but if I wait long enough, suddenly there is a beautiful tone or a novel turn of phrase which has made it worth my while to linger on. One can always learn, even from a poor alley player."

Expanding this thought somewhat, he said on another occasion: †

* Reprinted from *Problems of Tone Production* by Carl Flesch, by permission of Carl Fischer, Inc., copyright, 1931, by Carl Flesch, Baden-Baden, 1934, by Carl Fischer, Inc., New York.

† Reproduced by permission of *Etude, The Music Magazine*, from an article by Rose Heylbut, "Philosophy of Musicianship," copyright, 1944, by Theodore Presser Company.

Carl Flesch, 1873-1944

Flesch with unidentified students

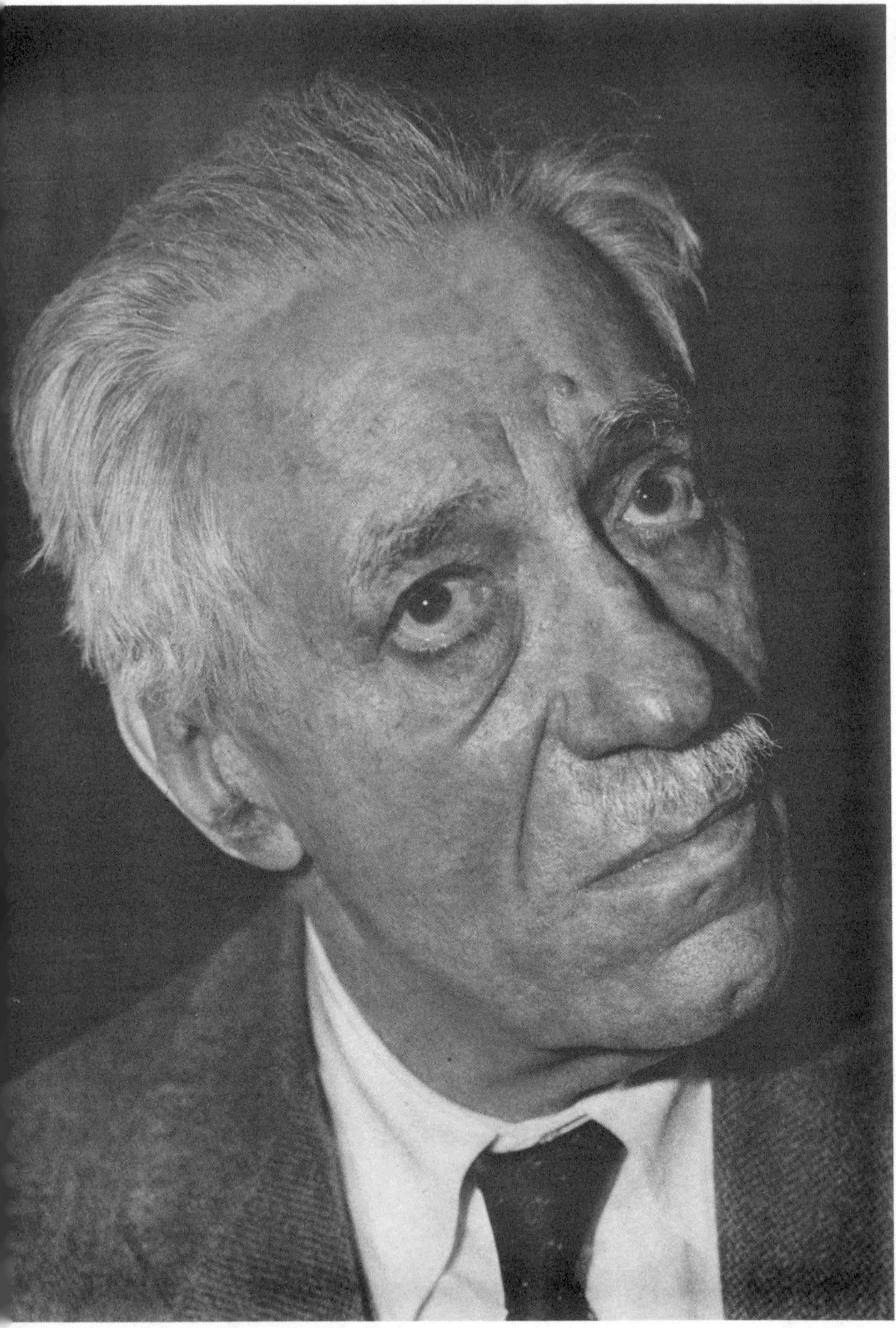

Kreisler in his later years

"Musicianship means constant alertness, constant learning. And there is no one from whom one cannot learn. More than once, I have stood near a poor street fiddler and have learned something from him. Certainly, his tonal and technical equipment was not of the finest—and yet in a human way inflections and emphases have come to light that have shown me something I did not realize before.

"To my mind, it all comes back to the conviction that musicianship is the most direct expression of personality. Thus one way of perfecting musicianship is to conquer oneself, to rid oneself of meanness, to live the sort of life one can admire. The 'artist's life' in its best manifestation is anything but a round of fun, parties, and gaiety! It is a constant problem of values, a constant desire to be the person one wants to be. Certainly no one ever reaches his ideal, but the act of striving does something to the spirit that can never be lost.

"The true artist is, in Henley's words, 'the captain of his soul.' And when those sheerly human qualities shine forth from his playing, he convinces others. Tone, technique, fleetness are never goals in themselves. They are simply the means by which the artist makes manifest those thoughts, feelings and aspirations for which he can never find words."

CHAPTER THIRTY-ONE

HOBBIES, HABITS, AND MISTAKEN IDENTITIES

FROM time to time a picture has been drawn for the reader of Fritz Kreisler's physical appearance in this or that decade, as seen by some keen contemporary. The uniqueness and the peculiarities of his art have been pointed out. His relation to his fellow men has been traced. His character has revealed itself through his words and actions.

Relatively little has hitherto been said, however, of his hobbies, his personal habits, his prejudices, if any. Yet these little things in the lives of distinguished contemporaries are of quite as great interest as are the big, outstanding things and events.

Dogs, with their fidelity and sympathetic understanding for their master, ranked high with Fritz during the many years that he kept them. No matter how busy he might otherwise be, he would walk them. Coming down the gangplank of an ocean liner, he often held his Stradivarius or Guarnerius in one hand, the leash for his dog or dogs in the other.

"Just imagine a human being with the character of a dog!" he said on one occasion.* "He would be loving, thankful, true, strong, graceful, and Heaven knows what else. A true demigod!"

He then recalled that Bismarck was once found lying on the floor crying because one of his dogs had died. "When my fox terrier died,"

* Reprinted from *Fritz Kreisler on Himself*, in the January, 1933 issue of *The Strad*, by permission of *The Strad*, London.

he continued, referring to Rexie's death in 1931, "I did not go to quite such lengths, though I found it quite natural to fly from Detroit to New York and to cancel some concerts so as to see my dog once more before it died. He was my wife's and my own very best friend."

It is a sign of the affection in which Fritz Kreisler is universally held that the news that Rexie had died caused many people to send telegrams of condolence. Some even sent flowers, all of which the Kreislers turned over to hospitals. This unusual expression of sympathy stirred even the French magazine *Comoedia* to describe the throngs that came to the funeral of a mere canine.

In January of 1932 Fritz Kreisler traveled to London to "find a successor to my best pal, Rex. It is as though I had lost a friend. I am now going to try to obtain one of his brothers or sisters. I must have another Rex and England is the best place to get a wire-haired terrier." He succeeded.

Yehudi Menuhin, outstanding representative of the younger generation of violinists, recently contributed this side light on the Kreislers' love for dogs in a personal letter:

> I remember one of our meetings when he and his wonderfully devoted Harriet came down a few floors in the Hotel Raphael in Paris to visit me. I heard the trample of many things, and a pawing and hoofing, which at first I could not explain. I opened the door to find Fritz and Harriet, accompanied by two great dogs.
>
> Both these people would have been the most wonderful parents and they must always be surrounded, even when they are most alone, with objects of tenderness and love, and there they were—tramping down the stairs to dinner with their two, I believe, most beloved companions—their two dogs.

In the course of his married life Kreisler has had three police dogs, several fox terriers, and an Airedale. His Rexie and his Jerry, which were shipped to him from Germany after World War II had broken out, attained the ripe old age of fourteen and thirteen years, respectively. None of the dogs appear to have shared their master's love for music—quite the contrary!

In one respect, however, dog and master had an affinity: they both got their thrill through their spine. In the course of an interview with the *Musical Observer* Kreisler said:

"There is only one critical judgment I can rely upon—the verdict of the spine. If I feel a thrill down my spine, from my own work or that of any other man, I know that it is good. Let the critics say what they will. There is no finer test. And if an artist never knows that thrill, or loses it, he is in the wrong business."

As if to prove his point, he called the interviewer's attention to Rexie, who was playing on the floor. "See," he said, "his tail is funniest when it lies flat on the rug and when he sways it—so. He gets his thrill through the spine!"

Doormen at the apartment house where the Kreislers live like to recall the days when Fritz used to take his dogs for a daily walk. "Often he would sit down on a bench," one of them said, "and the children of the neighborhood would come to play with the dogs. They hadn't the faintest idea that they were in the presence of one of the great men of our time."

Kreisler's love for animals was not limited to dogs. All over his beautiful Grunewald estate bird houses were erected and bird food was spread in winter as well as in summer. Kreisler even instructed his gardener that some cherries must be left on the cherry trees so that the birds, too, might get their share.

The outdoor life has always had a great appeal for Fritz. His various accompanists like to talk of the times when they strolled with him on long walks. He was then completely relaxed.

One pronounced hobby of his was his love for old clothes. At luncheons in Berlin he invariably wore the same dark gray business suit.

"I have become so attached to it that I don't like to part with it," he said to me in the 1920's. "The same thing applies to the dress suit that I wear during my concerts. I believe I have five new dress suits hanging in my wardrobe, which my wife insisted upon my having made whenever the fashion changed slightly. But I don't feel comfortable in them when I'm on the stage. So I always return to my good old dress suit, although the collar has had to be renewed twelve or thirteen times."

Occasionally, wrong conclusions are drawn from this love of old clothes. Vernon Crane, of *Collier's*, vouches for the accuracy of this occurrence which he related:

"Quite recently two of my lady friends were traveling in an eastbound Fifty-seventh Street crosstown bus in New York. It was a rainy day. Huddled in one corner, in an old, rain-bespattered coat and clutching a violin case, was a kindly old gentleman.

" 'Look at that poor old man,' one of the two ladies said compassionately. 'He has probably been standing out on the street all day playing and must now go home on account of the rain.'

"The other lady had another look. 'Why,' she exclaimed, 'that's Fritz Kreisler!' "

Kreisler never had valets or chefs accompanying him when on tour, nor did he engage special railway cars as did Paderewski. He would never permit his accompanist, Carl Lamson, to carry his baggage. "You have your own to carry," he would say, if perchance there was no porter around.

Lamson did, as a matter of fact, look after his friend Fritz in another way. "I always carried an extra set of cuff and collar buttons in my vest pocket," he said, "for Fritz was always losing his." He also revealed that he usually had to tie Fritz's cravat for him.

A so-called "road manager," assigned to him by his concert agency, was the only additional person he would permit in his entourage. This person not only saw to tickets, hotel accommodations, schedules, and so forth, but acted as a very necessary buffer between himself and pests who wanted to take advantage of his good nature.

At no period of his life did Fritz ever keep a diary, nor does he possess a scrapbook tracing his professional career. He did not even attach enough importance to his own manuscripts to preserve them. "Do you bother to keep the manuscripts of your books?" he countered when I chided him for this. The Library of Congress, at the time of his donating the original manuscripts of Brahms's Violin Concerto and Chausson's *Poème* in 1948, was more than eager to display, alongside these two treasures, some original work by Kreisler. Search as he might, Kreisler could find no manuscript of his own compositions!

Only at the eleventh hour, when this book was ready for the press, Charles Foley ran across a cadenza for a Mozart violin concerto, the only music manuscript by Kreisler in his possession. It is here reproduced:

1)

Concerto N° 3 (G-major) (Köchel N° 206)

Mozart

Cadenzas

I First movement (1 and 2)

Fritz Kreisler 1946.

Wolfgang Amadeus Mozart, 1756-1791

Pablo Casals visiting Kreisler in 1958

When asked whether he had any superstitions, such as artists usually have, Fritz Kreisler replied: "No, I have always fought against that."

"Any talismans or charms?"

"No. The only thing I always liked to have with me was a collection of pencils. One of them, at least, must have an eraser, I insisted, so that I might write down my musical inspirations immediately and make corrections as I went along.

"When I was younger, I always had a ring around my tie. Nothing modern: it had to be something ancient. This fad of mine started when an Egyptologist many years ago gave me a ring with the head of Medusa."

(Earlier photographs of Kreisler show a ring at the lower end of the knot of a four-in-hand tie.)

Besides being an inveterate moviegoer when on tour, Kreisler is fond of attending the theater with his wife, not, however, to steep himself in profound problems or to endure sex plays, but solely to amuse and divert himself.

That he loves card games of various kinds and is an excellent chess player has already become evident from various episodes related earlier. He can entertain charmingly with coin tricks. His passion for books will receive special attention in the next chapter.

Gretchen Finletter, a daughter of Walter Damrosch, from her long life with her father has arrived at the conclusion that all musicians are good eaters and often excellent raconteurs. She is certainly right about Kreisler. Fritz is noted among his friends as an amusing storyteller. And he loves good food. That is, after, and not before, a concert. Before a concert he merely sips a little tea and has a slice or two of toast.

Viennese cooking is understandably his favorite. But he loves Italian dishes almost as much. In New York, as already intimated, he is fond of going to Del Pezzo's Italian restaurant on West Forty-sixth Street, because of its delicious clams and also because of its special Zabboni wine. Everything, however, is within limits strictly prescribed by his wife, who knows his tendency to take on weight and who watches his blood pressure carefully!

Fritz always derived pleasure from those rare occasions when he could go through an evening unrecognized and be simply Mr. Kreisler. One day in the late thirties there was a dinner at the home of the American chargé d'affaires in Berlin. Seated next to Kreisler was an Italian-German baron who "sounded off" on every conceivable subject. Books, politics, music: on everything he considered himself an authority, and he did not hesitate to pontificate on any topic that arose.

When the baron proved utterly wrong on an assertion about some musical matter, Kreisler dared mildly to disagree. The baron clamped his monocle tightly into his eye, looked at his neighbor condescendingly, and said, "Oh, are you perchance a musician?"

With a mischievous twinkle Kreisler replied, "I fiddle a little." Only much later in the evening did someone bother to inform the baron who his table companion had been. He made his departure quite abruptly.

It was inevitable that frequent instances of mistaken identity should occur in Fritz Kreisler's life, all the more so in view of his similarity in appearance to Giacomo Puccini * and the similarity in pronunciation of his name to that of Walter Chrysler, the automobile magnate, and Herbert Arvin Crisler, football coach of the University of Michigan.

Hugh Gibson, former United States ambassador, one day gave a cocktail party to which, among others, a Polish count and Fritz were invited. The ambassador was at pains to tell his Polish friend, who arrived first, that he would see to it that he had a chance for a good chat with the famous Mr. Kreisler.

Kreisler arrived and Gibson managed to get the two men off into a corner for a huddle. Busy though he was receiving other guests and chatting with them, he nevertheless watched the proceedings in the corner with interest and, after a while, with some concern. As far as he could judge, the conversation between the two men was monosyllabic and dragging.

* See p. 134.

Fritz Kreisler had another engagement and left. As the company gradually thinned out, Gibson joined his Polish friend. "Well, how did you two make out?" he asked.

"Frankly," said the count, "I am a bit surprised at your great industrialists, if Mr. Kreisler is an example. I talked about motors and chassis and differentials and streamlined models, but Mr. Kreisler did not seem particularly interested."

Carl Lamson overheard in a hotel lobby how one traveling salesman said to another, "That's Fritz Kreisler over there." The person so informed replied, "Funny that he should be here; I thought this was Ford Week!"

Both Kreisler and Lamson stated that young people quite frequently come to Fritz to say: "You are the great football player, are you not? Do you still coach?" The Michigan Crisler is now generally nicknamed Fritz. Both "Fritzes" have been photographed together.

Legendary figure that Fritz Kreisler has become, certain anecdotes are associated with his name that may be good stories but have nothing to do with truth.

There is the story, for instance, of his allegedly entertaining a party all evening with card tricks. At the end of the evening one of the guests asked whether Kreisler would be willing to give a performance in his home. "Talk it over with my agent," is said to have been Fritz Kreisler's reply.

The night of the rich's man party came and Kreisler arrived with his violin. The host took one look at it and exclaimed, "Good heavens, and you can play the fiddle, too?"

Or there is the story of his playing in a Montana town where cowboys formed the greater part of the audience. His manager had placed the Chaconne by Bach on the program, but Kreisler, fearing this was too high-brow, substituted a lighter work.

That night, so the story goes, there was a rap at the door of his apartment in the hotel. When Kreisler opened the door, a huge, broad-shouldered cowboy, leading his ten-year-old daughter by the hand, entered, pulled out his six-shooter and said: "You cheated us. You played a different number from the one on the program. My daughter wants to hear what was on the program. You play it or—"

According to the legend, Kreisler played for some minutes, when the cowboy interrupted with, "Rotten," took his daughter by the hand again, and walked out.

Why include these two apocryphal stories? Their significance lies in the fact that legends are being woven around the name of Fritz Kreisler. Were he not such an outstanding man, nobody would bother to invent anecdotes about him.

The fact is, Fritz Kreisler has become a household word. It is taken for granted that every intelligent reader knows his name. For instance, in a recent article on Ed Macauley, St. Louis University basketball star, this significant sentence testifies to Kreisler's popularity even among sports fans: *

> They don't call him Easy Ed for nothing. . . . I have never seen a smoother player. *He handles a basketball as gracefully as Fritz Kreisler does a violin.*

* Reprinted from *Ed Macauley* by Paul Tredway, in the January 30, 1949 issue of *This Week Magazine*.

CHAPTER THIRTY-TWO

THE TWILIGHT

[1945-1950]

For sixty-one years Fritz Kreisler has stood on the concert platform—longer than any violinist in history. He and Harriet have reached the twilight of their rich and eventful lives. One might well wish that an old age free from sorrows and worries had been granted them. But such is not the case.

Harriet has been ailing for years, and of late has been spending more time in bed and at the physician's than ever. Fritz wrote from their annual summer residence in Stockbridge, Massachusetts:

> She is resting quietly and would certainly recuperate better if she did not excite herself constantly. Unfortunately, I am quite powerless in this respect, for even if I can segregate her from people and reporters, I cannot from the mail, the telephone, the papers and the radio. At any rate she feels much better in this quiet spot than in the turbulence and the turmoil of Babylon-on-the-Hudson.

The "turbulence and turmoil" in New York is no fiction. It is amazing how many people telephone to Harriet Kreisler for advice and assistance. The telephone next to her bed is seldom quiet. Her charities are as absorbing as ever, her concern about the problems of her friends as keen as ever.

Fritz, too, has not been well. An operation for appendicitis in June, 1946, seems not to have affected him much. But his grave traffic accident in 1941 has not only interfered somewhat with his memory (not his musical memory, fortunately, as has been emphasized before), but has resulted in a slight impairment of his hearing and has been the indirect cause of an eye condition which necessitated an operation

With proper treatment this condition, fortunately, improves constantly.*

But it is not only personal ailments that are casting a cloud over their old age. No sooner had World War II ended, than the full details of the destruction wrought in Berlin by air action became known to them. Their exquisitely beautiful home in Grunewald was a ghastly heap of rubble. With it were lost priceless mementos, art objects, Oriental rugs, a collection of china, costly tapestries, and all those intangibles that made the Kreisler home what it was.

Here again, however, Fritz Kreisler's inner strength of character, born of a deep religiosity and keen absorption of the philosophies of the ages, triumphed over adversity. His chief concern was not for the lost and destroyed property, but for the safety of his servants, for whose pay throughout the war he had made provision before he left Germany in 1939. He requested the writer, then on duty in Germany as war correspondent, to obtain all possible information about them, and in a letter expressed his joy that "our dear employes in the Bismarck-Allee, our maid and our chauffeur and his wife, are alive and in fairly good health."

In another letter he referred only incidentally to the destruction of the home, saying, "You can imagine that the news was sad for both of us, although one had to be prepared for everything." Once he had established contact with his servants, he wrote them that it was much more important for him that his wife was safe and sound at his side, than that his Berlin home be intact.

As they contemplate the state of the world today, Fritz and Harriet are somewhat resentful about the lighthearted, not to say callous, way in which the offspring of some of their dearest friends of earlier days are accepting a postwar situation replete with misery and suffering. They find it difficult to believe that the same persons who think nothing of paying $100 for a plate at some banquet where they will find

* Years ago, a ship reporter asked him, "Would you rather lose your hearing or your eyesight?" to which he replied without a moment's hesitation: "My hearing. I have heard much that is music, but there is still so much I wish to see. I love to read. There is much yet to be read. After all, I can hear music when I read it. I could do without my ears if there were a need. In fact, often I hear more beautiful things when I read music than when it is played."

The Kreisler home in Berlin, 1933 and 1945

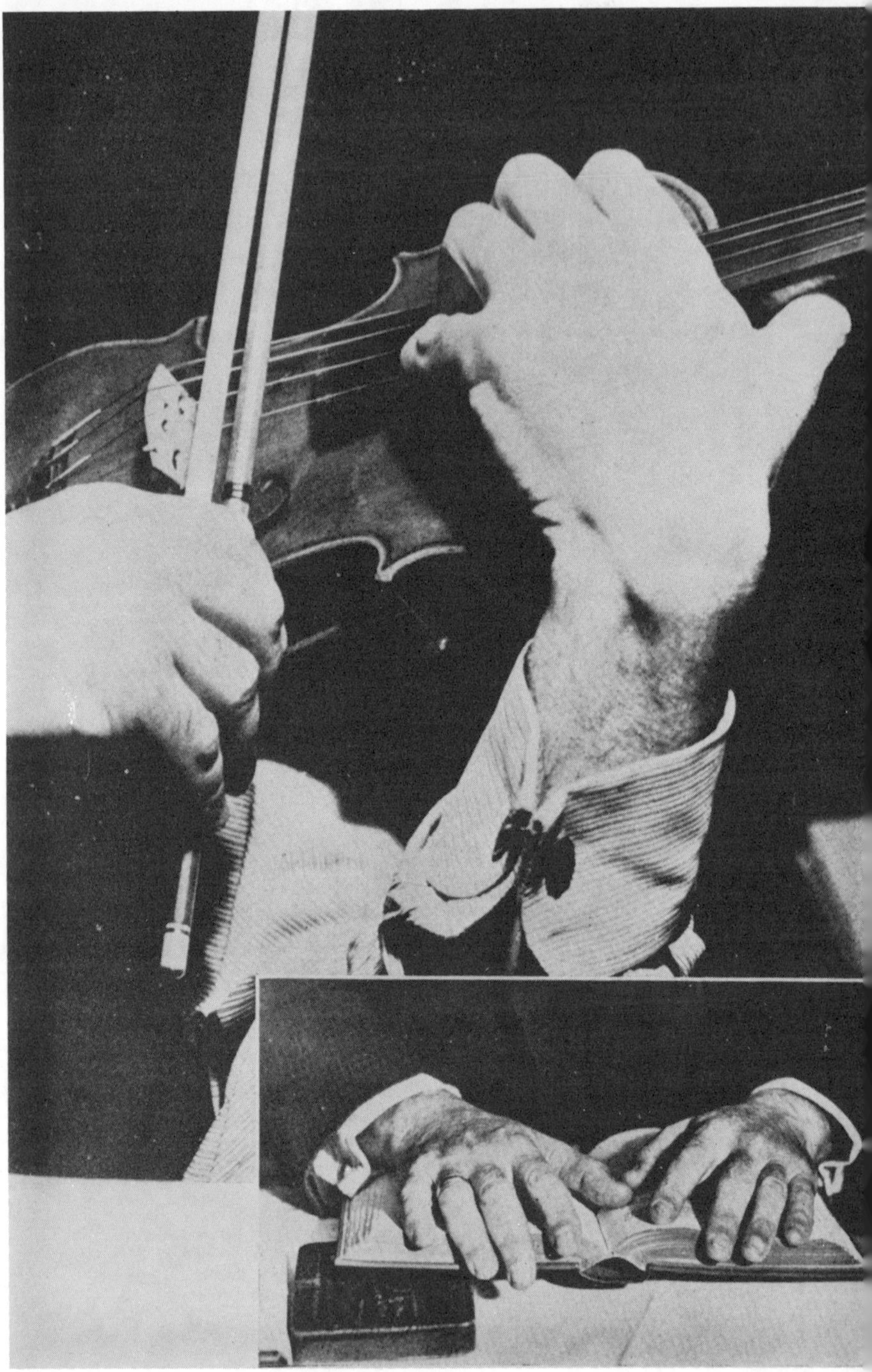

Close-range views of Kreisler's hands

themselves among, or next to, certain celebrities can ignore the suggestion that they make $10 available for this or that great servant of humanity whom the European upheaval has, without any fault of his own, pauperized.

Experiences of this sort make them more and more retiring. They seldom go out and just as seldom receive guests. They are always glad, however, if kindred spirits drop in upon them.

As after the Great War of 1914–1918, so also after the recent World War, Fritz and Harriet Kreisler are devoting large portions of their accumulated savings to the relief of distress in Europe. I chanced to come to the Kreisler apartment one day late in 1948 when Harriet had just bought two thousand pairs of shoes for destitute German children. One room in the apartment is set aside exclusively for gifts to Europe. It looks like a veritable bazaar, stocked with food, clothing, shoes, bales of cloth, and minor household utensils of the kind that Americans take for granted but that are now lacking in war-scarred Europe. There are also many toys, which go to the Martin Luther Hospital in Berlin-Grunewald, St. Dunstan's in England, to Cardinal Innitzer in Vienna for needy children, and to other institutions serving children. Fritz Kreisler's hands, which in younger years traveled many a mile up and down the fingerboards of his violins, now are engaged for many an hour in tieing relief packages.

When a friend called the attention of the Kreislers to the fact that many thefts of food have been reported from Europe, Harriet calmly replied: "What if some food is stolen; it is eaten by somebody! Even a dishonest postmaster has a family that must eat."

Instead of sending Christmas gifts to friends, the Kreislers now send a CARE package in the name of the friend to some needy family in Europe. The friend has a touching compensation for the nonarrival of a gift in the letter of thanks he or she receives from the family in Europe that has benefited from Kreisler munificence.

It goes without saying that American charities are not being forgotten amid all the concern of Harriet and Fritz for the suffering underprivileged of Europe. The greatest single gift of this kind is the sum of $120,372.50, allotted in January, 1949, to the Golden Rule Foundation and the Lenox Hill Hospital of New York City. It represents the proceeds from the sale of the famous Kreisler library of incunabula, rare early printed books and illuminated manuscripts, costly first editions and old prints.

Next to violins, worth-while books have been dearest to Kreisler's collector's heart. The 174 items auctioned on January 27 and 28, 1949, represent a painstaking effort covering some forty years.

"Collecting books in a sense makes one a slave," Fritz commented one day. "One never knows when to stop. It takes up so much time, and book agents pester you and you race around buying this and that until it is like a fever. I dare say five-eighths of my personal money—my spending money—went into books. I bought books in Marseilles, Florence, London, Paris, Berlin, Vienna—wherever the opportunity offered itself. The Brahms Concerto alone cost me $7,000. I must have spent about $4,000 a year on my books. Book collecting has been my greatest hobby besides music.

"Sometimes I even learned a language just because I wanted to know what was in a rare book I acquired. Take this Belgian manuscript of the fifteenth century on vellum." Here he took from a box he had just opened an enchantingly beautiful illuminated work embellished with ten full-page arch-topped miniatures, each surrounded by a floreated and pictorial illuminated border, the miniatures and borders executed in burnished colors. "I learned Flemish because I wanted to know what interpretation was placed in the manuscript upon various events chronicled in the Bible.

"As you see, the books are excellently preserved. I always handled them most carefully. I was more flattered, some years ago, when a bookseller's paper called me 'the erudite incunabulist' than I have been by many a critical eulogy of my playing.

"But Harriet says it is not right for me to hold on to costly books when there is so much misery in the world. She is right, of course, and so we are disposing of them for charity."

It might easily have happened that these books never reached the United States. For they were in Fritz Kreisler's study on the second floor of his Berlin home. Foreseeing a catastrophe, the Kreislers decided a short time before the outbreak of World War II to ship the collection to London. The Nazi Government at first objected. They did not want these treasures to leave Germany. They finally agreed to their export only on condition that, if they were sold within the ensuing five years, all proceeds would be turned over to the National Socialist régime. The collapse of the régime ended the stipulated obligation.

There was much red tape, too, to be overcome before the books finally received a clearance from the British authorities, who naturally would have preferred to have an English auctioneer entrusted with the sale. But in the spring of 1948 they finally reached Charles Foley's office, where Fritz Kreisler was on hand to have a look at his "pets" after a separation of more than a decade. There he stood, in vest and shirt sleeves, with a hammer in his hand, and as he opened box after box and took out volume after volume, he was lost to the world for some hours as he gently fondled the rare collection.

The Parke-Bernet Galleries, Inc., of 30 East Fifty-seventh Street, New York, were entrusted with the auction. They arranged a public exhibition from January 20 to the date of the first auction, January 27, in which the collection was shown to best advantage in individual glass cases, the books resting on rich velvet and the indirect lighting diffusing an inviting mellowness over them. Before each book there was mounted a description of its origin, content, and bibliophilic importance. Any interested person could ask an attendant to take any desired volume out of its glass case for detailed inspection.

Harriet Kreisler had always frowned somewhat upon her husband's passion for old books. Fritz more or less had to hide his acquisitions from her. Harriet once described amusingly how the servants would come to her with money they found that her husband had laid aside for book buying and then promptly forgotten. As she put it: *

"I can't do anything with him. When we were first married, and had hardly a dollar to spare, he would spend that dollar on some old book. And now, after all these years, when he goes to bed at night, you can't see the man for books. . . . He is honest as the day about everything but books. Whenever he finds himself with a bit of extra money in hand, he will hide it away for the

* Reprinted from *He Plays on the World's Heartstrings* by Beverly Smith, in the February, 1931 issue of the *American Magazine*, by permission of Beverly Smith and the Crowell-Collier Publishing Company, copyright, 1931, by *American Magazine*.

purchase of old parchments. He will hide it in books, or on top of the wardrobe, or under the rug. Then he will forget where he has hidden it. Months later the maid will come to me and say, 'Look, Mrs. Kreisler, here is some money I found hidden under Mr. Kreisler's dress shirts.' I always know what it is. It's book-money."

Fritz related with a chuckle: "One day after my return from a tour of the British Isles, where I had managed to branch off a part of my earnings for book money, I felt one of my pockets bulging with what I thought were reminder slips, receipted bills, and other accumulated pieces of now worthless paper. Without looking at them further, I tossed them into the waste basket.

"The German maid, who had never seen British five- and ten-pound notes, nevertheless sensed that my 'waste paper' was somewhat unusual. So she took it to Harriet and said, 'Could that be something valuable that the professor ought not to have thrown away?' That's how Harriet learned I had been saving for some more books!"

The late Professor Paul R. Pope of Cornell, who did not know that Kreisler had to acquire his rare books more or less surreptitiously, wrote me of a conversation he had with him in 1936:

At the dinner I told Kreisler of a book sale in England where I had bought an incunabulum (1488) and he replied that he just couldn't afford to get such books. As I knew he received as much for that concert as some Cornell professors get for a whole year's teaching, I was somewhat amused. Then we discussed the date of another book. My date did not agree with his, but he cut off the debate with a smile, saying that he happened to own the book in question.

"Harriet says I was always so secretive about the books," Fritz Kreisler confided. "Sometimes, in my obsession, it is true, I paid fancy prices; but then again poor old musicians would often present me with a rare book to show their appreciation of help given them. And after all, we bought houses in Berlin which have subsequently proven a total loss, and now we can't even get money on the mere ground on which our house in Berlin-Grunewald stands. Our cash was frozen by the Nazis; by the time it is 'thawed out,' it won't be worth anything. What more worth-while investment could I have made than the books? To me a bracelet worth $3,000 on a woman, for instance, does not mean much."

Altogether, Kreisler spent about $150,000 in the course of his artistic career on rare books.

On the night that Harriet saw the exhibition at the Parke-Bernet Galleries, she probably for the first time fully realized what her husband had been doing all these years. She suddenly understood that here was an amazing collection assembled by an amazing lay connoisseur of scarce and beautiful examples of the art of printing and of exquisite literary expression. Excitedly she rang us up and asked: "Have you seen the exhibition? . . . No? Well, you simply must. I tell you, it's out of this world. Such taste! Such discretion! I really must beg Fritz's pardon. I just didn't know his collection was *so* beautiful."

At that time, Arthur Swann, manager of the galleries, said: "Last night, when Mr. and Mrs. Kreisler came in after dinner to see the exhibition, I had everything appropriately illuminated. As Mrs. Kreisler entered the exhibition rooms, she simply gasped. 'Why, Pappi,' she said to her husband, 'you have been hiding something on me!' Mr. Kreisler's face lighted up as he looked at one item after another. He, too, had never seen everything assembled together. 'I got that from So-and-So, and that one from So-and-So,' he reminisced. It was quite a touching sight. Fritz Kreisler is certainly a man about whom I feel as though I had known him long ago, although our acquaintanceship has been very brief.

"Fritz Kreisler is one of the most remarkable book collectors I have come across. His collection is unique. Nothing like it has been offered to the trade in the way of 'small' collections. Anybody might have made a specialty of collecting fifteenth and sixteenth century works and could have gotten together quite a number of books. But Kreisler's great erudition and culture and taste produced something quite unique. Such knowledge! Such capacity for evaluating!"

The Parke-Bernet Galleries, besides arranging for a worthy exhibition of the Fritz Kreisler Collection, published an illustrated 128-page catalog which ought to be in every public library in the United States.

It is a veritable guide through incunabula and the early art of printing. In a Foreword Marion Caming wrote:

Even the most cursory examination of this catalogue will establish beyond a doubt the fact that this is no ordinary collection of old books. It will be quickly recognized also that the collector of it is no ordinary man, but one who, with wisdom, taste, and knowledge, brought together a most distinguished and rare library, which has its roots mainly in the fifteenth century.

Mr. Kreisler, man of genius and of the people, could easily have fitted into the rôle of one of the old scholastic monks poring over a beautifully engrossed manuscript, embellishing it with painstaking care, and contributing by its execution toward the dissemination of knowledge despite liturgical limitations. Such manuscripts are in this collection. We can also picture Mr. Kreisler fascinated by the transition of the creations of the pen into those of type. That too, is evident in this choice little library.

This collection is rich in fifteenth century illustrated books which never fail to interest and entertain modern scholars and collectors of incunables. Johann Bämler and Anton Sorg were Augsburg printers of such works; Johann Zainer of Ulm, Laurentius de Rubeis of Ferrara, and Johann Prüss of Strassburg were others. Lienhart Holle and Conrad Dinckmut were among the successful producers of pictured books in Ulm, despite the fact that the constantly recurring plague offered almost insurmountable obstacles. Peter Schoeffer of Mayence printed the *Gart der Gesuntheit*, which appears in this catalogue under the heading of *Hortus Sanitatis*. The remarkable woodcut frontispiece of this work illustrates a group of thirteen physicians, with the attribution laid to Erhard Reuwich.

Anton Koberger, well-known printer of the *Nuremberg Chronicle*, was said to have had twenty-four presses in operation at the same time, and perhaps as many as a hundred printers were employed by him. Fortune guided his choice when he settled upon two artists of distinction, Michel Wolgemut and Wilhelm Pleydenwurff. The *Schatzbehalter* or "Treasury of the true riches of Salvation" appears in this catalogue under the name form "Stephan Pater." It contains ninety-six magnificent full-page woodcuts by Wolgemut, master of Albrecht Dürer. It is difficult to leave the subject of the woodcut, in whose production artists in so many fifteenth century cities were involved, without again mentioning Albrecht Dürer of Nuremberg. Much of his genius was expressed through the woodcut, and his influence is exemplified in this collection. Samuel Johnson, in his preface to his English Dictionary, saw fit to remark: "When it shall be found that much is omitted, let it not be forgotten that much likewise is performed." It is utterly beyond the scope of this foreword to concern itself with every phase of this remarkable collection, or to indicate by more than a few words the startlingly fine condition of most of the books. Each catalogue description serves only in some measure as an introduction to the book or manuscript. The collection ranges from the fifteenth to the twentieth century and is replete with rarities. What could be rarer than the *Psalterium cum Hymnis*, or thirty-one leaves of the *Biblia Pauperum*, or Juan Gil's manuscript on poisons, or Monstrelet's *Chroniques*? There are also many bindings of great beauty and importance, such as the Lortic specimen on the Monstrelet "Chronicles" or the Jean Grolier example.

Mr. Kreisler loved all the books that he bought; he studied them and knew them. He could read and decipher their texts, and the books were handled with the same affection and care he bestowed upon his equally beloved violins. There are books of musical interest, and their variety and rarity show why they were sought for and collected.

In closing we would like to add a sentimental touch. Through the press and other couriers, it has been heralded that the proceeds derived from the sale of these books will be devoted to charity. It was because of Mr. Kreisler's wife, Harriet, and her long cherished wish to aid those in need, that Mr. Kreisler, as a tribute to her, gave his collection of rare books to The Golden Rule Foundation and the Lenox Hill Hospital by whose order the sale is now being held. The motive of this great artist and man may be summed up in his own words: "That which made possible the acquisition of such books came from the people, therefore, having served their purpose, what they accrue must go back to the people."

It should be added that with every item there is a lengthy description in the catalog, not only indicating the contents and general make-up of the work, but also setting it in its proper perspective historically and with reference to other works extant on the same subject or allied to it. From 42 of the 174 items listed, sample pages are reproduced in facsimile. Photographs of four especially artistic bindings are also included. These comprise *Les Chroniques de Monstrelet* (1503), of which it is believed that only two copies printed on vellum are extant; Matthaeus Bossus' *De veris ac salutaribus animi gaudiis dialogus* (1491), in an "exceedingly unusual and interesting specimen of sixteenth century binding suggestive of Canivari or Farnese attributions"; a manuscript of the twelfth century on vellum (southern French), bound in hand-wrought covers with metal work of the fifteenth century, the principal feature of which is the gilt figure of Christ, with a separately executed crown and small, black stones for pupils of the eyes, attached to a metal cross by four nails; and *Horae*

Beatissimae Virginis Mariae on vellum (1570) in a binding *à la fanfare mosaique*.

Among the books not mentioned in Marion Caming's Foreword, the following should be of general interest to the average reader: a first printed edition of the works of Horace (1498); a second edition of Nicolaus Jenson's Venetian printing of Caesar's *Gallic Wars* (1471); the first great printed work on Renaissance architecture, Leo Baptista Alberti's *De re aedificatoria* (1485); the Robert Hoe copy of Cicero's *Epistolae ad M. Brutum* (1470); the incunabular copy of the *Chronik der Sachsen* (1492); one of the rarest French illustrated books of the Romantic period—Honoré de Balzac's *Le Peau de chagrin: études sociales* (1838); a third edition of Francesco Petrarca's *Sonetti e canzoni Trionfoni* (1472); a first German edition of Ptolemy's *Cosmographia* (1482); an early French edition of Cervantes' *Don Quixote* (1780); a first edition of the following: The Bible in Greek (1518); *Chants et chansons populaires de la France* (1843); Fernando Cortez's *Third Letter on Mexico* (1523); Gluck's opera *Alceste* in full vellum (1769); M. de la Fontaine's *Contes et Nouvelles* (1762); the works of Molière (1734); a first edition of Sebastian Brandt's *The Ship of Fools* (1497).

It is interesting to note that there was not a single work in the English language in the collection. There were, however, various medical books, indicating Kreisler's continued interest in the medical sciences.

The auction was conducted in a dignified manner befitting the occasion. The auctioneer stood in a sort of pulpit beside a stagelike platform to which each book was carried before the bidding began. There it was once more exhibited against a background of dark velvet. At three lecterns in various parts of the auction hall stood employees of the Parke-Bernet firm to catch the signals of the bidders, many of whom merely indicated by a nod of the head that they were ready to go higher than the last announced bid. Kreisler was not present, but was represented by Charles Foley, who had previously obtained the best figures available as to the current market value of the auctioned books and then wrote against them in the margin of his catalog the actual prices obtained. His estimate of $120,000, volunteered to me on the first evening, proved almost 100 per cent correct, even though the prices for some works were far below their alleged market value, whereas for others there was bidding far beyond the most optimistic expectations.

For the most part the book dealers sat in the back of the large auction hall. In the front rows were ladies in evening dress and fur coats, accompanied by men mostly in tuxedos. One heard English, French, German, and Spanish spoken, but books in the German language brought relatively low prices, because dealers from Germany were absent.

German dealers had a reporter present, however, for the *Börsenblatt für deutschen Buchhandel* observed in its edition of March 8, 1949, that rumors had evidently been started doubting the authenticity of this or that book with the obvious desire of holding down the price. The organ of the German book trade commented:

> Of a vicious nature, for instance, was the gossip to the effect that there was something not quite right about the *Biblia Pauperum*. On the day of the auction the auctioneering firm had to contact the London firm of Maggs in order to obtain its certification of the genuineness of this blockbook. Need anyone be surprised that gossip of this sort can ruin a book? In this respect books are not less susceptible than a young girl or a woman. Even the certification of the genuineness of the *Biblia Pauperum* could not save it, and the $3,400 which a certain New York dealer risked on it corresponds to about one-tenth of its actual value!

The reporter for the German trade paper claimed that the total sum realized was approximately 15 to 20 per cent less than what, in the course of years, Kreisler paid for the collection. But he did not consider this slump surprising, since international competition was almost entirely lacking. Because of foreign exchange shortage, neither English, French, nor German dealers could bid. From his point of view the cheapest book was the *Chronik der Sachsen* (1492), which went for $800, whereas Kreisler had paid $2,400 for it.

One task which awaited Kreisler after the sales were concluded, and on which he had not counted, was that of autographing the 174 volumes. It developed that he possessed no *ex libris* stickers and had not even bothered to write his name as owner into these rare books.

"I never thought of having an *ex libris* designed for me," he said. "My field is the violin and not books. Many people have *ex libris* printed to enhance their own importance."

Two items which were taken out of the collection at the last moment before publication of the catalog were the manuscripts of Brahms's Concerto for Violin and Orchestra, Opus 77, and Chausson's *Poème*.

"Fritz was on tour," Harriet explained, "when an offer of $25,000 came to Parke-Bernet for the Brahms Concerto. Suddenly the thought that this priceless manuscript, as well as the Chausson *Poème*, was about to get into private hands and might possibly later become lost altogether, haunted me. I had read too often how later generations, unaware of the treasure they held in their hands, would first consign such manuscripts to the attic or basement and perhaps later sell them with other waste paper. So I had these two manuscripts taken out of the collection. Fritz, of course, heartily approved on his return. They were given to the Music Division of the Library of Congress, where they will always be available to serious students."

The news of these two rare gifts made the rounds of musical circles in America very rapidly, as may be seen from the fact that the program notes of the Nashville Symphony Orchestra concert on February 22, 1949, remarked that the original manuscript of the Chausson *Poème*, which Zino Francescatti was to play that night, was on exhibition in the Library of Congress, a gift from Fritz Kreisler.

The collection of rare books which was auctioned off is, of course, by no means all that Kreisler has of printed works. His "ordinary" library abounds in works of every description—chiefly philosophy, but also the classics, fiction, history, music, medicine, and even twenty-five-cent volumes. He will read Homer or Juvenal one moment and De Vere Stacpoole's novels the next. Romain Rolland, Anatole France, and Bernard Shaw are among his favorite authors.

Kreisler's vast erudition has sometimes led him to make discoveries which escape the less learned mortal. His most recent appearance in Nashville, Tennessee, was under the auspices of David Lipscomb College. Kreisler was intrigued by the fact that its president, Dr. Clay

Pullias, has a name that connotes Greek ancestry. How, he wondered, did a man whose family, he assumed, belonged to the Greek Orthodox Church, happen to become identified with the Christian Brethren under whose auspices David Lipscomb College is operated?

Then, during his stay, he was shown the buildings of the college. He noticed the absence of any organ or other instrument in the chapel. The Christian Brethren, he was told, do not approve of instruments for the house of worship.

He now put two and two together: "Obviously, at least as far as Church rites and practices are concerned, the Christian Brethren come closest to the Greek Orthodox Church," he reasoned, "for Orthodox churches and cathedrals also have no musical instruments."

It is unexpected comments like this which make chats and discussions with Fritz Kreisler so interesting and worth while. The wisdom and sagacity acquired in a long life of service to his fellow men is reflected in all he says.

We were discussing, for instance, the theoretical case of an atomic bomb destroying all music scores except three. Which, in the opinion of Fritz Kreisler, should be saved for posterity?

For a moment he mistook the question to mean which of his own compositions he would like to see secured at all costs. He therefore at first replied modestly: "Oh, I would not think of preserving any of my works. They are not worth it." When the question was rephrased in general terms, however, he replied: "Well, I have often thought of that. Supposing, for instance, a doctor were to say to me, 'You're going to lose your musical memory, but I can preserve it for a few favorite compositions.' I'd choose Schubert's 'Unfinished' Symphony, Brahms's First, and Beethoven's Fifth."

When I expressed surprise that no violin concerto was included, Fritz offered the following interesting explanation:

"I am not sufficiently objective when listening to a violin concerto. The fact that I am a violinist has tied me down in a certain way all my life. All of us, as a matter of fact, are tied down in one way or another, be it religiously, racially, ideologically, or nationalistically. I have tried to be objective and to eliminate myself completely, but that is hardly possible. I am the purest artist when I listen and not when I play. Whether I want to or not, the fact is that, unconsciously perhaps, I am somewhat egocentric. That is, subconsciously I am concerned not only with the work itself, but also with the way I am going to play it. When I listen, however, I give myself over to pure enjoyment of the work.

"I listen to derive pleasure and uplift, not to criticize. Even a mediocre performance of a great work gives me pleasure, for the work itself is there and cannot be wrecked by human imperfections. A false note does not disturb me. Anton Rubinstein played many false notes—yet what an artist he was!"

The remark about egocentricity led to another question: "When you play your own compositions, do you feel any differently than if you were playing, say, a Mozart work? Is your relationship to your own work when you are its executant a more personal one?"

"Not at all," he replied. "I am as detached from it as if I were playing Bach, Brahms, or Bruckner. I have no personal attitude when I stand on the podium. Naturally, every composition becomes individualized, as it were, by the temperament and interpretation of the executing artist. But when I play a Kreisler work, it is a *musical* composition that I am trying to interpret, not a *Kreisler* composition.

"The executing artist must, of course, stick to the main line and interpret a work as the composer envisaged it. But I do not object to different nuances in interpretation. When my own works are played by someone else, I can only learn from his interpretation, provided he has caught the general spirit. I am not dogmatic at all about details.

"The true sublimation is in playing. The real artist creates his music for himself alone. It is only incidental that it gives beauty to his listeners."

Kreisler's thoughts frequently revolve about the question of what he calls the "violinistic *Nachwuchs*"—that is, the fiddlers who are to take over from Thibaud, Enesco, Elman, Zimbalist, Spalding, Heifetz, Busch, Szigeti, and himself. He speaks in terms of high praise of Nathan Milstein, Yehudi Menuhin, Zino Francescatti, and Isaac Stern. But then he continues:

"You must remember that there are many besides these who as

mere technicians are great. But they lack background. Especially, they lack the divine fervor. They aim at mechanical perfection.

"That is, in a sense, the curse of our age. We are doing everything faster. But wasn't life also worth while when we had kerosene lamps, when we had time, when mechanical perfection wasn't what it is today? People often said, 'You must hear Kreisler. He draws an audience of so-and-so-many and his box-office receipts are so-and-so'; instead of saying, 'You ought to hear how Kreisler interprets this or that work.'

"It is so difficult to gauge the advance of human endeavor. Each generation brings its own ideals, and lives up to them as best it can. And each generation probably is right in selecting the ideals it will hold."

Kreisler is also much concerned about the attempts of the Soviet Politbureau to prescribe ideology-controlled music to composers like Sergei Prokofieff, Dimitri Shostakovich, and Aram Khatchaturian.

"The idea is absurd," he says. "When a Politbureau tries to tell the composer what to do, that is arrant nonsense. It is a sad state of affairs when an artist departs from real art and for reasons of politics or ideology tries to establish something new. If the motif is dishonest and not artistic, such a new venture will not last. Art is prophetic. It will not bow to political decrees.

"But then, history will take care of this situation. Later generations will detect what is genuine in Prokofieff's or Shostakovich's or Khatchaturian's music and what was written under duress. The latter will be forgotten."

During the concert season of 1948–1949 Kreisler went on tour as usual—his sixtieth year since his début in Boston in 1888 as a thirteen-year-old *Wunderkind*. The schedule was a leisurely one compared with his barnstorming tours of yore. Nevertheless, it took him among other cities to Washington, D.C., where one newspaper columnist pointed out that his appearance was "the week's social event—an island in Washington's great dismal swamp of culture, and it prompted a series of dinner parties that brought all the gold plate in town from the vaults." It also took him to Madison, Wisconsin, where he was the soloist in a season of concerts devoted to celebrating the one hundredth anniversary of the University of Wisconsin; to Chicago, where Felix Borowski, the veteran critic of the Chicago *Sun-Times*, observed that Kreisler's "fine musicianship, sense of style, exquisite taste . . . will remain with him until the end"; to Winnipeg, Canada, where he found time to acquaint himself with the humanitarian work of Dr. T. O. F. Herzer, chairman of the Canadian Christian Council for Resettlement of Refugees, in bringing displaced Europeans to Canada; and to Nashville, Tennessee.

At Nashville, Sydney Dalton of the Nashville *Banner* produced an apt summation of Kreisler's art after passing the seventieth milestone —a summation that probably reflects what all friends and admirers of the Nestor of the world's violinists feel he means to them when they now hear him:

> In this day of prodigious technical achievement and musical efficiency, when so many of the performers who press for recognition give evidence of having come off an assembly line, there is a breath of Elysian refreshment in listening to Kreisler. And when he decides to retire (he has already passed his seventieth year) something of the beauty and nobleness of fine musical interpretation will be lost.

When retirement was first suggested to Kreisler by some friends after his seventieth birthday, he said in an interview:

> "My friends often ask me, 'Why don't you retire—when are you going to rest?'" Here his eyes lit up, and leaning forward he said with conviction, "There is no time for rest."

As if to give added proof of his determination to continue, he played Jan Sibelius's Concerto in D Minor in tribute to the Finnish composer's eightieth birthday in his Carnegie Hall concert on October 20, 1945.

In a letter to my wife he had written a few weeks previously: "We return to New York because my autumn tour starts very soon. In a way I am glad, because when I exercise my musical profession I become (for a while at least) the captain of my soul."

That was five years ago. Now he is almost ready to leave the responsibility for artistic music making to younger generations. For one thing he no longer gives his annual concert in Carnegie Hall. His last

Kreisler after awarding a citation to 12-year-old Michael Tree, while Mrs. Parker O. Griffith looks on

Fritz Kreisler in his later years

appearance there was on November 1, 1947, when he played the difficult Bach unaccompanied Sonata in B Minor, the Chausson *Poème*, and the Schumann Fantasie, besides, of course, a number of his own compositions. He received a warm and affectionate welcome, the audience rising in tribute as he walked onto the stage, and played magnificently.

But although Carnegie Hall was eliminated, Kreisler did not quit abruptly. He was booked for a limited number of concert appearances and two radio broadcasts as late as the season of 1949–1950.

"The time is now approaching," he said to me three months before his seventy-fifth birthday, "when younger men must take over where we oldsters left off. At my time of life one becomes reminiscent; one looks back upon the joys and sorrows, the successes and the disappointments, the ups and downs of one's life.

"For my part, I feel that I have lived during a period when the arts achieved a new high, when its exponents were names to conjure with —Eugène Ysaÿe, Romain Rolland, Anatole France, Eleanore Duse, Herbert Beerbohm Tree, Auguste Rodin, Enrico Caruso, John Drew, Sarah Bernhardt, and all the rest. I am grateful to have been privileged to associate with Olympians like Johannes Brahms, Anton Bruckner, Antonin Dvořák, and Hans Richter. I believe that humanity lived more gracefully, more abundantly, and more deeply appreciative of what the arts meant for human uplift, during the period before 1914 than it could during and after the ravages of two world cataclysms. It has filled me with pride and joy that, while science, alas, has been mainly diverted during my lifetime to purposes of destruction, art, and especially the art of music, has been a healing factor, a powerful stimulus to overcoming national animosities, a harbinger of peace and international brotherhood.

"The giants of a Golden Age in music have for the most part gone to their deserved rest. The few who remain will be summoned sooner or later.

"If I have any one regret, it is that, in our present mechanical age, the growing generation of musicians may never be able to experience that indescribable, intangible something that made the profession of a musician so beautiful and satisfying in my time and age."

CHAPTER THIRTY-THREE

POSTSCRIPT: SEVENTY-FIFTH BIRTHDAY

ON the eve of his seventy-fifth birthday, Kreisler's friends and admirers in the Greater New York area paid tribute to him at a testimonial dinner in the ballroom of the Ritz-Carlton Hotel. In keeping with his own philosophy of giving, it was a benefit dinner for musicians in need of help.

There was an informal intimacy about this gathering of a kind seldom achieved at similar functions, a feeling of comradeship and fellowship that communicated itself to all participants, a happy oneness of thought in the oratorical and musical offerings of the evening, a rare grace and unceremonial dignity generated by the personality of the man whom we had gathered to honor.

Mrs. Lytle Hull, president of the Musicians' Emergency Fund, Inc., who presided, struck the keynote of the evening with words that reflected and epitomized what everyone present thought and felt:

"We extend our boundless admiration to Fritz Kreisler, not only for the joy he has given so many people all over the world with his great art, but also because he has never failed to stretch out a helping hand to his colleagues in distress."

Flanking the gracious Mrs. Hull on the dais were, in addition to Fritz and "my Harriet" (as the guest of honor fondly called her in his response), His Eminence Francis Cardinal Spellman; the speakers of the evening, Hans V. Kaltenborn, Georges Enesco, Bruno Walter, and Monsignor Fulton J. Sheen; and the artists who held the audience spellbound with a musical program after the speaking was over,

Kreisler nearing his 75th birthday

Kreisler, also about 1950

Nathan Milstein, violinist; Jennie Tourel, dramatic soprano; her accompanist Dimitri Mitropoulos; and Jorge Bolet, pianist.

Two distinguished Americans who regretted their inability to attend were President Harry S. Truman and Governor Thomas E. Dewey. The President telegraphed: "Hearty birthday greetings to one whom the power of music has given the spirit of eternal youth. Best wishes for many more years of health and happiness." Governor Dewey, in a longer letter, observed regarding Kreisler: "Of all the living musicians of our time, none has contributed more richly of his talents, nor has done more to maintain the highest standard of the arts in our country."

Cardinal Spellman, before invoking the blessing, informed the audience that Pope Pius XII had bestowed his special Apostolic Blessing upon Fritz (and with him, upon Harriet). The speakers, often interrupted by spontaneous applause from a receptive and enthusiastic audience, recalled various aspects of the birthday child's life and character in brief, pithy speeches, mostly of an impromptu nature. Kaltenborn spoke of his nobility of character and loftiness of sentiment shown during the hysteria of World War I. Georges Enesco stressed his long, friendly association with his colleague Fritz, "to whom the world owes so much." Monsignor Sheen paid tribute to the humility of the great artist, and smilingly expressed the hope that St. Peter would instruct the millions of angels of eight heavenly choirs to render the "Caprice viennois."

Dr. Walter, speaking from the perspective both of a celebrated conductor and an accomplished pianist, delivered a speech that is here incorporated almost in full:

"I look at you, my dear Fritz Kreisler, and I am aware—as we all are—that you are a legendary figure in the history of music. You are surrounded by an aura of your own, and well may we ponder how it happened that everywhere in the world the name Fritz Kreisler means a fascination for all music-minded folk. How come?—to say it in 'American.' Of course your name filled the concert halls everywhere in the world; you went through Europe and America from north to south, from east to west, and I don't believe that there exists on the globe a musical city where Fritz Kreisler has not played for an enthusiastic audience.

"But do external facts of life, like such an uninterrupted series of successes on the concert platform, explain how our friend reached that lofty position in the musical world? Do they explain how he became the 'legendary figure' I called him before? To understand this, I believe we must try to understand the inner, esoteric facts of his life's career.

"My friends, when I knew I should have to speak to you today on Fritz Kreisler, I 'went into a huddle' with myself; I called back my musical memories and my personal ones of our friend: I saw the two of us when, long, long ago, we spent charming and stimulating evenings together in Berlin, in the house of an old friend of Fritz Kreisler who was also a friend of mine; and there it often happened that, after dinner, Kreisler sat down at the piano. And how he played the piano! Like a real musician and an excellent pianist. And then, later in the night, when the spirits grew more and more alive and excited, then Kreisler took his fiddle out of its case and then he played—well, how to describe it? He did not only *play* the violin, he *became* the violin, or better, the violin became Fritz Kreisler. And I thought of the fantastic tale of E. T. A. Hoffmann—the same Hoffmann whom you see as the hero of Offenbach's opera 'The Tales of Hoffmann.' The third act of this opera tells the story of a girl who feels a mysterious relation to a violin. The story is mutilated in the libretto, so I shall tell it as the poet Hoffmann originally wrote it under the title *Rat Krespel* (in English, 'Councilor Krespel'). *Rat* Krespel collects and studies violins; he vivisects them, puts them together, and plays upon them. Among his many instruments there is one particularly beautiful, and when the girl, who has a beautiful voice, sings, her father accompanies her on *that* violin. Then the girl falls ill and is forbidden to continue singing. But she feels so identical with this violin that she begs her father to play it with the words, 'Father, I want to sing again.' And then *Rat* Krespel plays the violin and she feels it is her own voice which she hears from the fiddle.

"I mentioned this fantastic story because it is a poet's fiction of what seems to me to be the real fact, although an esoteric one, in Fritz

Fritz and Hugo Kreisler in a brotherly duet

The distinguished Kreisler

Kreisler's very existence: you hear Fritz Kreisler's voice when he plays the violin, you hear *him* sing.* Even when you hear from him the most brilliant passages, thirds, octaves, flageolets, you could say with every right: listen what a coloratura Fritz has! His is a mysterious identity with the fiddle. He was born with a right hand made for the bow and a left hand made for the finger board, and his soul—who knows from what former incarnation—was born for the element of music.

"From the first time on when I heard him play, I always had the impression of hearing the inner soul of music itself. Through the beauty of his singing tone, through the charm of his rhythm, through the natural simplicity of his expression, this very soul of music spoke to me. For he not only *makes* music, he *is* music; and he appears to me in some way as one of those mythological beings who populate the elements—he lives and is at home in the element of melody. To make music is for Fritz Kreisler what flying is for the bird or swimming for the fish, and I am sure it is this elementary quality which explains the spell that he casts over his audiences, that changes the passing events of his concerts into a profound, lasting experience.

"It was a lucky star that shone upon our musical world when Fritz Kreisler appeared in it, took his bow and his fiddle and played into the ears of generations his songs of beauty, of serenity, of affection, of gaiety, of transfiguration, of happiness."

And then Fritz Kreisler himself stepped before the microphone. Despite his white hair, he seemed younger than any of us had seen him in years. There was a certain radiance about him, a spirituality coupled with deep emotion, that is hard to describe in words. There was also that ineffable, beatific smile of his that he flashed on audiences the world over.

There he stood, erect and sturdy, without even as much as a note, and, carefully weighing every word, delivered an extemporaneous speech of thanks that was a gem of conciseness, wit, humor, and wisdom. One could well believe him when he asserted that "my health

* Note the similarity in Walter's approach to that of the Chicago *Tribune* critic's on page 127.

is very good," for earlier in the evening he had given evidence of his robust lungs by snuffing seventy-five birthday candles out in three puffs.

We were all so enthralled by his gripping words that nobody thought of taking notes. The speech would therefore have remained as an experience only for the privileged few who heard it had it not been for the happy circumstance that, unknown to the audience, a wire recording was made. I quote from this wire recording:

"Let me begin by thanking you from the bottom of my heart for coming here tonight and honoring me with your presence on the eve of my seventy-fifth birthday. Seventy-five years—three-quarters of a century—what a span of time and what an age! An age, if you think of it, which exceeds by many years the average general age allotted to mankind.

"Now let us consider what are the aspects of old age: unless I am mistaken, the chief aspects of it are: physical debilities, physical deficiencies, and moral obligations [prolonged laughter]. As to the physical deficiencies, I believe that Nature has dealt rather leniently with me, because, aside from the fact that both my hearing and my vision are somewhat impaired, my health is very good [laughter and applause], and up to now I have been able to exercise my profession, although lately in a very moderate and increasingly restricted way.

"As for the moral obligations [laughter], I have to confess that I have not acted in conformity with the code, demanded by custom and by social conventions, which demands that anybody who reaches a certain age should cease working and retire in order to make room for younger generations. Many of you, my dear friends, have probably surmised that I acted that way because I loved my vocation and because I wanted to retain the appreciation and the esteem in which my moderate artistic endeavors have been held by many of you. Since I am an average specimen of the human race and therefore tainted with all the weaknesses thereof, I will admit that to a certain extent your surmises were correct [laughter].

"But only partially so, because, to tell you the truth, my real motives in my actions were my fervent desire to exercise one of the inalienable rights of every artist; namely, the right to pursue his ideals

Kreisler nearing his 80th birthday

Fritz and Harriet at New York City celebration of his 85th birthday

and to seek new artistic experiences. You see, dear friends, music is a rather indefinable art. For instance, to give you only an example, how can an artist achieve an ideal performance of, let us say, a Beethoven concerto or sonata? There are no formulas for it. We have no paradigma. We have no examples which we could consult and copy. At least we have no universally acknowledged example to give. Therefore, any artist, according to his temperament and to his intuition, has to conceive and create his own ideals and follow them in the hope that some day he may be able to attain them. But assuming that he believes he has attained his ideal and wants to demonstrate it publicly—then he has to face the opposition of those who have different ideals and ideas.

"But that is not all, because an artist very often realizes that his own ideals have changed or that they have receded further from his reach.

"I remember a very interesting anecdote. Hans Richter, famous conductor, was once asked why he had conducted a certain piece differently and a little faster than he had done before; and he answered: Because the pulse of an artist is his only metronome—a metronome which changes according to his disposition, according to age, even according to the climate in which he performs.

"How true that is! Because I once myself thought I had come very near my own ideal in a certain performance, but I had to abandon all hopes of being able to repeat it because I realized how much I had been aided by fortuitous circumstances, such as my disposition, favorable atmospheric conditions, and even the acoustical propensities of the hall in which I played. You see, dear friends, the life of an artist is a theme on which many variations can be written. Some of them go in minor keys. Naturally, there are many variations that go in joyful major keys.

"I will only mention to you a few which I experienced in my own life. No. 1 is my Harriet, the best wife, companion, and friend that any man can hope and pray for. Incidentally, let me tell you that many charitable acts which have been ascribed to me have been really conceived and executed by her. No. 2 in my life was the influence of the quantity and the quality of a number of great, devoted, and loving friends. At this juncture allow me to tell you also how much joy and pleasure I derived from the realization that my beloved art of violin playing was not only maintained but that it was greatly increased, enlarged, and enriched by my younger colleagues" [long applause].

Harriet Kreisler, unexpectedly called upon, with a choking voice paid tribute to her Fritz by quoting, "I'm in love, I'm in love, I'm in love, I'm in love, I'm in love with a wonderful guy," from the popular musical comedy *South Pacific*.

The memorable evening came to a worthy close when, as the final number of a beautiful musical program, Nathan Milstein, accompanied by Hellmut Baerwald, played Kreisler's famous "Praeludium and Allegro in the Style of Pugnani," the work that led to Olin Downes's discovery of the celebrated hoax described in Chapter 26. Fritz afterward told me it was a "wonderful interpretation."

As the banqueters emerged from the testimonial dinner, they could obtain an early edition of the New York *Times* that contained an editorial, "Kreisler at 75," from which the following is quoted:

> Mr. Kreisler is a great human being, one of our most magnificent contemporaries. . . . In both his composition and his performance Mr. Kreisler has succeeded in making persons happy. It is a bit better to be alive for having heard him play; it is part of a more pleasant human experience to have listened to the things he has written. No one will ever know how many multiplied thousands of burdens he has lightened in a burdensome world.

On his birthday the following day a deluge of congratulatory telegrams and cables descended upon the Kreisler apartment as a small circle of us, consisting of a few intimate friends and Fritz's closest relatives, were discussing and reliving the inspiring scenes of the evening before.

There were, for instance, messages from famous ensembles with which Kreisler has appeared: the London Philharmonic, the Cincinnati Symphony, the Berlin Philharmonic, the London Symphony, the BBC, and the Hallé orchestras; and from the celebrated orchestra conductors: Sir Thomas Beecham, Serge Koussevitzky, Charles Münch, Dr. Wilhelm Furtwängler, Leopold Stokowski, Sir Adrian Boult, Sir John Barbirolli, Sir Malcolm Sargent, and Eugene Ormandy.

Then there were fellow artists, such as Jacques Thibaud, Albert

Sammons, Yehudi Menuhin, Erica Morini, Jascha Heifetz, Ernest Hutcheson, Alexander Brailowsky, Adolf Busch, Joseph Szigeti, James Melton, Sonia Essin, Louis Persinger, Elisabeth van Endert, Victor and Vitya Vronsky, Claudio Arrau, Zino Francescatti (to name but the best known), who remembered the day and occasion.

From Vienna came news that the Mozart Society had elected him an honorary member. Theodor Cardinal Innitzer of Austria sent a congratulatory message, as did Mrs. Eleanor Roosevelt and Jakob Goldschmidt. The director, faculty, and pupils of Kreisler's musical alma mater, the Conservatoire national de musique of Paris, felicitated their distinguished alumnus; and the Executive Committee of the Musicians' Benevolent Fund of London hailed his "unique services to the cause of British musicians."

The cable that most profoundly touched Fritz came from Queen Mother Elizabeth of Belgium. He has known the queen for some forty years and always found her an unfailing patroness of the arts, the constant helper of struggling artists. But what he admires most in this "very remarkable and noble woman" is the unusual fortitude and sublimity with which she always bore her personal tragedies.

"All my best and most affectionate wishes," Dowager Queen Elizabeth cabled from Laeken Castle near Brussels.

She voiced the sentiments of millions.

Kreisler with scroll received from New York City, about 1960

COMPOSITIONS, TRANSCRIPTIONS, AND ARRANGEMENTS

There are two catalogs of Fritz Kreisler's compositions, transcriptions, and arrangements in existence: one, by his European continental publisher, B. Schott's Söhne of Mainz, Germany; the other, by his American publisher, Charles Foley of New York.

The Schott catalog is useful to the lover of music who wishes to be reminded of the tune of a Kreisler work, in that the initial bars of most compositions are reproduced. It is therefore reprinted here in full.

Since, however, it was published before Kreisler's confession of his authorship of certain compositions, eight works are hyphenated as the joint product of some old, classical composer and his modern "arranger," when in reality they should be listed as original Kreisler works written "in the style of." They are:

Chanson Louis XIII and Pavane in the Style of Couperin
Andantino in the Style of Padre Martini
Menuet in the Style of Porpora
Praeludium and Allegro in the Style of Pugnani
Siciliano et Rigaudon in the Style of Francœur
Preghiera in the Style of Padre Martini
Tempo di Minuetto in the Style of Pugnani
Aubade Provençale in the Style of Couperin

The prices indicated no longer apply; they were based on the German reichsmark before World War II.

The Schott catalog also reveals that Kreisler edited all Beethoven sonatas for violin and piano. This edition is listed as Edition Schott No. 500.

The "illustrated" titles of many of Kreisler's works now follow:

(m) **Kreisler, Alter Refrain** (Volkslieder aus Österreich) *Viol. u. Klav. M. 1.30*

Andante con moto

(m) **Kreisler, Aus Wien** (Volkslieder aus Österreich) *Viol. u. Klav. M. 1.80*

Langsamer Walzertakt

(l) **Kreisler, Im Paradies** (Volkslieder aus Österreich) *Viol. u. Klav. M. 1.80*

Allegro moderato

(l) **Kreisler, Marche Miniature Viennoise** (Kleine Stücke 1. Lage) *Viol. u. Klav. M. 1.80*

Tempo di marcia

(l) **Kreisler-Couperin, Chanson Louis XIII et Pavane** (Klass. Manuskripte No. 1) *Viol. u. Klav. M. 1.80*

Andante

con sord. (ad libitum)

Pavane

Allegretto

Es bedeutet: (l) = leicht, (m) = mittel, (s) = schwer

(l) Kreisler-Padre Martini, Andantino (Klass. Manuskripte No. 2)

(m) Kreisler-Porpora, Menuett (Klass. Manuskripte No. 3)

(m) Kreisler-Pugnani, Praeludium u. Allegro (Klass. Manuskripte No. 5)

(m) Kreisler-Francoeur, Siciliano et Rigaudon (Klass. Manuskripte No. 6)

(s) Tartini-Kreisler, Variationen über ein Thema von Corelli (Klass. Manuskripte No. 9)

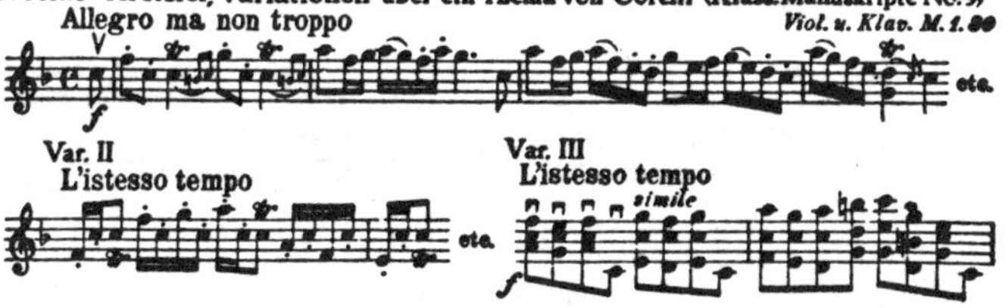

(m) Kreisler, Liebesfreud Alt-Wiener Tanzweisen No. 1 (Klass. Manuskripte No. 10)

(*l*) Kreisler, Liebesleid (Alt-Wiener Tanzweisen No. 2)(Klass. Manuskripte No. 11)

(*l*) Kreisler, Schön Rosmarin (Alt-Wiener Tanzweisen No. 3) (Klass. Manuskripte No. 11)

(*l*) Kreisler-Martini, Preghiera (Klass. Manuskripte No. 13)

(*m*) Kreisler-Pugnani, Tempo di Minuetto (Klass. Manuskripte No. 14)

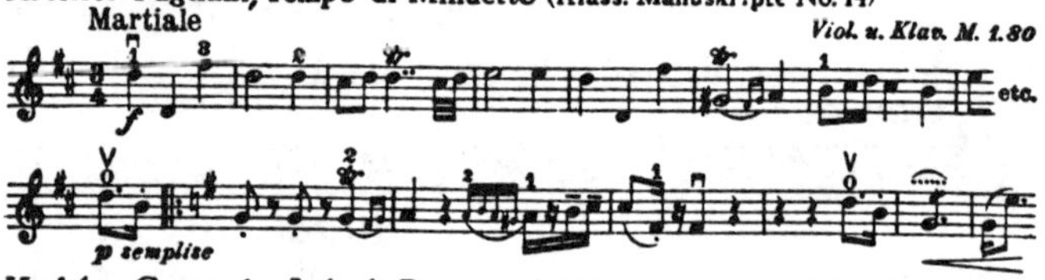

(*l*) Kreisler-Couperin, Aubade Provencale (Klass. Manuskripte No. 15)

(*m*) Bach-Kreisler, Grave (Klass. Manuskripte No. 17)

(*l*) Rameau-Kreisler, Tambourin (Meisterwerke der Violine No. 6)

(m) Mozart-Kreisler, Rondo (Meisterwerke der Violine No. 7) *Viol. u. Klav. M. 2.-*

Allegretto

(m) Gluck-Kreisler, Melodie (Meisterwerke der Violine No. 8) *Viol. u. Klav. M. 1.50*

Andante con moto

(m) Schubert-Kreisler, Moment musical (Meisterwerke der Violine No. 9) *Viol. u. Klav. M. 1.50*

Allegro moderato

(s) Kreisler, Caprice Viennois (Original-Kompositionen No. 2) *Viol. u. Klav. M. 2.-*

Allegro molto moderato

(s) Kreisler, Tambourin Chinois (Original-Kompositionen No. 3) *Viol. u. Klav. M. 2.50*

Allegro molto quasi Presto

(t) Kreisler, Rondino (Beethoven) (Orig.-Kompositionen No. 6) *Viol. u. Klav. M. 2.-*

Allegro grazioso

(l) Kreisler, La Gitana, Zigeunerlied. (Original Kompositionen No. 8)
Allegro giusto e ritmico — Viol. u. Klav. M. 2.-

Allegretto grazioso

(m) Schubert-Kreisler, Ballett-Musik a. „Rosamunde" (Transcriptionen No. 1)
Allegro moderato — Viol. u. Klav. M. 1.80

(m) Rimsky-Korsakow-Kreisler, Hymne au soleil (Transcriptionen No. 3)
Sostenuto Andantino (♩=76) — Viol. u. Klav. M. 2.-

(m) Rimsky-Korsakow-Kreisler, Chant Hindou (Transcriptionen No. 4)
Andantino — Viol. u. Klav. M. 2.-

(m) Rimsky-Korsakow-Kreisler, Arabisches Lied (Transcriptionen No. 5)
Andantino, quasi Allegretto — Viol. u. Klav. M. 2.-

(m) Rimsky-Korsakow-Kreisler, Orientalischer Tanz (Transcriptionen No. 6)
Lento Quasi Recitativo — Viol. u. Klav. M. 2.-
Andantino

(m) Kreisler, Londonderry Air, Altirisches Lied (Transcriptionen No. 7)
Andante con moto — Viol. u. Klav. M. 1.80

(m) Granados-Kreisler, Spanischer Tanz (Transcriptionen No. 8) *Viol. u. Klav. M. 2.-*

(m) Grainger-Kreisler, Molly am Gestade (Transcriptionen No. 12) *Viol. u. Klav. M. 2.-*

(m) Kreisler, He-Uch-la, Wolgalied u. anderes Volkslied (Paraphrase) (Transcript. No. 15) *Viol. u. Klav. M. 1.80*

(s) de Falla-Kreisler, Spanischer Tanz (Transcriptionen No. 18) *Viol. u. Klav. M. 2.-*

(m) Albeniz-Kreisler, Tango (Transcriptionen No. 19) *Viol. u. Klav. M. 1.80*

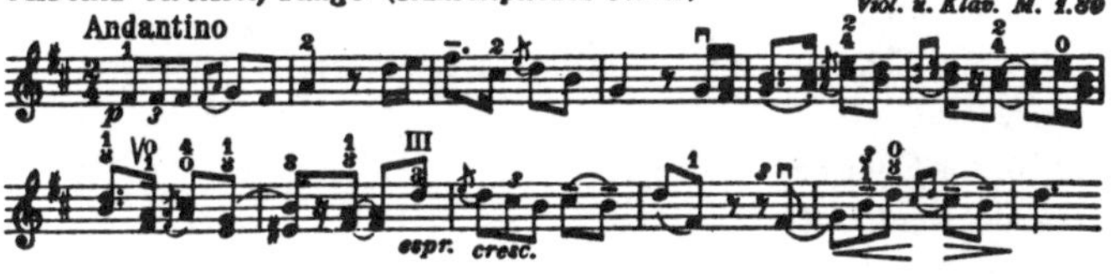

(m) Albeniz-Kreisler, Malagueña (Transcriptionen No. 20) *Viol. u. Klav. M. 2.-*

(m) Kreisler, Aloha Oe, Hawaisches Lied (Transcriptionen No. 25) *Viol. u. Klav. M. 1.80*

The "illustrated" catalog by no means exhausts Kreisler's creative work. Classified as cadenzas, string quartet, additional compositions, and additional transcriptions, the works not included in the foregoing are as follows:

CADENZAS

Three Cadenzas for Beethoven's Concerto, Op. 61, unaccompanied
Cadenza for Brahms's Concerto, Op. 77, unaccompanied
Three Cadenzas for Mozart's Concerto No. 3, in G Major, unaccompanied
Three Cadenzas for Mozart's Concerto No. 4, in D Major, unaccompanied
Two Cadenzas for Mozart's Concerto No. 5, in A Major, unaccompanied
Cadenza for Mozart's Concerto No. 6, in E Major, unaccompanied

ADDITIONAL COMPOSITIONS

Allegretto in the Style of Boccherini
Allegretto in G Minor, in the Style of Porpora
"Aucassin et Nicolette," Medieval Canzonetta
"Berceuse romantique"
Cavatina
Concerto in C Major, in the Style of Vivaldi
"Gypsy Caprice"
"La Chasse," in the Style of Cartier
"La Précieuse," in the Style of Couperin
"Malagueña"
"Marche miniature viennoise"
"Polichinelle Serenade"
Recitativo and Scherzo Caprice, unaccompanied
"Romance"
Scherzo in the Style of Dittersdorf
"Shepherd's Madrigal"
Study on a Choral in the Style of Stamitz
"Syncopation"
"Toy Soldiers' March"
"Viennese Rhapsodic Fantasietta"

STRING QUARTET

String Quartet in A Minor

ADDITIONAL TRANSCRIPTIONS

Albéniz, Tango
———, "Malagueña"
Bach, Gavotte in E
———, Prelude in E
———, Partita in E
Brahms, Hungarian Dance No. 17.

Chopin, Mazurka in A, Op. 33, No. 2.
———, Mazurka in A Minor (posthumous), Op. 67, No. 4
Corelli, "La Folia"
———, Sarabande and Allegretto
Dvořák, "Indian Lament"
———, Negro Spiritual Melody from the Largo of the "New World" Symphony
———, Slavonic Dance No. 1 in G Minor
———, Slavonic Dance No. 2 in E
———, Slavonic Dance No. 3 in G
———, Slavonic Fantaisie in B Minor
———, "Songs My Mother Taught Me"
Foster, "Old Folks at Home" (Swanee River)
Gärtner, Viennese Waltz Melody
Glazounoff, "Sérénade espagnole"
Haydn, Hungarian Rondo
Heuberger, "Midnight Bells" (from *The Opera Ball*)
Krakauer, "In Paradise" (Viennese folk song)
Leclair, "Tambourin"
Lehár, "Frasquita Serenade"
Mendelssohn, "Lied ohne Worte: May Breeze," Op. 62, No. 1
Moussorgsky-Rachmaninoff, "Hopak"
Paderewski, "The Bells" (La Clochette) Op. 7
———, Menuet
Paganini, "The Bells" (La Clochette), Op. 7
———, Caprice No. 13
———, Caprice No. 20
———, Caprice No. 24
———, Concerto in One Movement from Concerto No. 1 in D, Op. 6
———, "I Palpiti" (Theme and Variations), Op. 13
———, "Moto perpetuo" (Perpetual Motion), Op. 11
———, "Non più Mesta" (Theme and Variations), Op. 12
———, "Le Streghe" (The Witches' Dance), Op. 8
Poldini, "Dancing Doll" (Poupée valsante)
Rachmaninoff, "Album Leaf" (Marguerites), Op. 38, No. 3
———, "Preghiera" from Piano Concerto No. 2, Op. 18
———, Prelude in G Minor
———, Italian Polka
Rameau, "Tambourin"
Ravel, Habanera
Rimsky-Korsakoff, Fantaisie on Russian Themes, Op. 33
Schelling, "Irlandaise"
Schumann, Fantasy, Op. 131

———, "Romance" in A
Scott, "Lotus Land"
Tartini, "Devil's Trill" Sonata
———, Fugue in A
———, Variations on a Theme of Corelli
Tchaikovsky, Concerto Op. 35, revised, with new cadenza
———, Scherzo, Op. 42, No. 2
Weber, Larghetto
Wieniawski, "Airs russes"
———, Caprice in A Minor
———, Caprice in E-Flat Major (Alla Saltarella)
Winternitz, "Troika" Capriccio

All of the original compositions and transcriptions thus far listed are for the violin. Kreisler also wrote a few songs: "Drei Nachtgesänge" (Three Evening Songs), words by Eichendorff; "Ghasel" (words by Keller); "Ein altes Lied" (An Old Song) arrangement for voice of the "Caprice viennois."

Kreisler has also made arrangements of his best known works for the following instruments and combinations of instruments: piano solo, cello solo, trio for violin, cello and piano, and string quartet.

DISCOGRAPHY

A List of Recordings by Fritz Kreisler from 1910 to January, 1950

Throughout his professional career Fritz Kreisler recorded for RCA Victor and its European affiliates, the Gramophone Company, Ltd., "His Master's Voice" (Victor) of London, and the Electrola-Gesellschaft m.b.H. of Berlin. The serial numbers in this Discography are throughout those of RCA Victor.

The list comprises all Victor records released. Recordings made in Europe, the matrices of which were imported to America and released by Victor, are indicated by an "X" preceding the catalog number. When a record number is preceded by an asterisk (*), the number so marked has been cut from the catalog and is not obtainable. When there is no symbol before the record number, the disc is still available.

The meticulous, time-consuming work of compiling the Discography, which necessitated going through card indexes covering forty years and checking and rechecking to insure accuracy, was done by courtesy of the Record Department of the Radio Corporation of America, RCA Victor Division, Camden, New Jersey, under the personal supervision of Miss Elsie M. Garrison, to whom the author is especially indebted.

The Discography, as far as the author was able to ascertain, is incomplete in only one respect: it does not include the series of recordings of all Beethoven sonatas for violin and piano that Kreisler and Franz Rupp made for the Beethoven Society of London.

*64130	1325-B	* 722-A	"Old Folks at Home" (Swanee River) (Foster-Kreisler)
*64131	* 712-A		Hungarian Dance in G Minor (Brahms)
*64132	* 712-B		Gavotte in E (Bach)
*64142	* 716-B		"Chanson sans paroles" (Song Without Words) (Tchaikovsky)
*64156	* 710-A		Variations (Tartini-Kreisler)
*64202	* 713-A		"Aubade provencale" (Couperin-Kreisler)
*64292	* 713-B	14592-B	Chanson Louis XIII and Pavane (in the style of Couperin)
*64313			Melodie from *Orfeo* (Gluck)
*64314	1386-B	* 721-A	"Schön Rosmarin" (Fair Rosemary) (Kreisler)
*64315	* 710-B		Andantino (Martini-Kreisler)
*64319	* 711-A		"Berceuse" (Mme. Lawrence Townsend)

*64406	* 910-B		"Viennese Melody" (Gärtner-Kreisler)
*64408	* 910-A		Austrian Hymn ("God Preserve the Emperor") (Haydn)
*64488	* 723-B		Slavonic Dance No. 1 (Dvořák)
	(This was remade later for 1414-A)		
*64502	1320-A	* 720-B	"The Rosary" (Nevin-Kreisler)
*64503	* 724-A		"Sérénade espagnole" (Chaminade-Kreisler)
*64504	* 726-B		Mazurka in A Minor (Chopin-Kreisler)
*64529	* 720-A		"The Old Refrain" (Viennese popular song) (Brandl-Kreisler)
	(Remade, *see* 1465-A)		
*64542			"Song Without Words," No. 25 (May Breeze) (Mendelssohn)
*64556	* 724-B		Spanish Dance (Granados-Kreisler)
*64563	* 727-A		"Songs My Mother Taught Me" (Gypsy song from Slavonic Fantasy) (Dvořák-Kreisler)
*64565	* 711-B		"Berceuse romantique," Op. 9 (Kreisler)
*64575	1386-A		Rondino on a Theme by Beethoven (Kreisler)
*64600	* 715-A		Rondino (Kreisler)
*64601	* 715-B		Adagietto from L'Arlésienne (Bizet)
*64614	* 718-B		Minuet (Boccherini)
*64655	* 714-B		"Poor Butterfly" (Hubbell)
*64660	* 719-B		"Underneath the Stars" (Herbert Spencer; arr. by Josef Pasternack)
*64670	* 723-A		Ballet Music from *Rosamunde* (Schubert-Kreisler)
*64709	* 718-A		Paraphrase on Minuet (Paderewski-Kreisler; orchestrated by Joseph Pasternack)
*64730	* 708-B		"Dream of Youth" (Rêve de Jeunesse) (Felix Winternitz)
*64731	* 721-B		"Polichinelle Serenade" (Kreisler)
*64817	* 707-A		"Beautiful Ohio" (waltz) (Mary Earl)
*64824	* 722-B		"Nobody Knows the Trouble I See" (Clarence Cameron White)
*64842	* 709-B		"La Gitana" (Arabo-Spanish Gypsy song of the 18th century) (Kreisler)
*64857	* 709-A		"Gypsy Serenade" (Charles Robert Valdez)

*64873	* 708-A		"Forsaken" (Koschat-Winternitz)
*64890	* 706-A		"Chanson indoue" from *Sadko* (Rimsky-Korsakoff; arr. by Kreisler)
*64902	* 719-A		"Who Can Tell" from operetta *Apple Blossoms* (Kreisler)
*64924	* 714-A		"Love Nest" from musical comedy *Mary* (Louis A. Hirsch)
*64947	* 707-B		"On Miami Shore" (waltz) (Victor Jacobi)
*64961	* 725-B		Melody in A Major (General Charles G. Dawes)
*64974	1325-A	* 716-A	"Souvenir" (Franz Drdla)
*64993	* 727-B		"To Spring" (Grieg, Op. 43, No. 6)
*66023	* 725-B		"Paradise" (Viennese folk song) (Krakauer-Kreisler)
*66040	* 729-A		"Sérénade espagnole" (Chaminade-Kreisler); Hugo Kreisler, cello; Fritz Kreisler, piano
*66041	* 726-A		Waltz (Brahms, Op. 39, No. 15) (arr. by David Hochstein)
*66079	* 706-B		"Chanson arabe" (arr. by Fritz Kreisler from Rimsky-Korsakoff's *Scheherazade*)
X*66082	X* 729-B		Viennese Folk Song Fantasy (arr. by Hugo Kreisler); Hugo Kreisler, cello; Fritz Kreisler, piano
*66104	* 717-B		"Aucassin and Nicolette" (Canzonetta) (Kreisler)
*66127	* 728-A		"Pale Moon" (Indian Love Song) (Frederick Knight Logan; arr. by Kreisler)
*66137	* 728-B		"Toy Soldiers' March" (Fritz Kreisler)
*66149	* 717-A		"Midnight Bells" (Viennese melody) (R. Heuberger; transcribed by Fritz Kreisler)
X*66116	X* 956-B		"I'm in Love" from *Apple Blossoms*; Hugo Kreisler, cello; Fritz Kreisler, piano
X*66185	X* 956-A		Letter Song from *Apple Blossoms*, Hugo Kreisler, cello; Fritz Kreisler, piano
*66157	* 947-A		Mazurka, Op. 33, No. 2 (Chopin)
*66176	* 947-B		Melodie, Op. 16, No. 2 (Paderewski; transcribed by F. Kreisler)

*66196	* 966-A		"Cherry Ripe" (Cyril Scott)
*66197	* 966-B		Entr'acte (A. Walter Kramer)
X*66218	X* 987-A		"Liebesleid" (Love's Sorrow) (F. Kreisler); Hugo Kreisler, cello; Fritz Kreisler, piano
X*66219	X* 987-B		Serenade from *Les Millions d'Arlequin* (Drigo); Hugo Kreisler, cello; Fritz Kreisler, piano
*66231	* 994-A		"Love Sends a Little Gift of Roses" (John Openshaw)
*66232	* 994-B		"The World Is Waiting for the Sunrise" (Ernest Seitz)
*66250	*1010-A		Minuet (Haydn-Friedberg)
*66251	*1010-B		Old French Gavotte (Carl Friedberg)
*66269	1115-B		"From the Land of the Sky Blue Water" (Cadman-Kreisler)
*66270	*1122-B		Negro Spiritual Melody (adapted by Kreisler from the Largo of Dvořák's "New World" Symphony)
*74172	*6188-A		"Aus der Heimat": Bohemian Fantasy (Smetana)
*74180	*6181-B		"Humoresque" (Dvořák, Op. 101, No. 7)
*74182	*6186-A	6844-A	"Meditation" from *Thaïs* (Massenet)
*74196	*6182-A	*6608-A	"Liebesfreud" (Love's Joy) (old Vienna waltz) (Kreisler)
*74197			"Caprice viennois" (Kreisler)
(Remade and replaced by *6181-A, *6692-A; remade again in Europe and issued in U.S. under number X*14690-A)			
*74202	*6185-B		1. "Moment musical" (Schubert) 2. "Tambourin" (Rameau-Kreisler)
*74203	*6185-A	6844-B	"Tambourin chinois" (Kreisler, Op. 3)
X*74294	X*6187-B		Scherzo (Dittersdorf-Kreisler)
*74330	*6188-B		Chanson, "Méditation" (Cottenet)
*74332			Praeludium (Bach)
*74333	*6182-B	*6608-B	"Liebesleid" (Love's Sorrow) (Kreisler)
*74384	*6184-A		Largo (Handel-Kreisler)
*74387	*6186-B	7225-B	"Indian Lament" (Dvořák-Kreisler)
*74437	*6183-B		Slavonic Dance No. 2 (in E Minor) (Dvořák-Kreisler)
*74463	*6187-A		"Wienerisch" (Viennese Waltz) (Leopold Godowsky)

*74487	*6184-B	*8041-B	Andante Cantabile (from String Quartet, Op. 11) (Tchaikovsky)
*74720	*6183-A		"Hymn to the Sun," from *L'Coq d'Or* (Rimsky-Korsakoff; arr. by Kreisler)
*76028	*8040-A		Concerto for Two Violins in D Minor (J. S. Bach); Fritz Kreisler and Efrem Zimbalist
*76029	*8040-B		Part 2, Fritz Kreisler and Efrem Zimbalist
*76030	*8041-A		concluded, Fritz Kreisler and Effrem Zimbalist
*87191	*87545	*3021-A	Serenade, "Softly Through the Night is Calling" (Mattullath-Schubert); John McCormack, tenor; Fritz Kreisler, violin obbligato
*87192	*87546	*3021-B	"Ave Maria" (Mascagni) (adapted to Intermezzo from *Cavalleria Rusticana*); John McCormack, tenor; Fritz Kreisler, violin obbligato
*87230	*87547	*3018-A	Serenata (Moszkowski); John McCormack, tenor; Fritz Kreisler, violin obbligato
*87231	*87548	*3018-B	"Carmè" (Canto Sorrento) (arr. B. G. DeCurtis); John McCormack, tenor; Fritz Kreisler, violin obbligato
*87232	*87549	*3022-B	"Flirtation" (Meyer Helmund); John McCormack, tenor; Fritz Kreisler, violin obbligato
*87233	*87550	*3023-A	"Calm as the Night" (Carl Bohm); John McCormack, tenor; Fritz Kreisler, violin obbligato
*87245	*87551	*3019-A	Barcarolle from *Tales of Hoffmann* (Offenbach); John McCormack, tenor; Fritz Kreisler, violin obbligato
*87258	*87552	*3019-B	Serenade (Rosier-Raff); John McCormack, tenor; Fritz Kreisler, violin obbligato
*87571		*3020-A	"When Night Descends"; John McCormack, tenor; Fritz Kreisler, violin obbligato
*87573		*3022-A	"Since You Went Away" (James W. and J. Rosamond Johnson); John McCor-

			mack, tenor; Fritz Kreisler, violin obbligato
*87574		*3020-B	"O Cease Thy Singing Maiden Fair" (Rachmaninoff, Op. 4, No. 4); John McCormack, tenor; Fritz Kreisler, violin obbligato
*87576		*3023-B	"The Last Hour" (Jessie C. Brown, A. Walter Kramer); John McCormack, tenor; Fritz Kreisler, violin obbligato
X*87577		X*3017-A	"Farewell to Cuchullin" (Londonderry Air) (arr. by. F. Kreisler); Fritz Kreisler with Hugo Kreisler, cellist
X*87579		X*3017-B	Serenade (Jeral-Kreisler); Fritz Kreisler with Hugo Kreisler, cellist
*88479	*89103	8033-B	"Angel's Serenade" (Braga); John McCormack, tenor; Fritz Kreisler, violin obbligato
*88481	*89104	8032-A	"Ave Maria" (Bach-Gounod); John McCormack, tenor; Fritz Kreisler, violin obbligato
*88482	*89105		"Le Nil" (The Nile) (D'Armand Renaud, Xavier Leroux); John McCormack, tenor; Fritz Kreisler, violin obbligato
*88483	*89106	8032-B	Lullaby from *Jocelyn* (Benjamin Godard); John McCormack, tenor; Fritz Kreisler, violin obbligato
*88484	*89107	8033-A	"Ave Maria" (Schubert); John McCormack, tenor; Fritz Kreisler, violin obbligato
*88537	*89108	*8024-A	"Mighty Lak' a Rose" (Ethelbert Nevin); Geraldine Farrar, soprano; Fritz Kreisler, violin obbligato
*88538	*89109	*8024-B	"Connais-tu le pays?" from *Mignon* (Thomas); Geraldine Farrar, soprano; Fritz Kreisler, violin obbligato
*1029-A			"A Kiss in the Dark" (from *Orange Blossoms* (Victor Herbert)
*1029-B			"Waltzing Doll" (Poupée valsante) (Poldini-Kreisler)
X*1039-A			Melody in F (Rubinstein); Hugo Kreisler, cello; Fritz Kreisler, piano

X*1039-B	"La Cinquantaine" (The Golden Wedding, Gabriel Prosper Marie); Hugo Kreisler, cello; Fritz Kreisler, piano
*1043-A	"Slavonic Lament" (Schuett-Friedberg)
*1043-B	"Dirge of the North" (Balogh-Kreisler)
*1062-A	"Pierrot's Dance Song" from *Die Tote Stadt* (E. W. Korngold; arr. by F. Kreisler)
*1062-B	Chansonette (George Bass)
*1075-A	"Dance orientale" (arr. by Fritz Kreisler from Rimsky-Korsakoff's *Scheherazade*)
*1075-B	"Molly on the Shore" (Irish reel) (Grainger-Kreisler)
*1093-A	"Legend of the Canyon" (Charles Wakefield Cadman)
*1093-B	"Caprice antique" (Balogh-Kreisler)
*1122-A	"Song of the Volga Boatmen" (paraphrase, introducing "A Russian Folk Melody"; arr. by Kreisler)
1115-A	"Aloha Oe" (Liliuokalani-Kreisler)
1136-A	Menuet (Bach-Winternitz)
1136-B	Gavotte (Beethoven-Kramer)
1151-A	"Indian Love Call" from *Rose-Marie* (Harbach-Hammerstein II-Friml)
1151-B	"Deep in My Heart, Dear" from *The Student Prince* (Donnelly-Romberg)
1158-A	"Frasquita Serenade" (Lehár-Kreisler)
1158-B	"Kreisler Serenade" (Lehár)
1165-A	"At Dawning" (Cadman-Rissland)
1165-B	Andantino (Lemare-Saenger)
1170-A	"Albumblatt" (Rachmaninoff-Kreisler)
1170-B	"Humoresque" (Tchaikovsky-Kreisler)
1209-A	"Oriental Romance" (Rimsky-Korsakoff; arr. by Jacques Gordon)
*1209-B	"Invocation" (Owen-Kreisler)
*1233-A	"Blue Skies" (Berlin-Kreisler)
*1233-B	"Dance of the Maidens" (Friml-Kreisler)
*1244-A	"Malagueña" (Albéniz-Kreisler)
*1244-B	"Canción populare" (De Falla)
*1339-A	Tango (Albéniz, Op. 165, No. 2; arr. by Kreisler)

*1339-B		"Dance espagnole" (De Falla-Kreisler)
1358-A		"La Fille aux cheveux de lin" (The Maiden with the Flaxen Hair) (Debussy-Hartmann-Kreisler)
1358-B		"En bateau" (Boating) (Debussy)
*1414-B		"Songs My Mother Taught Me" (Dvořák-Kreisler)
*1428-A		"Ruralia Hungarica"—Presto (Dohnányi, Op. 32, No. 1)
*1428-B		"Ruralia Hungarica"—Molto vivace (Dohnányi, Op. 32, No. 1)
*1429-A		"Ruralia Hungarica"—Gypsy Andante, Part 1 (Dohnányi, Op. 32, No. 2)
*1429-B		"Ruralia Hungarica"—Gypsy Andante, concluded (Dohnányi, Op. 32, No. 2)
X 1465-A		"The Old Refrain" (Viennese popular song) (Kreisler)
(Also previously made here. *See* 720-A.)		
X 1465-B		"Midnight Bells" from *The Opera Ball* (Heuberger)
(Also previously made here. *See* 717-A.)		
*1501-A		"Dance of the Marionette" (Winternitz)
X*1501-B		"Polichinelle Serenade" (Kreisler)
X*1503-A		Chanson Louis XIII et Pavane (Couperin-Kreisler)
X*1503-B		"La Précieuse" (Couperin-Kreisler)
X*1505-A	X*26573-A	Ballet Music from *Rosamunde* (Schubert-Kreisler)
X*1505-B	X*26573-B	Larghetto (Weber-Kreisler)
X*1504-A		"Jota" (De Falla)
X*1504-B		"Sérénade espagnole (Glazounoff-Kreisler)
X 1891-A		"Danza española" from *La Vida breve* (De Falla)
X 1891-B		"Liebesfreud" (Love's Joy) (Kreisler)
X 1981-A		"Chanson indoue" (Song of India) (Rimsky-Korsakoff)
X 1981-B		"Poupée valsante" (Dancing Doll) (Poldini-Kreisler)
X 1950-A		"La Gitana" (Kreisler)
X 1950-B		"Liebesleid" (Love's Sorrow) (Kreisler)
X 2164-A		"Londonderry Air" (Grainger-Kreisler)

X 2164-B	Mazurka in A Minor (Chopin, Op. posth. 67, No. 4; arr. by Kreisler)
X*3035-A	"Miniature Viennese March" (Marche miniature viennoise) (Kreisler); Hugo Kreisler, cello
X*3035-B	"Syncopation" (Kreisler); Hugo Kreisler, cello
X*3036-A	"Evening Song" (Abendlied) (Schumann); Hugo Kreisler, cello
X*3036-B	"Nina" (Tre Giorni) (Pergolesi-Kreisler); Hugo Kreisler, cello
X*3037-A	Minuet in G (Beethoven-Kreisler); Hugo Kreisler, cello
X*3037-B	Andante in F Major (Beethoven-Kreisler); Hugo Kreisler, cello
X*6520-A and B to 6523-A and B incl.	Concerto No. 4, in D (Mozart); orchestra conducted by Sir Landon Ronald
*6692-B	"Humoresque" (Dvořák-Kreisler)
X*6706-A	"Lotus Land" (Cyril Scott)
X*6706-B	Hungarian Dance No. 17 (Brahms-Kreisler)
*6712-A	"Gypsy Caprice" (Kreisler)
*6712-B	"Shepherd's Madrigal" (Kreisler)
7225-A	"Slavonic Dance No. 3 (Dvořák-Kreisler)
X*Album M-13 (8074 to 8079 incl.)	Concerto in D Major, Op. 61 (Beethoven); Berlin State Opera Orchestra, conducted by Leo Blech
X*Album AM-13 (8138 to 8143 incl.)	Concerto in D Major, Op. 61 (Beethoven) (including, as final side in album, Adagio from Partita in G Minor, by Bach); Berlin State Opera Orchestra, conducted by Leo Blech
X*Album M-19 (8080 to 8083 incl.)	Concerto in E Minor, Op. 64 (Mendelssohn); Berlin State Opera Orchestra, conducted by Leo Blech
X*Album AM-19 (8126 to 8129 incl.)	Concerto in E Minor, Op. 64 (Mendelssohn (including, as final side in album, "A May Breeze" [Song Without Words], Mendelssohn-Kreisler); Berlin State Opera Orchestra, conducted by Leo Blech

X*8090-A	L'Arlésienne: Intermezzo (Bizet-Kreisler); Fritz and Hugo Kreisler, violin and cello duet
X*8090-B	"Sanctissima" (Corelli-Kreisler); Fritz and Hugo Kreisler, violin and cello duet
X*Album M-36 (8098 to 8102 incl.)	Concerto in D Major, Op. 77 (Brahms); Berlin State Opera Orchestra, conducted by Leo Blech
X*Album AM-36 (8115, 8118)	Concerto in D Major, Op. 77 (Brahms) (including, as final side in album, Romance in A Major, Schumann-Kreisler); Berlin State Opera Orchestra, conducted by Leo Blech
X*Album AM-45 (8106 to 8108)	Sonata in C Minor, Op. 45 (Grieg); Rachmaninoff and Kreisler
X* Album M-45 (8112 to 8114)	Sonata in C Minor, Op. 45 (Grieg); Rachmaninoff and Kreisler
*8163, 8164	Sonata in G Major, Op. 30, No. 3 (Beethoven); Rachmaninoff and Kreisler
*Album M-107 (8216 to 8218 incl.)	Sonata in A Major, Op. 162 (Schubert); Rachmaninoff and Kreisler
*Album AM-107 (8219 to 8221 incl.)	Sonata in A Major, Op. 162 (Schubert); Rachmaninoff and Kreisler
X*Album M-277 (8786 to 8788 incl.)	Concerto in E Minor, Op. 64 (Mendelssohn); London Philharmonic Orchestra, Sir Landon Ronald, conductor
X*Album AM-277 (8789 to 8791 incl.)	Concerto in E Minor, Op. 64 (Mendelssohn); London Philharmonic Orchestra, Sir Landon Ronald, conductor
X Album DM-277 (16689 to 16691 incl.)	Concerto in E Minor, Op. 64 (Mendelssohn); London Philharmonic Orchestra, Sir Landon Ronald, conductor
X*Album M-325 (14163 to 14168 incl.)	Concerto in D Major, Op. 61 (Beethoven); London Philharmonic, John Barbirolli, conductor
X*Album AM-325 (14169 to 14174 incl.)	Concerto in D Major, Op. 61 (Beethoven); London Philharmonic, John Barbirolli, conductor
X Album DM-325 (16878 to 16883 incl.) X 14168-B X*14690-B	Concerto in D Major, Op. 61 (Beethoven); (including, as final side, "Tambourin chinois") (Kreisler); London

	Philharmonic, John Barbirolli, conductor
X*Album M-335 (14249 to 14252 incl.)	Quartet in A Minor (Kreisler); Kreisler String Quartet
X*Album AM-335 (14253 to 14256 incl.)	Quartet in A Minor (Kreisler); (including, as final side, Scherzo à la Dittersdorf) (Kreisler); Kreisler String Quartet
*Album M-361 (14420, 14421)	Concerto for Violin (Paganini-Kreisler); Philadelphia Orchestra, Eugene Ormandy, conductor
Album DM-361 (18438, 18439)	Concerto for Violin (Paganini-Kreisler); Philadelphia Orchestra, Eugene Ormandy, conductor
X*Album M-402 (14588 to 14592)	Concerto in D Major, Op. 77 (Brahms); London Philharmonic, John Barbirolli, conductor
X*Album AM-402 (14593 to 14597-S)	Concerto in D Major, Op. 77 (Brahms); (including, as final side, Chanson Louis XIII and Pavane) (Couperin-Kreisler); Victor Symphony Orchestra, Donald Voorhees, conductor
(Also 11-9265-B, in Album M-1070)	
X Album DM-402 (16525 to 16529)	Concerto in D Major, Op. 77 (Brahms); London Philharmonic, John Barbirolli, conductor
X*14690-A	"Caprice viennois," Op. 2 (Kreisler)
X 15217-A	Andante Cantabile from Quartet in D, Op. 11 (Tchaikovsky)
X 15217-B	"Humoresque," Op. 101, No. 7 (Dvořák-Kreisler)
X 15487-A	*Le Coq d'Or*: "Hymn to the Sun" (Rimsky-Korsakoff)
X 15487-B	"Lotus Land" (Scott-Kreisler)
X 10-1022-A	Gavotte from Partita No. 3, in E (Bach-Kreisler)
X 10-1022-B	Rondino on a Theme by Beethoven (Kreisler)
10-1395-A	"The Rosary" (Nevin-Kreisler); RCA Victor Orchestra, Donald Voorhees, conductor
10-1395-B	"Stars in My Eyes" from Columbia film

	The King Steps Out (Kreisler); RCA Victor Orchestra, Donald Voorhees, conductor
DM-1044 (10-1202 to 10-1204)	Kreisler Program: "The Old Refrain," "Miniature Viennese March," Rondino on a Theme by Beethoven, "Midnight Bells," "Londonderry Air" Hungarian Rondo (Haydn-Kreisler); RCA Victor Orchestra, Donald Voorhees, conductor
DM-910 (11-8230 to 11-8232)	"My Favorites" (new orchestrations by the composer): "Caprice viennois," "Tambourin chinois," "Liebesfreud," "Liebesleid," "Schön Rosmarin," "La Gitana"; with RCA Victor Symphony Orchestra, Charles O'Connell, conductor
* M-1070 (11-9264, 11-9265)	Concerto in C (in the style of Vivaldi) (Kreisler); RCA Victor String Orchestra, Donald Voorhees, conductor
DM-1070 (11-9266, 11-9267)	Concerto in C (in the style of Vivaldi) (Kreisler); RCA Victor String Orchestra, Donald Voorhees, conductor (including, as final side, Chanson Louis XIII and Pavane) (Kreisler); RCA Victor Symphony Orchestra, Donald Voorhees, conductor
11-9952A, B	Viennese Rhapsodic Fantasietta (Kreisler); RCA Victor Orchestra, Donald Voorhees, conductor
X*Album M-623 (15759 to 15761)	Concerto No. 4, in D, K. 218 (Mozart); London Philharmonic Orchestra, Malcolm Sargent, conductor
X* Album AM-623 (15762 to 15764)	Concerto No. 4, in D, K. 218 (Mozart); London Philharmonic Orchestra, Malcolm Sargent, conductor
X Album DM-623 (15986 to 15988)	Concerto No. 4, in D, K. 218 (Mozart); London Philharmonic Orchestra, Malcolm Sargent, conductor
X*17220A, B	Rondo (from "Haffner" Serenade, Parts 1 and 2 in D) K. 250 (Mozart-Kreisler)

BIBLIOGRAPHY

BOOKS

1. DOMESTIC

Bauer, Harold, *Harold Bauer, His Book.* W. W. Norton & Co., 1948.
Bekker, Paul, *The Story of the Orchestra.* W. W. Norton & Co., 1936.
———, *The Story of Music.* W. W. Norton & Co., 1927.
Brook, Donald, *Violinists of Today.* The Macmillan Company, 1949.
Burch, Gladys, *Famous Violinists for Young People.* A. S. Barnes & Co., 1946.
Clemens, Clara, *My Husband Gabrilówitsch.* Harper & Brothers, 1938.
Dorian, Frederick, *The History of Music in Performance.* W. W. Norton & Co., 1942.
———, *The Musical Workshop.* Harper & Brothers, 1947.
Ewen, David, *From Bach to Stravinsky.* W. W. Norton & Co., 1933.
———, *Living Musicians.* H. W. Wilson Co., 1940.
———, *The Book of Modern Composers.* Alfred A. Knopf, 1942.
———, *Men and Women Who Make Music.* The Readers Press, 1945.
———, *Music Comes to America.* Allen, Towne & Heath, Inc., 1947.
Farrar, Geraldine, *The Story of an American Singer.* Houghton, Mifflin & Co., 1916.
———, *Such Sweet Compulsion* (autobiography). Greystone Press, 1938.
Finck, Henry T., *Masters of the Violin.* New York Mentor Association, 1916.
———, *Success in Music and How It Is Won.* Charles Scribner's Sons, 1922.
Finletter, Gretchen, *From the Top of the Stairs.* Little, Brown & Co., 1947.
Finn, William J., *Sharps and Flats in Five Decades.* Harper & Brothers, 1947.
Flesch, Carl, *The Art of Violin Playing.* Carl Fischer, 1924.
———, *Problems of Tone Production in Violin Playing.* Carl Fischer, 1934.
Gaisberg, F. W., *The Music Goes Round.* The Macmillan Company, 1942.
Geissmar, Berta, *Two Worlds of Music.* Creative Age Press, 1946.
Graf, Max, *Legend of a Musical City.* Philosophical Library, Inc., 1945.
Gronowicz, Antoni, *Sergei Rachmaninoff.* E. P. Dutton & Co., 1946.
Hughes, Adella Prentiss, *Music Is My Life.* World Publishing Co., 1947.
Jones, E. Stanley, *The Christ of Every Road.* Abingdon Press, 1930.
Kaufmann, Helen L., and Eva vb. Hansl, *Artists in Music Today.* Grosset & Dunlap, 1933.
Krehbiel, H. E., *The Bohemians—A Narrative.* The Bohemians, 1921.
Kreisler, Fritz, *Four Weeks in the Trenches.* Houghton, Mifflin & Co., 1915.

Littlehales, Lillian, *Pablo Casals—A Life*. W. W. Norton & Co., 1948.
Martens, Frederick H., *Violin Mastery*. Frederick A. Stokes Co., 1919.
McCormack, Lily, *I Hear You Calling Me*. Bruce Publishing Co., 1949.
Moore, Douglas, *Listening to Music*. W. W. Norton & Co., 1937.
O'Connell, Charles, *The Other Side of the Record*. Alfred A. Knopf, 1947.
Parker, H. T., *Eighth Notes, Voices and Figures of Music and the Dance*. Dodd, Mead & Co., 1922.
Phillips, Charles, *Paderewski, The Story of a Modern Immortal*. The Macmillan Company, 1934.
von Riesemann, Oskar, *Rachmaninoff's Recollections*. George Allen & Unwin, 1934.
Siegmeister, Elie, *The Music Lover's Handbook*. William Morrow & Co., 1943.
Slonimsky, Nicolas, *Music Since 1900*. W. W. Norton & Co., 1937.
Smith, Moses, *Koussevitzky*. Allen, Towne & Heath, 1947.
Smyth, Ethel, *Impressions That Remained*. Alfred A. Knopf, 1946.
Spaeth, Sigmund A., and John Tasker Howard, *The Ampico in Music Study*. Ampico Corporation, 1925.
———, *A History of Popular Music in America*. Random House, 1948.
Spalding, Albert, *Rise to Follow: An Autobiography*. Henry Holt & Co., 1943.
Stebbins, Lucy and Richard, *Frank Damrosch: Let the People Sing*. Duke University Press, 1945.
Stidger, W. L., *The Human Side of Greatness*. Harper & Brothers, 1940.
Stokowski, Olga Samaroff, *The Layman's Music Book*. W. W. Norton & Co., 1935.
Szigeti, Joseph, *With Strings Attached*. Alfred A. Knopf, 1947.
Taylor, Deems, *Of Men and Music*. Simon and Schuster, 1937.
Veinus, Abraham, *Victor Book of Concertos*. Simon and Schuster, 1948.
Wallace, Archer, *Hands Around the World*. Richard R. Smith, 1930.

2. FOREIGN

Bekker, Paul, *Das deutsche Musikleben*. Berlin, Schuster & Löffler, 1916.
Eberhardt, Siegfried, *Der beseelte Violinton*. Gerhard Keuthmann Verlag, 1910.
Farga, Franz, *Geigen und Geiger*. Zurich, Albert Müller Verlag A.G., 1940.
Flesch, Carl, *Die Kunst des Violinspiels*. Leipzig, C. F. Peters, 1924.
Friedländer, Max, *Zuccalmaglio und das Volkslied*. Jahrbuch der Musikbibliothek Peters, 1918.
Grünberg, Max, *Meister der Violine*. Stuttgart, Deutsche Verlags-Anstalt, 1925.
Hadden, J. Cuthbert, *Modern Musicians*. London, T. N. Foulis, 1913.
Hill, William, Arthur, and Alfred S., *The Violin Makers of the Guarneri Family*. London, W. E. Hill & Sons, 1931.
Mahler, Alma, *Gustav Mahler: Memories and Letters*. London, John Murray, 1946.
Pincherle, Marc, *Feuillets d'histoire du violon*. Paris, G. Legouix, 1927.
Scholes, Percy A., *Crotchets: A Few Short Musical Notes*. London, John Lane, 1924.

van der Straeten, Edmund, *The History of the Violin*. London, Cassell & Co., Ltd., 1933.

Weissmann, Adolf, *Die Musik der Sinne*. Stuttgart, Deutsche Verlags-Anstalt, 1925.

Ysaÿe, Antoine, *Eugène Ysaÿe, sa vie, son œuvre, son influence*. Bruxelles, Editions L'Écran du Monde, 1948.

Maine, Basil, *On Music*. London, John Westhouse, Ltd., 1945.

MAGAZINE ARTICLES

1. DOMESTIC

American Magazine, "He Plays on the World's Heartstrings," by Beverly Smith, February, 1931.

American Music Lover, "Virtuosi of the Violin," by Peter Hugh Reed, May, 1941.

Arts and Decorations, "Operetta's New Life," November, 1919.

Baton, The, "Fritz Kreisler, King of Violinists," by Elizabeth Stutsman, November, 1929.

Bookman, "Chronicle and Comment," May, 1915.

Catholic World, "A Connecticut Yankee of Our Lady's Court," by Elizabeth P. Walsh, May, 1949.

Current Opinion, "Kreisler and Riesenfeld Wield Cudgels Like Batons," October, 1924.

Delineator, "Radio's Million Dollar Music," November, 1935.

Esquire, "L'Amico Fritz," by David Ewen, August, 1935.

Etude, "Gallery of Musical Celebrities," April, 1929.

———, "Why Great Artists Succeed," by C. D. Isaacson, October, 1930.

———, "Kreisler and the Prodigy," by Carleton A. Scheinert, September, 1934.

———, "Who Wrote That?" by R. E. Wolseley, October, 1940.

———, "Fortunes in Melody," January, 1942.

———, "Philosophy of Musicianship," by Rose Heylbut, September, 1944.

Everybody's Magazine, "Heroes and Heroines of the Violin," by James Huneker, May, 1909.

Good Housekeeping, "Little Stories of Big Men," by K. Bercovici, January, 1934.

Harper's Bazaar, "Men and Women of Interest," January, 1910.

Harper's Weekly, "The Deep-Chested Austrian," Nov. 9, 1901.

———, "The World of Music," by Lawrence Gilman, Dec. 4, 1909.

Independent, "Ysaÿe, Kreisler, Vecsey," Jan. 19, 1905.

Jacobs' Orchestra Monthly, "A Musical Hoax," by Arthur C. Morse, March, 1935.

Journal of Religion, "Pseudonymity—A Modern Case," by C. Jackson, October, 1940.

Ladies' Home Journal, "My Musical Life," by Walter Damrosch, January and April, 1923.

Library of Congress Quarterly Journal of Current Acquisitions, "The Brahms and Chausson Manuscripts Presented by Mr. Fritz Kreisler," by Harold Spivacke, May, 1949.
Life, "Picture of the Week," May 12, 1941.
Literary Digest, "The Music of Shell-fire," May 29, 1915.
———, "States of Mind on Kreisler," Dec. 27, 1919.
———, "Kreisler Discusses America's Attitude Toward Him," Jan. 3, 1920.
———, "Kreisler Ending the War," June 25, 1921.
———, "Kreisler on German Intellectuals," Feb. 2, 1924.
———, "The Humility of a Great Musician," April 5, 1924.
Living Age, "Kreisler in Japan," June 30, 1923.
———, "Violinist in the Orient," March 1, 1924.
Mentor, "Fritz Kreisler's Emotional Art," by Henry T. Finck, May, 1916.
———, "Music and Life," by Fritz Kreisler, December, 1921.
———, "Personality of Kreisler," December, 1921.
Missionary Review, "Talents Not for Sale," June, 1933.
Musical America, "Fritz Kreisler Talks on a Variety of Subjects," Nov. 9, 1907.
———, "Independence Is What an Artist Must Have," Feb. 5, 1910.
———, "The Military Violinist," Nov. 19, 1910.
———, "Little Violin Music of Value Being Written," by A. Walter Kramer, Dec. 14, 1912.
———, "Two Ways to Play," an editorial, Feb. 4, 1914.
———, "Happy Is the Man Whose Profession Is His Hobby," by Henrietta Malkiel, April 26, 1924.
———, "L'Affaire Kreisler," an editorial, Feb. 25, 1935.
———, "Fritz Kreisler on Road to Recovery," Oct. 10, 1941.
Musical Courier, "Kreisler, A Colossus Among Violinists," Sept. 18, 1907.
———, "The Story of My Violins," by Fritz Kreisler, April 8, 1908.
———, "An Estimate of Kreisler," from the *London Strad*, Dec. 9, 1908.
———, "A Jolly Prank," by Leonard Liebling, June 9, 1909.
———, "Kreisler Talks About His Art," Jan. 26, 1910.
———, "Kreisler's Violin Art," an editorial, Nov. 26, 1913.
———, "With Fritz Kreisler at the Front," by Harriet Kreisler, October 14, 1914.
———, "Kreisler's Violin Art," Nov. 26, 1918.
Musical Forecast, "Kreisleriana," by George Seibel, December, 1946.
Musical Observer, "Fritz Kreisler," by W. E. B., September, 1909.
———, "Fritz Kreisler," by Edmund Severn, January, 1908.
———, "Fritz Kreisler—The Artist and the Man," by Cordelia Camp, August, 1925.
———, "The First Twenty-five Years Are the Hardest," by Ernö Balogh, November, 1930.
———, "Kreisler, Einstein, Mussolini," by Bernard Smith, May, 1931.

Musician, The, "Kreisler Interview," by Arthur Judson, March, 1910.
———, "Studies in Comparative Interpretations," by John Tasker Howard, February, 1935.
———, "The Kreisler 'Hoax,' " an editorial, February, 1935.
Nation, The, "Lion of the Musical Season," by Henry T. Finck, March 18, 1915.
———, "Three Violinists," Nov. 22, 1919.
———, "Fritz Kreisler," an editorial, Nov. 14, 1928.
Newsweek, "Modest Violinist 'Comes Clean,' " Feb. 16, 1935.
———, "Comeback," Jan. 26, 1942.
———, "Radio: Kreisler Capitulates," Feb. 21, 1944.
New Yorker, "Profiles: A Gentleman from Vienna," Nov. 24, 1928.
Outlook, "Two Great Violinists," by Richard Aldrich, May 6, 1905.
———, "Two Austrian Musicians," Dec. 23, 1914.
———, "Franz Josef and Fritz Kreisler," Dec. 27, 1916.
———, "Artist, Officer and Gentleman," Dec. 5, 1917.
———, "An Honorable Foe," Dec. 24, 1919.
———, "The Enjoyment of Music: About Good Violin Playing," by W. J. Henderson, Dec. 27, 1922.
Photo-Era, "Photographing Musicians," an editorial, March, 1926.
Reader's Digest, "The Maestro Plays On," by Doron K. Antrim, August, 1944.
Saturday Evening Post, "Genius Backstage," by Olin Downes, March 15, 1930.
Theater Arts, "Career of Fritz Kreisler," January, 1940.
Touchstone, "Fritz Kreisler Plays," poem by Grace Hazard Conkling, November, 1917.
Vanity Fair, "Stray Thoughts on Modern Music," authorized interview with Fritz Kreisler, August, 1924.
Variety, "Kreisler Returns to the Stage," Nov. 11, 1942.
Violinist, "The Story of My Violins," by Fritz Kreisler, September, 1923.
———, "Great Artists Under the Magnifying Glass," by Eugene Riviere Redervill, December, 1916.
Violins and Violinists, "With the Artists," by Samuel and Sadie Applebaum, October, November, December, 1947.

2. FOREIGN

Allgemeine Musik-Zeitung, items concerning Fritz Kreisler in the issues from March, 1899, to January, 1931.
Australian Musical News, issues from April to August, 1925.
Börsenblätter für den Deutschen Buchhandel, "Die Fritz Kreisler Versteigerung in New York," March 8, 1949.
Le Courrier musical et théâtral, "Société Philharmonique," by Paul de Stoecklin, Dec. 1, 1911.
———, "Le Violiniste Kreisler," by Raymond Ballinan, Nov. 15, 1924.

———, "Kreisler," by Yvonne Astruc, Dec. 1, 1924.
———, "Kreisler à l'Opéra," by Pierre Leroi, June 15, 1926.
———, "Kreisler Commandeur de la Légion d'honneur," June 1, 1926.
Dissonances, "Se méfier des contrefaçons," December, 1923.
Fortnightly Review, "Kreisler and the Critics," by Basil Maine, May, 1935.
Hellweg, "Fritz Kreisler," Vol. 52, 1924.
Illustrierte Monatsschrift für Kunst, Musik u.s.w.: "Der Meister der Geige," by Max Marschalk, December, 1927.
Le Ménestral, "Fritz Kreisler," by Émile Vuillermoz, June 5, 1936.
Musical Mirror, "Kreisler," June, 1921.
———, "Power of Interpretation," April, 1924.
———, "Musicians Who Don't Practice," September, 1924.
———, "Jazz Thieves," May, 1925.
———, "Kreisler About Marriage," February, 1927.
———, "Fritz Kreisler," by Ralph Hill, April, 1928.
———, "Kreisler and Snobbery," October, 1929.
———, "Kreisler and Mussolini," September, 1931.
Musical News, "Kreisleriana," May 21, 1921.
Musical News and Weekly, May 8, 1921.
Musical Observer (London), "Elgar's Violin Concerto," December, 1910.
———, "Kreisler at His Best," May, 1911.
———, "Violinist and Soldier," November, 1911.
Musical Standard, "The Richter Concert," by R. Peggio, May 17, 1902.
———, "Herr Fritz Kreisler," Dec. 27, 1902.
———, "Kreisler, the 'Kreis,' and the Kreis'chen," May 21, 1921.
Musical Times, items in the issues from June, 1902, to November, 1912.
Musikalisches Wochenblatt, "Fritz Kreisler: Eine Lebensskizze," by Ernst Mayer, Jan. 5, 1905.
Musikblätter des Anbruch, issues from 1921 to 1938.
Neue Musikzeitung, "Fritz Kreisler," by E. Honold, Vol. XXXIII (1912), p. 238.
Orchester-Magazin, "Fritz Kreisler," biographical sketch by Leopold Weninger, March, April, 1932.
Saturday Review, "Kreisler," by Robin H. Legge, Feb. 7, 1931.
Strad, The, "Chats with Eminent Violinists—Fritz Kreisler," November, 1902.
———, "Fritz Kreisler's Violins," by B. Henderson, October, 1908.
———, "Fritz Kreisler," by B. Henderson, October, 1908.
———, "Fritz Kreisler," by B. Henderson, March, 1927.
———, "Fritz Kreisler on Himself," interviewed by *Neues Wiener Tagblatt*, January, 1933.
———, items in issues from July, 1902, to July, 1924.
White Star Magazine, "Fritz Kreisler Plays for Passport Officials," 1932.

NEWSPAPER ARTICLES AND ITEMS

1. DOMESTIC

In addition to news items consulted, the following special articles were read:

Chicago *Herald*, "Fritz Kreisler's March to Glory—and Death," by Felix Borowski, Dec. 13, 1914.

Chicago *Tribune*, "Kreisler Hailed as a 'Mastersinger,'" by W. L. Hubbard, Jan. 9, 1908.

Christian Science Monitor, "Kreisler's Art," June 18, 1921.

———, "Fritz Kreisler, and What's in Him," by R. M. Hallet, Dec. 7, 1940.

Cleveland *Plain Dealer*, "Fritz is Getting 'Stingy,'" Nov. 28, 1912.

———, "Famous Violinist, Wounded in War, Reported Dead," Dec. 13, 1914.

Boston *Transcript*, "The Changing Kreisler," Jan. 25, 1915.

———, "The Genius of Kreisler," Dec. 8, 1918.

New York *Herald*, "Fritz Kreisler, Violinist, Tells of Slaying Cossack," Nov. 25, 1914.

New York *Herald Tribune*, "Kreisleriana," by Lawrence Gilman, March 31, 1935.

New York *Sun*, "A Soldier Violinist," Oct. 20, 1913.

———, "Kreisler on Holidays," Dec. 28, 1913.

———, "Old Master Kreisler," by W. J. Henderson, Feb. 16, 1935.

———, "Kreisler on Machine-Age Music," by William G. King, Oct. 23, 1937.

New York *Times*, "Kreisler, Wounded, Tells of War as He Saw It," Nov. 29, 1914.

———, "Fritz Kreisler's Tribute to His Emperor," Dec. 3, 1916.

———, "Kreisler on his Opera," Oct. 12, 1919.

———, "Kreisler Discusses Prodigies," Feb. 7, 1932.

———, "Kreisler Aroused by Critics' Taunts," Feb. 18, 1935.

———, "Kreisler's 'Classics,'" by Olin Downes, March 3, 1935.

———, "Talk with Kreisler," by Olin Downes, Nov. 8, 1942.

———, "Grand Master of the Bow," by Howard Taubman, Jan. 9, 1944.

New York *World*, "Not with Violin, but Pistol, Kreisler Played a Dead March," Nov. 25, 1914.

———, "Fritz Kreisler, Back from War, Offers Aid to Penny Lunch Fund," by Irene Loeb, Dec. 15, 1914.

Richmond (Va.) *Times-Dispatch*, "Interview with Fritz Kreisler," by Horace Melwin, Nov. 4, 1931.

Washington (D.C.) *Post*, "The Genius Who Came Back," by Doron K. Antrim, July 2, 1944.

2. FOREIGN

ARGENTINA

Buenos Aires *Herald*, "Interview with Fritz Kreisler," by W. B. R., May 30, 1935.

———, issues from May 24 to June 6, 1935.

La Prensa (Buenos Aires), "El Célebre Violinista Kreisler," May 24, 1935.

AUSTRALIA

Sydney *Morning Herald*, issues from May 2 to July 27, 1925.

AUSTRIA

Wiener *Freie Presse*, issue of Feb. 6, 1935.

BRAZIL

O Globo (Rio de Janeiro), "Cocktail with Fritz Kreisler," May 10, 1935.
———, "Great Violinist Greets Press," May 11, 1935.
Correio da Manhã (Rio de Janeiro), "Fritz Kreisler," May 9, 1935.
A Noite (Rio de Janeiro), issues of May 10, 15, 1935.
Jornal do Brasil (Rio de Janeiro), issue of May 7, 1935.
Jornal do Comércio (Rio de Janeiro), "Kreisler—Teatro Municipal," May 11, 1935.
São Paulo *Estado*, issues of May 8 to 15, 1935.

BRITISH ISLES

Glasgow *Bulletin*, "Said It with Violin," June 20, 1929.
Glasgow *Daily Record*, "Kreisler Plays to Students," June 20, 1929.
Glasgow *Evening News*, issue of June 19, 1929.
Glasgow *Evening Times*, "Famous Violinist 'Capped,'" June 19, 1929.
Glasgow *Sunday Mail*, issue of June 23, 1929.
London *Daily Chronicle*, issues of Dec. 13, 1902; May 5, 12, 1921.
London *Daily Express*, issue of May 12, 1921.
———, "Caesar with a Violin," May 5, 1921.
London *Daily Graphic*, issues of May 6, 7, 1921.
———, "Wonderful London Yesterday," May 5, 1921.
London *Daily Mirror*, issue of May 5, 1921.
London *Daily News*, issues of May 13, Nov. 11, Dec. 4, 13, 1902; May 10, 18, 21, 1921.
———, "The Return of Kreisler," May 5, 1921.
London *Daily Telegraph*, issues of May 5, 18, 21, 1921.
———, "Kreisler as Composer," Nov. 11, 1921.
London *Evening News*, issue of May 5, 1921.
London *Evening Standard*, issue of May 5, 1921.
London *Morning Post*, issues of May 5, 10, 12, 18, 21, 1921.
London *Observer*, issues of May 8, 12, 22, 29, 1921.
———, "Kreisler's New Quartet," May 15, 1921.
London *Pall Mall Gazette*, "The Richter Concert," Nov. 11, 1902.
———, "Elgar's Violin Concerto," Nov. 11, 1910.
———, issues of Nov. 7, 1902, to May 12, 1921.
London *Sunday Times*, issues of May 18 to Dec. 14, 1902; Nov. 12, 1905; Feb. 17 to May 17, 1907; Nov. 13, 1910; May 19, 1912; April 27, 1913; May 26, 1914; May 8, 15, Dec. 11, 18, 1921.
London *Star*, issues of May, 1921.

London *Westminster Gazette,* "Kreisler Recital," Dec. 13, 1902.
Manchester *Guardian,* "Kreisler's Return," by Ernest Newman, May 6, 1921.

CHINA

Peking *Daily News,* issues of May 9 to 28, 1923.
Shanghai *Celestial Empire,* issues of April 28, June 5, 9, 1923.
Shanghai *China Press,* issue of June 2, 1923.

GERMANY

Berlin *Vossische Zeitung,* issues of Dec. 24, 1932; Jan. 10 to Dec. 9, 1934.

JAPAN

Osaka *Mainichi,* issue of May 12, 1923.
Japan Advertiser (Tokyo), issues of April 22 to June 10, 1923.

NEW ZEALAND

Wellington *Evening Post,* issues of May 27 to June 19, 1925.

INDEX